Gabriela Mistral's
Struggle with
God and Man

Gabriela Mistral's Struggle with God and Man

A Biographical and Critical Study of the Chilean Poet

MARTIN C. TAYLOR

McFarland & Company, Inc., Publishers
Jefferson, North Carolina, and London

ALSO OF INTEREST: *Language into Language: Cultural, Legal and Linguistic Issues for Interpreters and Translators*, by Saúl Sibirsky and Martin C. Taylor (McFarland, 2010)

All photographs appear courtesy the Gabriela Mistral Legacy, Biblioteca Nacional de Chile. The Franciscan Order of Chile authorizes the use of the work of Gabriela Mistral. An amount equivalent to the value of the copyright has been donated to the Franciscan Order of Chile for the children of Montegrande and of Chile in conformity with the will of Gabriela Mistral.

Frontispiece: Gabriela at 65 (1954).

LIBRARY OF CONGRESS CATALOGUING-IN-PUBLICATION DATA

Taylor, Martin C., 1932–
    Gabriela Mistral's struggle with God and man : a biographical and critical study of the Chilean poet / Martin C. Taylor.
    p.   cm.
    Includes bibliographical references and index.

    ISBN 978-0-7864-6485-2
    softcover : acid free paper ∞

    1. Mistral, Gabriela, 1889–1957. 2. Authors, Chilean — 20th century — Biography. 3. Mistral, Gabriela, 1889–1957 — Religion. 4. Belief and doubt in literature. 5. Secularism in literature. 6. Religion in literature. I. Title.
PQ8097.G6Z8519   2012
861'.62 — dc23   2012024860
[B]

BRITISH LIBRARY CATALOGUING DATA ARE AVAILABLE

© 2012 Martin C. Taylor. All rights reserved

No part of this book may be reproduced or transmitted in any form or by any means, electronic or mechanical, including photocopying or recording, or by any information storage and retrieval system, without permission in writing from the publisher.

Front cover image © 2012 Shutterstock

Manufactured in the United States of America

McFarland & Company, Inc., Publishers
  Box 611, Jefferson, North Carolina 28640
  www.mcfarlandpub.com

To the memory of Lucila from Elqui and Gabriela from Chile. Intertwined, they surpassed, through synergy, the boundaries of the *patria chica* through perseverance and intellectual and humanitarian works to create a new *persona*, a global icon who prevails in the twenty-first century.

Lucila Godoy's/Gabriela Mistral's
Sacred/Secular Manifesto

Tengo un corazón grande y en que sólo germinan grandezas: inmensos odios, amores, y dolores; son bestiales los primeros, divinos los segundos, sublimes los últimos. — "Alguien" (a pseudonym of Lucila Godoy Alcayaga).*

[I have a huge heart in which only great things germinate: immense hates, loves, and pains; horrible are the first, divine the second, sublime the last. — "Somebody"]

---

*"Página de un libro íntimo" ("Page from an Intimate Book"). From *La Voz de Elqui* (29 agosto 1906). Reproduced in *Recopilación de la obra mistraliana, 1902–1922*, ed., Pedro Pablo Zegers B. (Santiago: RIL Editores, 2002), 103.

Contents

Acknowledgments	vii
Preface	1
Part One: The Secular	
I. Personal Abnegation and Spiritual Fulfillment	7
II. A Pathway to the Sacred and the Secular	18
III. Family and Personal Matters	26
IV. Self-Education and Survival	46
V. Antofagasta: Desertic North and Arid Behavior	57
VI. Life Changes in Los Andes	62
VII. Sexuality, Humanity and Existential Choices	70
VIII. Punta Arenas: Exile in Land's End	82
IX. Temuco: A Staging Area	93
X. The Transformation: Chile and Beyond	100
Part Two: The Sacred	
XI. Critical Perspectives	113
XII. The Hebraic Tradition	115
XIII. A Quest for Religious Harmony	146
XIV. The Poetry of Sacrifice	183
XV. Conclusions on the Sacred and the Secular	215
Appendices	
A. The Theosophical Society of La Serena	219
B. Zacarías Gómez: A Personal Correspondence	223
C. The Bible: "An Intimate Experience"	228
Chapter Notes	236
Bibliography	256
Index to Mistral's Works	277
Index to Names and Places	280

Acknowledgments

I thank Editorial Aguilar, of Madrid, Spain, for having given me permission to quote from its *Poesías completas de Gabriela Mistral* (1962), edited by Margaret Bates, for two of my publications, *Gabriela Mistral's Religious Sensibility* (Berkeley & Los Angeles: University of California Press, 1964), and its expanded and corrected version in Spanish: *Sensibilidad religiosa de Gabriela Mistral* (Madrid: Editorial Gredos, 1975). The present work — updated and greatly revised — on Gabriela Mistral draws upon Aguilar's *Poesías completas* (1962) and the volumes from the University of California and Editorial Gredos. Although research has confirmed that the "complete poetry" in the 1962 Bates edition was far from complete, it was deemed the best at that time because the poet had actively collaborated on it so that it could also be labeled "definitive." The 1962 Aguilar edition contained several errors, and shortly after was superseded by a second and third edition (1966), which had a different prologue but few changes of substance. Although most textual citations herein of Mistral's poetry come from the 1962 edition, I will point to exceptions when reference is made to Mistral's prose and poetry in the individual volumes of *Desolación, Ternura, Tala, Lagar, and Poema de Chile*, and in other collections and anthologies.

Part One, "The Secular," presents an organization and documentation of the major personal, psychological, and social currents in Mistral's life and times, mostly during the Chilean years, but also abroad, from witnesses, her own writings, and articles about her. Many revelations of her personal life in Chile derive from the major compendium of her early writings: *Recopilación de la obra mistraliana, 1902–1922*, edited by Pedro Pablo Zegers B. (Santiago: RIL Editores, 2002). The quotations and references in the Notes and Bibliography may be referred to simply as from/in/see *Recopilación,* followed by a page number. Mr. Zegers edited also *Gabriela Mistral: Álbum Personal*, a pictorial history of the poet and her friends, relatives, and writings. I am most grateful to Pedro Pablo Zegers Blachet for written permission to quote freely from *Recopilación*, and to publish photos and other material from the *Álbum personal*.

Two clarifications are in order: In Part Two, "The Sacred," many quotations derive from the articles in the *Anales* of the University of Chile (Volume CXV, Number 105 [1957]). This compilation is referred to as *Anales*. Unless otherwise specified, Santiago refers to Chile, not to Spain or Cuba.

Except where noted, the author assumes responsibility for Spanish to English translations of Mistral's poetry and prose and of other citations in Spanish. The translations, primarily in Part One, facilitate a smooth flow of the biographical narrative in some sensitive areas for those readers whose native language is not Spanish. Every attempt has been made to translate gracefully, but short of that, clarity and meaning are the objectives.

The 1968 edition of *Gabriela Mistral's Religious Sensibility* owes a great debt to academics — unfortunately now deceased — at the University of California, Los Angeles and Berkeley who, directly and indirectly, gave moral and intellectual guidance, sponsored the research, and supported its publication. At the Los Angeles campus, I refer to professors John A. Crow, Donald F. Fogelquist, Joseph Silverman, and Marion A. Zeitlin. At the Berkeley campus, professors Luis A. Monguió, Edwin S. Morby, and Arturo Torres Rioseco provided assistance.

Extensive research took place in Washington and Chile. I remain grateful to the Solnit Fund of Yale University for awarding me a travel grant that permitted me to investigate source material in Washington. The former directors of the Hispanic Foundation of the Library of Congress, and of the Columbus Memorial Library of the Pan American Union, respectively, Francisco Aguilera and Arthur Gropp, allowed me to utilize their extensive resources. A travel grant from the Horace H. Rackham School of Graduate Studies, University of Michigan, and a fellowship from the Organization of American States, enabled a stay in South America from May to December 1966, to amplify and correct the 1968 edition.

A special word of appreciation goes out to those Chileans who, in 1966 and afterward, graciously and unstintingly offered assistance: Mario Bahamonde, Isolina Barraza de Estay, Alfonso Calderón, Hernán Díaz Arrieta, Alfonso M. Escudero, Guillermo Gómez Marzheimer, José Santos González Vera, Augusto Iglesias, Gerardo Infante, Luisa Kneer, Enrique Lafourcade, Pedro Lastra, Ricardo Michell Abós-Padilla, Carlos Parrau Escobar, Roque Esteban Scarpa, Raúl Silva Castro, and María Urzúa.

During trips to Santiago, Chile, in 2005 and 2008, I benefited from the generosity, wisdom, and companionship of the following persons: Oscar Agüero Wood of the Ministry of Culture lent his spiritual, intellectual, and material support from near and afar. Grace Dunlop, editor of the *Revista Pat–*

rimonio Cultural, Biblioteca Nacional de Chile, accepted my article, for which I remain appreciative. Héctor Hernán Herrera Vega, who gifted me with his autographed *Gabriela Mistral, Vicuña y su gente (1945–1954)*, promotes Mistral scholarship in the Norte Chico with articles and political energy. Luis Vargas Saavedra, indefatigable Mistral scholar and professor at the Pontificia Universidad Católica de Chile, has offered assistance and friendship for decades. Part One owes its strength and clarity to his expert review. Jaime Quezada, president of the Fundación Premio Nobel Gabriela Mistral, is a companion and author of many valuable publications. Pedro Pablo Zegers Blachet, curator of the Archivo del Autor and of the Legado Gabriela Mistral at the Biblioteca Nacional de Chile, deserves special mention for his generosity and guidance. Researchers and scholars owe him a great debt of gratitude for his dedication and organizational abilities.

I am again most appreciative to the University of California Press for relinquishing, in 2010, publishing rights to me. Gary Eyrich, proprietor of the print shop, Sir Speedy, in Pembroke Pines, Florida, labored expertly to produce a clear, digitized manuscript. The reference librarians of the Broward County Library system of Florida have provided great assistance via Interlibrary Loan.

My wife Beth has borne with me, time and again, in my efforts to produce another work that might justify the trust others have placed in me. Her care, patience, and computer skills made this labor of love possible.

Preface

To examine the personal, intellectual, and spiritual trajectory of Gabriela Mistral (1889–1957)—the final pen name of Lucila de María del Perpetuo Socorro Godoy Alcayaga—South America's and Chile's first Nobel laureate in literature (1945), I have had to cull out and interweave information from many hundreds of divergent sources (among thousands) in order to focus on her involvement with sacred and secular matters. Religious, moral, and ethical sensibilities are central to any discussion of Lucila and Gabriela, who developed personalities and courses of action relative to two major time/space schisms.

Until 1922, people who knew Lucila Godoy Alcayaga associated her with her native Coquimbo province, the Norte Chico, two hundred miles north of Santiago, the capital. Between 1904 and 1914, friends addressed her as Lucila Godoy, known under various pen names as the author of 84-plus magazine and newspaper articles and poems, who also toiled as a low-paid schoolmistress in various Chilean villages, towns, and cities. From 1914 to 1922, Lucila Godoy was developing an enviable reputation—not without her share of conflicts and petty jealousies—as a non-traditional teacher and educational developer. Lucila Godoy, in 1914, also won a poetry contest in which she displayed her pen name, Gabriela Mistral, to an elite audience who inquired on a large scale about this author of cutting-edge language and dramatic content.

After 1922, she became hailed as Gabriela Mistral, no longer from Coquimbo but from Chile, the author of promising books and essays who officials from Mexico invited to develop educational systems. In consequence, after 1922, her travels on diplomatic and educational missions re-cast her as from Chile but not necessarily of Chile. Her travels abroad—in self-imposed separation from Chile—through Latin America, Europe, and the United States brought her in direct contact with leading international intellectuals and institutions through letters, speeches, publications, and conferences, all of which led to being awarded the first Nobel Prize in Literature (December 10, 1945) from South America after the Second World War.

Over the decades, in a vast array of articles, poetry, and letters, Gabriela Mistral elaborated sacred themes, such as love and the role of God and the divine in man's issues of life, being, travails, and death. Her search for the sacred was not confined to isolated aspects of her conduct and literary production, but rather so permeated her being that it cannot be easily overlooked, regardless of what topic is written about her. After a review in Part One of her life and times, Part Two examines in depth, among other themes mentioned, the poet's utilization of and sensitivity to Old and New Testament sources and non-Christian beliefs. The reader will explore a field of the sacred that has had many disguises and nuances. The object is to unify a complex subject that hitherto has been both recondite and dispersed.

A pursuit of secular matters ran concomitantly with the sacred. She advocated for underprivileged workers, women, and children. Education was her linchpin for Latin America's development. She dwelt upon in her life and works man's penchant for suffering, treachery, and anguish. Early economic privation forced her to concern herself with financial survival for herself and her family.

Writers about Mistral up through the seventies seldom entered into many of the extremely delicate personal matters of Mistral's private life concerning, for example, finances, sickness, and sexuality. These sensitive subjects are explored here. Undocumented personal sexuality, especially, remained taboo and beyond public discussion, and was left to gossip. With regard to possible intimacies, this writer had held to the prudent position of avoiding gossip, because the objective was not to ferret out evidence of indiscretions, rather, to regard her, like countless other writers from a literary perspective, as the symbolic "virgin-mother." She appeared to eschew sexuality and sublimated by praising, defending, and writing about defenseless children of the Americas. Many of the prohibited topics from the sixties to the present time, however, have — with greater social openness, the "sexual revolution," and newly-discovered documents and testimony — since her demise become subjects for discussion among journalists, academics, and friends of the poet.

One topic that continues to elicit discussion concerns the nature of the relationship between Lucila and her purported boyfriend, Romelio Ureta, because the theme impinged upon the fame and long trajectory of her poetry, celebrity, and personal anguish. (See Chapter II, "A Pathway to the Sacred and the Secular," section "Romelio Ureta: A Friend Dies, a Legend Lives"). But the Romelio Ureta incident, important for having been attributed to the "Sonetos de la muerte," now seems a bit diminished in the light of evidence in the love letters that reveals the distinct probability of other relationships in Chile and abroad, ranging from a year-long flirtation and correspondence as an impressionable teenager with the married, forty-something lothario

Alfredo Videla Pineda to more meaningful — albeit unrequited — relationships as a woman in her twenties with two Chileans (Jorge Hübner Bezanilla and Manuel Magallanes Moure), and in her thirties possibly with another married man, the Catalonian Eugenio d'Ors. (See Chapter VII, "Sexuality, Humanity, and Existential Choices," sections on the aforesaid men and "Other Suitors.")

If, indeed, physical intimacy occurred with these men — beyond amorous correspondence, ardent admiration, and alleged flirtations — another explosive matter has emerged that shatters the publicly-held position regarding the image of the "virgin motherhood." The overriding question concerns the allegations from close associates that Mistral's adopted "nephew" or "godson," Juan Miguel Godoy Mendoza, nicknamed Yin-Yin, was not as she and the documents state, the son of her half brother Carlos Godoy, but might have been her own offspring, the fruit of a liaison with Eugenio d'Ors, or with, perhaps, an unknown Italian Don Juan. (See Chapter III, "Family and Personal Matters, section "Juan Miguel Godoy Mendoza: The Tragic Illusion of Motherhood.") The text lays out the research and choices. Still very important, but of secondary concern in this matter, then, is the boy's sudden death. Did he commit suicide, or as Mistral firmly believed, was he killed? These intertwined events determined the course of Gabriela Mistral's writings and psyche.

Even more startling, since my 1968 edition — but perhaps less so given the tendency to current shock journalism — is that a dozen or so researchers involve her with lesbianism and "queerness." (See, again, Chapter VII, section "A Fractured Sisterhood.") In doing so, these modern researchers have not only undercut — they would say "clarify"— her public image of asexuality, but also have impugned the obvious heterosexual patterns in her writings and conduct, and have moved beyond these two to an alleged, but never proven by documents and testimony, bisexuality and homosexuality. Among those who focus on these matters is, for example, Licia Fiol-Matta. Do they label her correctly or libel her as a "closet lesbian"? Without going into details at this point, these writers draw evidence from her way of dressing, her symbolic language, and her complicity in failing to confront the "macho" political *status quo* to which, some claim, she was both contributor and victim. They cite, for example, her lack of traditional femininity in that she did dress in a dowdy fashion, wearing jackets over long skirts, men's shoes, and heavy stockings. She cut her hair short, like a man's, and avoided makeup and jewelry. The fact that she, perforce, was accompanied by female admirers, secretaries, and assistants provided further visual confirmation. These critics unabashedly tout her "tendencies" towards lesbianism. An attempt will be made in Chapter VII, "Sexuality, Humanity, and Existential Choices," to make fair sense of this second allegation by letting the evidence speak for itself. Is it based upon fact or conjecture? Does it impinge upon her artistic production?

Before a complete and systematic study of her life, poetry, and prose can be undertaken, Mistral's innumerable essays, newspaper articles, letters, and unedited poems have had to be collected, analyzed, and incorporated into an overarching work. Today's writers on Mistral must pay a debt to the dozen or so assiduous collectors and compilers who have passed away, such as Doris Dana, Alfonso M. Escudero (O.S.A.), Roque Esteban Scarpa, and Gastón Von dem Bussche. Their perseverance prepared the path for many others, among them, Magda Arce, Elizabeth Horan, Patricia Rubio, Jaime Quezada, Luis Vargas Saavedra, and Pedro Pablo Zegers B. The latter form part of the cadres of advocates who continue to unearth, rescue, organize, and analyze documents, essays, letters, and poems.

Gabriela's final companion and executrix of her estate, Doris Dana, died November 28, 2006. The two had met briefly on, May 7, 1946, at a course Mistral delivered in Barnard College, and after 1948 they developed a firm friendship over the years. This is discussed in depth in Chapter VII, the section "Doris Dana's Reason for Being." Ms. Dana, zealous guardian of Mistral's effects and reputation, bequeathed the poet's literary and personal legacy to her niece, Doris Atkinson, of South Hadley, Massachusetts. Faced with these historic and extensive documents, Ms. Atkinson veered away from her aunt's guardedness.

She turned to the Government of Chile as their repository, because Chilean President Ricardo Lagos had rescinded (January 2003) General Augusto Pinochet's onerous decree (1979) banning the publication of Mistral's works unless the rights to them belonged to the state. The Pinochet decree would have abrogated Mistral's wishes, stated in her will, that the rights be transferred to the Order of Saint Francis. With the support of President Lagos, Ms. Atkinson felt open to consider granting custody to Chile. She started by inviting professors Elizabeth Horan of Arizona State University and Luis Vargas Saavedra of the Pontificia Universidad Católica of Santiago to review the documents contained in dozens of boxes in order to suggest recommendations regarding their eventual custody and publication. With the aid of U.S. Embassy officials in Chile, and with the generous political, financial, and logistical support of President Lagos' government, a signed legal arrangement permitted Ms. Atkinson to award custody of her legacy to the National Library of Chile.

Under the supervision of Pedro Pablo Zegers B., curator of the Archivo del Escritor and supervisor of the Gabriel Mistral Legacy, the library's technical support personnel has been scanning, digitizing, and organizing the material. Among the many examples of Mr. Zegers' dedication to Chilean pride and devotion to Mistral and her international image, he arranged, in 2008, a public symposium and an exhibition of letters, photos, and memorabilia.

Pedro Pablo honored me with an invitation to both events, where I gave two talks on Mistral in the elegant Salón Ercilla. He also introduced me to Grace Dunlop, editor of the Library's *Revista Patrimonio Cultural*, who kindly published an article on Mistral's religious sources for the magazine's special homage edition to Mistral (46, Año XIII [Verano 2008]).

The archive that Mr. Zegers directs is required to send copies of its documents to the U.S. Library of Congress. The Library of Congress is now doubly blessed. In the sixties, Doris Dana gifted the library custody of trunks full of letters, books, and memorabilia — now on microfilm — the result of a trove that Magda Arce had discovered and organized in Mistral's former residence in Santa Barbara, California.

On the basis of this long-sought and coveted treasure about Chile's first Nobel laureate, new discoveries are emerging and will continue to surface over the following years to re-shape the long-held, previous impressions of Mistral. Professors Horan and Vargas Saavedra, the first scholars to review and transcribe many materials in the boxes, have already started the transformation. Dr. Vargas Saavedra published in a handsome, large-format edition *Almácigo* in 2008, the first compilation and organization of newly unearthed poetry from the archive. From the same sources, Dr. Horan is pursuing a biography.

As indicated earlier, Lucila Godoy Alcayaga, in her official last will and testament (a.k.a., Gabriela Mistral, in parenthesis), stated that the Order of Saint Francis, in Santiago, retains control of the rights and accruing financial benefits from the publication of the writer's legacy. The Franciscans are obligated, in turn, to invest the revenues to benefit the children of Gabriela's remote village at the western edge of the Andes, Montegrande, where she grew up, was initially educated, and is now entombed.

This present work explores findings from the Gabriela Mistral Archive and from additional recent sources in order to expand, update, and revise the revelations in *Gabriela Mistral's Religious Sensibility*. The present work attempts to further clarify the legend and facts surrounding Chile's first Nobel laureate.

Gabriela Mistral was an icon of the first half of the 20th century for a wide-ranging international audience. She remains an icon as well in the first half of the 21st century for an audience which respects and appreciates a female figure who surpassed her humble beginnings and, despite financial hardships and injustices from private and public media, reached, through intelligence, perseverance, and very dedicated work, the Nobel Prize of her chosen field. Gabriela Mistral continues to serve as a model for Chileans and for humanity.

PART ONE: THE SECULAR

CHAPTER I

Personal Abnegation and Spiritual Fulfillment

Asceticism and Worldliness

Pain and anguish recur constantly, almost to surfeit, in the dramatic poetry of Gabriela Mistral. Suffering, though, was for her no mere literary theme; for years it suffused her whole being. Pain made existence unbearable, yet in its absence, paradoxically, life had little meaning. While desperately striving to achieve serenity, she seemed to delight in pain, to be proud of the bondage that martyrdom, exile, and public asceticism imposed. As a martyr and pariah she stood alone, apart, proud of a stoic attitude that internalized her anguish and made consolation impossible. And so the cycle renewed itself.

Gabriela gave the appearance of an ascetic by eschewing adornment and makeup. To intensify her gaunt, almost masculine, features, set off by an aquiline nose, deeply penetrating green/brown eyes [?], she tied her hair straight back in a knot or cut it short.[1] Her clothing was usually coarse, loose-fitting, and monotonously brown or gray, like a monk's sackcloth. A description at the age of fifty-eight stresses adherence to lack of adornment and simplicity: "That morning she had a shawl over her shoulders, wore a loose brown dress, cotton stockings, and men's shoes. There was not a single feminine adornment on her person, not a trinket or a jewel. And yet she gave the impression of being a beautiful woman [by her attractive smile] in her Franciscan simplicity."[2] As she avoided artificiality in her dress, so, too, did she avoid artificiality in her later, mature poetry.[3]

Self-debasement and self-vilification were fixed characteristics, evident not only in her dress, but also in references to her features and humble beginnings. One telling example of this comes out in her epistolary relationship with the married poet from the town of San Bernardo, Manuel Magallanes Moure. Despite years of ardent correspondence to him, harboring the delusion that he would reciprocate, she finally revealed to him that her ugliness ("*fealdad*") would prevent him from returning that ardor. Indeed, one critic asserted that her lifelong bitterness derived from her "*complejo de fealdad*," i.e., her psychological complex of feeling ugly.[4]

Still other reasons may be adduced for her austerity: a lifelong sense of self-righteousness, apparent renunciation of carnal desire, and an insistence on continual self-purification.

Some critics believe that Gabriela's emphasis on love for God and Jesus in her personal habits and writings is no reason to consider her a recluse or ascetic. She was not given to visions or trances, except perhaps, when envisioning poetic creation. Notwithstanding the hagiographic labels of "saint" and "divine ("*Santa Gabriela*," "*Divina Gabriela*")— labels that some authors ascribed to and which she rejected — Gabriela never believed in the hyperboles nor claimed to be saintly or divine.[5]

She did not, like her admired Santa Teresa de Jesús, the Discalced Carmelite nun from Ávila, Spain (1515–1582), assume vows of poverty, chastity, and obedience. As a child abandoned by a father and working as a rural teacher half her life, she had a grasp on near-poverty, but not because she desired it. Chastity, a controversial matter, will form the subject of Chapter VII on "Sexuality, Humanity and Existential Choices." Rather than obedience, intransigence better described her nature. Respectable public at that time frowned on ladies who smoked. But she did, excessively, in public and indoors behind screens. She also sipped Coca-Cola and wine and delighted in buying handsomely-bound books. Over a life time, she believed that her major vices were — minor, really, in comparison to others which will be explored — buying books and extensive traveling.

Money and Finances

In support of her asceticism, devoted admirers affirm that Lucila/Gabriela "never touched money" nor was attuned to finances. (Read the comment in Appendix B.) Dozens of letters and one or two poems indicate the contrary, that she was totally sensitive to money and finances during a lifetime. To reinforce a minimum life style for herself, her mother and sister, she started working at fifteen as a low-paid teacher's assistant for a monthly government check and never stopped working and thinking of funds because of a felt obligation to be the family's rainmaker and because money offered power and personal independence.

One telling example occurred with the Nobel Prize stipend (December 14, 1945). The amount consisted of 116,335.20 (SEK), i.e., Swedish Krona, at that time approximately U.S. $38,352.00.⁶ She was proud, indeed, to receive the award, which vindicated her literary skills and mollified many personal grievances. But she guarded that sum avidly to pay off current debts and to consider investing in real estate. In picturesque Santa Barbara, California, the site of her consular post (1952–1954), she compared buying a home to fulfill a dream for a long-sought place of repose with the possibility of that asset as a source of potential rental income. The Nobel funds eventually went towards the hillside house overlooking the Pacific Ocean on 729 Anapamú Street.

Among other financial matters, she dealt with budgets, royalties, commissions or the absence thereof from articles, loans from/to friends, and rates of monetary exchange. In Appendix B, which details her relationship with Zacarías Gómez, she asked her trusted friend to oversee insurance money, to pay doctors with travelers' checks for her sister Emelina's care in Chile, and to find out why the newspaper editors delayed her commissions. This ongoing honest concern for money is again exemplified in a letter from Monrovia, California, where she served as consul from 1948 to 1950. In it, she elaborated skillfully and at length the dollars required for the financial complexities of living on a small, fixed government salary ($100.00/month) and of paying a variety of bills for personal and job maintenance in the United States.⁷ From this preoccupation with finances, one can infer that among the worldly, perhaps, she might have been considered ascetic, but among the truly ascetic, worldly.

Dilemma of the "Chosen One"

Because Gabriela tried to lead a life as a free-thinking, dedicated teacher and writer, and because her physical appearance inspired awe, many people sang her praises. Novelist and friend Pedro Prado labeled her the "chosen one."⁸ The term is both flattering and unfortunate. The chosen one is always envied by those left out, the unlucky and the incompetent. It is a matter of record that Gabriela Mistral, accidentally or by choice, found herself in the minority on many issues and was often subject to harassment by her countrymen. She bore the scars of mistreatment all her life, not only because she found it difficult to forget and forgive, but also because the humiliations were so heinous. It is important to examine the origin of her suffering because the incidents that caused it played a large part in shaping her attitude toward life and art.

Stoned at Nine, Poisoned for Life

A life-long Chilean friend, the journalist Hernán Díaz Arrieta (1891–1984), known by the pseudonym Alone, wrote that one of the most decisive events in Mistral's life occurred at the age of nine in the school she attended.⁹ The principal — her teacher and godmother — Doña Adelaida Olivares, who was blind, falsely accused her chosen paper monitor of stealing official sheets of paper in the face of a shortage at semester's end. Doña Adelaida, blind also to her own shortcomings, suddenly forgot the long friendship with Lucila's family, and blinded by rage, believed that Lucila had duped her. The principal ordered Lucila from the classroom and incited the children to throw stones at her and to shout, "*ladrona, ladrona*" ("thief"). She recorded officially that the malicious child was mentally defective ("*débil mental*"), a judgment that would blemish her on seeking to apply to other schools. Battered, and in a state of shock from the accusation, Lucila hid at first and then ran home. Her family, who had befriended Adelaida, was devastated. Afterward, forlorn and distrustful of other teachers and schools, she attended elementary school in Montegrande where her half sister Emelina taught.

Díaz Arrieta's quotation that follows reveals that the sordid situation turned into a poisoned thorn buried deep in Lucila's flesh from which blood and pus would ooze forever. From that moment forward, Alone believed, Lucila/Gabriela would become the eternally persecuted one, the offended and humiliated person, the poor and weak creature against whom were aligned external powers who would not be able to find a resting place nor many persons to whom she could turn to for succor:

> *Sean como hayan sido las cosas en esa Escuela semirural donde Gabriela tiene la revelación de la crueldad humana, es allí donde aprende, con las primeras letras, el dolor, la injusticia y los trágicos errores de que está lleno el mundo. Una envenenada espina se le hunde en las carnes y sangrará para siempre. Será, desde entonces, la eterna perseguida, la ofendida y humillada, la pobre y débil criatura contra la cual se conjuran las potencias exteriores y que no halla a dónde volver los ojos para* pedir *auxilio*.¹⁰

By a curious turn of fate, Gabriela was visiting Vicuña, Chile, in 1938 — her birthplace — when Doña Adelaida was laid to rest. A friend, Santiago del Campo, reported that Gabriela approached the coffin in the church, placed some violets on it, and when asked if she remembered her teacher of decades past replied, with derision, "—*Claro está que la recuerdo; yo nunca olvido*" ("Of course I remember her; I never forget.").

She again became painfully aware of the childhood incident upon being awarded, *in absentia*, Chile's National Prize for Literature in 1951. Three striking aspects became apparent. First of all, she snubbed the ceremony refusing to travel from her consular post in Rapallo, Italy, to receive the award personally. Second, the principal reason for not returning to Chile might well have been that the National Prize was awarded belatedly and grudgingly, six years after receiving the Nobel Prize. And third, the Chilean officials compounded that embarrassment when they decided to spend the prize money, 100,000 pesos (U.S. $1,108.00, at that time), on a library in Vicuña, the site of the stoning and not, unfortunately, on a library in Montegrande, the village where she grew up and which she revered more than her place of birth.

> *¡Pensar que mi Valle de Elqui, mi Monte Grande,*
> *donde me crié de cuatro a diez años que es mi único*
> *recuerdo dulce de esa infancia, nada va a tener;*
> *todo se lo darán precisamente a la ciudad donde*
> *fui echada de la escuela y apedreada en su plaza por ...*
> *unas diez condiscípulas azuzadas por una maestra ciega!*[11]

She neither forgot nor forgave the stoning and often retold the story to demonstrate Chile's early disdain for her.

It is ironic that Gabriela would never see in her lifetime the children of Montegrande benefit from her prizes, royalties, and revenue from books. Only upon Mistral's death would sums from her estate flow legally, according to her will, to the children of tiny Montegrande, a task that the Order of Saint Francis of Santiago is entrusted to carry out.

Attacked Publicly

It can be shown that certain Chileans treated Gabriela with hostility and that, ironically, representatives of other countries were quicker to recognize her talents. From 1921 to 1922, for example, the *"criollas,"* her label for the vindictive, upper-crust "creole" women in Santiago associated with Amanda Labarca's vilification campaign, taunted her and discredited her in seventy vile, anonymous letters. This incident took place with regard to her promotion to principal of a prestigious girls' school in Santiago. (See Chapter X, section "Labarca Hubertson's Opposition," for a full discussion.)[12]

The Santiago newspapers, *El Mercurio* and *El Diario Ilustrado,* to which she had sent articles for many years, refused to publish her contributions, thereby depriving her of an income. Their reasons: She had attacked the regime of President Gabriel González Videla (1940–1952), for persecuting Senator Pablo Neruda, the eminent poet and future Nobel laureate (1971), and for labeling as Communists and summarily dismissing hundreds of public employees. Gabriela denounced the editor, Rafael Maluenda, and his "tedious" and "embarrassing" paper: *"Ya le conté que, con toda elegancia, M. [Maluenda] me ha cortado de El Mercurio. Leer el diario da de un lado tedio, del otro sonrojo."* Unable to restrain her bitterness, she lashed out at President González Videla, who, she believed, had secretly engineered the destitution after having sent articles for 28 years:

> ¿Sabe Ud. que a mí me han echado de ese diario sin una sola palabra, no publicándome, lo que les mando? Así, después de 28 años, como a una sirvienta. Estoy segura, AUNQUE SIN DATOS, de que la orden ha debido venir de lo alto ... es decir de Lo Bajo [González Videla].[13]

Chilean critics attacked her literary production and, until 1923, publishers were hesitant to come forward to admit to her literary worth, unless forced to do so. Most damaging to her reputation were three studies by the prominent critic Raúl Silva Castro, who directed the Chilean section of the National Library. His first article, "Aspectos de la poesía ...," was based upon the Chilean edition of *Desolación* (1923); he painted an unflattering portrait in *Literary Portraits* (*Retratos literarios* [1932]); and his *Estudios sobre Gabriela Mistral* (1935) dealt entirely with her works to that time. The influential critic ridiculed her, especially for blaspheming against accepted religious principles regarding suicide, and displayed little understanding of poetry despite his arrogant claims to the contrary. Doubtless, Silva Castro's opinion, among that of other journalists, influenced Chilean publishing houses.[14]

Mistral's first volume of poetry, *Desolación*, appeared first in the U.S. (1922), to be followed, in 1923, by its publication in Chile. Her only volume of poetry to appear first in Chile was *Lagar* (*Winepress*, 1954), three years before her death. *Tala* (*Felling of Trees/Havoc*) first appeared in Buenos Aires in 1938. *Ternura* (*Tenderness*, 1924), the *Poesías completas* (1958 and 1962), and the *Poema de Chile* (1967), were printed originally in Spain.

Distancing and Itinerancy

Except for brief return visits in 1925, 1938, and 1954, she spent her last thirty-four years outside Chile. In referring to that self-imposed distancing and life-long itinerancy, she wrote solemnly of being cast out, and she justified that by an understatement, intimating that the spirit of her father's wanderlust had been passed on to her, as if in her DNA: "*Me lanzaron, y como tengo un fondo de vagabundaje paterno, me eché a andar y no he parado más.*"[15] She referred to herself, with some pride, as "*la descastada*" ("the outcast"), to contrast with the scorn the word had acquired on the lips of those Chileans who had coined it to mock her. In the same vein, repugnance for her suffering in Chile led to statements that dismissed out of hand a return to Chile, the country that she loved: "*No regresaré a la tierra mía que amo, porque allá me hicieron sufrir muchísimo.*"[16] These words reflected her attitude at the end of a long career abroad, but even in 1922, on the eve of her first departure, that to Mexico, acrimony and unrelenting anguish dominated her personality:

I. Personal Abnegation and Spiritual Fulfillment 13

> *Despedazándome he luchado por la paz y la he adquirido incompleta después de largos padecimientos; y ha llegado un poco tarde. Vivo días serenos y apacibles; ya nada temo, ni nada espero. ¿Penurias? Las he conocido tan desesperantes. ¿Desengaños de las gentes? Ya han rebosado mi vaso de amarguras.*[17]

In "Nocturno de la consumación" ("Nocturne of the Consummation"), she dramatizes disillusionment toward Chilean officials.[18] The poem portrays the poet as a Christ-like figure severed (*"rebanado"*) from her spiritual fatherland (Chile): "*...despojada de mi propio Padre / ¡rebanada de Jerusalem!*" ("...stripped away from my own Father / sliced off from Jerusalem!"). Chile symbolized the poet's Jerusalem. She compared her suffering and destitution to that of Jesus, who was taunted by the populace and suffered ostracism. The interpretation finds support in the double repetition of the verb *rebanar* (to slice/cut off/sever), used in the following portion of a letter to suggest a violent schism between herself and the maximum representative of Chile, President Carlos Ibáñez del Campo (1887–1960), who had cut her consular salary for six months:

> *... mi jubilación rebanada por el Sr. Ibáñez...... Y viví. Dios es grande, es el amigo de los abandonados y de los perseguidos. Ya vuelve el Sr. Ibáñez, ídolo de la chilenidad y yo volveré a vivir el trance de que me rebanen del presupuesto.*[19]
>
> ... my retirement sliced off by Mr. Ibáñez... And I lived. God is great, the friend of the abandoned and of the persecuted. Now Mr. Ibáñez comes back, idol of the Chilean people, and I shall again pay the price of being cut off by them from the budget.

Gabriela was alluding to an incident long-forgotten by many, but, in 1952, still of concern to her. President Ibáñez had cut off payment of her pension for a half year during his first term in office (1927–1931). The president entwined that miniscule saving, incredibly, with an exaggerated desire to save money for the almost bankrupt treasury. But he was acting hypocritically, since he and the Armed Forces had looted it. The salary severance was an excuse, actually, to chastise Gabriela for some remarks she had directed against his authoritarian government. The fear of another punishment from the colonel who had fired her from her job as consular officer—according to her letter to her long-term friend Zacarías Gómez (October 20, 1951, in Appendix B)—added to her adamant refusal to return to Chile:

> *No quiero "toparme" con aquel soberbio Señor que me trató con [illegible] en Brasil.... Y casi lloro cuando leo que el próximo patrón es, precisamente aquel otro que me destituyó del cargo de Cónsul hace años; fue "mi Coronel." Parece que Chile pierde más y más su sensatez y ... su memoria histórica.*[20]
>
> I don't want to "run across" that haughty Lord who treated me with [illegible] in Brazil.... I almost wept on reading that the next boss is, precisely,

that guy who fired me from my job as consul years ago; he was "my Colonel." It seems that Chile loses more and more its good sense ... its historical memory.

Her fear, though, that Ibáñez would stop her pension in 1952, when he was elected for a second term (1952–1958), proved groundless. What had stopped him from doing so? Gabriela surmised that the glory of the Nobel award ("*el Sueco*") had prevented him. In any event, because of the stipend from the prize and royalties from books, she had less cause for alarm. What is essential here is the literary-psychological repercussion. In 1930, she blamed President Ibáñez for cutting her ties with the fatherland. In her imagination and creation, "Nocturno," she appeared to associate that rupture with her native land with the abandonment that Jesus Christ had suffered in Jerusalem.

Official Recognition

Gabriela Mistral's expressions of hostility must be evaluated in the light of evidence that the Chilean bureaucracy did not forsake her completely. Although she lacked a traditional university degree, the Minister of Education, her friend Pedro Aguirre Cerda (1879–1941), awarded her a State certificate of teaching competence for having organized two elementary schools that had been disrupted, ironically, by teachers with degrees. Aguirre Cerda, who later was elected president (1938–1941), entrusted her with directing schools in the cities of Punta Arenas (1918), Temuco (1920), and Santiago (1921). He also had recommended her for the educational revitalization project in Mexico to that country's Minister of Education, José Vasconcelos, whom she had already known through correspondence and his book *Indología*.

The highest levels of the national government eventually recognized her capabilities after the mission to Mexico ended successfully in 1924. In 1925, she returned to Chile, where the Congress, through a special act, awarded her the gift of a pension at the age of 36, which covered 20 years of teaching (1904–1925), instead of the usual thirty.

Soon after, Chilean officialdom started grooming Mistral as its representative to international conclaves. She represented the Ministry of Education and Culture, in 1926, as Secretary of the Literature Division of the International Institute of Intellectual Cooperation (IIIC) of the League of Nations. From 1927 to 1928, she attended educational congresses in Locarno, Switzerland, the Federation of Universities in Madrid, and the Cinematographic Educational Council in Rome, among others.

The foreign ministry also took note of her abilities and value to the nation. The chronologies prepared by the National Library of Chile (*Gabriela Mistral, a cien años de su nacimiento, 1889–1989*), and another at http://www.biografiadechile.cl/especiales/gabrielamistral/cronologia.php, outline her multiple diplomatic postings. The ministry sent her, first, as consul in Genoa, Italy (1932), a country then under Benito Mussolini's yoke. In Italy, she did not exercise her official role having declared herself as anti-fascist. In July 1933, the ministry sent her briefly to Madrid, where she left hurriedly under negative pressure, and then to Lisbon (1933–1935). To celebrate her valuable services, the Chilean Congress, through a special act (September 24, 1935), elevated her to second consul, or minister plenipotentiary, which permitted an exercise of authority from any place she chose for life.

Gabriela, at 49 (1938).

From 1936 to 1940, Gabriela flitted from Guatemala City (1936), to São Paolo (1937), to Buenos Aires (1938), to St. Augustine, Florida, and five other U.S. cities (1938), and on to Nice (1939). From 1940 to 1945, to avoid war-torn Europe, she chose Brazil, first at Niteroi and then Rio de Janeiro, for her official postings, much to the disappointment of her European friends. She lamented Brazil forever, because her adopted nephew, Juan Miguel, committed suicide in Petrópolis (1943). After the Nobel Prize in 1945, the foreign ministry ceded once more to her personal considerations. She abandoned South and Central America and elected the United States (California: Monrovia [1946–1948], and Santa Barbara [1952–1954]; New York City and Roslyn Harbor [1954–1957]). From the U.S., she took side postings to Veracruz, Mexico (1948–1950) and Rapallo, Italy (1951). Always requesting consular service outside of Chile, a roving, international ministry suited her desire for travel, change, and celebrity.

Wherever she traveled — Europe, Latin America, the United States — she merited adulation, banquets, and awards. In addition to the honorary doc-

Garbiela (center) in Rio de Janeiro in 1945 before receiving the Nobel Prize.

torates conferred from the University of Florence (1946), Mills College (Oakland, California, 1947), and Columbia University (1954), she was awarded the "key" to New Orleans and the Legion d'Honneur from France. On her three brief, return visits to Chile in thirty-five years abroad (1925, 1938, 1954), both critics and friends made pilgrimages to her home. Although some carried grudges, most preferred to listen in awe to her monologues rather than to speak during gatherings held in her honor. Héctor Hernán Herrera Vega, a native like the poet of Coquimbo province, describes in detail the exuberant celebrations from friends and from enthusiastic crowds who lined the streets to catch a last glimpse of "*nuestra Lucila*" when she visited (1954) the towns along the Elqui valley, from coastal La Serena, to her birthplace Vicuña, and last to her revered Montegrande at the foothills of the Andes.[21]

Upon her death (January 10, 1957), President Ibáñez declared three days of national mourning. Solemn official ceremonies extolled her greatness, and her body lay in state while thousands of people — friends, opponents, and strangers — filed past the flower-strewn bier to glimpse the legendary "la Mistral."

It is possible to blame certain individuals for arrogance and shortsightedness, but evidence has been presented to prove that most officials, critics, and the common people of Chile generally respected their most prestigious poet. The praise might have come sooner, more often, and with greater fervor, but, in all fairness, adds Hernán Díaz Arrieta, a loyal supporter, a person who cultivates dissatisfaction, remembers gossip, and demands attention cannot easily be gratified.

Poema de Chile: Mistral's Paradise

At the same time, Mistral displayed an immense love for Chile, the Chile of her dreams, of her childhood in Montegrande, the stylized, poetic Chile that could exist only after a violent break, after a separation in time and space. Her poetic heritage is Chilean: the rural metaphors, the allusions to nature, the dedications, the themes, and the people.

The poet's book-length georgic poem, *Poema de Chile,* edited by her companion and heir, Doris Dana, and published posthumously (1967), amply shows the love the poet reserved for her country.[22] Having absorbed natural history texts of Chile, she carefully and methodically organized the poem into geographical zones. She wrote as if she were the Biblical Adam of Chile, the "name-giver," who identified in "Chileno" the fruits, flora, and fauna peculiar to each region. Into this linguistic framework, she wove a plot featuring an innocent Indian boy, in part, a symbol of her adopted Yin-Yin, who, because of his suicide, never toured Chile to identify with his Chilean mother's heritage. On this tour went a Chilean deer, the *huemul,* another symbol of peace and innocence. The poet — who believed in reincarnation — had descended from on high as a ghost to lead the boy and deer from the Atacama Desert in the north to Punta Arenas on the Straits of Magellan through the different provinces learning of the greatness and splendor of that country and countryside. Unable to find a nesting place in Chile, the de-territorialized Mistral returns in her poetry to locate a hearth, but also to find social justice for the deracinated Indian boy via a plot of arable land. One of his many insistent queries to the mother-figure is why they are wandering and never finding roots: "*No te entiendo, mamá, eso / de ir esquivando las casas / y buscando con los ojos / los pastos o las mollacas* ..."; ("I don't understand you, mommy, / your avoiding houses / and your eyes searching for / land for pasture and crops..."). The posthumous *Poema de Chile,* once again, manifests the sacred (Adam, spiritual quest, reincarnation, and innocence) juxtaposed to the secular (flora, fauna, and social justice). In spite of her voluntary, enforced separation, Gabriela never left Chile spiritually or poetically. Her poetry, personal idiom, and dreams of Chilean greatness offer eloquent testimony that she was proud of her heritage.

Chapter II

A Pathway to the Sacred and the Secular

Romelio Ureta: A Friend Dies, a Legend Lives

Not all the poet's suffering was due to a lack of recognition, or to the wagging tongues of the envious or less-gifted, or to malicious criticism of her ideas. A major source of public attention and contention was self-generated. It originated from her relationship to Romelio Ureta Carvajal, who committed suicide and whose death gave rise, allegedly, to "Sonetos de la muerte" ("Sonnets of Death"). Indeed, scholars often cite the bizarre and tragic relationship with Romelio Ureta to explain Lucila Godoy's early unhappiness and her aversion to male company. Unfortunately, legend has obscured the facts. Because, in later life, Gabriela, through prudence or modesty, consistently hedged about the details, one can only conjecture from the scant evidence.[1] An often-mentioned clue is a postal card. Although the official police report does not say so, the investigating authorities purportedly found on his remains or among his belongings a postal card bearing the name "Lucila Godoy."

Romelio Ureta Carvajal.

The composite story reveals that the seventeen-year-old Lucila first met Ureta in the coastal city of La Serena — 290 miles north of Santiago, and 20 miles west of Montegrande — where, as baggage clerk, he collected the freight money. Later in 1906, she encountered the 22-year-old Ureta again in the town of La Cantera, where she taught school. It is difficult to tell whether the reunion was accidental or planned. They boarded in the same pension in which she had a room over his. She reportedly saved a seat for him in the dining room and they probably talked. When asked later, her sister Emelina was unaware of any affection she harbored for Ureta. Gossip, hearsay, and imagination hold sway beyond these few details. One author reports a real or invented dialogue in which Lucila rejected Romelio for dressing like a dandy and living beyond his means to court a spoiled fiancée who came from a wealthy family.[2] The report, one of many in this vein, is another attempt to malign Ureta and to account for his untimely death.

Three years after their meeting, Ureta shot himself (November 25, 1909). What led to his self-inflicted wound? An audit of the funds under his supervision had turned up a shortage of 1501.11 pesos. Two hours after being confronted with the loss, he returned to his room in the boarding house, locked the door, and shot himself in the right temple. The police report in *La Reforma* (November 26, 1909), hinted that he was a showoff and a person who lived beyond his means and got caught embezzling.[3] Others declare that he had loaned the money from the railroad to a friend, Carlos Omar Barrios, who had promised to repay him then reneged. In any case, Ureta chose suicide rather than endure shame over the embarrassment and the loss of honor.

Poetry of Death and Life: "Sonetos de la Muerte"

The supposed effect of Ureta's death on Lucila the person and on Gabriela the poet did not surface until five years later, after the public heard recited "Sonetos de la muerte." This airing took place at the first Juegos Florales (Floral Games) in the regal Teatro Santiago on the hot summer evening of December 22, 1914. The Society of Artists and Writers, presided over by the poet Manuel Magallanes Moure, organized the competition to enhance the poetic tradition, to acquaint the public with new creative artists, and to permit aspiring poets a chance at prominence. As an incentive to entice a larger and more illustrious audience, the organizers invited Don Ramón Barros Luco, the president of the republic and his wife, among other notable political and society figures, literati, journalists, and critics. In conjunction with the poetry contest, the organizers held a beauty contest where young, high-society ladies competed for queen. The Art Nouveau-style program, reproduced as *El Libro de los Juegos Florales*, captures the beauty of the moment, as it features the texts of the cast of poets and photographs of the beautiful ladies of the court.[4]

That evening the tuxedoed gentlemen and bejeweled ladies fanned themselves and suffered in the unusual heat. The unease, in part, arose from bearing with a lengthy program. Maestro Tritini started off with the overture to *William Tell* and directed many other numbers. The attendees then had to listen to a dramatic play and several speeches. The queen, María Letelier del Campo, received the crown.

Then poems in the traditional Romantic tradition, including Julio Munizaga Ossandón's "Prayer to the Virgin" were read. After the "Prayer," the moderator called to the stage Gabriela Mistral to read the "Sonetos." Nobody came forward. Following an awkward pause and apology, the poet Víctor Domingo Silva read the three sonnets written by his friend from the printed program. In contrast to the reverent "Prayer," the stunned audience heard about unrequited love, betrayal, suicide, death deserved, and a glacial body in a deep frozen grave that only the poet could or would rescue or redeem.

When it came time for the judges to choose, Miguel Luis Rocuant voted for the "Prayer." Domingo Silva and Magallanes Moure opted for the more audacious "Sonetos." Independent of whether Magallanes Moure liked the poetry, he voted for an avid admirer from their personal association in his literary circle, El Ateneo de San Bernardo, whom he favored for also being native to Coquimbo. Unknown to the other two judges, Gabriela, in advance of submitting her poems to the Floral Games, had corresponded with Magallanes Moure and had received his approval. His tie-breaking vote validated an underlying and unrevealed conflict of interest.

Magallanes Moure, however, got more than he bargained for. He had inadvertently selected the person with whom he could not or would not separate himself from for the next nine years. She not only cherished his vote, but would also take that vote as permission, as a token of love, to continue to write him clandestine letters. The secret correspondence between the two, upon being aired and analyzed publicly, in 1978, revealed a tormented, but unrequited, relationship.[5] (The story between Magallanes Moure and Lucila Godoy unfolds in Chapter VI, "Life Changes in Los Andes.")

Gabriela, embarrassed, never came down from the balcony of the Teatro Santiago. She remained in the darkness to survey the events. Mireya, Magallanes Moure's own daughter, heiress and guardian of his letters, painfully relates Lucila's inability to show herself as further evidence of her father's disloyalty. Lucila, she moaned, was present in the Teatro Santiago, but not to hear her poetry read, nor to claim a prize, but to get a glimpse of her father from a distance and to hear his voice. Gabriela's letter—in Spanish and in the English translation — confirms the vicarious tryst. It is dated December 23, the afternoon following the Juegos Florales[6]:

> *Manuel:*
> *Fui solo por oirlo. No por oír mis versos (los había escuchado leer); no por aquello de los aplausos de una multitud (unos momentos sólo entre la multitud me hacen daño); por oírlo a Ud., por eso fui.... No saqué de esa noche sino que una frase de Ud. sobre mis sonetos me abriera de nuevo la llaga central de mi corazón. Nada más. L*

> Manuel:
> I went just to hear you. Not to listen to my verses (I had already heard them); not for the applause of the multitude (even a few moments among the multitude do me harm); to hear you, for that I went.... The only thing that I took out of that night would be that a word from you on my sonnets would have opened again the central wound of my heart. Nothing else. L[ucila]

She never approached Magallanes Moure that night of the Floral Games nor on many subsequent opportunities in the years that followed because, she declared in a letter to Manuel, of her personal unworthiness, her ugliness (*"fealdad"*), and a sense of sin at participating in forbidden love. One can surmise that a sense of personal *"fealdad"* — mentioned earlier as a key to her personality — overwhelmed her that evening as a reason for not stepping onto the stage to read her "Sonnets" and for not accepting the prizes. That inferiority complex involved her green/brown eyes, her tall appearance (five feet six and one half inches), her long, coarse skirts and an absence of makeup and jewelry. On stage, she would have appeared in a very grotesque light in front of the lovely, slim ladies, of the right height, who were dressed in fashionable gowns, contestants for queen.

Then there was social and class inferiority. Most of the audience and all of the contestants proceeded from elegant families and the finest city schools. Lucila, in contrast, came from poor folks and was educated in rural, public schools. She had to work hard to support herself and her mother at low-paying teaching jobs and by contributing articles to local papers and journals for paltry sums or just to prove herself.

Nor was she a "daughter" of the mothers and aunts who witnessed the contest. The women in the audience united customarily in the dilettante Círculos de Señoras or the Círculos Literarios. Many of these idle rich women, *gente bien* ("the smart set"), lived in nice houses acquired with funds from huge sales of nitrates (*salitre*) from mines in northern Arica Province.[7] The mothers and relatives of the young women in the beauty contest did not chat about nitrates, the business of their tuxedoed husbands, but wittily about the latest books and fashions, and about raising pretty daughters who would marry men of society.

What Lucila lacked in finery and refinery, she made up for in pride of her intellectual abilities. She would not fit well into the Literary Circles, but into other groups that she frequented, such as the Theosophical Society [of Antofagasta, La Serena, and Santiago], and the Ateneo de San Bernardo, founded by Magallanes Moure, environments where discussions about ideas and spirituality prevailed. The upper social classes were not Mistral's foes, but her antithesis, the opposite of where she came from and what she did and stood for. Even so, she knew that in order to gain the recognition that she craved for her creative activities and for her profound need to improve public education, she would have to depend on the goodwill of the ruling and moneyed elites.[8]

The Juegos Florales half-concluded, Gabriela fled from the balcony into the night. The first prize — the gold medal and the laurel crown — was retrieved by an old family friend, Isauro Santelices. In the poet's mysterious absence, the strong verses and the curious pseudonym motivated the audience, judges, and journalists the next day and subsequently to discover the winner's history and the source of the poetry. The "Sonnets" would also catalyze serious comments and polarize progressives and conservatives. Two questions were at stake. One would be whether treating suicide as a poetic theme, however well done, violated moral and religious traditions. The second would concern the role of women as protagonists in a male-dominated culture.

Since that time scholars started searching to find clues to the person and the poetry. The most obvious clue, but not necessarily the correct one, is Mistral's poetry. Led by such eminent critics as Julio Saavedra Molina, writers have tried to piece together all the events in her life through the poetry in *Desolación*, especially the "Sonetos" and the poems of the section "Dolor" ("Pain"). Critics have rearranged the poems to discover a "logical series" that correspond with conjecture.[9] The poet's life and her art do happen to coincide at several points, but, as will be discussed in Chapter XI, "Critical Perspectives," poetry cannot be judged solely in terms of its conformity to biography. Poetry is not biography, for, if it were, it would merely record facts and information and would thereby lose its uniqueness.[10] This subject will be discussed at length in Chapter XI, "Critical Perspectives."

Another clue is the postal card with the name "Lucila Godoy." How conclusive could this be to establish a relationship?[11] If the card bearing her name indicated a trace of an amorous link, friends and admirers of Gabriela discount it in order to dissociate Gabriela from a morbid affair. The poet Erna Fergusson called Ureta a "weakling" and noted that he was inferior to her "intellectually."[12] The Cuban Dulce María Loynaz, more sentimental than most, believed that there was a mutual love — albeit platonic — and that, on the eve of marrying another woman, Clementina Herrera, Ureta committed suicide to keep a vow he had made never to marry anyone but Lucila Godoy. Her source is Gabriela. Miss Loynaz justified her conclusion that his death was a worthwhile sacrifice — whether or not there was a love affair — because without the death *Desolación* would never have been written, nor would "Gabriela Mistral" ever have reached international heights.[13]

Augusto Iglesias' considered opinion is that Gabriela, inspired by her readings and her passion for the dramatic wove a fantasy, a myth that assumed a life independent of the facts. This myth, or *"ensueño,"* transfigured by the process of creation, became the truth, a poetic truth more lasting, genuine, and superior than any concrete fact: *"No obstante, la obra de arte sobrevive a su creador, por ingrato que éste sea con su propia creación, y es superior, por eso mismo a los caprichos del artifice."*[14]

Whether or not Iglesias' opinion will someday be borne out, it is not likely to change the view that Romelio Ureta's suicide was a catalytic force that elicited and crystallized latent feelings of loneliness and despair. Iglesias supports his opinions by referring to some of Lucila's favorite novelists who were involved with themes of death, suicide, and eroticism, such as the excitable and sensuous Colombian José María Vargas Vila (1863–1933), who wrote *Ibis*, and the Italian Gabriel D'Annunzio, who gained fame with *The Triumph of Death*.[15]

Perhaps the death of Ureta evoked the pain associated with her truant father. On a conscious and more practical level, Gabriela realized that an artist, in order to attain eminence, must fashion a particular theme — in her case, grief for the dead lover — and make of a particular event something universal. Some of or all of these forces must have coalesced after she won the Juegos Florales for "Sonetos de la muerte." Her imagination was fertile enough to generate their artistic possibilities. They could be extended and elaborated to include disappointment over frustrated motherhood, the clash between the traditional Christian opinion of suicide and her own, the role of God toward the deceased and the despairing, and the eventual apotheosis of the loved one. If this hypothesis is valid, Ureta's suicide unified and channeled her raw emotions, and his death provided a central theme for the poetry in *Desolación*, especially for the section describing pain, "Dolor."[16]

Her hidden feelings about the matter came out in a hitherto secret love letter, in 1917, to Manuel Magallanes Moure. After six years of artfully twisted public explanations, but well-hidden true thoughts, she wrote, on January 4, 1917, that she had loved Ureta, but, in exchange, he returned love "in a pool of blood, ruined by vice and thievery, besides his suicide.... When we separated, he went straight to the muddy earth" (*"...en una charca de sangre, envilecido por el vicio y hasta ladrón, además de suicida.... Cuando nos separamos, fue derecho al fango"*).[17]

The prize, which made her a celebrity, also turned out to be a Pyrrhic victory in many ways. Without a doubt, the triumph opened doors to privileges previously closed in education, literature, and special positions as an emissary, first to Mexico and later from Chile to the world. The trophy also opened her to personal scrutiny, exaggeration, jealousy, and derision for a long time. For a country teacher and prolific writer, especially a female, who sought recognition, seeking and attaining fame came with a price.

"Gabriela Mistral" Fuses the Sacred and the Secular

After having written under a variety of disguises in the magazines and newspapers of Coquimbo, starting in 1904, Lucila, confronting the Juegos Florales ten years later, decided upon one name, "Gabriela Mistral," as mysterious in origin as it was elusive to the attending public and subsequent researchers. One asks, with "Gabriela Mistral" was she trying to hide or was she taking steps to reveal to a wide audience her poetic voice? Before discussing the final choice, it would be useful to review briefly a trajectory of her *personae*.

Between August 11, 1904, and February 21, 1911, after four years of tutoring from Emelina and on the verge of beginning teaching in a rural school, Lucila published 84 pieces in a dozen newspapers and magazines of Coquimbo province.[18] She had begun developing her craft by practicing writing in 1902. After two years of sentimental scribblings, using variations of her given name, she launched herself at the age of fifteen (1904), with "El perdón de una víctima" ("The Forgiveness of a Victim"), in the newspaper *El Coquimbo*, of La Serena. She explained her rites of passage in stark terms:

> Me inicié en la enseñanza a los 15 años (...) en una escuela rural de campo, sola, sin familia. En este ambiente impregnado de tristeza y de silencio empecé a escribir, él me hizo espiritualmente lo que soy.
>
> I initiated myself in teaching at 15 (...) in a rural country school, alone, without a family. In this environment, impregnated with sadness and silence, I began to write; it made me spiritually what I am.

In "El perdón" and in five other pieces in 1904, and in thirty five from January through December 1905, she veiled herself as "Soledad" ("Solitude") and revealed herself as Lucila Godoy Alcayaga. In 1906, she wrote ten selections, in 1907, eight, and in 1908, thirteen, sanctifying herself with "Alma" ("Soul"), and posturing in a materialistic, secular way as "Alguien" ("Somebody"), the pseudonym that marks the book's opening Epigraph/Manifesto. The assertion of "posturing" gains greater validity with regard to "Alguien."

Pedro Pablo Zegers B. claims this pseudonym is an anagram — a scrambling of letters — to playfully and furtively involve the initials of her full name, i.e., LGA.[19]

The first recorded appearance of "Gabriela Mistral" occurred June 10, 1908, in *La Constitución* of Ovalle, with the poem "Rimas" ("Rhymes"); the second appearance took place the next day for a prose piece "El crítico de Barros Arana." Her full legal name, intertwined with "Soledad, "Alma," and "X," and her recently adopted "Gabriela Mistral," appeared sporadically over the next five years. In Chapter V, "Antofagasta: Desertic North and Arid Behavior," we will discuss how the typesetter of the start-up newspaper *El Mercurio* misread the flourishes and loops of the handwritten "Mistral" and believed it to be "Mistral*y*," thus giving rise, erroneously, to another pen name. In publications in 1913 (August 30, and October 30), and afterwards, Lucila finally surrounded herself in the life-lasting and life-giving appellation.

Three groups of researchers offered different opinions regarding the source of the final pseudonym. One group held that Lucila combined the given name of the Italian novelist of *The Triumph of Death*, Gabriel D'Annunzio, with the surname of Frédéric Mistral (1830–1914), the Provençal poet of *Miréio* (1859), and Nobel laureate (1904). Another group held that she combined Dante Gabriel Rossetti, the English Pre-Raphaelite, and Frédéric Mistral to give rise to the name. Lucila finally cleared up the provenance, in 1946, after years of tortuous elaborations and hesitations. She declared, in accord with a third group, that the name derived from a *"nombre de arcángel con apellido de viento"* ("the first [name] from an archangel, the last, a wind"). The mistral wind flows north from Africa and crosses the Mediterranean toward France. She re-fashioned herself in sacred and secular symbols. "Gabriela Mistral" fused materialized divine essence (the archangel), with earthly, but invisible, matter (the mistral).[20]

CHAPTER III

Family and Personal Matters

Function and Dysfunction

This short preview of Lucila's family life will serve as a guide to the details that follow. Her grandmother and father left important impressions on her, despite their premature departure from Montegrande and the family. With regard to her mother and half sister, a lifetime of love and affection was replaced by pain, when Gabriela was unable to attend their funerals. Finally, Juan Miguel Godoy Mendonza (or Mendoza in Spanish), the boy Gabriela adopted, cared for, and nicknamed Yin-Yin, took his own life. A mention and understanding of these personal matters leads to an understanding of the comments in the text that follows about the person and the poetry.

Isabel Villanueva Godoy: Biblical Tales

Lucila's grandmother on her father's side, Doña Isabel Villanueva Godoy, opens this brief discussion of the family and sets the tone for a fuller discussion in the chapter "The Hebraic Tradition" and in Appendix C, where in the context of Jewishness, Isabel's influence on Lucila's religious and intellectual development will be made clearer. The objective here is to set the scene regarding an old woman of stern temperament who rocked her granddaughter on her lap while reading to her passages from the Old and New Testaments and reciting tales of Biblical heroes and heroines during the child's early formative years.

When Lucila's father abandoned the family after three years of marriage, Isabel, to her regret, accompanied him. However, Lucila's recollections of the age when this event took place, as she reported in Appendix C, oppose those of the critics. Lucila said the reading took place at nine years of age. It is true that she missed her grandmother very much. She never forgot Isabel's permanent influence and incorporated Biblical tales and language into her corpus and speech.

Juan Jerónimo Godoy Villanueva: A Father's Desertion, a Poet's Vindication.

The first family crisis concerned Lucila's father, Juan Jerónimo (1857–1911), who married Petronila, in 1888, a widow with a fourteen-year-old daughter from a previous marriage named Emelina Molina.[1] It was a mismatch from the beginning. Juan Jerónimo was 27; Petronila was 42. He studied to be a teacher; she worked as a seamstress. The arrangement appeared to be a marriage of urgency and convenience, owing to Petronila's pregnancy.

Gabriela's father and grandmother, Juan Jerónimo and Isabel Villanueva.

Juan Jerónimo worked as a schoolteacher and, for entertainment, strummed a guitar, told tall stories, and did his best to write poetry.[2] In 1892, he left home to pursue a job and new adventures in northern Copiapó, returning only occasionally until his death, in 1911, at the age of fifty of pneumonia in the city's hospital. He gave excuses for the desertion, such as to escape from a carping wife whose recriminations robbed him of sleep and verses for his guitar.

> ... su padre dejó el hogar, acaso por gustarle la vida errante, tal vez porque su mujer, de temperamento nervioso, solía alterar sus ensueños con quejas y recriminaciones copiosas que, fuera de impacientarlo, le ahuyentaban rimas singulares casi en el instante de asirlas.[3]

His departing legacy to his three-year-old daughter consisted of a fountain he had constructed, some avocado trees he had planted, and a handful of poems. In 1884, he had already heralded in verses the landscape of La Serena and, on Lucila's birth penned several bittersweet creations that prefigured marital unhappiness and personal separation:

> *Oh dulce Lucila, que en días amargos*
> *Dichosos los cielos te hicieron nacer,*
> *quizá te preparen para ti, hija mía,*
> *El bien que a tus padres no quiso dar.*

> Oh, sweet Lucila, despite the bitter days,
> Heaven bless that you were born,
> Maybe what awaits you, my child,
> Is the goodness your parents never had.

His legacy also consisted of his creative soul, a background as an elementary schoolteacher, and a vagabond nature.[4] Godoy Villanueva's desertion caused serious alterations in Gabriela's life, but, curiously, she does not blame her suffering directly on him. No poems refer to him by name, as do sections of poetry to her mother, the putative sweetheart Romelio Ureta, and her "adopted godson" Juan Miguel Godoy Mendoza.[5] Although this lack of attention could imply indifference, actually her father's absence inflicted a deep wound. The mother tried to shield Lucila from the disdain she herself felt for her husband. Mistral recalled, in 1953, that her mother's stoic forbearance and silent martyrdom caused anguish to both of them, as is evidenced by the charged language of the following attempt at vindication:

> ... siempre creí que mi madre debía haberse ahorrado los sufrimientos que le dio mi padre.... siempre ella se rehusó al divorcio [para] no despojar al esposo de sus derechos de padre y esperar una reacción en sus hábitos. Esto no llegó, pero yo no oí jamás una sola queja de esa mujer ... tampoco un solo juicio contra el compañero ingrato. Ella evitó siempre el que yo creciese alimentando un resentimiento amargo en mi espíritu. En la aldea donde crecí era común el caso

> *del padre ausente, ligado a otra mujer y la reacción de las víctimas era la misma de mi madre, es decir, un silencio "per vita."*[6]

In 1933, she referred to her father in a way that pinpointed the two emotional orbits of her own life, i.e., bitterness and estrangement. They existed alongside admiration and filial tenderness: *"Mi recuerdo de él pudiese ser amargo por la ausencia, pero está lleno de admiración de muchas cosas suyas y de una ternura filial que es profunda."*[7]

Lacking a constant father, could it be that she looked for solace from the steadfast *"Dios Padre,"* a God the Father who was stern and loving, righteous and merciful? Jerónimo escaped from a purportedly oppressive atmosphere at home to gratify physical pleasures and to attempt to refine a mediocre talent. In the daughter's own wanderings, she lived modestly, helped others, and worked with a grim tenacity to succeed as a poet and as a teacher — occupations in which her father had failed.

The absence of masculine guidance conditioned Gabriela to financial self-reliance and, at the same time, made her suspicious of male constancy. During the long period of financial hardship after the father's desertion, her half sister Emelina contributed her modest teacher's salary to sustain the family. Lucila was forced to seek work at fifteen to lend support. In the following poem, she laments having to sell her soul to commerce to bring a loaf of bread to the table:

> *Para que tenga mi madre sobre su mesa*
> *un pan rubio, vendí mis días lo mismo*
> *que el labriego que abre el surco.*
> ("Coplas," p. 108)

In that family, as in others in rural Chile, fidelity and constancy were not the norm. Examples permeated the family, e.g., her paternal grandmother had left home because her grandfather had been sleeping with the maid. In short, Lucila grew up among widows and frustrated wives whose belief that men were inconstant made a profound impression. The irony is that Lucila would also become an active conspirator in the alienation of affection of several married men.

Mistral never married, although several suitors presented their pleas. It appears that spiritual love offered more gratification and less anguish than carnal desire. But the desire for physical love existed in her, as evidenced by the ardent correspondence with Manuel Magallanes Moure. Later on, the discussion will treat the reported physical loves, but they, too, failed to satisfy her because spiritual love and constancy were absent in the relationships. She reacted against her father's denial of responsibility toward his family by becoming, for a public audience, at least, the perfect teacher and, symbolically, the "virgin-mother" who cared passionately for the welfare of children throughout the world.[8] It is worthwhile reiterating a fragment of Pedro Prado's prescient eulogy upon his friend's departure for Mexico in 1922. A faithful friend, Prado underscored Mistral's chaste appearance likened to Mary of Nazareth, her inability to let a man or men shackle her, an absence of earthly desire, and her unique nature as the "chosen one":

> Ultimo eco de María de Nazareth, ... a ella también la invade el divino estupor de saberse la elegida; y sin que mano de hombre jamás la mancillara, es virgen y madre; ojos mortales nunca vieron a su hijo; pero todos hemos oído las canciones con que le arrulla.[9]

Petronila: A Mother's Forbearance

On July 7, 1929, Lucila suffered the loss of her mother, Petronila Alcayaga Rojas, who died at age eighty four. Doña Petronila's demise is noteworthy because it gave Gabriela the celebrity the opportunity to blame, once again, Chilean government officials, such as the Minister of Education, Jorge Matte, for having forced her to go abroad against her wishes to the Institute of International Sciences conference while her mother lay dying: "*Yo salí de Chile 'obligada y forzada' por don Jorge Matte, Ministro de Educación. A causa de aquel nombramiento para el Instituto de Ciencias Internacionales de París. Quería quedarme con mi madre hasta su muerte.*"[10] There was a certain amount of capriciousness in Mistral's arbitrary condemnation of Chilean officialdom as unfeeling and insensitive. Her mother had been lingering near death for a long time, and ample opportunity existed to return beforehand, had she been so inclined. The truth lies somewhere in between her exaggerated claims

Gabriela's mother Petronila

of persecution and the Chilean government's increasingly stern treatment of her for having been outspoken in her criticism of its political and economic policies. The Chilean government, for its part, largely ignored the potential genius of its most renowned woman poet. And Gabriela, for her part, had always harbored a smoldering grudge against the institution of government. Her mother's death merely aggravated that ire. As a result, she had no incentive to return to Chile and continued in voluntary exile, having lost the strongest tie to her country. By remaining abroad, she made reconciliation almost impossible.

Her mother, in life as in death, meant more to her than anybody else for received affection and tenderness. Some of the finest poetry commemorates her mother's death. In "Muerte de mi madre" (in *Tala*, 1938), the poet hopes God will be as benevolent to her mother as he has been to the biblical women who ascended to heaven.[11] The death and resurrection of Jesus Christ inspire an exhortation to him to spare her mother all pain because, in her purity, her mother can be compared with Christ's mother. Although she does not desire her own resurrection to avoid the pain flesh is heir to, Gabriela believes that Doña Petronila merits a more sublime destiny, having led an exemplary life of simplicity and honesty. With the physical bond broken, mother and daughter commune, in these poems, in a silent spiritual bond of penance and perseverance.[12]

Emelina: A Sister's Stoic Connectivity

Emelina Molina Alcayaga (1874–1947), played a decisive role in her younger half sister's early development and continued to be a source of strength and connectivity to her *patria chica*— Coquimbo and the Elqui valley— for years afterward, more so during the writer/diplomat's half-life absence from the *patria grande*, Chile. Emelina, fifteen years older than Lucila, a teacher

Gabriela's half-sister Emelina.

and the family's early breadwinner, played a large part in influencing Lucila's evolving education and social life. Emelina motivated her half sister to develop skills in the Spanish language, books, ideas, and teaching.

Despite their long relationship, Gabriela did not travel from her consular post in Monrovia and Santa Barbara, California to attend Emelina's funeral proceedings. She had already witnessed Emelina's frail health since her second return trip, years before, and had been worried about it. Over the years, the two exchanged numerous letters that covered gossip, relatives, and regular payments from the wealthier relative to defray household expenses and medical bills. In Gabriela's last letter before Emelina's demise, she chided her sister for harboring "*una tribu*" ("a tribe") of lazy relatives and hangers-on who would not lift a finger to take care of her, or the garden, or the dirty dishes. Gabriela wrote that she was not above doing the daily chores, like tending the plants, because, despite her salary and job, she could not afford in expensive California a full-time servant or a gardener. Gabriela demanded that Emelina ask for more effort, rather than more money, from her caretakers. Gabriela might have regretted that Emelina's death came upon the heels of her scolding letter.[13]

Notable figures from local educational, political, and intellectual circles eulogized Emelina at her funeral in La Serena, in March 1947. While Gabriela remained in California, the shadow of her accomplishments dominated the proceedings. The praise for Emelina symbolized reflected glory of the younger sister. The ceremony for Emelina included praise and sensitive comments from local representatives of the central government, the Alianza de Intelectuales de Chile, the newspaper *El Regional*, the retired teachers association, the City of Vicuña, and a poet from the university.[14]

The hard-scrabble early lives of Emelina and Lucila were no predictors of the celebratory eulogies that awaited each in their final days. Both were born into a rural society where men abdicated responsibilities, families were dysfunctional, and financial hardship prevailed. Ill-starred from birth, Emelina came forth from the secret liaison between her unmarried mother and her younger sister's husband, Rosendo Molina Rojas. Rosendo, after ruining the lives of three female relatives, deserted them. Petronila's skills as a seamstress sustained the family and permitted the only daughter to train as a rural teacher. Starting at age 17, Emelina added to their wellbeing with a modest salary as a teacher's assistant.

She got promoted at age 18 to principal of the elementary school in Montegrande and remained there from 1892 to 1900. By 1889, Lucila had been born, and the three — absent male financial support and companionship — benefited financially and emotionally from living in the state-provided two-bedroom house in Montegrande, where the adjoining bedroom served as classroom for about two dozen students. Emelina also taught Lucila there after she was thrown out of Adelaida Olivares' school in Vicuña over the matter of lost sheets of paper and the stoning. After Montegrande, the family followed Emelina to a series of teaching posts in different towns: Diaguitas (1900), La Serena (1901), Coquimbo (1902), and El Molle (1903).[15]

Emelina and Petronila avoided male companionship for a long time. Given her bad luck with Rosendo and Jerónimo, Petronila did not approve of the only man who interested Emelina. It happened that when a trusted family friend died, Petronila gave Emelina her consent to marry the widower, José de la Cruz Barraza (1901), because he was a person with a solid trade as blacksmith in the town. But tragedy followed soon after. Following Emelina's birth to two daughters, her husband died (1906). That caused financial and emotional hardships, made harsher by the death, shortly after birth, of her first-born, Marta Amelia and the medical bills for her second daughter, Graciela Amalia Barraza Molina (born March 7, 1903). Graciela was sickly and larger than normal children owing to a genetic defect of the pituitary gland. She died prematurely. When is not clear; some say in 1923, others say years later.

Lucila, sensitive about her role as Graciela's aunt, dedicated to her the poem "En la siesta de Graciela." Rather than focus on the beauty and peace of the sleeping child, she transformed her niece's nap into a meditation on the fleetingness of existence, especially her own.[16]

> If tomorrow time shortens my being,
> I will be glad if you calm the grief
> That flows from my soul and if you
> Dry my tears when I sadly weep.
> "On Graciela's Nap"

Lucila paid tribute to Emelina's personality and perseverance as the revered and persevering mother and schoolteacher. She became the subject of the iconic poem, "La maestra rural" ("The Country Schoolteacher"). At first, some observers said the poem was a self-portrait. It might have been, but it could not have been. The poem extols a teacher's humility and greatness. Lucila recognized her own shortcomings in humility by seeking recognition. The first series of adjectives refer to Emelina and glorify her as *"pura," "pobre," "alegre,"* and *"dulce"* ("pure," "poor," "joyful," and "sweet"). Each of the positive tags is not gratuitous. To earn them, the rural teacher pays the price of sacrifice and pain: *"Los hierros que le abrieron el pecho generoso, / ¡más anchas le dejaron las cuencas del amor!"* ("Metal rods opened her generous heart, / but wider still remained the valleys of love.") Moreover, if the poem had been a mirror into Gabriela's heart, it would have reflected pain, not pleasure.

Juan Miguel Godoy Mendoza: The Tragic Illusion of Motherhood

Another family tragedy beset Gabriela's life, obscured in conflicting testimony, documentation, and speculation which, when explored fully, promises to be significant. It dealt with Juan Miguel Godoy Mendoza a boy who Gabriela cared for as a devoted mother from the time she "acquired" him to his death at the age of eighteen (April 1, 1925–August 14, 1943).

Like the conflicts surrounding Juan Miguel's origin and death, his names and his relation vis-à-vis Mistral also caused confusion. For example, Mistral affixed to his death certificate in Petrópolis, Brazil, his biological mother's Portuguese surname, Martha Mendonza, thus, "Juan Miguel Godoy Mendonza." But for travel purposes, she Hispanicized the Portuguese surname to "Mendoza" for the official joint passports. Mistral also altered the boy's first name, giving him the melodious nickname Yin-Yin, a word that Isolina Barraza de Estay interpreted as "faithful" in Hindi. The public perceived him as Mistral wanted him to be perceived, either as her "*sobrino*" ("nephew") or as an "*ahijado*" ("godson").

Gabriela and Yin-Yin frolicking (1936).

How did Gabriela come to "acquire," support, and dedicate herself to this boy from childhood to adolescence? Two conflicting and controversial versions persist, each with its supporters and detractors. The first group holds that Juan Miguel *Godoy* was the son of her half brother, Carlos Miguel *Godoy*, whom Lucila *Godoy* [surnames emphasized] adopted. This version finds support in unusual coincidence, credible public opinion, and, most importantly, official documentation.

In stark contrast, the conflicting version, based upon low probability, secrecy to avoid scandal and punishment, lack of supporting documentation, and revelations by former associates after Gabriela's demise, declared that Juan Miguel was Gabriela's biological child. Both versions merit exploration.

The publicly-reported version supported by coincidence, public opinion, and documentation is that Lucila's father, Jerónimo, after abandoning Petronila and the family following three years of marriage, moved north to Copiapó with his mother Isabel and lived with a woman who bore them a son named Carlos Miguel Godoy Villegas. One off-shoot scenario holds that, years later (1924?), Carlos got married in Chile to Marta Muñoz Mendonça [a.k.a. Martha Mendonza], from Barcelona, Spain. Carlos remained in Chile after Marta gave birth (1925) to their son, Juan Miguel. Marta, on returning to Barcelona on the ship "Aconcagua" with her son, met and befriended Gabriela. Gabriela pledged to take care of the son of Carlos and Marta should she become incapacitated by tuberculosis. Marta, in her last moments, entrusted Juan Miguel's care to Gabriela. Carlos, meanwhile, set out for Barcelona from Chile a year later to inquire about his lost wife and son. After searching and not finding them, he applied for a return visa in the Chilean consulate where Gabriela officiated. It was there that both Godoys met by chance, learned of family ties, and found out about Marta's and Juan Miguel's circumstance.

A documented variant of the preceding scenario, developed by Luis Vargas Saavedra, is that while serving as consul in Madrid (1933–1935), Gabriela learned that a Carlos Miguel Godoy, accompanied by a baby, was applying for a visa to Chile. Their paternal heritage and family ties, owing to the same surnames, came out. Her newly-discovered half brother, Carlos, voluntarily surrendered the child to Gabriela for permanent care, since Marta, the mother, had died of tuberculosis in Switzerland [or in Barcelona?].[17] Vargas Saavedra adds and underlines that Gabriela accepted the adoption under the condition that Carlos, who would be traveling to North Africa [perhaps with the French Foreign Legion, 1926–1927?], should renounce all further claims to Juan Miguel. Professor Vargas Saavedra has graciously provided notarized documentation to support the birth, adoption, and death of Juan Miguel. These ought to be convincing and conclusive.

Professor Vargas Saavedra and Mistral's friend from Vicuña, Isolina Barraza de Estay, rejected the following undocumented version, based upon oral comments. But the undocumented view, that Juan Miguel was Gabriela's biological offspring, gains credence from former friends and associates. Gabriela's trusted companions, assistants and some writers allege guarding the secret birth until well after Gabriela's death in 1957. Her companions and the years associated with her follow: Doris Dana (1948–1957), María Urzúa (1945–1945), Palma Guillén (1922–1957), Laura Rodig (1917–1923), and Ema Cossío de Villegas (1925 forward). The Chilean critic, Ricardo Latcham, among others, declared that the public story of the boy's maternity and paternity was a closely-guarded invention. Ms. Dana, heir to Gabriela's legacy, freed from keeping secrets after Gabriela's death, revealed on Chilean television (1999) and in an interview (2002) that her dear friend had given birth to Juan Miguel in France assisted by Palma Guillén. She declared that the story about Carlos Miguel Godoy was a fiction necessary to protect her literary reputation, her official position and salary, and the legend of the "virgin-mother." Comments attributed to Doris Dana about the Nobel Prize winner's "supposed motherhood" to a "supposed nephew" made headlines in Chilean newspapers for two days and continued to be a source of concern.[18]

Ana Pizarro reinforced the preceding with the following sweeping sarcastic comment: "As she would throughout her life, Mistral used subterfuge on this issue in order to lead the life she envisioned for herself, and to be able to claim what she needed. She used the 'strategies of the weak,' and avoided a situation that otherwise would have limited her life."[19]

Subterfuge and irony aside, if there was a father, who was he? In addition to Ricardo Latcham, Volodia Teitelboim and Maximino Fernández Fraile ventured, without offering documentation, that the father might have been the prominent Catalan philosopher and prolific writer Eugenio d'Ors (1882–1954). But the Catalan's daughter, María Eugenia, in 1984, thirty years after his death and thirty-seven years after Gabriela's, declared that such public declarations were inventions, "pure lies" by Chileans meant to discredit both parties and/or to sell newspapers.[20]

One can pursue the matter further based upon circumstantial evidence using time and space as markers. When and where could they have met? They most probably joined forces at the International Institute of Intellectual Cooperation (IIIC), a division of the League of Nations. Indeed, in 1926, Gabriela headed the Secretariat of Literature of the IIIC in Geneva. Vargas Saavedra reports that Gabriela's status made it possible for her to recommend Eugenio as the representative from Spain. He further states that she admired his affinity for the classical tradition and his elegant prose style, so similar to that of her dear Mexican friend Alfonso Reyes: "*Trabajan juntos. [Ella] compartía su revitalización de la tradición clásica, y admiraba su prosa, clara y elegante como la de Alfonso Reyes.*"[21]

D'Ors, for his part, by 1925, had read Mistral's poetry and the controversies surrounding it, declaring that her supporters encouraged a "prophetic mood," whereas he saw and preferred a secularizing tradition. In 1927, Eugenio d'Ors attended the IIIC's meetings in Paris. Thus, chronology, places, and sharing of ideas roughly coincide. If any physical contact ensued that bore fruit, then the time frame also correlated with the conception of Juan Miguel.

The attraction for Gabriela, if indeed one existed, would be due to the fact that the handsome and eloquent Eugenio d'Ors was one of the most brilliant thinkers on the Iberian Peninsula and one of the most controversial politically. Gabriela was no stranger to brilliance and controversy. The major obstacle was that, as with Manuel Magallanes Moure — who had died in 1924, thus leaving her vulnerable emotionally — he was already married. She, for her part, bore stoically the publicly-imposed and self-inscribed image of "virgin-mother," was labeled "casta" ("chaste") by Pedro Prado in his farewell eulogy, "Divina Gabriela" by Virgilio Figueroa as his book's title, and "Santa Gabriela" by the Ecuadorean writer Benjamín Carrión in the title of his book. Scandal would have shriveled Gabriela's image politically and income financially. If subterfuge were called for, she had reasons enough logically to maintain secrecy and to create a fictional narrative of Yin-Yin's origin and her role.

Let us imagine for a moment how an unmarried prominent figure could keep a pregnancy secret? Did her long, ample skirts and dresses provide cover? If the revelation would have been so destructive, then why not terminate the pregnancy? If Gabriela were indeed pregnant, she would have continued until birth, because in her heart she was imbued with the Catholic tradition against abortion, and in her soul she believed in letting children, even those born out of wedlock, live. She never advocated abortion, even for the many underprivileged women in Chile, a country that suffered a very high mortality index for mothers and children.

And where, if this account were true, could she deliver a baby and nurture him? Doris Dana's version is that Palma Guillén escorted her friend to France for delivery. Another version, from Maximino Fernández Fraile quoting her secretary, María Urzúa, lent stock to the theory that she gave birth in Algeria.[22] This involves a most bizarre and unexplained coincidence, because Carlos Miguel Godoy was supposed to have spent two years in the French Foreign Legion in Algeria.

These speculative tidbits come from present-day books, letters, and newspaper reports freighted with a degree of improbability. Doris Dana rejected the possibility that written documentation existed in the many boxes that were in her home and are now in the custody of the Biblioteca Nacional de Chile. Ms. Dana stated that Gabriela mothered Juan Miguel by an anonymous, impassioned, and forgotten Italian Don Juan who never surfaced after the fecundating interlude: "'*No tiene nombre. No es una persona conocida. Ni ella [Gabriela] recordaba su nombre. Fue un italiano.... Palma Guillén la acompañó a dar a luz en Francia.... Ema Cossío de Villegas, también [lo sabía]. Pero no lo dijo por escrito.'"*[23]

However improbable, perhaps a careful researcher might come across — among the thousands of digitized and indexed documents in the Biblioteca Nacional — the medical and personal records that answer these puzzling questions? Even if the pregnancy should prove real, the fact would change the image represented in the biography, but not the literary power and scope of the writer's poetry and prose. Until such time, the documented records presented by Luis Vargas Saavedra and Isolina Barraza de Estay have great validity, despite inconsistencies of time and place.

Gabriela accepted this boy and raised him with the aid of her assistants Consuelo Saleva and Palma Guillén. The photos of the pair together playing and hugging, and the comments about them in correspondence indicate that she showered great affection on Yin-Yin over the years. Perhaps the overweening affection and protection caused unfortunate character disturbances that made him take his life. Perhaps the fact that Gabriela moved often in her consular postings caused emotional alterations. She blamed the Second World War for having abandoned France, where he grew up with French, to live in Portuguese-speaking Brazil, causing the foreign language and cultural inadequacies he sustained. Some of this is suggested in two letters that her close Mexican friend, the diplomat Palma Guillén, wrote just before he killed himself. Palma directed the first to Gabriela, criticizing her for spoiling him and for exercising great control over his life. Palma pointed out to Gabriela, in her strongly-worded letter, that her attention was excessive in burdening him with money and gifts and defending him even when he was rude and lazy. Palma mentioned that her discipline with him was lax, to the point that the young man acted rudely, felt that he could do what he wanted, and showed no inclination for work or studies.

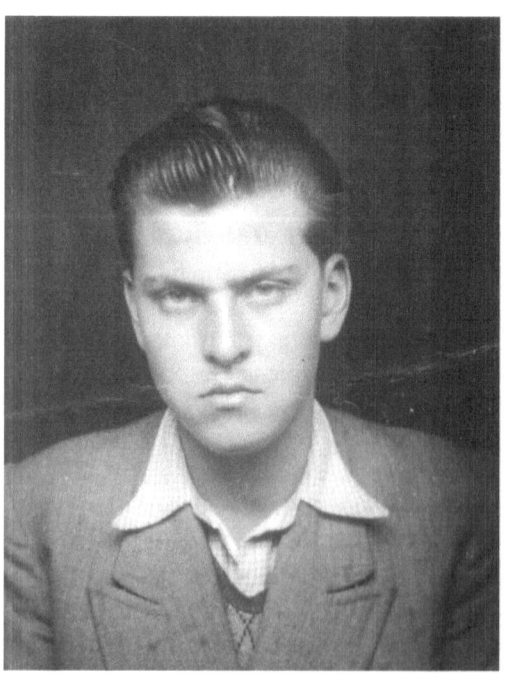

Yin-Yin in Petropolis, Brazil (1943)

Palma's letter to Yin-Yin

arrived three months before his death. In a caring tone, she suggested he take action to improve at school and to set achievable goals. But Yin-Yin's adoration for Palma and the fact that he knew she would soon arrive in Brazil did not suffice to placate his internalized suffering.[24]

The academics turned psychologists among Mistral's observers held that Yin-Yin fulfilled her maternal need and satisfied her longing for a child. Thus she achieved, albeit vicariously, the motherhood denied her by her promise to remain true to an unattainable lover and her distrust of physical love.[25]

After the unexpected death of Yin-Yin (August 14, 1943), at the age of 18 years in Petrópolis, Brazil, the issue of the cause of his death became clouded in a battle between Mistral, who continually insisted that he had been assassinated, and the police, who officially classified the act as self-induced arsenic poisoning in Death Certificate Number 01492.25.[26]

Mistral's companions, Consuelo Saleva, Palma Guillén, and María Urzúa — that is, the people closest to her — also attested to the boy's suicide. They said he had killed himself because he felt culturally isolated in Brazil, his French useless, and frustrated also because the law required him to repeat schoolwork already completed in France. The Brazilian poet Manuel Bandeira suggested to me another reason for his unease. Bandeira remarked that a deformity of the spine — which Gabriela acknowledged to Esther de Cáceres — caused a nervous condition that eventually led to self-destruction.[27] Some reported that Gabriela's negative commentary on a draft of his novel shattered his self-esteem and drove him to tear up the manuscript. Imagine, for a moment, a distraught and sensitive sixteen-year-old attempting to measure up to a Nobelist in literature. Some report that he had called her "Buda" to emphasize her glacial attitude and enforced righteousness and purity.

To these reasons one must add the double suicide of the exiled Austrian-Jewish refugees, the acclaimed international writer of *Amok*, Stefan Zweig (1881–February 23, 1942), and his young second wife, Charlotte Altmann. The Zweigs, having fled the rampaging Nazis in Austria and France, became disillusioned to discover fascism flourishing in Brazil under President Getúlio Vargas (1883–1954). The couple, pacifists, despaired of finding a safe haven away from war and its ravages. Stefan and Charlotte found comfort in the intellectual conversations over tea and dinners with Gabriela and Yin-Yin, who resided a few houses away. Zweig, a friend and associate of another Austrian, Sigmund Freud, had studied psychology and philosophy. But formal psychology did not avail in their personal struggle of *eros* and *thanatos*; the latter won out. With all the travails they endured, the couple could not embrace a philosophy that vouchsafed survival. Stefan, speaking for both, penned the following statement that justified their irreversible decision to die by ingesting poison: "It seems to me, therefore, better to put an end in good time and without humiliation to life in which intellectual work has always been an unmixed joy and personal freedom earth's most precious possession."[28]

The double suicide affected Gabriela and Yin-Yin profoundly. She commemorated the Zweigs days after the tragic event in a personal eulogy.[29] Yin-Yin felt the pain to a greater degree, but kept his anguish within because Stefan had befriended him and tried to understand him. Stefan had become, in the absence of paternal affection, the boy's surrogate father and a counterweight to Gabriela's "glacial affection." In the months after Zweig's passing, one imagines that the sensitive youth felt abandoned by this older and wiser friend, alienated from his busy and intellectual mother, and, as noted below, estranged from his classmates. In retrospect, Zweig's epitaph might have motivated the boy's own self-inflicted poisoning six months later. One can find flashes of Zweig's final self-justification and stoicism in Yin-Yin's scant note to his mother, in which he surrendered in the face of great odds having received from her the best that life had to offer:

> *Querida mamá:*
> *Creo que mejor hago en abandonar las cosas como están: No he sabido vencer, espero que en otro mundo exista más felicidad.*
> *Cariñosamente, tu Yin-Yin. Un abrazo a Palma.*[30]

> Dear mommy:
> I believe it is better for me to abandon things as they are: I haven't known how to overcome, I hope that in another world a greater happiness exists.
> Affectionately, your Yin-Yin. A hug to Palma.

The preceding thoughts are validated by a sympathetic article in Portuguese in the local paper, which appeared one day after Juan Miguel's death. Written by a classmate who expressed friendship and sadness, it implied that his friend was a sufferer fated to a tragic ending owing to the death of his natural mother, i.e., Marta Mendonza, and an absence of paternal guidance and care:

> *Morrera o Godoy, êsse companheiro dedicado das bancas escolares em todas as horas, fiel expressão de um predestinado a viver, no alvoecer dos anos, os grandes dramas íntimos que caracterizan os sofredores de todos os tempos. Paradoxalmente, êsse menino louro abrigava um espírito avançado, como se os meses se houvessem transformado em anos, êstes, por sua vez, em lustros intermináveis. Este, sem dúvida alguma, o destino daqueles que anelam no coração as dores da terra, as múltiples paixões das almas inquietas e trazendo no olhar amortecido aquele mistério insondável que tanto desafia a argúcia dos que blasonara surpreender ou desvendar os sofrimentos alheios. O Godoy morreu ôntem ... orfão de mãe e divorciado dos carinhos paternos, óra em terras distantes.... quisemos falar dêle e para êle, como una homenagem á sua tristeza e ao seu*

grande drama íntimo, drama que é o reflexo do mil e um males coletivos, definindo-se como símbolo das grandes tragédias de todos os dias.[31]

In opposition to official declarations and the testimony of friends and witnesses, Gabriela clung tenaciously to the opinion that the boy had enjoyed good physical and emotional health. Thus, she insisted, he had no reason for anguish which would lead to suicide. She found justification for his death — "he had good physical and emotional health"— not in suicide but in homicide. She told of one or more youths on different occasions, troubled by their conscience, who informed her personally that a gang of young neo–Nazi "youths," called precisely "Mocidades," had taunted Juan Miguel because of his refusal to join them, his white skin, and the wealth and reputation of his family. Finally, they had said he was a bastard.[32] In an interview Mistral indicted the Afro-Brazilian boys of the high school Juan Miguel attended of bigotry and envy toward wealthy boys from white-skinned families and foreign countries ("*...estaba lleno de muchachos negros y mulatos que hostilizaban a los pocos blancos que había.*"). But how could he have been in good health — physically and emotionally — if, as she was well aware, he suffered harassment and bruises, the result of attacks by those same school mates?: ("[*Regresó a casa*] ... *lleno de moretones a causa de los golpes de los demás.*") She gave the following reasons for his depression and death:

> *Y era porque vivía rodeado de comodidades que los demás no tenían. Esto despertó la envidia de sus compañeros, el deseo de vengarse de lo que se llamaba 'la banda.' Una noche me lo trajeron muerto. Dijeron que era suicidio, pero yo supe que lo mató 'la banda,' porque no podían perdonarle que él poseyera lo que ellos no tenían.*[33]

Gabriela insisted that this fanatic group killed Juan Miguel. In veiled language she revealed this intrigue in an article that warned of the dangers of xenophobia and in many letters to friends.[34]

As if the death — from whatever cause — were not burden enough, the poet suffered grievously on learning that the Catholic Church refused to allow the boy, a true Catholic and believer despite his final action, to be buried in sacred ground. A death by suicide, argued the priest, notwithstanding a person's beliefs, violated links to a Church-sanctioned burial. Higher governmental and ecclesiastic powers, however, prevailed in the sensitive conflict, and Juan Miguel was laid to rest in hallowed ground. In 2005, his remains were disinterred and sent to rest in the mausoleum alongside Gabriela's in Montegrande. Distraught over the death and the Church's initial refusal to accept him in its bosom, she wrote two long, impassioned prayers to "Our Lord" and to "Jesus Christ" to vindicate this act and to safeguard his soul. The two prayers in Spanish are powerful and, ideally, should be read in that language for maximum emphasis. But perhaps the following translation of three short paragraphs of "Our Lord" can capture the passion[35]:

> Jesus Christ, Our Lord, at dawn we commend to thee Juan Miguel, and before sleeping we hand him over once again..... After us he was yours, J. C.; but now he is only yours. Look out for him, provide for him, watch over him. Before, he was among us women, or wherever he was he remained within our view. Now he has the first white day one of Eternity, beyond the reach of our poor eyes.... Before, Christ, it was up to us to watch over him, listen for him, look out for him. Now he finds himself entirely under your governance and submerged in your mercy.

The cause of death notwithstanding, the aftermath dogged her forever.[36] She even felt emptiness on hearing news, in October 1945, of winning the Nobel Prize: "*¿Para qué lo quiero ahora?*"[37] In a letter to her dear Argentine friend, Victoria Ocampo, twelve days after the boy's demise, she revealed the existential and irretrievable loss involved with Yin-Yin's death, whether by his own hand or by others in my translation of the letter:

> *... this child wasn't a portion of my life; he was life itself. In him began and ended my reason for working, my joys and my worries..... The house was for him; the day, him; reading, him. I know that God rudely punishes idolatry and that this doesn't just mean the cult of images.*
> Oh, but I have to return to my old heresy and believe in the karma of past lives in order to understand what phenomenal crime of mine has punished me so suddenly, with my Juan Miguel's night of agony....[38]

Illnesses, Debilitation and Death

Juan Miguel's passing produced even greater physical and psychical damage. On an emotional level, report Elizabeth Horan and Doris Meyer, she suffered, as a result, from delirium, weaknesses, and forgetfulness. The illnesses that continued to afflict her for years — diabetes, kidney pains, blurring eyesight — intensified. She believed that she could mitigate her grief by traveling and by increasing her charitable works. Having failed to save her son — whether hers or her half brother's — as she had been unable to save Romelio Ureta thirty-four years earlier, she preserved the boy's image and her love for him in *Lagar* (*Winepress*), in a poem titled "Luto" ("Mourning," pp. 703–722). The death inspired a return to the poetry of divine suffering. She likens him to the archangel Michael who was transported to heaven to attain, in the poet's eyes, celestial beauty. She also continued, after his death, to work on the *Poema de Chile,* where, in line with her belief in karmic principles and reincarnation from Buddhism and Theosophy, she transformed herself into a ghost who repented from misdeeds by guiding an innocent boy [Yin-Yin?] and his *huemul* (a Chilean deer) safely through the difficult Chilean landscape. (This theme was analyzed in Chapter I, "Personal Abnegation and Spiritual Fulfillment.")

Precarious health played a significant part in Mistral's attitude toward life, death, and suffering. Diabetes, perhaps inherited from her mother, was not diagnosed until 1930. The disease brought her to the edge of grave illness at several points in her early life. Intensified by the diabetes, heart trouble nearly caused her death in 1948: "[*Sufrí*] *un colapso hepático-cardíaco. Viví el más dulce estado que yo haya concebido en este mundo, todo eso antes de la adrenalina que me resucitó. Ya no tendré ningún miedo de la muerte. Estoy mucho mejor y me cuidan de más.*" Three years later, she reported to a friend that an incurable loss of eyesight, owing to poor circulation [arteriosclerosis?] had brought on blurred vision and consternation: "*Hay días, mi amigo, en que todo el mundo es para mí borroso como una nube. Dicen que esto viene de una circulación muy mala de la sangre en los ojos.*"[39] Finally, in 1957, she succumbed to cancer of the pancreas.

Mistral bibliographer Patricia Rubio, in her analysis of Mistral's correspondence, makes much of her illnesses. She labels Mistral's frequent references to ailments and body parts in her correspondence as "pathographies," symptoms and consequences of deeper socio-psychological concerns, rather than as debilities and sicknesses that afflict many people who find limited relief in writing about them to friends and relatives, perhaps to gain sympathy, perhaps as a catharsis. Rubio considers it psychologically strange that Mistral could reveal weaknesses and ailments to friends in letters, but could not voice them aloud or publicly because enemies in the bureaucracy would see in them an inability to carry out her consular duties and roving ambassadorship, which would result in destitution.[39]

Rubio — who confesses to not being a psychologist — applies Mistral's ailments and vulnerabilities expressed mainly in her correspondence to a psycho-pathology based on fear.[40] Rubio believes they explain and underscore her "marginality, her sense of displacement, her isolation, her feelings of vulnerability, her paranoia." She compares Mistral's reactions to illness to those of the American essayist Susan Sontag, author of *Illness as Metaphor*, who also succumbed to cancer. The analogy lacks balance because Sontag, on voicing her illness publicly, did not fear losing her job, indeed, she made money from that book while showing that "illness is not a condition, but a place."

But in these differences of opinion, one has to give credit to Professor Rubio's more cogent argument about illness and "place." Rubio's poetic, spiritual coda coincides with this writer's central theme of Mistral's concepts of religiosity and God: "...we enter this new *place* [emphasis added] without knowing it, without feeling we have crossed a border.... the power of the mind is a mirage, sickness is all-powerful..... The individual in the kingdom of the sick has only God to rely upon — Mistral's refuge as she struggled to escape from the imprisonment of physical decay."

Owing to Mistral's physical disabilities, she required traveling companions over her lifetime to attend to her medicines, meals, finances, itineraries, lodging, and general well-being. On her trip to Mexico, from 1922–1924, for instance, Laura Rodig and Amantina Ruiz accompanied her from Chile. Joining them in Mexico as official escorts and facilitators were Palma Guillén and Eloísa Jasso. The 7,000-foot altitude of Mexico City caused her breathing difficulties, so she could not remain in the capital to participate in the administration of Mexico's rural school and library system. She operated then, as she would do in a consular visit in 1948, from the coastal area of Veracruz. Overcoming fatigue to comply with her commitments to José Vasconcelos, the Minister of Education, she traveled by car and bus along dusty roads and over peaks and through valleys to visit village schools.

Over the years, she journeyed constantly, not only to escape boredom and to achieve spiritual satisfaction, but also to find a hospitable climate. She mentioned three such places: Petrópolis, Brazil, Naples, Italy, and Santa Barbara, California. Under the threat of death from anyone of her illnesses, it is surprising that she lived sixty-seven years, and that she could pursue an active career. An incident in 1953, when she attended a conference in Havana dedicated to the Cuban poet and martyr José Martí, the Congreso de Escritores Martianos, illustrated her constant alertness to error. Fatigue had prevented her from delivering a message, and, apparently half asleep from exhaustion, she interrupted a speaker who had misread a line of her poetry.

She looked thin and wan when, in 1954, she returned to Chile to receive, belatedly, the Premio Nacional de Literatura, i.e., three years after having been awarded it. In her acceptance speech, she rose above the slights and shortcomings received in Chile and referred to what was uppermost in her mind and spirit, that is, the welfare of underprivileged and overworked peasants, miners, and mothers.

She persevered in spite of her debilities and tragedies and pushed herself beyond her physical capacities, always giving her thoughts and care to those who needed them most. An early poem, "Credo" ("Creed"), captures the essence of her lifelong attempt to rise above the limitations imposed by physical defects. In this expression of belief, to regenerate hope and love in man, action should be rooted in willpower, creative activity, and faith in God:

> *Creo en mi corazón, ramo de aromas que mi*
> *Señor como una fronda agita, perfumando de*
> *amor toda la vida*
> > *haciéndola bendita.*
>
> I believe in my heart, bough-laden aromas that
> my Lord like a frond shakes, perfuming
> life with love
> > making it blessed.
>
> *Creo en mi corazón, el que no pide nada porque*
> *es capaz del sumo ensueño y abraza en el ensueño*
> *lo creado*
> > *inmenso dueño!*
>
> *Creo en mi corazón, que cuando canta hunde en*
> *el Dios profundo el flanco herido, para subir de la*
> *piscina viva*
> > *como recién nacido.*
>
> *Creo en mi corazón siempre vertido, pero*
> > *nunca vaciado.*

One key line from the preceding sums up her beliefs and feelings: "I believe in my heart, always flowing, but never empty" (*Desolación*, "Credo," pp. 31–32).

CHAPTER IV

Self-Education and Survival

An Inquiring Mind

Gabriela Mistral's formidable intellectual depth, breadth, and reach did not germinate from the child Lucila steadily climbing a structured and graduated educational ladder from elementary school, to *liceo* (high school), to university, with institutions peopled by degreed professionals who steadily and incrementally recognized her talents and provided lots of games, books, libraries, and exams, which led, finally, to certifications and degrees. Her formal and informal ascent, instead, took accidental and disturbing starts and stops, turns and twists.

Lucila led forth the advancement of her own education [Latin, *educere*, to lead forth] by observing, absorbing, and trying to understand nature's wonders in the rural Elqui valley. The precocious child, in addition, asked questions of teachers in the family, i.e., grandmother, father, and sister. After her sister taught her to read Spanish, she devoured as many books as were available. From the age of five or six to about fifteen, she attended formal schools sporadically, mainly in the Elqui valley, but a large part of her learning took place from a conscious decision to study alone. Upon receiving the Nobel Prize, many who examined her career pointed out with great surprise that Lucila/Gabriela was mainly an autodidact, a self-motivated and self-taught person who, once having grasped the nuances and power of language and an early understanding of her own persevering nature, began to learn and to create by herself.

First of Many Bookstores

Lucila propelled herself to books. While Lucila lived and worked in La Cantera, in 1904, a unique chance and opportunity struck. She discovered the well-stocked bookstore run by Domingo Gallo in the nearby town of Guayacán. It might seem odd to find in this off-the-beaten-path bookstore 19th century writers from many countries. But the not-too-distant port city of La Serena (founded 1543), and some 260 miles north of the capital, attracted a wide-ranging commercial and touristic population.

On days off from teaching, or when not writing, she frequented the shop, and with her meager earnings from teaching and writing began to buy paperback editions of local and foreign writers, which she read eagerly, and whose ideas permeated her writings from that period onward. Her literary formation blossomed from the material she harvested in Gallo's bookstore.

For his readers, Gallo would have acquired, most probably, French Romantics, Symbolists, and Parnassians, such as, Victor Hugo, Paul Verlaine, Arthur Rimbaud, Leconte de Lisle, and Frédéric Mistral the Nobelist (1904). Readers might have found turn-of-the-century writers from Spain: the poet Gustavo Adolfo Bécquer; the novelist Benito Pérez Galdós; and the essayist Miguel de Unamuno.

Curious Chileans took an interest in other Latin American writers, among them, Cuba's José Martí, Colombia's José María Vargas Vila and José Asunción Silva, Mexico's Amado Nervo and Enrique González Martínez, and, of course, Nicaragua's Rubén Darío. Gallo's patriotism would have prompted him to stock the shelves with older and younger Chilean writers. He offered, of course, the traditional writers: Alonso de Ercilla's epic poem, *La Araucana*, and the treatise on spelling by Andrés Bello. He assuredly stocked Lucila's generation, with the poetry of Miguel Luis Rocuant and Manuel Magallanes Moure.

Many of the above mentioned Latin American, Spanish, Chilean, and French authors whom Lucila first knew in paperback would spring alive some day, since, in the course of time, she encountered them in person or integrated their ideas into her own writings. In 1935, in Madrid, she met and respected, but later had a falling out with, the illustrious Miguel de Unamuno, rector of the Universidad de Salamanca. The Cuban patriot Martí, who had suffered martyrdom in the battle of Los Ríos (1895), was memorialized in "La lengua de Martí," an article on his prose style. Vargas Vila's philosophy of death and eroticism captivated her. Nervo's interests in Theosophy and Buddhism would find a place in her poetry, as discussed later in Chapter XIII, "A Quest for Religious Harmony." And the other Mexican, the Ambassador to Chile, Enrique González Martínez, whose poem "Tuércele el cuello al cisne" ("Twist Off the Swan's Head") would challenge and diminish Rubén Darío's emphasis on Parnassian themes, recommended her to José Vasconcelos for the mission to Mexico (1922–1924). She, of course, read Darío's *Azul* (1888, *Azure*), as did every other literate Chilean, since the Nicaraguan had spent three years in Santiago (1886–1888), where he published his pioneering poems in prose. In 1914, Darío would invite Mistral to collaborate on *Elegancias,* his Parisian magazine. The two Chilean writers (Rocuant and Magallanes Moure), soon-to-be friends, would participate in the Juegos Florales. And, of course, Frédéric Mistral, who wrote *Miréio* and won the Nobel Prize, is long associated with Mistral's pen name.

Ossandón's Influence

Chance and opportunity struck again in Lucila's early intellectual and artistic growth — a period of rude awakening and great potential. In 1904, at the age of fifteen, on a train ride to La Serena, she bumped into Don Bernardo Ossandón, editor of the newspaper, *El Coquimbo.* Following their conversation, the journalist remained impressed with the young girl's enthusiasm and inquiring mind. Don Bernardo invited her to read books in his library and to submit articles for publication. He made good on his offer. In 1904, the first year of their chance encounter, he published all six of her submissions, from August 11, to December 17. For the next six years, starting January 26, 1905, until February 21, 1911, the editor accepted twenty-eight articles and poems in his newspaper.

Successes and Failures in Teaching

In 1904, Don Bernardo recommended Lucila to the school inspector for a position as *ayudanta* (assistant) in the country school of La Compañía, a few miles from La Serena. So this young girl, mostly self-taught and lacking formal credentials stood before students for the first time to teach reading to those less fortunate than herself, i.e., by day to children of farmers and at night to their parents who came in from the fields.

This period of rude awakening was not only artistic and intellectual. She could no longer afford to foster childhood dreams of being sheltered from family and financial difficulties. Just as she launched herself into books, readings, and artistic productivity, she thrust herself into the cold world of earning a living by teaching. Evenings and weekends she prepared her reading lessons and also researched and wrote articles and poems.

The year she spent teaching in La Compañía turned out to be unsatisfying for reasons not easily understood. They might have had to do, on the one hand, with her sense of personal unsuitability owing to physical unattractiveness, and, on the other, with her lack of formal preparation. At the

Coquimbo and Elqui valley

end of the year, she either quit or was not re-hired, and applied, in late 1904, for entrance, starting March 1905, into the teachers' training school, La Escuela Normal de Preceptoras, under the direction of the Catholic Church. The credentials she offered were, to all appearances, impeccable, and included a letter of support from Bernardo Ossandón and six articles in 1904, and three in the first months of 1905, all in Ossandón's newspaper *El Coquimbo*. Her energy and intellectual ability were laudable, but some articles reflected traces of pantheism, a theme that the Church opposed. Her approach to nature caused the director, Capellán Manuel Ignacio Munizaga, to reject her application.

That was an unexpected blow, a threat to her freedom of expression and a menace to her livelihood. She took the rejection personally, because her first opportunity to become credentialed was thwarted. This rejection planted the seed of her alienation from the Church and the clergy. It was another quiver in her bow aimed at Chile's officialdom. The rejection also transformed into a literary and philosophical theme regarding the Church's ideological control over ideas and public education and coincided with existing external historic conflicts, aside from Mistral, between liberals and conservatives.

Notwithstanding the rebuff, Lucila persisted in finding employment. Two openings presented themselves. She taught in La Cantera in 1905 and 1907, and worked as staff in the city of La Serena, 1906 and 1908. La Cantera was, like La Compañía, an agricultural area. Because of her previous experience she adapted more readily to the farming students and their parents, to the reading schedule and curriculum, and to the school administrator.

City schools were another matter. The school in the city of La Serena, larger, more formal, and more complex than farm-area schools, presented unexpected challenges and difficulties during 1906 and 1908. Lacking credentials, Lucila's duties did not involve teaching. She worked, instead, in the admissions office and served as hall monitor, standing-in occasionally, whenever needed, as *profesora interina* (interim teacher). Her physical makeup and personal conduct, rather than her professional performance, gave rise to difficulties. Her tallness, which was unalterable, seemed to bother her shorter colleagues. But it was her refusal to alter her frozen silence toward colleagues that caused the most concern. Lucila withdrew and refused to communicate.

Years later, when Gabriela was asked about the job in La Serena, she claimed that she had kept silent and aloof because of feeling intimidated. She reasoned or rationalized that her silence was a shield from Ana Krusche, the German-born principal, who treated her badly and who considered her a threat because of intellectual superiority. The three reasons she proposed for the difficulties — height, silence, and intellectual superiority — were important, but not necessarily the critical one. The teachers gossiped about Lucila also owing to the *relación rara* (strange relationship) she had developed with a teacher twenty years her senior, Fidelia Valdez Pereira. It was Fidelia who had recommended Lucila in the first place and who defended her from the principal, Ana Krusche.

The two developed a very close personal relationship which eventually led to both of them resigning, deciding to move on, and living together at future teaching posts. However, this decision presented practical challenges. Fidelia did not have another immediate teaching assignment; Lucila did not possess teaching credentials. Fidelia recommended that Lucila stand again for another exam. This time around, Brígida Walker's Instituto Pedagógico had revamped the exam and replaced the German methodology and schoolteachers.

This important narrative regarding Lucila and Fidelia and their teaching together will resume after a clarifying intervention, a discussion of the people and ideologies in Chile's educational system that made it possible for Lucila and Fidelia to reach their decision to obtain credentialing and to move on in tandem.

Chilean School Systems (1840–1890)

Lucila's difficulties with a church school director and with a demanding German principal beg the question regarding the development, quality, and ideology of the Chilean school systems of the mid–19th and early 20th centuries. In brief, how did first a German, followed by a Venezuelan, by an Argentine, and by a Frenchman come to play key roles? What were the roles of religious leaders and secular leaders in the training of children and adults? Who were the major Chilean contributors to national education.

These general questions beg the overriding singular questions: Would Lucila have received a good education if she had moved forward through the system, or was she better off educating herself? Could a precocious, question-asking, inquiring *girl* [emphasis added] find a place in a structured system that required young women, but not young men, to train for obedience, household duties, and motherhood?

Another matter is the quality of the schools. Quality ranged from adequate to good in the cities, but in the rural areas, front-line teachers faced poor housing, low pay, and scarce supplies. These inadequacies made it difficult to attract, in number and quality, certified personnel for rural schools. Many of the instructors were young "*ayudantes*" and/or *preceptoras*" ("assistants," "tutors"), like Lucila herself, drawn from the local countryside who substituted for scarce professionals and performed as well as they could given existing conditions. Each year or so, rural teachers—Emelina and Lucila are examples—would be transferred to new postings, either willingly or as the system demanded, so that students and instructors lacked loyalty and continuity. In these educational disruptions, Lucila was lucky. Emelina served as Lucila's ongoing and constant mentor, so she received personal, above average instruction and attention.

To give a very brief idea of the educational systems that influenced Chileans, especially Emelina and Lucila, one must turn to three foreign and two local influences that shaped Chile's educational systems in the 19th century after the new nation declared its independence from Spain (1810). At the university level, the Venezuelan Andrés Bello introduced the European tradition. At the high school (*liceo*) and vocational school levels, the American-inspired, democratic ideas of the Argentine Domingo Faustino Sarmiento found a place. At the teachers training and elementary school levels, in addition to the U.S. tradition, German, French, and Chilean ideologies prevailed.

The two Chilean officials who most brought to bear their influence and power in implementing educational ideologies and systems during the era in question were Foreign Minister Diego Portales and President Manuel Montt. Diego Portales, in the belief that Chile's higher educational system needed development, invited to Chile, in 1829, the Venezuelan polymath, Andrés Bello (1781–1865), tutor to the young Simón Bolívar and author of patriotic odes and intellectual essays. Portales rescued Bello from his involuntary exile in London, where he studied and wrote at the British Museum. Bello's erudition, plus his support of independence from Spain, made him an excellent candidate to strengthen higher education. Bello became, first, a senator and later founder of the University of Chile (1843). As rector, he developed programs in the humanities, classics, and laws designed to train *licenciados*, that is, the professors, lawyers, and new intelligentsia, among them, José Victorino Lastarria. Bello, furthermore, utilized his knowledge of languages and laws in the emerging nation to also write tomes that organized and codified systems.

His seminal *Gramática castellana* (1847) clarified Spanish grammar for Latin- and Anglo-Americans, thus promoting better international communication. The *Código civil* systematized laws and regulations to guide the general populace. His *Ortografía castellana*, the work on spelling, unified and streamlined the style of spelling and writing.

Unlike Andrés Bello, Doming Faustino Sarmiento (1811–1888) did not get to Venezuela by boat at the invitation of the Chilean government with a promise of high-level employment.[1] In 1831, he crossed the cold and barren Andes on foot and by cart, fleeing Juan Manuel de Rozas' dictatorship (1832–1852). Reared in poverty, Sarmiento arrived penniless to Chile, but while working menial jobs, this autodidact published newspaper articles on governance and education, subjects he taught himself. Bello and Sarmiento differed in background, experience and objectives. Bello's privileged training favored developing the elites. Bello was shaped by classical traditions and writers of the English and French Enlightenment, such as John Locke and Jean-Jacques Rousseau.

However much that Chile required lawyers and intellectuals, President Montt believed that Chilean youth needed to be trained, also, as productive members of the labor force in practical schools for teacher training, vocational skills, and engineering and science. The articles of the exiled Argentine, Sarmiento, about improving public and vocational instruction impressed the president, so he sent for him. But before implementing any plans, President Montt dispatched Sarmiento, from 1845 to 1848, on a mission to the U.S. to survey school and library standards, where he befriended and learned from Horace and Mary Mann, important educators from Massachusetts. By the way, a statue of Sarmiento graces Boston, a tribute to his contributions to education and to solidarity between the U.S. and Argentina.

On his return, Sarmiento, the self-taught elementary schoolteacher, wrote *Las escuelas, bases de la prosperidad y la democracia de los Estados Unidos* (1848; *Schools, Bases of the Prosperity and Democracy of the U.S.*), *Educación popular* (1849; *Popular Education*), and *Educación pública* (1852; *Public Education*). In 1854, Sarmiento's concepts took root in President Montt, who ordered established Las Escuelas Normales de Preceptoras, a series of teachers' training schools and a system of free educational schools where rich and poor alike could learn practical and vocational arts. Like Sarmiento, Montt was in favor of technical, agricultural, and scientific institutions. Chile needed a post-revolutionary school system to reach the masses, to increase literacy, and to develop a capable labor force that would lead the country to economic growth.

Bello and Sarmiento had died by the time Lucila was born. Their influence, however, persisted. Lucila, along with the general populace, adhered to Bello's spelling rules and wrote her surname as "Godoi Alcayaga," substituting the Latin "*i*" for the Greek "*y*"; much later she, like other Chileans, were required to modernize the spelling, thus Godoy Alcayaga.

Lucila absorbed Bello's spelling rules, but Sarmiento's ideas left a more enduring impression on the schoolteacher and on the future educator. They were born into similar social circumstances, having risen from obscurity and poverty to become teachers, educators, authors, and leaders. If she was the iconic and metaphorical "*maestra rural*" ("country schoolteacher"), he became known in Argentina, after being elected (1868–1874), as the "teacher-president" whose slogan was "*gobernar es educar*" ("to govern is to educate").

Mistral and Sarmiento received U.S. honorary doctorates, she from Mills College (1947), he from the University of Michigan. Both agreed that early- and mid-level training systems for teachers could be created that stimulated positive attitudes and fairness of opportunity toward all levels, from manual laborers to future poets. From her teaching post in Los Andes, she paid homage to Sarmiento by visiting the small Andean schoolhouse in Pocuro where he first taught. There she meditated on the valuable national edifice that Sarmiento had bequeathed to the foreign country that had sheltered him in exile and had implemented his ideas. Sarmiento's edifice was an educational system that encouraged positive attitudes toward manual labor and equality of opportunity achieved through free, democratic schools. Where Sarmiento implemented secular learning systems for efficient and effective mass education, she added humanity and morality to education by including in its philosophy the sacredness of teaching through love and dedication.

In 1854, at the same time that President Montt decided to invest in Sarmiento's ideas about U.S. high school and vocational training for the emerging labor force, he also invested in the already mentioned Escuelas Normales de Preceptoras (Normal Schools for Preceptors). Up until mid–19th century, the Hermanas del Sagrado Corazón (Sisters of the Sacred Heart) directed these schools and provided an education to young girls that included marital fidelity, religion, and the dutiful attention to household tasks. This curriculum might have trained girls as lay nuns, faithful wives, and breeders of children, but not as leaders and thinkers.

Chilean School Systems (1890–1922)

By 1890, a different political regime replaced the Sisters of the Sacred Heart with a system from Germany. German school mistresses, like Ana Krusche, Lucila's principal, continued the training in virtuosity and household domesticity, but added math, reading, spelling, and physical education. This curriculum and ideology answers the earlier question about Lucila/Gabriela that was "begged" at the start. Under these structures, could the precocious and inquiring Lucila have developed into a free-thinking, independent writer and thinker?

By the time Lucila was applying to enter the Escuela Normal de Preceptoras in La Serena, under Ana Krusche, other political and ideological shifts were taking place. Two Chilean pedagogues had entered the fray to improve public school education and to move it way from German methodology and personnel. They were Teresa Prats de Sarratea, who wrote *Educación doméstica de las jóvenes* (1913; *Domestic Education for Young Girls*), and Brígida Walker, who translated from the French Jean Aubert's *Curso de pedagogía y y metodología* (1915; *Course of Pedagogy and Methodology*).

Brígida Walker, influenced by Jean Aubert, introduced the *lycée* system. The system involved night classes, lectures, and course cycles. Its structure included six years in primary school and six in high school *humanidades* (humanities). She also changed the methods by which certification could be obtained, which helped Lucila enormously. Walker centralized the process of applying and testing for certification as a high school teacher in the Instituto Pedagógico (Pedagogical Institute), located in Santiago. Rural school districts, on the other hand, could still establish regulations and requirements that permitted hiring interim or short-term teachers and posting them frequently to different towns. Under this system, rural teachers, such as Emelina and Lucila, had been hired under special conditions of exigency and capability and traveled often. But Lucila, by now, sought certification to be able to teach outside of the rural areas.

Lucila, Fidelia and Certification

At this point in the discussion of the poet/teacher's educational development, the Chilean school system unites the lives of Lucila Godoi, Fidelia Valdez Pereira, and Brígida Walker. Fidelia, who had become a close friend and protector in the high school in La Serena, aware of Lucila's earlier inability to obtain credentialing at the school directed by Capellán Manuel Ignacio Munizaga because, he said, her articles "*tenía sabor a panteísmo*" ("smacked of pantheism"), recommended that she apply at the Instituto Pedagógico in Santiago, under Brígida Walker's direction, for a special credentialing exam for gifted persons, which took the place of years of course work. It was a desperate gamble to enable Fidelia and Lucila to go forward in their plans to work together and to live together. Unless Lucila was also credentialed and had earning power, the future for them looked bleak.

IV. Self-Education and Survival   55

Fidelia Valdez Pereira (center) and Gabriela (right) with an unnamed companion in Los Andes.

Lucila accepted Fidelia's idea and appeared for the credentialing exam, but with apprehension. The first part of the exam no longer required answers to factual questions, as it had under the prior German system and methodology, but did require an understanding of the candidate's spirit. Director Walker, prompted by Víctor Domingo Silva, administered the exam to Lucila personally aware of the woman's talents as an author. She asked her to complete the first section in verse and then proceed to the second section. Lucila, relieved, passed both successfully. Brígida Walker awarded her a special Certificate of Competence to teach humanities at the *liceo* level, with a specialty in *castellano* (Spanish), and to serve as *inspectora general* (a regal term for "overall monitor").[2] The Minister of Education validated the certification, and the official notice appeared in *El Mercurio* of Antofagasta (1911).[3]

The event made it possible for Fidelia and Lucila to live and to work together, and opened a new chapter in Lucila's life, one in which she depended less on Emelina and Petronila and more on her fortyish live-in companion. At first, they resided together, in 1911, but did not find jobs at the same institution until the year was almost over. In that same year, Lucila was hired for a series of short-term teaching assignments: Barrancas, near Santiago (March to July), and Traiguén, south of Concepción (August–September).

CHAPTER V

Antofagasta: Desertic North and Arid Behavior

Unbearable Heat

Fidelia, unsuccessful in gaining employment until 1911, was appointed *directora* (principal) and "*profesora de historia y geografía*" at the Liceo de Niñas in Antofagasta, where her younger companion, "*señorita Lucila Godoi Alcayaga*" was named "*inspectora general*" and "*profesora de castellano*."

Antofagasta, the northern coastal city on the Pacific Ocean, center of activity to the waterless and wind-swept Atacama Desert, serves as port to ships that load nitrates that travel to the U.S. and Europe and that offload food, water, and other supplies from Valparaíso, hundreds of miles to the south, and from European suppliers with commercial interests. At the turn of the 20th century, Antofagasta was transforming itself from a wild-west port city of sailors, merchants, and miners, into one that was home to a newspaper, concert hall, new foreign consulates, and a Liceo de Niñas. The only unchanging and unchangeable aspect was the asphyxiating heat and a sense of isolation for its inhabitants, which Mario Bahamonde characterized as "*...una tierra sin salvación para enmarcar vidas irredentas*" ("...a land without salvation that frames irredeemable lives.")[1]

According to Mario Bahamonde, Fidelia had preceded her friend, the new *inspectora general* (hall monitor) and Spanish teacher, and welcomed her after arriving on the "Panamá" (January 11, 1911). The two came as teachers and administrators to replace previous personnel who, according to city officials, had been unsuccessful or had resigned. The assignment should have lasted at least two years, but only endured one and a half years for reasons that will become apparent. The two departed as they had arrived, entwined but on different dates and ships. The principal boarded for Valparaíso, May 10, 1912, and her subaltern for La Serena, June 1912. Did they depart under pressure, or did they escape for a better assignment?

At the school on Calle Bolívar 654, with its 204 pupils, Fidelia introduced the arriving teacher to the staff, who met her new colleagues with a certain air of superiority. The condescension remained over the coming year. The teachers repaid the disdain and ongoing rebuffs at their *despedida* (farewell party). Detractors pointed to the famous but personally unpopular Spanish teacher, with the long skirts and hair tied in a bun, as an oddity. They gossiped about her large frame and lack of gracefulness, which did not allow her to perform the quick-stepping *cueca*, Chile's traditional flirtatious, handkerchief-waving dance. Kindly put, that was unpatriotic. Fidelia, however, on her final days received regrets and sympathy. The teachers and local organizations pleaded with the authorities to retain Fidelia. But it was not to be, because Santiago had already approved her request. The two women came and left as a couple.

Literary and Personal Achievements

From the outset, Lucila got along famously with Don Fernando Murillo Le Fort, editor of the new start-up newspaper, *El Mercurio*. Lucila's journalistic reputation had preceded her, and she submitted, three days after arriving (January 14, 1911), a light prose piece, "Navegando," dedicated to her mother, based upon her voyage on the good ship "Panamá." An embarrassing incident, immediately corrected, listed the author of "Navegando" as "Aníbal" Godoy Alcayaga. As if that were not bad enough, another error occurred with her name. The same neophyte typesetter, facing another handwritten article signed "Gabriela Mistral," interpreted the scribbled surname as "Gabriela Mistral*y*." Critics Raúl Silva Castro and Mario Bahamonde took this literally as a new pseudonym and promoted the concept of "Gabriela Mistraly." Having inspected the document, I believe that the typesetter misread the final "l." Gabriela adorned the final "l" with an exaggerated flourish, loop, and swirl which made it look like a "y." Typesetting errors and a start-up newspaper in a remote place, notwithstanding, Lucila submitted eight more pieces in prose and poetry to *El Mercurio*, thus increasing her weight as an author.

Fidelia, sensitive to the grumblings regarding the condition of the school she inherited, arranged for officials from the city to view the instruction and the teachers. On August 3, 1911, a former magistrate, the chief of the carabineros and his aide, and other officials paid a visit. Of all the teachers they talked to, the only one highlighted in the newspaper *El Mercurio* was "señorita Lucila Godoy Alcayaga." The observers commented positively on her "método práctico," which awakened in the students an interest in their studies ("*despertar a sus alumnas el interés por el estudio*"). The visitors remarked, in their final congratulatory summary, that "*la profesora de castellano*" had presented literary pieces as examples of grammar and style, thus forging in the pupils "*el buen gusto literario*" ("good literary taste"). Even before entering the school, the visitors had known about Lucila's articles. They sought her out, and her celebrity added value to the school and the principal.

Fidelia, masterful at promotion, was pleased that the paper reported that her school "...*ha recuperado el prestigio que debió tener siempre*" ("...has recovered the prestige that it should have always had"). She impressed the political decision makers with its progress, and, in so doing, had underscored also Lucila's teaching talents. Lucila was on her best behavior for her own sake and to protect Fidelia. Her literary and teaching skills allayed misgivings, if any, from the officials about having paid for her trip and salary. Lucila enjoyed the spotlight and official praise. Was Fidelia trying to give Lucila a wake-up call to take a greater interest in teaching, or was the demonstration an attempt to dispel adverse publicity from city administrators?[2]

Condescension and Avoidance

Can a leopard change its spots? From the first, Lucila became as one with the isolated, arid environment. The temporary publicity did not alter the habits Lucila had practiced in La Serena, that is, she continued to avoid unnecessary communication and did not pander to popularity and social graces. After finishing her teaching duties and administrative tasks, she shunned unnecessary social communication with students, teachers, and other staff, and went off to her small room, where, wreathed in cigarette smoke, got absorbed in her books and writings. Bahamonde described her as "*voluntariosa*" ("willful"). Her obstinacy and self-centeredness, he believed, derived from her background. Gabriela, a self-taught individual who came from humble beginnings, who never attained a university degree, had to prove herself at all costs (*contra todo, contra todos*), by writing even at the expense of teaching and not being social.

Does her inferiority complex rationalize these acts of petulance, or can one bring to bear the French term *je m'en foux* (I don't give a care.)? However one justifies the actions, judging from allegations of indifference to teaching and students during these early years, it was becoming clear that the stipend from teaching and administrative duties also served as a means to an end, that of permitting economic survival and providing the support mechanism to cultivate more important intellectual activities.

The reported peevishness regarding teaching obligations did not reflect, at this time, the future noble actions of the self-effacing schoolmistress, as represented in the poet's principled and much vaunted "Decálogo de la maestra" ("Decalogue of the school mistress"), but that of the self-absorbed writer. From all reports, she belied in her actions in La Serena and in Antofagasta what she later expressed in the first of the ten points: "*Ama. Si no puedes amar mucho, no enseñes niños.*" ("Love. If you can't love a lot, don't teach children.")

A Dispute over Catholicism and Theosophy

Two social and intellectual groups dominated Antofagasta and sparked strong differences between Lucila and Fidelia. In Don Pedro Olegario Sanchez's group, Fidelia felt at home. Don Pedro Olegario Sánchez, director of the Liceo Fiscal de Hombres, hosted parties for the area's most important political, religious, and intellectual figures. The attendees, conservative and Catholic, formed part of Antofagasta's high society. The high-profile principal, a fervent Catholic, resented her friend and employee for not attending the meetings at Don Olegario's house, nor Mass, nor partaking of the Church's practices. Her ire increased upon discovering that Lucila preferred the Theosophical Society's members, ideas, and rituals.

Lucila, indeed, found greater personal and intellectual satisfaction attending Don Carlos Parrau Escobar's Theosophical Society. At the Logia Destellos, Lucila met and befriended Zacarías Gómez, whom she would encounter again in La Serena and would become a lifelong confidant on personal, financial, and intellectual matters.[3] (See Appendix B: "Zacarías Gómez: A Personal Correspondence.")

From Zacarías and others in attendance, she first learned the exoteric and esoteric concepts as handed down from the movement's leading female exponents and adepts, Mme Héléna Petrovna Blavatsky and Annie Besant. With the latter, she began a series of communications. Yoga and other physical exercises formed part of a self-awareness regimen to heal her mind and body. The Yoga practices began to ease the shame long felt about her body. It is reported that she disrobed to practice meditation and took long walks. Vegetables rather than meat became a large part of her diet. For years after their encounter in Antofagasta, Don Zacarías continued to send books and other materials from his Librería Orientalista in Santiago, and was a trusted guide in many private and family matters.

A Quick Retreat

The reader can infer from several of the points mentioned the factors that might have prompted Fidelia and Lucila to escape a year or more later.

They included the gossip regarding the social estrangements and differences over a personal attachment to Fidelia. Bahamonde imagined Lucila "*asfixiada en este Antofagasta opresivo y salitrero añorando su tierra campesina ...*" ("...asphyxiated in this oppressive and nitrate-centered Antofagasta, desirous of her native lands").

But if there were external and internal factors that pushed them toward the door, there was also in the wings an external magnet. Their friend Víctor Domingo Silva had notified them of a vacancy for a high school principal and a teacher in Los Andes, a small, but growing town some 50 miles from Santiago, the cultural and economic heart of Chile. Fidelia accepted for both of them. And so the 43-year-old spinster and the future old-maid, now 23 years old, began two hegiras, the first physical of 1,000 miles to a six-year assignment in a small town, and the second a journey that would unite them for that period and then concluded by separating them for a lifetime as one faded into anonymity and the other achieved international fame.

Chapter VI

Life Changes in Los Andes

An Unchanging School Building

In 2008, Oscar Agüero Wood and his wife Panchi drove their friend visiting from Florida fifty miles from Santiago on smooth highways some 8,800 feet up into the cordillera to the town of Los Andes. This easy ascent contrasted with the journey Fidelia and Lucila endured, in May 1912, by mule-drawn cart over rutted roads with their books and belongings to begin their teaching assignment. A small bronze plaque marked the doorway of the school building on the narrow Calle Esmeralda 138. The plaque heralded the famous teacher/poet, but did not mention the driving force of the journey and the school, the principal, Fidelia Valdez Pereira.

The original structure had one story and extended well-back into the narrow lot, offering two interior patios, the first, with facing classrooms on either side. The second sat behind with residences for some of the teaching and administrative staff. The building, by 2008, had a second story. We climbed the narrow staircase to a loft, where, the guide told us, Gabriela once lived. We surveyed the interior, the patios, and the vestiges of a trellis-supported grapevine, imagining what the site might have looked like and how the place had hummed with students and teachers 96 years before. No shouts of students reciting their lessons, or of playing games, or of eating lunch echoed forth from the swept, but empty, slowly deteriorating historic site.

Initial Resistance to Change

The French have a saying, "*Plus ça change, plus ç'est la même chose,*" translated loosely as, "The more things change, the more they stay the same." On reaching Los Andes, the teacher had served in at least six teaching positions since starting as an *ayudanta* in La Cantera in 1904. Notwithstanding the physical changes, she continued to persist in habits and rituals which defined her nature and personality. Six habits and rituals, at minimum, continued to dominate her personality and actions: As in Antofagasta, she usually ate her meals unaccompanied, either in the school patio or at Mme Borie's pension — immersed in a book or magazine — meals that the other teachers did not want to partake of, mainly vegetables, nuts, and fruits, a continuation of her Theosophical regimen.

Having been credentialed on the basis of merit and via the political leverage of Víctor Domingo Silva and Brígida Walker, and with dozens of publications to her credit by this time, Lucila/Gabriela continued to act like a diva. For many years at Los Andes, she played helpless, refused to lift a hand to move furniture, and was incapable, according to witnesses, of sewing a dress or boiling an egg. She clung to her adopted petulance — her colleagues would have called it laziness — even in the face of strong faculty opposition, in 1915, which will be described later.

Habituated to cigarettes, she smoked incessantly to the discomfort of others, morally and physically, to the point that a separate room was eventually refurbished in an adjacent building to accommodate her habit and her increasingly large collection of books which she read and wrote about well into the night.

In a changing sea, Lucila relied on two major constants, Fidelia and her own family. The principal and her teacher acted like sisters rather than employer and employee, although some teachers gossiped about the employee dominating and pushing around the employer, which was part of an intimate enactment that transcended barriers and norms. At Lucila's insistence, Fidelia invited Emelina to teach at the school, which brought, of course, Petronila and her daughter Graciela to Los Andes, where they found quarters on Calle Las Heras 181. It is logical to assume that Lucila resided with her family for closeness and to reduce costs.

Tagore Catalyzes Changes

In Lucila's first year of teaching in Los Andes, she displayed the same aloofness to students fostered in earlier teaching assignments. In the second year, however, a transformation took place. One can attribute the change to a greater maturity and preparation, to the Theosophical teachings of Mme Héléna Petrovna Blavatsky and Annie Besant, the founders, respectively, of Theosophy in India and the United States, and to soothing Yoga "Prácticas." But the real transformation began with the literary and pedagogical prominence of Rabindranath Tagore (1861–1941), the Bengali poet/teacher who penned the influential *Gitanjali* (*Song Offerings*), for which he received the Nobel Prize in 1913. Tagore attracted attention and garnered appeal from photographs. He appeared as the venerable father figure, whose long flowing white hair and silvery gown or tunic made him appear otherworldly.

Gabriela/Lucila, absorbing this, must have had an epiphany which set two currents in motion. The first current was long-range and literary. Gabriela, the writer, fashioned her poetry and prose around Tagore's ideas. In 1917, four years after his Nobel Prize, she wrote six commentaries on the Hindu poet for Raúl Ramírez's book on Tagore. An analysis of three commentaries appears in Chapter XIII, "A Quest for Religious Harmony."[1]

Lucila Godoy, the teacher, set in motion the second current. She communed spiritually with educators worldwide who were as fascinated as she with Tagore's educational ideas and practices in Santiniketan, his outdoor school. The formerly dismissive teacher adopted Tagore's radical techniques. Her coldness to her students thawed; she called them "*mis chiquillas*" ("my little girls"), and began developing pleasant, some called them "captivating," teaching patterns.[2]

Disregarding the scorn of colleagues who preferred the security and tradition of four walls, Lucila, with Fidelia's approval, took over the space of the shaded grapevine in the patio to impart lessons. The first ten days were uncomfortable for everybody concerned; the students joked and made fun, believing it was a short-term game. But on the tenth day, they acceded to and enjoyed the novel situation and began to take seriously nature's contributions to the learning process.

Gabriela, age 28 (1917), Los Andes.

Her open-air school concept reveals persistent efforts to invigorate teaching, emulating Tagore, with existing natural materials and under Spartan conditions. It is apparent from the following translated paragraph of her article, with its telegraphic style, the struggle she began to learn and impart a new style of teaching:

> ... on cold days, the girls did ten minutes of [outdoor] exercises.... The relief map, drawn on the dirt, was unforgettable.... The class was losing its formality ... an advantage. I hate ... "obscuring" studies. [The class] was losing its "unreality"; it was real and more human. [An] environment of trust, the only one possible in which to educate, was established with greater ease.... "Holy" is [the school's] business.... Everything that does not translate into "life," physical and spiritual, is deception and betrayal to the [human] race and to God.[3]

The outdoor school also underlined a commitment to sacred and secular growth for her students and of education in general which, she hoped, they would carry out in their studies and in social activism.

San Bernardo Hastens Changes

From Los Andes, observers stood in awe of the 22,848-foot snow-capped Mount Aconcagua, some forty-five miles away. Los Andes, with its scenic pathways and natural, untrammeled beauty, held much more attraction for Lucila than cosmopolitan, crowded, and politicized Santiago. If Lucila felt the need to get away, the town of San Bernardo afforded a compromise, with its tree-lined avenues, intellectual societies, and poet-friends. Both San Bernardo and Santiago, some ten miles apart, offered bookstores as well as human diversion.

Shopping for books in Los Andes, as well as in San Bernardo and Santiago — as she had done in Antofagasta and La Serena — held a fatal attraction, constrained only by meager earnings or the ability to obtain credit. In Los Andes, Adelina Fajardo's shop was a limited source for essays and poetry from Chile and from Uruguay and Argentina. A very popular author at the time was the Uruguayan, José Enrique Rodó, who penned the philosophical essay *Ariel* (1900).

San Bernardo's and Santiago's book stores offered additional temptations to buy originals and translations of many writers. Researchers privy to Mistral's books have encountered the following foreign-language authors, among hundreds of others, who made their mark at the turn of the century: French (Romain Rolland, Paul Verlaine), Russian (Feodor Dostoevsky, Leo Tolstoy, and Maxim Gorky), Portuguese (José María Eça de Queiroz, Abílio Manuel

Guerra Junqueiro), American (Walt Whitman), and English (Oscar Wilde). The poet's bookshelves also held some foreign-language authors who specialized in Theosophy and the occult, but she would find many more in Santiago, at the Librería Orientalista of Zacarías Gómez. (See Appendices A and B for the titles of many books she read or held on esoteric religion.)

The bookshops stocked Domingo Faustino Sarmiento's *Facundo* and *Recuerdos de Provincia*, two among fifty-one books that he published over a lifetime. Sarmiento reminded her of their struggles and perseverance in overcoming adversities as educators and as authors. To pay homage to the former president of Argentina, who espoused the slogan "governing means educating," Lucila, from Los Andes, traversed Mount Aconcagua to visit the rundown, one-room school house in Pocuro, envisioned as a shrine, where Sarmiento had taught.

Several years after that visit in 1915, she would be surprised to find out, in 1918, in a private interview in Santiago that Pocuro's landowner was the Minister of Education, Pedro Aguirre Cerda. In that future interview with Aguirre Cerda, Lucila learned of several surprises and coincidences. Prior to his entering politics, Aguirre Cerda had studied education and directed the boys' Liceo de Varones in Los Andes. He revealed that his status as a landowner, as an educator, and as minister had motivated his writing the tract *La cuestión agraria* (*The Agrarian Question*). In the book, he recognized, as did Lucila in her writings on literacy and compulsory primary education, that successful land reorganization meant turning illiterate *campesinos* into literate farmers. In that future interview, Minister Aguirre Cerda offered her the position of *directora* of El Liceo de Niñas de Punta Arenas, in the southernmost territory of Magallanes, in Patagonia. She also learned of his plan to re-habilitate her special shrine in Pocuro and to turn it into an agricultural Escuela-Granja Sarmiento (the Sarmiento Farm-School).[4]

Her success in Punta Arenas and afterwards in Temuco, prompted Aguirre Cerda to recommend her to another Minister of Education, Mexico's José Vasconcelos. Vasconcelos chose Gabriela, in 1922, to promote his own idea of the *escuela-granja-hogar* (residential farm school) in rural areas of Mexico. Aguirre Cerda was instrumental in transforming the course of her life. But first, she had to leave Los Andes successfully.

Changing Relationships

Fidelia, as her name suggests, maintained fidelity to Lucila starting in 1908, so long as she was able to endure her younger friend's willfulness with respect to teaching and administrative chores, her propensity for literary glorification, and her loyalty and respect. In 1915, three years into their shared assignment in Los Andes, the older principal, now a *solterona* (an old maid), and the twenty-six-year-old teacher began a slow falling out that would lead to separation in 1918.

The differences between them had already been egregious in Antofagasta, causing them to argue and to flee. But they carried over the differences to Los Andes. Fidelia, staunchly Catholic, regarded Lucila's Theosophy, as defiant blasphemy. The principal, who reported to the Education Ministry, had a fiduciary relationship regarding the school's image, finances, staff, and students. The teacher, taking advantage of their friendship, defied responsibility, had a fleeting regard for colleagues, and most of the students except her favorites, but a major allegiance to salary and private time for writing and conversations with intellectual mentors or peers.

Fidelia's devotion had been very strained over Lucila's personal and open attachment to Jorge Hübner and her secret epistolary alliance with Magallanes Moure. The Hübner affair, never out of mind but out of sight in Santiago, remained tolerable. But Lucila's excessive attachment to Laura Rodig, in 1918, a pretty and artistic student, broke her spirit. Fidelia found a grotesque way to lash out.

The anger between the two friends, and between the staff and the celebrated writer, ignited over a minor affair that Fidelia could have solved if she had not been blinded by her pride and devotion. The Juegos Florales brought visitors to see Lucila/Gabriela at the school. The guests not only wanted to meet her but to remain to discuss ideas over drinks and snacks at the traditional, afternoon Chilean *once*. "*Tomar once*," literally to "take eleven," is a euphemism to skirt saying in Victorian Chile, *tomar aguardiente* (to take afternoon whiskey). *Once* replaced the word for whiskey, *aguardiente* in Spanish, which is spelled with eleven letters.

The teachers became jealous of Lucila's literary recognition. They could not compete with her fame, but they could point to her as just another teacher, one who did not even have a university title. They also complained about spending limited school money on Lucila and her friends, which meant less for them. But they rebelled openly when Fidelia ordered them to tidy up after the mess left from Lucila's guests.

Fidelia, over the years, eventually lost all patience with regard to the depleted *once* funds and, worse, with Lucila's open and warm friendship for Laura Rodig. Fidelia played a friendship-ending trick, witnessed by José Santos González Vera. He recalled that Fidelia served a "chicken" salad one afternoon at *once*. Fidelia declared that, owing to limited funds, she prepared the salad using a *paloma,* a pigeon. Lucila began to shriek and howl; the cooked *paloma* turned out to be her favorite pet. An American saying is that revenge should be served cold, but not necessarily as cold chicken salad. This was Fidelia's pay-back after many small cuts. The deepest cut, Laura Rodig, caused her to snap once and for all.[5]

Laura Rodig and Long-Lasting Changes

The constants heretofore in Lucila's changing sea, that is, Fidelia and the family on Calle Las Heras, disintegrated when Lucila, deeply disturbed over the pigeon incident, decided to alienate herself from Fidelia (December 1916). The rancor also affected the family. Emelina submitted her resignation and, with Petronila and her sickly daughter Graciela, moved back to warm La Serena, a respite after the icy climate of Los Andes. Lucila rented a second-floor apartment in nearby Coquimbito, where, at night, she could reflect on the role her actions had played in alienating her from the constants in her personal life.

Laura Rodig learned, as others did after the Juegos Florales, that the mysterious Gabriela Mistral lived in her home town of Los Andes. The fifteen-year-old read Gabriela's poetry and traveled from Santiago to meet her. They began to communicate on a deep level. Lucila enrolled her and protected her as a special student, an act that estranged not only Fidelia, but also some of the teacher's other special female students. Laura, gifted in the plastic arts, especially sculpture, forged a close relationship with her older and wiser teacher turned mentor. Estranged from her parents and distant from relatives in Santiago, Laura reported that she turned eventually to Gabriela for shelter and comfort in her rented rooms in Coquimbito. Rumors spread among the students and staff, out of jealousy perhaps, that the teacher/student relationship covered up a deeper meaning. But Laura, in her various writings on this period disparaged a sexual relationship and indicated that she just served as a devoted messenger for the teacher/writer's trivial needs and as an acolyte who held at bay the loneliness that each felt. Laura remained by her mentor's side for at least five more years and accompanied her to Punta Arenas (1918–1920), to Temuco (1920–1921), to Santiago (1921–1922), and on the boat trip to Mexico (1922).

Despite the nasty rumors from students and staff, Lucila/Gabriela defied them with silence, both in person and in the writings. Neither denial nor confirmation of a love affair arises, but confusion does. Years apart, Lucila dedicated one prose piece and one poem to two Lauras. The first, "Adiós a Laura," on March 11, 1906, is an unknown Laura, who, judging by the early date, could not have been Laura Rodig. But if one believes the rumors that pervaded El Liceo de Niñas in 1917, the prose piece, "Adiós a Laura," for its content and passion, could have applied more to Laura Rodig than did the poem she dedicated to Rodig, called "El pensador de Rodin" (1919, "Rodin's Thinker").[6] "Adios a Laura," an elegy on Laura's death, or a lamentation to a lost lover named Laura, begins with burning love phrases and continues with many more ardent lines. Who could have imagined that the seventeen-year-old country schoolteacher could and would write lines such as the following to a young woman?

> *"Adiós, la dulce compañera de mis soledades y mis penas, mi confidente única, mi sola íntima porque solo tú me has comprendido y has podido por lo tanto amarme; adiós!"*
>
> Good-bye, sweet companion of my solitudes and my sufferings, my only confidante, my only intimate one, because only you have understood me and have been able, for this reason, to love me; good-bye!

Mistral's poem dedicated to Laura Rodig, on the other hand, celebrated the sculptress's professional interest and influence. Laura channeled Gabriela's poetic creativity, first to Auguste Rodin's "El pensador de Rodin," then to the Torinese sculptor, Leonardo Bistolfi (1859–1933), who was fascinated by tombs, death, and crosses. Bistolfi's crucifix at Villabasse (1901), gave rise to Mistral's "La cruz de Bistolfi," a poem on Christian sacrifice. Since both Rodin and Bistolfi are treated at length in Chapter XIV, "The Poetry of Sacrifice," it would be useful to conclude these brief comments by saying simply that Mistral attempted to go inside both sculptors' secular, visual representations to capture in her words and images the sacredness involved in man's grief.

And as Lucila's sojourn in Los Andes was winding down, so did her symbiotic relationship with Fidelia. The relationship between the older woman and the younger devolved into a rivalry for power and control, between a straight-laced organizer/administrator *versus* a free-thinking creator/teacher. Power and control also permeated the symbiotic liaison with Laura Rodig. With the roles reversed, an older and dominant Lucila controlled a malleable, young and pretty girl who, absent parental guidance, doted on her matronly and celebrated friend.[7]

Chapter VII

Sexuality, Humanity and Existential Choices

Manuel Magallanes Moure: An Epistolary Affair

After buying books and supplies in San Bernardo on weekends or during vacation periods, Gabriela, accompanied most of the time by Fidelia, would attend cultural meetings at the farm home of Manuel and Amalia Magallanes Moure. Magallanes Moure, referenced earlier in the subsection "Sonetos de la muerte," with his tie-breaking decision in favor of Gabriela Mistral at the Juegos Florales (December 1914), initiated their deep personal association at his home, in 1913, a year before the Juegos Florales. Lucila attended meetings of the Ateneo de San Bernardo, which Magallanes led. Tall, bearded, deep-voiced, and very smart, he radiated energy and enthusiasm. Lucila and others looked to him with admiration. Outside of his intellectual pursuits — author of seven books of poetry — he also presided over La Liga Protectora de Estudiantes, El Centro Cultural Victoria, the Club de Tiro (Gun Club), and a Tolstoy-like, Bohemian life style that involved growing crops for personal use and the needy.

When their daughter died (1912), and when his sister passed away (1915), Magallanes did not relieve his depression on the consoling shoulder of wife Amalia, older by seven years. Rather, he sought relief for his despair and depression in greater cultural activity and in at least one other woman, Sara Hübner Bezanilla. He pursued Sara, the radiant and eccentric sister of Jorge Hübner Bezanilla. She was, to all outward appearances unavailable, but, much to the grief of Amalia, often attainable.

Sara's charms also eclipsed by far those of the tall and ungainly twenty-four-year-old single poet and school teacher from Coquimbo who traveled from Los Andes to attend meetings of the Ateneo. Lucila, conscious of her physical shortcomings and inferior social status, had begun to fantasize about

Manuel before the Juegos Florales. The afternoon after winning the competition, in the wake of his vote in her favor, she acted upon her fantasy by beginning a nine-year (1914–1923) epistolary love affair in which she recognized her limitations, but was disposed to surrender herself if he so desired.[1]

At his request, she destroyed all his letters, but five. So the true feelings of this thirty-five-year-old philanderer can not be ascertained, except by conjecture and inference from her letters. Although it was most probably a physically unrequited mutual affair, Lucila professed guilt for her "*adulterio mental*" ("mental adultery").[2] From Lucila's perspective, the love was strong and enduring and if it had been possible, permanent and physical. But it never came to pass. The exchange and the relationship ended when, in 1923, on the final leg of her mission to Mexico, she wrote of her decision not to return to Chile, the source of pain and emotional emptiness.

An inveterate smoker, Manuel suffered from pleurisy and died of angina in 1924. Of course his death ended any further contact with Gabriela, but it left her open to other possibilities, including a probable relationship, in 1925, with Eugenio d'Ors, which was discussed in the section related to Juan Miguel Mendoza. As a very personal friend to Manuel, she signed her letters "Lucila Godoy," "Lucila," or "L" straight-up or at an angle, never her literary name, "Gabriela," according to Luis Vargas Saavedra's analysis. In the eighty letters, she exposed the depths of her soul and her capacity for loving a man, notwithstanding his unwillingness to leave his wife and her inability to break up a marriage.

Jorge Hübner Bezanilla: A Mismatched Exchange

Lucila's romantic escapade with the poet Jorge Hübner Bezanilla (1892–1964), from 1915 to 1918, ran concurrently with her clandestine epistolary involvement with Manuel Magallanes Moure. If there were letters between them, they have been unavailable or unearthed; he and his heirs have preferred silence rather than possible controversy over what the family considered indiscretions. The fragments of their public life are pieced together from snippets from friends at the time and later by academics, like Margot Arce de Vázquez, Angel Cruchaga Santa María, Hernán Díaz Arrieta, José Santos González Vera, and Augusto Iglesias. The aforementioned combined direct knowledge, gossip, and inferences based on the collective poetry and prose of both poets.

It was most likely and, if so, a great irony, that the two met at the Ateneo de San Bernardo, where the host carried on with Lucila and Sara Hübner, Jorge's sister, while Lucila carried on with Manuel and Jorge. It was a scenario worthy of an operetta or a movie script.

While Manuel's intellectual abilities suited Lucila's desire for a platonic relationship with a married man, Jorge offered an entirely different dimension in contrasts rather than similarities. Twenty-three-years old, in 1915, Jorge, unmarried, loquacious, outgoing, a *bon-vivant*, well-dressed, and a good chess player, appealed to Lucila's sense of fun and gregariousness, elements undeveloped in her. Not only was Jorge three years younger, he was several inches shorter. He moved with quick steps; she moved with a long-gliding pace. One could not conceive of a more mismatched pair physically, in tastes, and in social status.

They did share a general love of poetry and the arts. By the time he was seventeen (1909), the public considered him a wunderkind, having published, in collaboration with Hernán Díaz Arrieta (Alone), one book of poems.

Jorge came from a family of writers and diplomats. Owing to his social background, he was invited to parties, the theater, and concerts in Santiago. At times, he went accompanied arm-in-arm with Lucila Godoy. Sometimes, they met, as if by chance, in museums, discreetly, to avoid gossip. Other times, they preferred quiet meetings in out-of-the way places, where they could talk.

One such intimate encounter was witnessed by José Santos González Vera. In his book of boyhood tales, *Cuando era muchacho*, José Santos testified that Jorge had invited Lucila to drive up to San Cristóbal Hill, a quiet place overlooking Santiago, usually frequented by *pololos* (lovebirds). As she arrived to be picked up, he reported, Lucila was surprised to see him there also. Undaunted, he nudged his way uninvited into Jorge's chauffeured limousine. The rear of the long car had extra rows of backseats. The couple made it clear that they wanted to sit in the front row by themselves to talk confidentially. The intruder confined himself to the very back row. His embarrassment increased when, he reported, her large frame overshadowed his small one and the tone of the conversation turned "violent." He discovered in later talks that neither party preferred to speak of their encounter openly and publicly.[3]

Some critics have claimed to find in their poems hints of mutual recognition and celebration. The claims may be speculative, because Jorge pursued other women who may have entered his poetic vision; and Lucila's poetry contained palpable tracks of only Romelio Ureta and Manuel Magallanes Moure. Vargas Saavedra, in an invidious comparison of Lucila's existing letters from/to Magallanes Moure with the inexistent ones from/to Hübner, notes wryly that the missing ones would have proved more intense and conflictive. Vargas Saavedra, on the same page 182, quotes Lucila's first and last remark on the three-year affair: "*Como estos montes me tienes de tajeado y negro el pecho.*" ("Like these mountains, black and chopped off, that is how you left my bosom.")

Jorge, in 1918, finally decided upon marriage to Ofelia Schiavetti Gallo, a woman he had once rejected, but now welcomed on his return from Paris and down on his luck from gambling and stock market reverses. He was persuaded by her family's wealth. After 1918, Lucila and Jorge separated forever with no trail of letters or tears. His marriage and Lucila's departure for a teaching post in Patagonia ended the mainly secretive and ambiguous link leaving few traces of what was probably a superficial and tempestuous relationship that produced guilt and shame given their social, intellectual, and emotional differences.

Other Suitors

In Chile, Lucila had been courted by at least a dozen suitors, almost all in the grip of some sort of urge to conquer this woman. We already know how she perceived herself physically, that is, as unattractive by traditional standards of beauty. What did the few men who chose to pursue her see? The intellectual types, such as Manuel Magallanes Moure, Jorge Hübner, and Eugenio d'Ors, who knew of her writings, wanted to get close primarily because they admired her intrinsic beauty, intellectual capacity, and energy. Hübner, from what others have described, was the spoiled dilettante and playboy who enjoyed intellectual as well as amorous interests. The narcissistic types, such as Alfredo Videla Pineda, Santiago Aste, and Romelio Ureta, following traditional male dominance patterns, pursued her for personal pleasure.

Perplexities and incongruities arise from Lucila's relationships with these men and with others in future attachments. Her own life story should have been a warning and moral lesson in men's inconstancy. She did not heed her own screeds urging women in general not to consider themselves as love objects. As an adolescent, she appeared to behave recklessly in flirting with Alfredo Videla Pineda, the older married man described as a lothario when they came in contact in La Serena (1904–1905). She pursued relentlessly the married Magallanes Moure, who was, in turn, seducing Sara Hübner. Lucila was conscious of her humble beginnings, yet she conspired in the intellectual, sexual, and social meanderings of high-born men ("*jaibones*"), like Magallanes Moure and Hübner. Judging from these few documented details, the label of "virgin-mother" was a fictional construction, one that certain writers cultivated and one she abetted, but one that the facts should put to rest.

Besides Magallanes Moure and Jorge Hübner, more than a half-dozen suitors are recorded publicly as expressing their positive feelings, among the previously mentioned, the older married man from La Serena, Alfredo Videla Pineda, the suicidal Romelio Ureta (La Cantera, 1906), the grocer Santiago

Aste (Los Andes, 1913–1922), and the Catalan philosopher, Eugenio d'Ors (France, 1925–1926).[4] Via letters and personal associations, she attracted and was surrounded by scores of Chilean intellectual males, including Eduardo Barrios, Víctor Domingo Silva, Hernán Díaz Arrieta, Zacarías Gómez, José Santos González Vera, Eugenio Labarca, Carlos Mondaca, Pedro Prado, and Isauro Santelices.

A Fractured Sisterhood

Lucila/Gabriela's many overt displays of heterosexuality increases the doubt that she was a "closet lesbian," despite the label that Licia Fiol-Matta and other academics have applied to her.[5] It would be useful to go over that allegation from various perspectives. The extant epistolary exchanges to date with female assistants (the Mexican Palma Guillén, the Puerto Rican Consuelo Saleva, and the American Doris Dana), and with female writers from Argentina and Uruguay reveal affection, trust, and a willingness to treat serious intellectual and social concerns, but not an amorous attraction. Mistral's correspondence with the Argentine Victoria Ocampo and with eight Uruguayan female writers, among them, Esther de Cáceres, for whom she had a special affection, does not reveal overt or covert physical love.[6]

Out of fear of exposure and ostracism, for social and economic reasons, she could have asked the women with whom she corresponded to mask their love interest, as she did and had asked Magallanes to do, with code words.[7] But none of that is evident. What is evident from the letters and articles from/to Lucila/Gabriela that have been made public, starting in Chile and continuing through her residences abroad, is female bonding on social, political, and intellectual matters. She participated in an epistolary sisterhood of women who celebrated unshackling themselves from supporting roles to males and quasi-enslavement by them for eons. Her cohorts were intellectual females who, like her, found the time and the means to express themselves to others — male and female — in literary salons, letters, and books without being martyrized for witchcraft or Satanism, as had happened in America's Colonies and during Torquemada's Inquisition.

This is distinct from the "unspeakable" "female bonding" into lesbianism movement that Sylvia Molloy coyly hinted at in, what she called Gabriela's "self-projecting" "Locas mujeres." Molloy appeared to label as "unspeakable" a reference in that one specific poem to a female's "madness" in discarding family and disavowing socio-sexual norms. Maybe, as in the literary theme of "*loco amor*," Gabriela played with another literary motif, i.e., "locas mujeres," rather than with self-analysis.[8]

Doris Dana's Reason for Being

Gabriela's nine-year (1948–1957) intermittent relationship, at first, and ultimately lengthy co-habitation with the vibrant, elusive, and clever Doris Dana (1920–Nov. 28, 2006), gave rise to additional rumors of a gay relationship. Nothing of the kind occurred, according to Ms. Dana, in an extremely candid interview with Cherie Zalaquett Aquea (2002). Ms. Dana, with Gabriela long-deceased (Jan. 10, 1957), and few of her own years remaining, denied all rumors of her own lesbianism and, to her knowledge, Gabriela was not a lesbian nor was she sexually active during their time together: "*Si ella tuvo, tal vez en su juventud, experiencias homosexuales, puede ser, yo no sé. No*

Gabriela (left) and Doris Dana, Santa Barbara, California (1947).

puedo decirlo. Sí puedo afirmar que nunca le conocí esas conductas de adulta."[9]
But what story emerges from their intimate epistolary exchange?

As stated in the "Preface," Doris Dana's will left their letters and other effects to her niece, Doris Atkinson, who graciously awarded them to the Biblioteca Nacional de Chile (2008). The Biblioteca published their epistolary exchange (2010), as *Niña errante,* with a sensitive prologue by Pedro Pablo Zegers B. and a penetrating family portrait in the epilogue by Ms. Atkinson. Of the two-hundred-fifty communications in their nine-year courtship, Gabriela — the obsessive-compulsive communicator — wrote two hundred-thirty-five, or 94 percent, averaging one every two weeks. Doris, according to *Niña errante,* transmitted only fifteen short messages. Doris initiated the exchange on February 9, 1948, with the first of six letters in a row in Spanish (Numbers 1, 3, 4, 6, 8, and 9). But she sent only nine messages in the remaining eight years — averaging 1.67 letters per year.[10]

Doris' initial letters began with the endearing and humbling salutation, "*Mi querida maestra,*" which set the tone of engagement of a fascinated Barnard College graduate for a Nobel laureate. The unexpected, ennobling, and affectionate words lit a fire in Gabriela. The flames intensified when Doris spoke of introducing Gabriela to the novelist and Nobel laureate (1929), Thomas Mann (1875–1955), author of *The Magic Mountain* and *Death in Venice,* among others. The solicitous six letters from the student attracted Gabriela like a moth to a flame. She became as excited to meet the American student who had translated to English her article, "El otro desastre alemán," for the critical compilation, *The Stature of Thomas Mann,* as she was to meet the German-American novelist. Furthermore, Doris enticed Gabriela by promising to introduce her to Mann, a resident of Los Angeles, as part of an overly-ambitious car trip with Doris driving from New York, to Santa Barbara, to Los Angeles, and on to Mexico.

At the time, Gabriela remained bereft of old trusted friends in Santa Barbara, California, after Consuelo Saleva left for Puerto Rico and Palma Guillén (1898–1975) for Mexico. As a result of her emptiness, she pursued and intensified this new avenue of friendship and growth with many letters to "*Cara Doris.*" The poet found in Doris youthful energy, intelligence, and, as a practical matter, a guide for the linguistic and cultural challenges in the United States. Doris, for her part, guarded the ongoing stream of friendly and affectionate letters reciprocating one or more per year after the first six. After receiving dozens in a steady stream, Doris must have realized the increasing harnessed power residing within the affectionate language of an elderly and self-exiled Nobel laureate and became possessed of possibilities and fantasies. It is not inconceivable that Doris thought that if she nourished the relationship, Gabriela would eventually become her calling, her reason for being. And so it happened.

VII. Sexuality, Humanity and Existential Choices

Gabriela's compulsive obsession with letter writing since leaving Chile went hand-in-hand with her errant life. Via thousands of letters to men and women of distinction on four continents, she overcame, what Karl Marx pithily called, "the annihilation of space by time," in which "connectedness became more urgent than rootedness." Gabriela, the "*descastada*," having abandoned space in her native land, afterwards connected in time and with time to hundreds of persons, among whom she now included the enigmatic and rejuvenating Doris.

Although the correspondence dwells mainly on trivial chit-chat, medical problems, money matters, travel plans, and intellectual subjects, they also opened pathways to love, affection, jealousy and anxiety over Doris' unexplained lack of replies and absences. Gabriela bared herself in the passionate letters as she also recognized an ambiguous relationship, owing to differences of culture, language, age, experience, achievements, affluence, and energy levels.

Letter 52 (p. 118), (May 1949), illustrates the matter:

> *Mi vida:*
> *Tú eres de una raza que se controla; yo no. Tú estás segura de mí; yo no tengo seguridad alguna de ti.*
> *Pero hay más: yo necesito de tu presencia de una manera violenta, como del aire. Parece que [yo] estuviese viviendo una asfixia. Es eso exactamente.*
> *Tal vez fue locura muy grande entrar en esta pasión. Cuando examino los primeros hechos, yo sé que la culpa fue enteramente mía. Yo creí que lo que saltaba de tu mirada era amor y yo he visto después que tú miras así a mucha gente. Loco fui, insensato; como un niño,*
> *Doris, como un niño*
> *Tu Gabriela*

The passionate and obsessive tone and substance of this letter, and the one that follows, do not erase the question of lesbianism, but require one to think more about the social and psychic dynamic of an older and isolated Gabriela's need for friendship, trust, and companionship as life-giving oxygen.

From letter Number 163 (p. 286), August 13, 1952.

> *Has hecho muy dulce mi pobre vida; me has sacado del pozo negro en el cual yo vivía, me has traído una especie de segunda juventud.*
> *Todo es vida, calor, ligereza de aire desde que yo te hallé.*
> *Un abrazo Gabriela*

> You have sweetened my poor life; you have pulled me out of the black well in which I was living; you have brought me a kind of second youth.
> Everything is life, warmth, lightness of air since I found you.
> A hug Gabriela

Ms. Dana's own sexual orientation, however, begs the question without a definitive answer. Neither Cherie Zalaquett's prior direct question and denial

Gabriela and Doris Dana, Naples, Italy (1951).

(2002), nor Elizabeth Horan's pointed question to her niece, Doris Atkinson, six years later, elicited an affirmation on that orientation. Ms. Atkinson replied obliquely to Dr. Horan that her aunt partied away her years in Naples, Florida, surrounded "*exclusivamente*" by wealthy [septuagenarian] widows and spinsters, some "*lesbianas.*"[11] Aunt Doris, according to her niece, four decades after Gabriela had died, still cultivated and "enjoyed the cultural prestige that came from having been the closest friend and supposed lover ("*supuesta amante*") of a woman who was a famous Latin American writer." Doris Dana nourished her reflected glory, her reason for being through her twilight years, and with cultivated evasiveness and indirection admitted obliquely their individual and collective shadowy sexual orientations.[12]

Gabriela the Risk-Taker

The aforesaid summary leaves open the possibility, but not the probability, that Lucila/Gabriela — undoubtedly a life-long high risk-taker in literary, social, and educational matters — might have found comfort in the vicinity of one or more women. One might ask hypothetically that if Lucila/Gabriela was capable of masking in code her long epistolary exchange to/from Magallanes Moure and hush up her three-year furtive escapade with Jorge Hübner, then she might have had alternate types of liaisons which would have required even more secrecy because of imploding danger from scandal. But all this and the aforesaid sections are in the realm of conjecture. Unless and until other documentation and human testimony come to light, logic should allay allegations of her being repulsed by men and attracted to women, that is, a "closet lesbian," or attracted to both genders (bisexual), or to neither (the asexual "virgin-mother").

Licia Fiol-Matta, insistent on affirming her hypothesis, repudiates her own thesis when referring to Mistral's departure for Mexico: "Although hard documentation of her sexuality simply does not exist, it's quite possible that Mistral's exile was in part sexual" (p. xxii). But beyond those conclusions on her sexuality provided by careful documentation, testimony, and observation, it is prudent to proceed carefully before labeling her a "closet lesbian" to satisfy personal and social ideologies of a current wing of the feminist movement that seeks allies among powerful historical figures. It is especially disturbing to label a deceased international figure who cannot defend or explain herself.

Instead of concentrating on Gabriela's sexuality — closeted or uncloseted — her major efforts as a feminist in Chile and in Latin America deserve greater examination and praise. From her earliest writings she advocated for the development and benefit of women, not merely as housewives and breeders, but as persons who, with the proper education, training, and opportunity could assume roles in society that would bring them, their families, and the nation dignity and pride. At the age of seventeen (March 8, 1906), she wrote from Vicuña, her birthplace, this passionate assessment of woman's place in history and the challenge that lay ahead — for women and for Lucila/Gabriela — to change historical and personal circumstances:

> *Retrocedamos en la historia de la humanidad buscando la silueta de la mujer, en las diferentes edades de la Tierra. La encontraremos más humillada y más envilecida, mientras más nos internemos en la antigüedad. Su engrandecimiento lleva la misma marcha de la civilización; mientras la luz del progreso irradia más poderosa sobre el globo, ella, la agobiada, va irguiéndose más y más. Y, es que a medida que la luz se hace en las inteligencias, se va comprendiendo su misión y su valor y hoy ya no es la esclava de ayer sino la compañera, la igual. Para su humillación primitiva, ha conquistado ya lo bastante, pero aún le queda mucho que explorar para entonar un canto de victoria.*[13]

Let us go back into the different ages of the history of humanity on Earth to search for the silhouette of woman. The further back we go the more we will find her humiliated and debased. Her enhancement advances as civilization advances; while progress's light shines ever brighter on our globe, so, too, does she, the downtrodden one, rise further and further. And the fact is that in the same fashion that light illuminates intelligence, one continues understanding her mission and her value, and nowadays she no longer is yesterday's slave, but the companion, one who is equal. Since her primitive humility, she has conquered quite a bit, but much still remains to explore before singing a triumphal hymn.

The preceding derives from a collection of fifty articles that spans more than four decades of defending feminine pride and prowess, a testimony to her efforts. Not one article in the collection, from what this reader can ascertain, deals with advancement via lesbian activity, but via praising and supporting women who have emancipated themselves intellectually in the eyes of men and women. Lucila counted herself among them. The intellectually capable woman captures Mistral's conception of feminism at its best.

And what opinion does Mistral display of groups of women clamoring for justice, or the vote, or a right to employment? Luis Vargas Saavedra unearthed the following long article on Mistral's philosophical perspectives of feminism, which merit attention and may answer these questions[14]:

> *Para mí, es el feminismo hasta ahoy [1925] como una casa que no me inspira confianza grande.... El feminismo llega a parecernos a veces, en Chile, una expresión del sentimentalismo mujeril, quejumbroso, blanducho, perfectamente invertebrado, como una esponja que flota en un líquido inocuo.*
>
> For me, feminism is to date [1925] like a house that does not inspire a lot of confidence.... Feminism to us in Chile seems an expression of womanish sentimentalism, whining, mushy, and perfectly spineless like a sponge that floats in an innocuous liquid.

Vargas Saavedra punctuated the prior quote with a strong editorial: "*Otra tribu que la dañó tremendamente fue la de las feministas que querían usarla de pedestal, estatua, bandera y volante electoral.*" The translation reads: "Another tribe [public group] that harmed her a great deal was the feminists, who wanted to use her as a platform, statue, banner, election flyer." It is clear that Mistral acted negatively toward the feminist movement in Chile captained by her outspoken and well-connected adversary, Amanda Labarca Hubertson, who founded the Partido Cívico Femenino, Acción Femenina, and wrote *¿A dónde va la mujer?* (1934). (The disagreement is captured in Chapter X, "The Transformation: Chile and Beyond.") But it is not clear whether the thirty-six-year-old Mistral rectified her ideas when, twenty-years later, she became associated with the United Nations, a supporter of women's rights as part of human rights. But the vehemence and condescension displayed towards feminism in 1925 persisted and cannot be overlooked.

Existential Choices

This controversy surrounding Lucila/Gabriela's sexuality, looked at objectively and non-judgmentally as part of a larger picture of conduct, points to a human being who is calculating and needy of affection and attention. Although aware of existing social/sexual mores, she was willing to evade them, in effect, to satisfy her own heterosexual needs and socio-psychical insecurities. This hypothesis carries over with regard to her early teaching assignments. Lucila/Gabriela, a larger than life character possessed with a desire for fame, overrode a teacher's obligation to devote herself, especially in her early teaching assignments, to the morale of the young people in her charge and cared more for her personal needs of writing articles and poetry. One could argue about relative and categorical morality and ethics. Does one develop an image of public purity or does one satisfy a hunger for human warmth? These choices extend to satisfying the immediate and the important, that is, the obligations of a time-bound teaching job *versus* satisfying a dream of belonging to the writers of the ages?

Il faut choisir, insisted the existentialist Jean-Paul Sartre; "choosing" is man's fate. Choices through actions, according to Sartre, define a person's identity. And what did Lucila/Gabriela choose? How did she act? What was more compelling: the immediate job and tasks of daily living or the pulsating life force? From the aforesaid descriptions of her early conduct in life's decisions, it appears that frail humanity and artistic calling compelled her to enter into all sorts of devious arrangements and compromises — sexual, aesthetic, and social — within a male-dominated hierarchical society, weighing all risks and rewards, to forge her social, economic, intellectual, and aesthetic identity.

CHAPTER VIII

Punta Arenas: Exile in Land's End

A Presidential Commission

The fictive encounter and interview (*circa* 1915) enacted (Chapter VI, "Life Changes in Los Andes") between Lucila and Pedro Aguirre Cerda at Pocuro, her "shrine" to Sarmiento, turned into a real possibility in December 1917. Minister of Education Aguirre Cerda chose the only distinguished woman in Chile he could find to head a team to direct the Liceo de Niñas de Punta Arenas in the southern-most Territory of Magallanes. The region was named for Fernando Magellan (1480–1521), the Portuguese explorer who sailed through the eponymous Straits that linked the Atlantic with the Pacific.

Minister Aguirre Cerda, after a final vetting, recommended Lucila Godoy to President Juan Luis Sanfuentes as *directora* to a post that entailed great personal challenges and physical risks. The decree, signed February 15, 1918, authorized the teacher of Castilian to propose to the Government any and all changes to personnel and management "*...que estime convenientes para asegurar la buena marcha del establecimiento*" ("...that she may deem necessary to ensure the proper functioning of the institution"), and to "Chileanize" the schools and the surrounding populations.[1]

For the first time Lucila Godoy's lack of a university degree was not an issue or an impediment. Aguirre Cerda required an educator with imagination, with strong will, and with the ability to lead a school in a hostile physical and human environment. From personal talks with her in Los Andes, in 1915, Aguirre Cerda knew that his candidate had overcome all sorts of hardships. Her writings, actions, and honors spoke for her: high intelligence, perseverance, a social conscience, a commitment to education for the masses, articles on compulsory education, innovative teaching methodologies, winner of the Juegos Florales, and endorsements by trusted advisers.

In the first week of May 1918, Lucila Godoy led her carefully chosen seven-member Consejo Presidencial Sobre la Educación to the steamship "Chiloé," in the harbor of Puerto Montt, for a two-week voyage to the tip of South America.

Exile within Chile

Roque Esteban Scarpa, the maximum authority on the poet's stay in Magallanes, presciently titled his monumental two volumes, *La desterrada en su patria* (*The Exile in Her Own Country*).[2] All things considered, she underwent three physical exiles from her sunny and vine-laden Elqui valley and one additional exile of an emotional sort.

If Punta Arenas is her second exile, the first one, surely, must have been Antofagasta, where she had choked on the rainless desert heat in a nitrate-centered town in which its first newspaper and concert hall just appeared. In Punta Arenas, in contrast, she would gag on rainy torrents in extremely cold weather and nine months of twilight. In Punta Arenas, as with Antofagasta, she underwent the additional emotional exile from family, friends, and from Manuel Magallanes Moure. As yet unperceived, the third physical exile would take her to Mexico (1920–1922), and from there to her self-imposed and life-lasting de-territorialization in Europe, Brazil, and, finally, the United States, before coming home to Montegrande for final repose in 1957.

In 1918, on arriving in Punta Arenas, province of Magallanes, she mailed a postal card to Pedro Prado in which she defined her sense of emotional as well as physical exile: "*Estoi tan sola i en pleno destierro.*" ("I am so alone and totally exiled."[3]) This could have been a play on words, that is, in 1918 she still felt close to [Manuel] Magallanes the man, but not the place of the same name. Volodia Teitelboim acutely pointed out the ironic twist of words: "*Parte a Magallanes escapando de Magallanes.*" Interpolating, "she leaves for Magallanes [the place] while escaping from Magallanes [the lover]."[4] In 1923, she was totally sensitive to the double verbal irony coined by Teitelboim, that she was "deported" from her unattainable lover, Manuel Magallanes, to a land that bore his name but not his presence or essence.

Her love persisted, despite rumors of his attachment to other women. But it was a bittersweet love, embittered by being able to visualize the betrayal, as expressed in "Balada":

Él pasó con otra;	He passed by with another:
Yo le vi pasar.	I saw him pass by.
Siempre dulce el viento	The wind ever sweet
y el camino en paz.	and the road at peace.

| ¡Y estos ojos míseros | And these wretched eyes |
| Le vieron pasar! | Saw him pass by! |

"Balada" was written in Punta Arenas and included in *Desolación*.[5] "La otra" could well have applied to Manuel's dalliance with Sara Hübner. Thoughts of him may have warmed Lucila from time to time in frigid Patagonia, but following a two-year, letter-less vacuum, in which betrayal was on her mind, a personal coldness set in that never thawed. In her last letter from Mexico, in 1923, she bade a final farewell, to him and to Chile.[6]

Maturing Leadership

No longer could Lucila count on Fidelia to straighten things out. On accepting a leadership position in Punta Arenas, she became accountable, for the first time, for the well-being of students, teachers, and the administration of an institution in an inhospitable environment. Gabriela the poet was already mature. The teacher, Lucila, needed to mature as an administrator, counselor, motivator, and community organizer. Sink or swim, Lucila could no longer shy away from obligations and people who were not her intellectual equals or gifted with special aptitudes. The small cadre of incoming teachers would, with the ongoing staff, turn their attention to the children, illiterate adults, and the native Alcalufs.

In contrast to the lonely and solitary receptions at prior teaching assignments, Lucila was greeted, May 18, by the military governor of Punta Arenas, by Dr. Luis Aguirre Cerda (the minister's brother), and by political and business notables, who feted the Commission at a banquet and offered their assistance in carrying out the president's goals. The band of teachers would need all the help it could muster from the military, political, and business communities.

But the first in a series of many concerns consisted of adjusting to the harsh climate, the semi-darkness, health issues, and eating and sleeping routines. In second place, but not less important, the arriving team was concerned with integrating itself among the existing teachers, organizing a division of labor and responsibility, and scheduling classes at the Girls' Liceo on Calle Waldo Seguel so that it could re-open on April 1, after having been ordered closed by an investigative commission that found serious physical and sanitary deficiencies.

Lucila had inherited a failed school as part of a failed school system. She could not correct the system, but she set out to correct her unit's problems as quickly as possible. The previous *directora*, having fled an untenable scene of poor sanitary conditions, lack of space, and demoralized staff, caused the school to close. The new *directora* and her team were sent to provide invigoration and new direction so that the school could open on April 1. Problems abounded with equipment, teachers, and parents which could not be solved easily or overnight. The heating stoves, for example, were necessary, but created a double burden. They did not provide adequate heat and yet gave off fumes. Open windows dissipated the toxic smoke in the rooms but led to shivering people within. She found teachers demoralized over poor leadership, pay, and benefits. Parents of some forty children, who suffered from tuberculosis and malnutrition, were reluctant to return them to school, in part owing to inadequate systems, but in the main, because their children were needed to labor over sheep-shearing obligations to bring in needed money for the families. There was no law as yet that compelled parents to send their children to school.

In two articles (1909 and 1910) on the need for a law on compulsory primary education, Lucila had obliquely petitioned the national legislature to solve the serious *cuestión social* of parents who kept their children out of school so that they could work to bring in money on farms or in factories. She followed up the first sentimental article of 1909, "Ideas de una maestra" ("Ideas from a Schoolteacher"), with the second, tightly-reasoned second one (1910), "Ventajoso canje" ("Beneficial Trade-Off"). The first appealed to pathos, the second to the long-term socio-economic benefits to the nation of compulsory education.[7]

Ideas from a country schoolteacher from La Serena found no root within the Conservative and the Radical powerbrokers in Santiago, although the Liberal Party had supported such an idea starting in 1907. Three years after her arrival in Punta Arenas, starting May 1, 1915, the Federación de Instructores de Instrucción Primaria increased pressure on the legislature for the law that Mistral had previously envisioned. In 1919, the legislature finally passed the law on compulsory education: Instrucción Primaria Obligatoria.[8]

At some point, and for the first time, she joined the poorly-attended and poorly-funded Sociedad de Instrucción Popular de Magallanes. At their monthly meetings, according to an undated *"Editorial,"* she urged on the membership less social entertainment and more emphasis on sobering matters, like night extension courses for working men and women and prompting the business community to provide funding. The evidence is not clear, but it is possible that she also sought and obtained the aid of the Sociedad in cleaning up El Liceo de Niñas for it to re-open with the furniture rearranged, the students tested, and the classes assigned to teachers. Lucila's personal energies with the Sociedad de Instrucción Popular, with the teachers, and with the reluctant parents erased doubts among the skeptics that the children would return for the start of school on April 1. And so it was.

Socio-Political Aspects of Education

What socio-economic and socio-political conditions prompted President Sanfuentes and Minister Aguirre Cerda to dispatch the Consejo Presidencial Sobre la Educación to this austere austral land? And what did the senior governmental officers expect eight additional educators to accomplish?

If Lucila had known in advance what President Sanfuentes and Minister Aguirre Cerda already knew about the economic and demographic power structure in Punta Arenas, she might not have accepted this daunting position. The highest governmental authorities were asking for the heroic efforts of a dozen educators to tip the power structure in the government's favor by improving education and by Chileanizing some of its citizens. If she had read the census report, she would have learned that political and numerical strength did not always equal economic strength. Chilean citizens in Punta Arenas were in the majority, but the wealth to run, repair, and expand the schools, institutions, and city and national governments resided in the foreign population, most probably exempt or delimited from the tax structure.

The demographics revealed a population of approximately 20,000 Chileans, which represented 80 percent of the 25,000 inhabitants. The Chilean majority, according to census reports, controlled only 5 percent of the estimated commercial and landed wealth, totaling almost 20,000,000 pesos. In order of concentration of wealth, an estimated 3860 foreigners, or 1.55 percent of the population, controlled 85 percent of the wealth. In descending order of economic power, the population consisted approximately of the following nationalities: 400 Germans, 500 Austro-Hungarians/Slavs, 1,500 Spaniards, 1,100 British, 200 Italians, 160 Swiss, 360 Argentines, and some 800 persons of diverse origin. Would the foreign, moneyed population — huddled in their socio-linguistic enclaves — support schools when most were males living without families in this inhospitable environment?

The President of Chile was very sensitive to another element of foreign encroachment that affected overall revenues and Chile's importance in international affairs. By the time Lucila's team arrived, May 1918, the Panama Canal, built by the United States, had been open for four years. The Canal was being used more and more for time- and cost-saving ocean-to-ocean commercial and military transportation. The new Canal diverted shipping from going around stormy Cape Horn or through the turbulent Straits of Magellan, the principal portals for hauling bulk goods and people and stopping at Punta Arenas and at Valparaíso for provisions.

President Sanfuentes, aware of Chile's diminishing competitive geo-political and geo-strategic edge, stationed a well-provisioned garrison to safeguard the economically privileged, mostly foreign investors, and to maintain order within the itinerant labor force. The military, in fact, during Lucila's stay, in 1919, suppressed with violence an organized labor protest in nearby Puerto Natales. And again, in 1921, one year following her departure, the army was called out, this time in Punta Arenas, to put down striking workers.[9]

Socio-Political Aspects of Chileanization

The teachers had no obligation to Chileanize the foreigners, who were more eager to take money than to take roots. As "outside investors," the very wealthy minority groups probably avoided taxes and were not required to enhance the community, which accounted for the dire economic conditions that crippled school systems and offered a downtown Puntas Arenas devoid of trees and community sprit. Did the Spanish-speaking majority, at the bottom of the economic pyramid, resent and take action against the wealthy "outside investors"? It appears so from the violent labor strife in 1919 and 1921.

Once the school system was organized to permit minimal functioning, Lucila turned to the mission that Minister Aguirre Cerda assigned to her as leader of the Consejo Presidencial, i.e., that of Chileanizing the natives. Lucila organized free night classes for some Alcaluf Indians. The lessons involved the Spanish language, Chilean history, conversation, and reciting oral traditions. Lucila knew the history and literature of Judeo-Christian and Eastern traditions. On the other hand, she encountered for the first time the native oral tradition among the Alcalufs. The Indians were reluctant at first, but as time passed more and more came to Lucila's classes, some to hear her monologues, others to recite tales of strange animals and struggles against the cruel *puelche* wind. These unscripted accounts, listened to and endorsed by a government official in an official building, formed the basis for eliciting loyalty to the Chilean regime from tribesmen in the southernmost region. Lucila knew that the oral tradition represented the most authentic vehicle for harnessing the literary imagination. Without realizing the bond she was forging with the Alcalufs over the year, the night classes catalyzed some students into forming a pressure group to air grievances to the civil and military authorities. A part of the civilizing process, therefore, included offering disenfranchised groups and tribes the opportunity to acculturate themselves slowly through the Spanish language and classes on Chilean history and learning how to address and focus their social concerns. This slow and careful civilizing process in a hostile physical and economic environment was designed to lessen, but not eliminate, revolts by the underprivileged.

The lessons had unanticipated consequences. When overall socio-economic conditions worsened, the Alcalufs participated with other low-wage workers in revolts and demonstrations. At that point, the disciplined Chilean military stepped in to control strikers and anarchistic groups. If Chile's armed forces had triumphed in the War of the Pacific (1879–1883), overcoming the combined military of Bolivia and Peru, arrogating to itself the nitrate- and copper-rich provinces of Tacna and Arica, and sacking the city of Lima, then it had the will and the skill to overpower rebellious workers and Indians.[10]

Lucila Godoy, to all appearances, supported the process of Chileanization advocated by President Sanfuentes and Minister Aguirre Cerda. The process, as she envisioned it, took shape as a voluntary, peaceful means to instruct less fortunate individuals into the Chilean way of life. If Lucila and her instructors could advance the cause of peaceable progress, then it was worthwhile. She stated to Roque Esteban Scarpa in her prologue to his book, *La desterrada en su patria*, that she undertook the task of Chileanization pressured by authorities in Santiago. She may have done so "under orders," but she complied.

She knew as did all literate persons that Chile's military was also "under orders" to put down indigenous people and unionizing protestors opposed to harsh working conditions and slave wages and therefore a danger to the state, to wealthy Chilean landowners, and to foreign investors. Difficult labor-management conflict conditions also existed in Chile's northern territory of Antofagasta, among the nitrate miners in Iquique (1906–1907), maritime workers in Valparaíso (1905), and students in Santiago (1905). Unrest prevailed, also, in the southern territory of Magallanes, where lumber and cattle workers endured personal hardships, which resulted in the riots of Puerto Natales (1919).

The strife was caused by abysmal working and living conditions and poor pay, whether in the mines, on farms, aboard fishing fleets, or in factories. In addition, unsanitary housing, epidemics, high infant mortality, unemployment and underemployment, uncontrolled inflation, and indentured slavery afflicted Chileans. Not limited to Chile in this time frame, in other countries dissatisfied laborers gave rise to the Industrial Workers of the World (the "Wobblies," December 24, 1919), the Mexican Revolution (1910–1917), the Russian Revolution (1917), and to generalized anarchists' attacks in Spain, Italy, the United States, and elsewhere. In Chile, when landholders protested to the politicians, when foreign investments underwent risk, and when state security appeared to be threatened, the president called out the army to suppress laborers, teachers, students, and Indians. As Mario Garcés Durán emphasizes in his book about turn-of-the-century Chile, *Crisis social y motines populares en el 1900*, the elites, the Conservative Party, and the Catholic Church "*no reconocen la cuestión social.*"[11]

Mistral, in this context, warned years later about the danger to Chilean society's wellbeing if the government ignored workers' rights. Was Lucila/

Gabriela duped, or was she in concert with the government authorities who advocated Chileanization by force if necessary? Neither idea makes sense! Did she support a "Europeans-only" program of immigration like that advocated by President Domingo Faustino Sarmiento (1868–1874), in Argentina? That is possible. If so, could she or should she be accused of not supporting miscegenation or of favoring genocide against natives so that Europeans might prevail? If so, no evidence has appeared. But it seems to be the allegation espoused by Licia Fiol-Matta, when she states that Mistral favored, wittingly or unwittingly, perplexed or not perplexed, her support for [assimilating or annihilating] "indigenous peoples in "...the state's racial project....":

> Mistral spoke rancorously about her stay in Magallanes, yet the same national prerogatives that she occasionally decried governed her public and private discourse until her death. Though Mistral evinced perplexity at her role in this endeavor, she internalized and enacted it thoroughly, to the point that her own feelings meshed with the state's racial project.[12]

One possible cushion to the allegation by Fiol-Matta — giving Lucila/Gabriela the benefit of the doubt — is that she compartmentalized her feelings and thoughts. On the one hand, Chileanization, which meant teaching history, Spanish, and literature benefited the Alcalufs, the prisoners, the illiterates, and the women socially and intellectually and made them better citizens and prepared for the work force. On the other hand, education meant raising the social consciousness of the students to the point where they might have themselves chosen to act as a pressure group on government. Did she and other teachers, by carrying out their paid assignments as directed, increase or channel the pent up rage the poor Indians felt? If this was the case, and there is no proof, she might have contributed, perhaps obliquely, to their social revolt to improve their well-being.

Achievements That Leave Tracks

Most teachers realize that great efforts spent on students, including preparation, presenting and testing material, and energizing or corrective conversations, leave little trace or residue or palpable reminders, after the class is over. So the great efforts that Lucila made with the day students and the conversational night-classes with the Alcalufs have left few footprints. But Lucila left visible marks in areas of community action.

On March 19, she inaugurated the Biblioteca Infantil (Children's Library) with a gift of encyclopedias from the Librería Cervantes, books from the Argentine Consulate, and a contribution from her own personal collection. The generosity of others motivated the city government to pay a monthly stipend for library personnel.

The lack of reading materials among the sick in the hospital and among the prisoners in the city jail prompted Lucila to extend her literary enrichment campaign to those institutions with the aid and generosity of a local magistrate. She might have put her own name on the door, but chose instead to highlight a recently-deceased Spanish female, Concepción Arenal (1820–1893), an advocate of reform for the indigent and imprisoned. Her successes in these campaigns — part of the civilizing and literacy-enhancing missions — and her humility in carrying them out was sure to impress Minister Aguirre Cerda. She did not have her name engraved on the library's door, but she probably burned it in the minds of the officials who had appointed her.

As if the literacy campaigns in and out of school were insufficient to fulfill the Commission's charge, Lucila launched a public beautification project of planting trees downtown. With the financial support from the managers of banks, restaurants, and other shops on the main thoroughfares, who discovered that planting trees was in their economic self-interest, she collected the money to buy them. The staff and students planted them along the Avenida Colón and around the Plaza Magallanes. It was a cheerful touch intended to brighten up a drab area, which benefited all concerned and garnered praise for Lucila. The old-timers in Punta Arenas still point out "*los árboles de Gabriela.*"

Health and Living Conditions

Laura Rodig, who accompanied her best friend to Punta Arenas, published articles in later life that permit a reader to recapitulate an understanding of their life together in Punta Arenas under ordinary and exceptional conditions.[13] The daily routine consisted of trying to stay as warm as possible. During the cold nights, they covered themselves with vicuña pelts. Lucila wrote from under the blankets. Laura, after finishing her art classes, had to sculpt standing in the middle of the cold room; with hands freezing she tried to shape hard clay.

The cold weather took its toll by sapping physical stamina and served as a constant reminder of their vulnerability. Lucila's yoga exercises permitted her to retain relative good health. Laura, in contrast, delicate in health and temperament, suffered from issues related to colds and coughing. During the school vacation period in February 1919, Laura became very ill, and Lucila had her transported north to a warmer and sheltered area to be attended to by a couple recommended by Dr. Luis Aguirre Cerda. Laura's sickness worsened, so Lucila remained by her side for the rest of the vacation period. Lucila's concern for health, hers and Laura's, played a large part in seeking to leave Punta Arenas.

Literary Outpourings

During this vacation time away from the school, Lucila concentrated on writing more poems and articles and correcting manuscripts. She had constantly pondered the question whether she could find, with all her responsibilities, time to continue the one activity that possessed her soul: writing. The answer lay in her productivity. In Punta Arenas, she founded and wrote articles for the magazine *Mireya*— named in honor of Frédéric Mistral's poem. To break the isolation from friends, Lucila corresponded often with novelists Pedro Prado (*Alsino*, 1920), and Eduardo Barrios (*El niño que enloqueció de amor*, *El hermano asno*), and with the poetess María Enriqueta, among many others. She did not write, oddly enough, to Magallanes Moure. He resided in her thoughts during the year and a half absence and motivated her to match him in artistry and in ardor by being creative during those months of frigid Antarctic darkness. Lucila produced more than eighty poems, eighteen of which formed part of her first book, *Desolación*, three years later (1922), for Federico de Onís in New York. These writings were reasons enough for critics to believe that the title, *Desolación*, extended not only to the harsh Patagonian landscape, but also to her cold emotional inscape, thawed mainly by recollections of the sunny Elqui valley and her family, informal conversations with Laura Rodig, and labors civilizing town streets and libraries, children, women, Indians, prisoners, sick persons, and farm workers.

A Farewell to Exile

Lucila felt, in the course of 1919, that she had done her best to improve conditions and wanted to depart as soon as an appropriate opening was available. The Liceo was functioning as well as could be expected under tight budget constraints, and the physical and sanitary improvements prevented the school from being closed as unsafe. The morale among teachers, students, and parents was strengthened. She had developed community ties by establishing libraries for the children, the hospital, and the prison. Some downtown merchants could point to "Gabriela's trees" as a reminder of her efforts to offer beauty to a commercial center dedicated to enriching itself.[14]

Although much more remained to be achieved, she had set an unparalleled pace and prepared to pass the baton to her replacement, Celmira Zúñiga. Health problems affecting Laura motivated her even further to make an effort to depart. Gabriela/Lucila conceived of an indirect and a direct plan to inform Minister Aguirre Cerda of her desire to transfer to another post. María Enriqueta, a poet and friend, reported years later that, in 1919, she had "leaked" a private letter to the press that Gabriela Mistral, Chile's well-known writer was "exiled and abandoned in Patagonia," much to the distress of admirers. Laura Rodig engineered the direct approach. She traveled to Santiago on a "mission of mercy," to convince the Minister and friends to transfer a sick and "*postrada*" ("prostrate") Lucila to La Serena, or Los Andes, or another site, before she succumbed to the cold.[15]

Aguirre Cerda took notice and, after negotiations, brought her out of her *destierro* to a post directing the Liceo de Niñas in Temuco, a town some 300 miles south of Santiago. Just as the band had played in her honor when she arrived, so, too, did it play on April 15, 1920—eight days after her thirty-first birthday. Gabriela and Laura boarded the "Orcoma" to sail north out of exile.

Chapter IX

Temuco: A Staging Area

Comparing Cautín to Magallanes

Lucila believed that her new post in Temuco, starting April 1920, would be a positive change and would relieve much of the stress and tedium that she and Laura had experienced in Punta Arenas. The major stressors — the very cold climate and the long twilights that confused a person's biological rhythms and contributed to illnesses — disappeared in Temuco. Other stressors replaced them. The rain in Cautín Province was not cold, but it was as abundant as in Magallanes; and in both cities rain was a blessing to the ever-present farming, timber and cattle industries.

A census report credited Temuco with a population of 32,000 at that time, 7,000 more inhabitants than Punta Arenas. As in Punta Arenas, European foreigners had emigrated, between 1883 and 1901, from a dozen countries, including Switzerland, Spain, France, and Germany.

An editorial of the newspaper *La Mañana* (April 30, 1920), welcomed the "notable" Lucila Godoy, alias of the "distinguished" writer Gabriela Mistral, firm in the conviction that she will guide the students, as she always had done, on the road to "*el perfeccionamiento moral e intelectual.*" But, in contrast with Punta Arenas, no brass band or politicians greeted the new principal and Laura Rodig. This trip the two women did not arrive bolstered by a governmental decree and a commission which mandated fulfilling a state security mission, that of re-opening and restoring a failed school in three weeks, Chileanizing people under very difficult socio-political circumstances, and restoring hope to a recalcitrant business community through civic actions.

A merchant class similar to that in Punta Arenas existed in downtown Temuco. But, according to her written comment to Minister Aguirre Cerda, it was much inferior in quality and civic ideals. She was under no allusions that farmers, lumberjacks, and cattlemen would give forth intellectual and spiritual giants. In that same subtle letter, she turned a first negative impression into a sign of hope, in that, the low quality of life, including lots of poorly-dressed and unwashed persons in the smelly marketplace, offered her [and Aguirre Cerda?] an opportunity to better it, as perhaps, she had done in Punta Arenas. Was Lucila offering the Minister an opening to restore to her in Temuco the noble title and mission she had just abandoned in Punta Arenas? That did not happen, and perhaps Gabriela wondered whether she should have taken up Constancio Vigil's generous offer from Buenos Aires to be editor-in-chief of three magazines, *Atlántida*, *El Gráfico*, and *Billiken*. But she turned down Vigil because she could not leave Chile nor her family, not just yet.[1]

Pleasure and Pain in the Liceo

At the Liceo, Lucila remained captive to activities that had become part of her behavior, with two important exceptions. One exception was that at the start the staff, instead of showing hostility as had happened in previous assignments, felt comfortable having a principal who was an important author. The second exception consisted of the principal, not any more just a teacher, greeting every young girl dressed in radiant white by their name. The principal ingratiated herself with every student who lined up to say, "*Buen día profesora, bienvenida*" ("Good morning teacher, welcome.").

But Lucila remained a prisoner of two major habits that provincial mores could not accept. The first was that women smoking, drinking, and going outside bareheaded were frowned upon. The second related to Laura Rodig. Some teachers opposed the hiring of Rodig because of inappropriate qualifications, others because of cronyism. Perhaps the reasons were excuses to mask the main point, which was "unspeakable," to use Sylvia Molloy's euphemistic adjective. The question had dogged the two women in Los Andes and Punta Arenas. Were they very close friends or lovers?

Lucila's aura, physical presence, and increased confidence as an administrator had calmed down the pre-existing dissension among the teachers over pay and benefits. In Punta Arenas, the intolerable frigid weather had dominated most conversations instead of gossip over personal relationships. But in conservative, temperate Temuco, the once quarrelsome teachers focused their attention over the relationship of the two women. As if that dissension were not sufficient, the principal added to the conflict upon hiring Luisa Fernández, a young, eager devotée from Santiago. With Luisa aboard, the relationship between Lucila and Laura became strained and contentious. This triangle of women competing for favors and superiority could not have escaped the attention of the staff, which added to the gossip and confusion.

Araucans and Indian Rights

If Lucila wanted to justify to Minister Aguirre Cerda restoring her authority as head of a Presidential Commission to carry out the Chileanization program in distant Temuco — to Santiaguinos still considered the Wild West — as she had with the Alcalufs, she could have justified it with the Mapuches and Araucans. Both groups had native roots in the Temuco area. The Araucans were the remaining descendants of the conquered tribes heralded in two major epic poems, Alonso de Ercilla's *La araucana* (1569, 1578, 1589), and Pedro de Oña's (1570–1643) *El arauco domado*. In the former, Ercilla (1533–1594) created living characters who suffered at the hands of the encroaching Spaniards. Fictional names from Ercilla's famous epic poem, like Caupolicán and Colocolo, still live, etched with pride on the jerseys of sports clubs and on street signs. Pedro de Oña's somber approach and his praise for the subjugation of the Araucans has not endeared him to post–Colonial Chileans.

Mistral, in her "Recado," or "Message," titled "Música araucana," sided with Ercilla and berated both Spanish *conquistadores* and current despoilers of Araucan lands and human rights. Mistral's encounters with impoverished Indian populations led years afterward to a larger role as defender of Indian culture through writings and speeches. She carried this theme forward in Mexico, whose pre–Columbian tribes inspired her to write "Recado sobre los Tlalocs" and "Recado sobre Quetzalcóatl."[2] Her growing sensitivity to Indian rights, and the Sanfuentes government's problems with tribal unrest, might have justified setting up another Presidential Commission for the purposes of Chileanization in Temuco.

Years later, in Spain, when serving as consul, she defended Indians in strong terms against the inconsiderate racist remarks of several Spanish intellectuals at a public gathering. Their derision was the last straw. Perhaps the slander reminded her of Miguel de Unamuno's denigrating comments about the brilliant Nicaraguan poet and ambassador to Spain, Rubén Darío. Unamuno, the rector of the University of Salamanca, slammed him for his native heritage as "*un poeta chorotega sin plumas*" ("a featherless Chorotegan poet"). Her recollection of that insolence and others motivated her to detail the matter in a supposedly confidential letter to Armando Donoso and María Monvel in Chile.[3] Gabriela's "friends" published the letter in *Familia* magazine, which caused an uproar. The Spaniards residing in Santiago complained to the Ministry of Foreign Affairs. The affair led to her quick transfer to a consular post in Lisbon just before the Spanish government declared her *persona non grata*. The irony is that Pablo Neruda replaced her as consul, a poet who also praised Indians, the Incas, in his "Alturas de Machu Picchu."

Four Visitors: Díaz Arrieta, Winters, González Vera, Neruda

The limited reports about Lucila's life in Temuco mention brief encounters with four men who played a role in her life: journalist Hernán Díaz Arrieta (pseud., Alone), poet Augusto Winters, student agitator/essayist José Santos González Vera, and student agitator/poet Pablo Neruda.

Díaz Arrieta entwines Lucila with Augusto Winters in his account of a vacation visit to Temuco, probably December 1920. From Temuco, Alone and Lucila traveled to Lago Budy, where Winters lived. Lucila and Augusto coincided in having published poems in *Selva lírica* (April 1917). The two poets also shared a love of nature and a desire to help the less fortunate.

González Vera flitted in and out of Lucila/Gabriela's life for decades. We had seen him last cowering in the back seat of Jorge Hübner's limousine, an uninvited and unwelcome witness to and reporter of their conflictive meeting. He had traveled once before a great distance to Lucila's doorstep, to Punta Arenas, seeking refuge then as he did in Temuco. Once again he was fleeing from a police roundup of student agitators among the Federación Nacional de Estudiantes. Chilean university students, in the style of their earlier Argentine cohorts in Cordoba, Argentina (June 1918), demanded many reforms, among them a voice over appointments of administrators and professors, and a declaration of the inviolability of the campus from the police. Lucila, never having attended a university, was not involved in student unrest, but was no stranger to police violence. She had witnessed police action in Punta Arenas against union workers.

González Vera's political flight to Temuco also brought him in contact with Lucila's fourth important visitor, Neftalí Ricardo Reyes, the birth name of Pablo Neruda. At the time, González Vera went to visit him about taking student political action in Temuco similar to that occurring in Santiago. Lucila and Neruda had met a year earlier, but in an academic setting. Neruda, a student activist at the age of sixteen, was already advocating social action that he would clarion later in life as a member of the Communist Party. And Neruda, like González Vera, in later life would be fleeing the police, but across the Andes Mountains on horseback into exile. Neruda and González Vera shared ideas about social justice through revolts and anarchy, themes that involved low-paid, unemployed, union workers and the underclass before and after the First World War.

Gabriela would defend Neruda at all costs, even, she said, "if it meant my own life." She carried out her promise by protecting him from the Chilean government's persecution. But she did not share his belief in violence for its own sake, or to create a revolution, or to subvert the state. Her belief in human rights, for example, did not encompass marching through the streets, or standing on soap boxes, or yelling "fire" gratuitously in a public place, like the activist Emma Goldman. Lucila, having been raised poor and being dependent on a steady government check for personal and family sustenance (800 pesos monthly as *directora*), having been attacked for ideas publicly (Juan Duval in Santiago, among others), having been born a woman in a male-dominated society, expressed in her writings sympathy for the poor wage earner, for permitting people to express their ideas freely, and for women who were subjugated by men. She could, however, prove to Neftalí Ricardo Reyes, who was about to assume the pen name Pablo Neruda (the future Nobel Prize winner [1971]), that she had taken action in Punta Arenas to improve society without tearing it down first.

The sixteen-year-old student from the nearby Liceo de Hombres, Neftalí Ricardo Reyes, was president of the Ateneo Literario. He sought out Lucila Godoy (May 1920) to award her an honorary membership. She never forgot that gracious act or his humble questions about the worth of his writings. He came by El Liceo de Niñas frequently to ask her opinion about his poems, or to borrow a book by a Russian author, or to comment on social injustice. With regard to his early writings, Gabriela recollected taking pride in encouraging him to keep writing so that he would pass through the portals of literary fame.

Years later, from memory, Neruda painted a flattering portrait of the tall teacher, whom he first spied striding, with her floor-length skirt and bobbed hair, down the street in Temuco, home to the Araucans: "When I was introduced to her I found her a good-looking woman. Her tanned face showed her predominant Indian blood. Like a beautiful Araucan pitcher, her translucent white teeth stood out in a full generous smile that lit the room."[4] Neruda, the second Nobel laureate from Chile, was as proud of Gabriela, the first Nobel winner, as she was of him.

Contemplating the Future

After Lucila gained the tactical advantage of no longer living in exile 1,500 miles from Santiago, she began thinking beyond the completion of their one and a half year assignment (April 1920 to August 1921). From Temuco, a long train ride to Santiago, she traveled several times for business and personal reasons. She sought every opportunity — after the success in Punta Arenas and Temuco as principal — for the Ministry of Education to offer her a position as headmistress of a school in Santiago, or Los Andes, or perhaps Valparaíso. In her defense would be new publications and old friends. The major barriers remained: the absence of a university degree and jealousy. Could excellent literary productivity, powerful friends, hard work in Punta Arenas attested to by the minister's brother and her tenacity, overcome a major educational shortcoming and the personal rivalries? Would high-level friends come to the rescue? Again and again, she must have thought whether living 300 miles south of the capital — instead of 1,500 — would place her objective closer. Many questions about the future, post–Temuco, gave her pause for reflection for a year and a half.

Final Testimonials and a Prayer

The departure of Gabriela Mistral the poet as well as Lucila Godoy the principal for Santiago surprised and shocked Claudio Antúnez, according to his article — and the ten others that soon followed — in the Temuco newspaper *La Mañana* (*The Morning*), April 28, 1921.[5] Appearing to speak for the community and the childrens' parents, citizen Antúnez praised the writer and ennobled the principal for educational and civic efforts beyond the call of duty in the *liceo*, in the workers' forum Casa del Pueblo, and in the city jail's literacy program. Antúnez, apparently unaware of ongoing personal conflicts in the Liceo, also singled out Lucila's ability to bring harmony to the previous quarrelsome and unproductive staff: "*En su corta estadía, ... hizo el milagro de la resurrección de la tranquilidad y cordialidad entre el personal docente.*" ("In her brief stay, ... she made a miraculous resurrection of tranquility and cordiality among the teaching staff.")

One angry writer blamed herself and the community's apathy for the principal's departure. This anonymous, ashamed female believed that the principal was leaving because so few citizens had answered her appeal for help with funding. In a glimmer of hope, the writer urged the community to do more for the incoming principal.

La Mañana recorded several emotional farewells, or *despedidas,* by workers at the Casa del Pueblo (May 24, 1921). Many recalled Lucila's efforts to take books to the prisoners to rescue them from being forgotten and from illiteracy. On May 25, an Araucan student praised the teacher for her fine work and blamed herself and her friends for not living up to the high moral and intellectual standards being offered. With the departure, it was too late to make amends.

In *La Mañana* of May 24, Gabriela the author and Lucila the principal united in voicing a sacred and secular prayer in and out of time and space. The prayer did not only reach the citizens and teachers of Temuco, but eventually and discreetly made its way to the Chilean Minister of Justice and

Instruction, who, on reading it made a major decision that shaped the principal's destiny, as we shall see in the next chapter. The joint prayer was "La oración de la maestra" ("Prayer of the Schoolteacher"). The powerful opening unites Jesus' mission with the humble teacher: "*Señor, Tú que enseñas, perdona que yo enseñe, que lleve el nombre de maestra que Tú llevaste por la tierra.*" ("Lord, Thou who teach, forgive me for teaching, for bearing the name teacher which Thou carried on Earth."). And in the coda the poet emphasizes that Christ's preaching, like that of the teacher, is an act of pain and sacrificial love*: " Y, por fin, recuérdame, ... que enseñar sobre la tierra es llegar al último día con el lanzazo de Longinos en el costado hendido de amor.*" ("And, finally, remind me ... that teaching on Earth means reaching the last day with the thrust of the lance of Longinus in your side rent with love.") Signed, Gabriela Mistral.[6]

Lucila was well aware of the secular basis for moving on — inadequate funding for education, deficient classrooms, lack of citizens' support, and internal quarrels — but her practical and optimistic side hoped for better conditions in Santiago. Gabriela, who conceived and signed the "Oración," was imbued also with sacred reasons for being a teacher. Aligning herself with deeply-rooted, messianic Christian beliefs, she echoed Christ's message of spreading the Word. And she hoped to do just that. Her prayer would be answered in a 300-mile pilgrimage to her dreamed of shrine in Santiago de Chile, not to a far off cathedral in Santiago de Compostela.

CHAPTER X

The Transformation: Chile and Beyond

Prelude

This brief prelude prefigures the unusual structure of this chapter's sections, made necessary to explain the key, multiple events that transpired simultaneously and in succession within one year. The different themes within each of the following sections begin with her arrival in Santiago from Temuco and conclude with her official departure from Chile.

In May 1921, the president-elect approved Lucila Godoy's nomination by the Minister of Instruction as *directora* of the Liceo de Niñas No. 6 in Santiago. By June 1922, owing to a smear campaign, the elected president dismissed her. A fall from that prestigious, long-sought, post made her unavailable or unsuited for other teaching jobs within Chile. The highest officials, embarrassed over their vigorous initial support of a renowned poet and accomplished educator, arranged a face-saving way out of the predicament for all parties concerned. They arranged, and she accepted, without recourse but with relief, a position as an educational emissary to Mexico.

This last official and public rejection, this culminating assault and fall from grace — however dressed up — pained her to the quick. The thirty-three-year old teacher-poet spent thirty-five years abroad. She returned four times briefly to Chile, three on personal/official visits, the last, permanently, in a bier to redemptive national honors and universal glorification.

That posting to Mexico eventually led to her transformation. Her personal life and professional mission, with time, perseverance, and great intellectual efforts — previously described — led to her ascension to national and international prominence.

Santiago: A Temporary Way Station

Lucila/Gabriela, having served in hellish Antofagasta, frozen Punta Arenas, and frontier Temuco, felt herself an outlier. After twenty years in second-tier schools and environments, she believed she merited the summit, i.e., directing a *liceo* in Santiago. To further that end, she wrote for newspapers and magazines, furiously and well, earning recognition for her efforts in print, in the classroom, and as head of two schools. She traveled often from Temuco to Santiago to persuade influential friends to grant her the opportunity to show her capabilities in a *liceo* in Santiago, the Chilean equivalent, perhaps, of New York's Carnegie Hall. The visits and the efforts met with success, but at a tremendous cost personally and emotionally. She did not realize in May 1921 what she learned by June 1922. She learned that once coveted Santiago was merely a way station to bigger and better steppingstones abroad.

To merit the positions abroad, she possessed qualities that exceeded the capacities of most Santiaguinos, male and female. One might draw a verbal analogy with the Cuban writer and patriot, José Martí. Martí's capabilities so out ran those of his compatriots, such that when he left Cuba, writers about him used the following wordplay to describe him: "*Martí no salió de Cuba, sino que se salió de Cuba.*" Roughly, Martí did not leave Cuba, nor did Gabriela leave Chile, rather they overshadowed their peers, and "left" by exceeding the limitations imposed by their respective environments.

When she arrived in Santiago from Temuco and had no place to live, friends and admirers who were aware of her literary and educational successes seemed eager to have her reside with them, even temporarily. Among them were the family of her employee in Temuco, Luisa Fernández, and the very wealthy María Luisa García de Huidobro. Doña María Luisa, by the way, was the mother of the celebrated poet Vicente Huidobro (1893–1948). Vicente authored *Altazor,* founded Creationism, and linked himself to French Vanguardists and Spanish Ultraists. Just as Lucila, the poor principal, and María Luisa, the wealthy matron, traveled in different social circles, so, too, did, Gabriela and Vicente, who crossed paths from time to time, travel in different literary circles.

Until she could find her own quarters after winning the job as headmistress of the Liceo Número 6 de Niñas, Lucila resided with the sisters Virginia and Alice Trewhela, spinsters who headed the Trewhela School for Girls, an academy that trained wealthy girls in British English and the European way of life and culture. In appreciation, Gabriela dedicated "El himno cotidiano," in the volume *Ternura,* to "*la señorita Virginia Trewhela.*"

Subsequent to being appointed headmistress, Lucila lived first at the *liceo* and then in a private house. A lack of means and a desire to remain close to the school prompted her to occupy the fourth floor of the Liceo, at Calle Chiloé 1879. The building, titled the Palacio Bravo after its owner Exequiel Bravo, belied the physical surroundings. Built in the 19th century, when the area consisted of elegant homes, population shifts placed the Palacio Bravo in the Matadero [slaughterhouse] District. A "palace" in name only, it needed considerable renovation.

By December 1921, Lucila regretfully moved to a house she could ill afford in the Huemul district in order to take care of her mother. Petronila, escorted by Laura Rodig, had traveled from La Serena to live with her daughter after many years of separation. Within a month, homesickness on Petronila's part and the increasing bad health from the effects of hyperthyroidism on Graciela, Emelina's daughter, obligated Lucila to send her mother back to La Serena. Santiago would be their next-to-last meeting place before Petronila passed away in 1928.

Lucila, for the first time in years, lived alone in the house. She filled the evening solitude with long walks, corrected poetry to be selected for *Desolación,* and prepared for the next day's full academic and administrative schedule. Lucila also had time to reflect on the incessant "*clamoreo,*" the "clamoring" from detractors who had opposed and continued to oppose her appointment as *directora.* Decision points were looming large, once again, regarding separation from a job, friends, and even Chile to an uncertain future.

Lucila Godoy Wins Support

Contacts in Santiago informed Lucila in Temuco of the opening of a two-story school, Liceo Número 6 de Niñas. Obtaining the job at the Liceo became her prime objective. After several discussions, she forwarded to the new Minister of Justice and Public Instruction, Armando Jaramillo Valderrama — who replaced Pedro Aguirre Cerda, now a senator — reports of her achievements regarding rapport with teachers, adherence to budgets, community activities with women, children, and workers, Chileanization projects, and references from, among others, Pedro Prado, and, of course, numerous publications.

On April 6, 1921, Lucila's name was penciled in on a draft budget proposal to become *directora* of Liceo Número 6 when it opened May 21. High officials were aware that, alone among the applicants, she lacked a university degree, but agreed that without one had mounted successes that *directoras* with one could never match. Presidential-designate Arturo Alessandri and his staff were expecting disagreements but were prepared to support the appointment. They never imagined the storm of nasty political, journalistic, and personal attacks which the nomination would soon incur.

Attacks and Ripostes

The multi-level attacks began almost immediately. Josefina Dey de Castillo, very upset over not having won the appointment, whined to her husband, Luis Castillo, a prominent Mason and secretary of the political party Junta Central Radical. Mr. Castillo wrote to Minister Jaramillo Valderrama and accused him of failure to follow the law, which required a *directora* to have a certificate from the Instituto Pedagógico. Mrs. Dey de Castillo's major qualifications, her husband pointed out, were that she had passed the required courses, obtained a certificate, and served as *directora* in Arica Province. Left unsaid was that his letter posed a political threat. Mr. Castillo soon found added support from the Masonic Order and the prominent educator Amanda Labarca Hubertson, among others.

Mr. Castillo failed to understand that Lucila Godoy's merits, entirely dissimilar from those of his wife, had prompted the minister to appoint her. Unmarried, she could dedicate time to a new enterprise. Her lack of roots in Santiago meant fewer enemies and fresh ideas from the field. Her overriding merit was having accomplished so much intellectually, pedagogically, and administratively without a degree from the Pedagogical Institute. And importantly, she imparted Christian beliefs unwedded to Catholic or Masonic dogma.

Lucila, disturbed by this public commotion, made two quick and high-risk pre-emptive strikes. She tendered her resignation publicly (May 27, *La Mañana*) to calm the enemies and to protect the minister. He could now accept the resignation, save face, and make another selection. She also wrote to Mrs. Dey de Castillo to extol her merits, lament her loss, and, in explaining her life story, based on merit and hard work, asked for fair play. How could Dey de Castillo, in the face of Lucilas's generosity in resigning and chivalry in writing to her, accuse her of being less than noble?

Minister Jaramillo Valderrama responded publicly in *Zig-Zag* (No. 850, 4 junio 1921), that, despite *"el clamoreo"* ("the [public] clamoring"), the appointment was justifiable to "the great Chilean poet" and would not be rescinded.[1] The inference was clear that to do so would be to surrender to public and secret political influences and to give in to an attack on the judgment of the officials involved in the decision. The minister also refused to accept the resignation. If he had, it would have been an admission of bad judgment and of breaking the law. The appointment was official and final on the basis of exceptional and meritorious service, without diminishing the importance of graduating from the Instituto Pedagógico.[2]

Recently uncovered information has clarified that a covert twist overrode the opposition and clinched the decision. Minister Jaramillo Valderrama, in reaffirming the appointment was influenced by Carlos Silva Cruz, who showed him Gabriela's passionate "Oración de la maestra," analyzed at the close of the previous chapter. The minister was impressed by the author's eloquence, humility, and Christian virtues in carrying out in her teaching the Lord's message. Not by coincidence did the secular and the sacred enter once more into the teacher/poet's sense of being, in that she was appointed not merely to a job, but also to carry out Christ's mission.

Liceo Número 6 to Teresa Prats de Sarratea

One of the new principal's first objectives was to transform a numbered school — sixth in a series — into one with a branded name. The inaugurating principal desired the staff, students, and public to recognize a figure to be proud of. The principal could think of no greater guide than Teresa Prats de Sarratea. A day following the inauguration (May 14, 1921), a respectful article appeared in *El Mercurio* (May 15), which expressed Gabriela's heartfelt sentiment for the minister to change the name. He did so.[3]

If new wine should enter new casks, then female students entering "Teresa Prats" could expect, in addition to a secular academic education, a training that Prats recommended regarding hygiene and sacred issues, such as moral and spiritual guidance. Young, impressionable female students would now form the cadres of a new feminism, with their own heroines as guides, with courses shaped to their needs, and with two strong women as their mentors, one, Teresa Prats, with her name over the door, and the other, Gabriela Mistral, within the door and guardian of it.

Why Teresa Prats? Prats had written, in 1913, *Educación doméstica de las jóvenes* (*Domestic Education for Young Girls*), a manual so influential that, in the year of its publication, she was named head of all girls' *liceos*. Her philosophy of education was not novel, but was held in high regard because it reinforced ideas and practices that the community had already sanctioned, including the separation of the sexes, practical training for young women interested in marrying, facts about hygiene, and the moral and spiritual guidance of young ladies. Lucila would accept and put into practice in her teachings the practical, that is to say, the secular aspects of Teresa Prats and much of the sacred or spiritual philosophy.

One month before resigning as *directora* of "Teresa Prats de Sarratea" and departing for Mexico on her first international mission, Gabriela wrote a commemorative article for *El Mercurio* (May 15, 1922). The article, "Teresa Prats de Sarratea," paid homage to her on the first anniversary of the school's name change. Gabriela declared, "Not only did I admire her, I loved her profoundly."[4]

Gabriela's ascension vindicated the plight of Teresa Prats, who, like Lucila, despite working herself hard for the sake of Chilean education, was also denied the title of *maestra* because she lacked a diploma. In her eulogy, Gabriela noted that Teresa Prats rose to her glory by educating and elevating the masses. In the eyes of some high-level Chileans, Gabriela's promotion seemed to take to task an educational hierarchy that handicapped the laboring majority physically and intellectually to further an elite, non-laboring minority. In summarizing her last and final year at "Teresa Prats," Gabriela stressed having put into practice her mentor's ideas and ideals, which included avoiding rote memorization in the classrooms, training females to think independently, and learning to love simple things devoid of material worth. She concluded in her exiting message to the students that they not sit idly by, but take an active role in advancing their cultural heritage through moral suasion.

Labarca Hubertson's Opposition

Lucila/Gabriela may have guarded the door to the Liceo "Teresa Prats de Sarratea," but Amanda Labarca Hubertson (1886–1975) had blocked her entrance from the first and would continue to labor for a year for her destitution. She joined forces with the opposition: Josefina Dey de Castillo, her husband Luis and his Radical party, the Order of Masons, and a future Minister of Labor, Fernando G. Oldini, who wrote that Gabriela was "badly informed and ill-advised" in her quest. ("Carta abierta a Gabriela Mistral," in *Claridad* [June 4, 1921]).[5]

Gabriela had to take Amanda Labarca Hubertson seriously. She would be a formidable foe, socially, economically, politically, and intellectually. Singly, she would have been difficult, but having married Guillermo Labarca Hubertson, an official of the Radical Party, who would soon join Arturo Alessandri's administration as Minister of Justice and Instruction, she would appear to be unstoppable, if not immediately then in the near future.

What had occasioned Amanda to oppose the nomination? She was not a candidate, but could have aspired to be one, since she was experienced directing the Liceo Número 5 de Niñas. By supporting Luis Castillo's petition on behalf of Josefina, she increased her political stance. Those reasons aside, what really moved her were a deep-rooted sense of class superiority, personal rivalry, and revenge for a rebuke suffered years before.

The rebuke was related to the Círculo de Lectoras, which Amanda helped found (1915). The Ladies Reading Circle had sponsored (1916) a poetry contest in which Gabriela's contribution received second place. Despite wounded pride, Gabriela did not complain. Soon after, Amanda's novel, *En tierras extrañas,* appeared. To get even, but slyly, Gabriela wrote a review with exaggerated, faint-hearted praise. Amanda captured the words and the music. The review was a subtle political exercise in retribution by a recognized and intelligent female member of the underclass to a female member of the upper class.

Class warfare existed by definition between the two women. Gabriela ascended by her bootstraps to social importance and literary fame from Coquimbo, through rural and remote schools, to a prized school in Santiago. A resident of Santiago, Amanda enjoyed the fruits of the wealthy- and socially-connected Labarca Hubertson family. She had the talent and the means to attend the Instituto Pedagógico, Columbia University, and the Sorbonne. Based upon academic studies in the U.S., she wrote *La escuela secundaria en los Estados* Unidos (1919). This publication enhanced her relevance within national educational circles.

In opposing Lucila's nomination to direct the Liceo Número 6, Amanda had cited educational reasons — not personal payback for a review or veiled class reasons — that is, the absence of her formal training in pedagogy and education and the corresponding diploma. The veil obscured the true reasons. On a personal level, for one, Amanda felt threatened and rivaled by Gabriela, another woman, with a voluminous intellectual output that out matched her own. Amanda, a graduate of Columbia and the Sorbonne, refused to be outshone on paper and in the papers by a woman who had not even graduated from high school.

Amanda Labarca believed that her vendetta was justified. She represented a caste system that could not tolerate a woman, however talented, who supported workers, the poor, prisoners, and illiterate women to direct a school in class-conscious Santiago. The appointment might have been appropriate in rural areas and in cities distant from the capital, but not in the capital. Amanda and her followers did not approve handing-out a sensitive assignment to a social reformer who might serve as a model which would disturb the maintenance and status of a middle- and upper-level class system. The attack resulted in a life-long enmity between the two.[6]

Labarca Hubertson might have lost the battle but not the war. Over the next year she persisted politically and socially to undermine the teacher/poet who, ultimately could only find relief by abandoning the school and her native land. Amanda gained political leverage over Gabriela's fate when President Alessandri appointed her husband, Guillermo, to the post of Minister of Justice and Public Instruction, once held by the man who had insisted on appointing her, Minister Jaramillo Valderrama.

Amanda attacked also from another direction. As she had organized feminist organizations, starting 1915, with the Ladies Reading Circles, so too, in

1922, did she advance herself and feminine causes with the Partido Cívico Femenino (Feminine Civic Party) and the newspaper *Acción Femenina*. The latter two would be instrumental in a letter-writing campaign libeling the principal of Liceo Teresa Prats de Sarratea and demanding her ouster. Labarca Hubertson did not have a clue that she gained a Pyrrhic victory ousting the country schoolteacher. Although she dominated Chile's educational field with Mistral's absence, Mistral eventually dominated Chile's heart and soul.

Gabriela, in denouncing Chile from exile, referenced seventy public letters written by "*las criollas,*" probably the same "creole women" who had allied themselves with Amanda's Partido Cívico Femenino.[7] A whispering campaign started. Detractors lobbied representatives of Alessandri's government murmuring about the diploma situation and incompetence. But the cruel blow concerned inferences about homosexual and heterosexual activities. The message to resign also took a menacing turn. In 1954, when old and memory was slipping, Gabriela wrote a letter to Mercedes Dublé Urrutia on her last visit to Chile. She recalled a stranger who, in 1922, had stalked the house in Huemul to intimidate her to "leave the country." And she did leave and never came back, except as a final resting place.

Desolación and Departure

By 1922, Gabriela Mistral had written more than one hundred articles and poems in a dozen magazines and newspapers in Chile and abroad. Negative opinions about her poetry and controversy surrounding her person had diminished chances that a publishing house in Chile would collect and publish her material in book form. In an odd twist, her first book, *Desolación*, which led to her national and international literary fame, did not come to fruition in Santiago, but in New York. That printing contributed to her star power at home, catalyzed the invitation from Mexico's government, and eventually played a decisive role in the decision of the Nobel Committee in 1945.

One version of the happening is that Arturo Torres Rioseco, the Chilean writer and future professor at the University of California, Berkeley — who had written seven articles praising her — carried a selection of Mistral's poetry and prose to New York to show to Federico de Onís (1885–1966), director of the Instituto de las Españas at Columbia University.[8]

Two pieced-together complementary versions, taken from Professor de Onís's prologue to *Desolación* and from a report in *La Nación* (September 18, 1921), reveal that de Onís learned of Mistral's poetry from Chilean magazines and other sources. De Onís, after reading the poems at a meeting of the Sociedad Norteamericana de Profesores de Castellano and at a student forum to great acclaim, decided that he wanted to translate them into English and to publish them in Spanish. At the meeting of Columbia University students, de Onís reported making an unusual proposal to them, i.e., that he would publish the poems under the imprimatur of the Instituto de las Españas if the students, as an act of faith, would subsidize the printing. The students consented.

When de Onís requested Gabriela's permission to authorize the publication, she hesitated. The vacillation was due, in part, to personal and historical reasons. One can infer her personal reasons from the ironic slant of *La Nación's* editorial (September 18, 1921): "...'our first poet' ... will be edited for the first time in another hemisphere where her eminent value is recognized with greater unanimity."[9] The not-so-subtle irony was not lost on those who followed her conflict. It lends credence to the saying, "Nobody is a prophet in his own land."

The historical reasons derived from Gabriela's awareness of Chile's ambivalent socio-political affairs with the United States. On the positive side, Chileans favored the U.S. because its mediators had resolved lingering border disputes with Bolivia and Peru in Chile's favor after the War of the Pacific (1879–1883). In addition, Chilean businessmen and politicians cherished, in 1920, U.S. capital investments and loans. Indeed, Chile was a recipient of forty-percent of U.S. investment capital in Latin America, and except for Panama's Canal Zone, more than any other country. Ironically, the U.S. involvement with Panama raised a negative reaction. The opening of the U.S.-created Canal, in 1914, had siphoned away, by 1922, shipping revenues from Chile's ports, which exacerbated a fiscal and political crisis owing to international loans. Tensions also flared over the tragic outcome of the U.S. Navy's involvement in the "S.S. Baltimore incident," which resulted in the death of a Chilean military officer.

When all that was filtered, Gabriela thought that her devotion to Chile had borne bitter fruit. The politicians in power were opposed to her, including the Minister of Public Instruction and his wife Amanda Labarca Hubertson and her feminist cohorts. They were squeezing her out of the most desirable position that she could have imagined since starting to teach at the age of fifteen. The philosophical question that she faced was that in Chile she had to struggle constantly in her efforts to fulfill her sacred mission as a teacher and her earthly ability as a writer to eke out a grain of man's bounty. Should she, then, rely on foreigners in the U.S. for a book and on strangers in Mexico for a job?

She relented, finally, to the requests from Arturo Torres Rioseco and Federico de Onís to publish in the U.S.[10] Thus was born *Desolación*. In 1922, Mistral's first book came out first in the U.S.[11]

X. The Transformation: Chile and Beyond

In 1923, Georges Nascimento, of Santiago's Editorial Nascimento, sensing an audience and sales, published *Desolación*. An angry Gabriela, from Mexico, considered the delayed recognition another slap in the face. Perhaps it was a rebuke, however ineffectual, to Minister of Justice and Public Instruction Guillermo Labarca Hubertson that she dedicated the book to a previous government's minister. She saluted, fittingly, former Minister of Public Instruction Pedro Aguirre Cerda, the only high government official who, after friendly private talks in Los Andes, had enough faith to approve her leadership in Chile's educational system and who promoted and blessed her international mission to Mexico.[12]

Chile Rejects and Mexico Redeems

When the Minister of Justice and Public Instruction, Guillermo Labarca Hubertson, revealed to President Arturo Alessandri the many letters and whispers against the principal of the Liceo "Teresa Prats de Sarratea," he had to break a promise. The year before, then President-elect Alessandri had approved the appointment from Minister Jaramillo Valderrama that recognized that Mistral was Chile's "great poet" and therefore merited the post as principal despite not having a degree. But the public and private clamor fomented by Amanda Labarca Hubertson and others over the year was causing problems for President Alessandri.

Having already reached the summit in education, none of Mistral's supporters was able to rescue her and themselves by finding her a more prestigious teaching job within Chile. Their double solution to a double problem was, first, to elevate her to a position of greater eminence, and, secondly, reduce the internal clamor by sending her abroad. In this maneuver, Senator Pedro

José Vasconcelos, Mexico's Minister of Education in the 1920s.

Aguirre Cerda and other colleagues played a principal role in organizing her mission to Mexico.

Chile's rejection prompted Mistral to accept the redemptive and face-saving offer that Pedro Aguirre Cerda had arranged with José Vasconcelos. The official celebration took place June 20, 1922. Chilean and Mexican dignitaries made speeches in praise of the nominee, as reported in the article "El Homenaje a Gabriela Mistral."[13] Gabriela would be the minister's guest and take part in the plan to establish rural farm schools (*escuelas-granjas*) and libraries during the reconstruction period following the Mexican Revolution (1910–1917). Vasconcelos ordered a residential school named for her, the Escuela-Hogar "Gabriela Mistral" de México, and ordered a statue of her to grace the school's patio. Mexico displayed convincingly its official respect for Gabriela Mistral in ways that Chile never conceived, by paying permanent homage to her past accomplishments and, in advance of her trip, to the successes that she would contribute to Mexican women and children.

Gabriela in Veracruz, Mexico (1948)

A Student-Teacher Farewell

What appears to be a final ceremonial photograph portrayed the principal at the bottom and center of the marbled, twin staircases that snaked upward to the classrooms of the former Palacio Bravo. Dozens of smiling students, who line both staircases, surround the principal at the bottom-center and face the camera for the final remembrance. The principal forces a smile regarding a happy, but short-lived period of closeness to her school and her "*chiquillas.*" High morale appears evident despite the internal sadness. The positive attitude resulted from Lucila's method of forging young girls through high energy, care, and interesting projects.

The final student farewell was followed by a staff *despedida*. The teachers dedicated the farewell tea not only to a poet, but also to an amiable companion, "*una amable compañera.*" Only Lucila, however, was positioned to compare the sour and scornful *despedidas* from the teachers of Antofagasta and Los Andes with the present fondness and admiration of the teachers in Santiago. Did Lucila/Gabriela wonder about how her emotional growth and maturity in the preceding years had led to this conviviality, albeit tinged with sadness?[14]

A Final Transition

Her life-long, self-imposed separation from Chile began on June 22, 1922, as she boarded the train at Mapocho Railway Station to travel to Valparaíso, where she would embark on the "Orcoma" for stops in Lima and Havana, before arriving in Veracruz, Mexico, July 22, to a warm and festive welcome.[15]

Pedro Prado wrote a beautiful farewell address in her honor (June 22, 1922), when she departed Chile at the age of thirty three for Mexico. The eulogy, in poetic prose, has stood as a template against which many subsequent comments are measured. Prado's comments are still worth quoting at length because his comparisons augured a new Gabriela on her first international mission, freed from the rebuffs and criticisms received in Chile. After that moment, according to Prado, she belonged, not merely to Chile, but to the world, and her reputation was to be fashioned by those who saw in her apostolic, even divine, qualities.[16]

> *La veréis llegar y despertará en vosotros las oscuras nostalgias que hacen nacer las naves desconocidas al arribar a puerto; cuando plieguen las velas y, entre el susurro de las espumas, siguen avanzando como en un encantamiento lleno de majestad y ensueño.*
>
> *Llegará recogido el cabello, lento el paso, el andar meciéndose en un dulce y grave ritmo..... Cuencos llenos de agua que la noche roba a las estrellas, claros, azules, verdes y grises, sus ojos brillan con el suave fulgor de un constante amanecer.*
>
> *Tiene la boca rasgada por el dolor, y los extremos de sus labios caen vencidos como las alas de un ave cuando el ímpetu del vuelo las desmaya..... Ultimo eco de María de Nazareth, eco nacido en nuestras altas montañas, a ella también la invade el divino estupor de saberse la elegida; y sin que mano de hombre*

> *jamas la mancillara, es virgen y madre; ojos mortales nunca vieron a su hijo; pero todos hemos oído las canciones con que le arrulla.*
>
> *¡La reconoceréis por la nobleza que despierta! ... No hagáis ruido en torno de ella, porque anda en batalla de sencillez.....*
>
> *Los taciturnos montañeses de mi país no la comprenden, pero la veneran y la siguen, ¡oh! ingenua y clara ciencia.*

At the beginning of her international journey, in 1922, as at the end of days, in 1957, Gabriela's face — like that of a statue weathered by time — revealed her burdens. She had her eye on a distant star and, although surrounded by many who tried to fathom her nature, she remained, in Prado's words, *la elegida*, the unfathomable chosen one.

Postlude

This short offering concludes Part One. The preceding narration has offered details of Lucila/Gabriela's earthly struggles with Man and milieu so that she might carry out God's mission as she envisioned it. Part One has opened the path to Part Two, an in-depth and focused study of the elaboration of the Sacred and Secular in her poetry and prose.

PART TWO: THE SACRED

CHAPTER XI

Critical Perspectives

Tradition versus the New School

Tradition, morality, religion, and social norms have guided Chilean critics from the thirties through the fifties in evaluating Gabriela Mistral's poetry and prose. Manuals of rhetoric, which link poetic worth to adherence to fixed rules, have shaped evaluations. The legacy of tradition is evident also in numerous examples of what the New School critic Ivor A. Richards calls "stock responses" and "doctrinal adhesions," which evaluate her poetry according to the critic's morality, or use the poet's work as a pretext for personal digression.[1]

Further, Mistralian criticism continued for a long time to chain poetry to biography. The effect has been a slavish paralleling of text to life and has involved rearrangement of her work for biographical purposes and for psychoanalysis, as well as indiscriminate substitution of artistic ideation for the poet's actual beliefs. Indeed, many critics have considered Mistral's personal life and humanitarian works more significant than her poetry.

Biography plays a useful role and tool in literary criticism and is of considerable importance in this study. In the fashion and rigor of the New School critics, biography is used to examine the poet's religious beliefs in anticipation of formal study of her use of religious symbols, metaphors, and imagery. To completely ignore the personal, human aspects would be a travesty of literary criticism, because poetry, as Gabriela Mistral herself put it, is fashioned in intimate and reciprocal harmony with the totality of one's being and blood and experiences: "*Darás tu obra como se da un hijo: restando sangre de tu corazón.*"[2] The poet Louis MacNeice strikes a similar note: "A poem, though an individual thing, derives from and has to be referred back to life, which means, in the first instance, the life of the poet. In the same way, the life of the poet, though also an individual thing, derives from and has to be referred back to the life outside him."[3] As the work, then, reflects the author, so the search for the core of Gabriela Mistral's literary expression begins in the person, because the poet has determined in advance the bases of her method of creation and has, at the same time, suggested the means by which that creation can best be understood. Only after an exposition of pertinent biographical and historical data does the present work proceed to a direct analysis of the poetry.

Although it is possible to examine poetry for indications of a poet's religious faith and the degree of its adherence to prescribed theological doctrines, this approach justifies the poetry in terms of religion only. The problem then becomes: Is the poetry good or bad theology? Does it accord with formal pronouncements by theologians? Chilean critic Raúl Silva Castro, for example, denounced an impassioned line in Gabriela's poetry, which asked God to pardon a suicide, as a grave theological error: "*nuevo y más grave error teológico.*"[4] Unless the intent of a poet is theology, it seems otiose to measure poetry against formal religious doctrine. Doing so deprives a poet of his right to choose what seems appropriate for the conditions of his art. In the same way that religion, when practiced without coercion, entails a personal quest whose goal is self-knowledge, so individual poetic expression is the culmination of a poet's desire to externalize the unconscious. A passage from Stuart Holroyd's *Emergence from Chaos* illustrates the point: "The question of the truth of a religion or of its dogmas does not arise, for religion is not justified by its truth but by its efficacy. A religion is anything that a man can live by, and in being lived it finds its truth, which, because it is existential, is irrefutable."[5] André Gide states it more pithily in his novel *Les Faux Monnayeurs*: "*Faire, et en faisant, se faire.*" What to apologists of prescriptive, thus proscriptive, criticism may be "*grave error teológico,*" to me, at least in this particular instance, indicates Gabriela's freedom to appeal to God at any time, regarding any question, without need of formal invitation or the intercession of a priestly caste. For her, the validity of the appeal to God derives, not from Thomas Aquinas, but from the poet's need for a personal encounter with God, a need fashioned in her own soul.

It seems more fruitful, therefore, to consider the religious allusions in the poetry of Gabriela Mistral as manifestations of her personal quest for expression of the meaning of religious truth. Her poetry is religious art in the sense that it is dedicated to transcendental and ontological matters. The poet speaks to the Hebrew and Christian versions of God in her own way. Jesus Christ is given utmost reverence. Love, charity, and humility are extolled. Her art, because it developed unfettered from religious strictures and dogmas, and thus avoided the incongruities of formalized religion, is able to transmit a responsible reply to the meanings of God, Jesus Christ, life, death, and the universe. In a sense, her *art* is her religion. Still, it upholds those virtues any religion might possess.

CHAPTER XII

The Hebraic Tradition

The Old Testament

In the formative period of Gabriela Mistral's life, the years in which a person acquires ineradicable impressions and habits, the Bible was the principal literary source of moral instruction and poetic inspiration.[1] The book offered stern instruction on right conduct and emphasized duty, honesty, and obedience. Isaiah and other Prophets taught what God required of every man: To do justly, to love mercy, and to walk humbly. God's mighty and terrible wrath, his vengeance on unbelievers and evildoers, instilled fear. The child Lucila could not fail to be impressed by the Bible's rigid code of moral and religious behavior. She listened with awe to the account of Job's laments to a reproving God. The heroic feats of David, the escape of Jonah, the Jacob-Joseph saga, and the adventures of Ruth were wondrous tales to the sensitive and imaginative girl.

Lucila learned the Bible from the people she trusted and loved most, with the result that she came to trust and love the Bible. Lucila's paternal grandmother, Doña Isabel Villanueva,[2] her father, Jerónimo Godoy Villanueva,[3] and her half sister, Emelina Molina,[4] would read to her constantly, so that she memorized entire passages. In later life, the poet carried with her the Bible she had bought in Antofagasta, Chile, where she lived from 1911–1912.[5] That book remained at her bedside and became her "libro de cabecera."[6] At the front of this Bible, several paragraphs in her handwriting clearly indicate that the poet found in the Scriptures the love, strength, comfort, and wisdom she eagerly sought:

> Libro mío, libro en cualquier tiempo y en cualquier hora, bueno y amigo para mi corazón, fuerte, poderoso compañero. Tú me has enseñado la fuerte belleza y el sencillo candor, la verdad sencilla y terrible en breves cantos. Mis mejores compañeros no han sido gentes de mi tiempo, han sido los que tú me diste: David, Ruth, Job, Raquel y María. Con los míos éstos son toda mi gente, los

> que rondan en mi corazón y en mis oraciones, los que me ayudan a amar y a bien padecer. Aventando los tiempos viniste a mí, y yo anegando las épocas soy con vosotros, voy entre vosotros, soy vuestra como uno de los que labraron, padecieron y vivieron vuestro tiempo y vuestra luz.
> ¿Cuántas veces me habéis confortado? Tantas como estuve con la cara en la tierra. ¿Cuándo acudí a ti en vano, libro de los hombres, único libro de los hombres? Por David amé el canto, mecedor de la amargura humana. En el Eclesiastés hallé mi viejo gemido de la vanidad de la vida, y tan mío ha llegado a ser vuestro acento que ya ni sé cuándo digo mi queja y cuándo repito solamente la de vuestros varones de dolor y arrepentimiento. Nunca me fatigaste, como los poemas de los hombres. Siempre eres fresco, recién conocido, como la hierba de julio, y tu sinceridad es la única en que no hallo cualquier día pliego, mancha disimulada de mentiras. Tu desnudez asusta a los hipócritas y tu pureza es odiosa a los libertinos, yo te amo todo, desde el nardo de la parábola hasta el adjetivo caudo de Los Números.[7]

The preceding quotation suggests the existence of an essential oneness between the poet and the Bible, which is borne out not only in the poetry, but also in the everyday speech of Gabriela Mistral. Indeed, many critics have compared Gabriela with biblical characters. José Santos González Vera's observations echo and confirm the poet's own feelings about her closeness to the biblical figures, like Joshua, Job, and Moses: "*Por instantes son Josué, Job, Moisés ... quienes reviven en las palabras.*" Again, to describe her pessimism, her unwillingness to come to terms with reality, her self-imposed martyrdom, and also, perhaps, the sense of mission and prophecy which characterized her life, González Vera links her to Jeremiah: "*Jeremías sopla en su espíritu.*"[8] Hernán Díaz Arrieta, a close friend, remarks: "*...después, predilecciones íntimas y quién sabe qué secreto atavismo la llevaron definitivamente hacia la fuente encendida de la Biblia, y tuvo a Job en la carne y el 'Cantar de los cantares' en la sangre.*"[9] With acuity, Díaz Arrieta is at once pointing to two complementary facts. First, she is the afflicted of Jehovah, who remains steadfast in her love of God, like Job, despite the unjustified burdens he imposes. Second, she is the bride of Christ, wedded to his pain and dedicated to carrying out the acts of mercy and charity about which he preached. Berta Singerman (1901–1998) — a famous actress in her time who declaimed Spanish and Latin-American poetry before auditorium-sized publics, and to whom Gabriela had repeatedly expressed her love for the Old Testament — compares her friend, in her strength of character, to Ruth the Moabite and the prophetess Deborah.[10] The preceding comparisons are not gratuitous, nor should they be construed as flattery. They represent only a fraction of many serious comments in this vein, and further, they offer insight into the spirit of Gabriela Mistral, a spirit shaped by constant devotion to the Bible:

> *¡Biblia, mi noble Biblia, panorama estupendo,*
> *en donde se quedaron mis ojos largamente,*
> *tienes sobre los Salmos las lavas más ardientes y*
> *en su río de fuego mi corazón enciendo!*
>
> *Sustentaste a mis gentes con tu robusto vino y*
> *los erguiste recios en medio de los hombres, y a mí me*
> *yergue de ímpetu sólo el decir tu nombre, porque de ti yo*
> *vengo he quebrado al Destino.*
>   ("Mis libros," pp. 33-34)

Much divergent opinion exists with regard to Mistral's possible Jewish origin. Her mother was of Basque descent and her father was born to Spanish parents. Nothing definite is known of their religious affiliations, but it is assumed that they were Catholic. However, her paternal grandmother, Doña Isabel Villanueva Godoy, who read the Old Testament to her regularly, was rumored to have been of Jewish extraction. A woman of strong temperament, she had her granddaughter recite whole chapters by heart. It is thought that the grandmother's influence set the tone for the poet's interest in the Jews.[11] Colombian writer Germán Arciniegas opposes the theories of her Jewish origin and calls Gabriela "*una mujer alucinada*," a woman prone to exaggerating and enlarging her own fanciful world: "*Cuando ella hablaba de la abuela y de las lecturas de la Biblia, hacía siempre un cuento distinto. La abuela era otro fantasma suyo.*" Carlos Hamilton was less cynical than Arciniegas, but supportive of his evaluation. Hamilton, however, demanded proof of Mistral's Jewish and Indian origin: "*El origen judío de Gabriela, que nadie ha demostrado, me parece tan mitológico como su origen indio.*"[12]

The doubt was never totally dispelled by the author herself, who, asseverations notwithstanding, belied in her playful tone and oblique manner what she affirmed in words. To Berta Singerman, she explained that her ability to quote passages of the Old Testament reflected the influence of her Jewish grandmother: "*Y de repente se puso traviesa y su cara se llenó con esa sonrisa amplia y grande cuando me dio la explicación: 'Es por mi abuela judía.*'"[13] Still, the term "*traviesa*" ("playful") and the smiling, sly expression on Gabriela's face described by Miss Singerman, give rise to suspicion. A similar playful attitude was present in a conversation between Gabriela and her friend, the Brazilian poet, Cecília Meirelles:

> "*Que raça poderosa, á dos judeus: apenas uma gota dêsse sangue basta para explicar muitas coisas....*" *E contou-me certa conversa com un escritor chileno que lhe perguntara: "V. não é Villanueva? E que são os Villanuevas senão judeus?" Isso parece ter-lhe causado grande impressão. Como de costume depois de expor o tema, deixava-se estar quieta, por um momento, como a caminhar pela imaginação, atrás dos seus antepassados.*[14]

The "*grande impressão*," noted by Miss Meirelles, seems unwarranted in someone whose lineage should be clear. The first comment by Gabriela appears to be tongue in cheek, and the last description by Meirelles indicates, tactfully, a certain premeditated pose, one quite familiar to Gabriela's acquaintances. Well aware of the controversy, and also of the legends that surrounded her name, Gabriela further confounded the issue by saying her "*abuela materna [sic] era una Rojas*" ["*materna* should have been "*paterna*"]. "*Este apellido lo da un libro español por hebreo también.*"[15] To ambiguously link her maternal [sic] grandmother's surname with the Spanish writer Fernando de Rojas, the author of the *Celestina*, who was a Jew forced into Christianity, simply cast more doubt on her grandmother's true religion. Thus, without more adequate proof, it is difficult to accept her alleged Jewish ancestry.

Despite the influence of a grandmother, whose Jewish origin was real or imagined, it is clear that Gabriela never followed the Jewish social or religious tradition. The importance of the grandmother lies, not in her problematic Jewish origin, but in her having introduced the young girl to the Bible and to its rigid Mosaic code of morality, which influenced Gabriela. Gabriela learned to identify herself in life and in poetry with biblical characters. The Bible's multiple allusions to nature became synchronous with her own time and place, and she "talked" with its unswerving, righteous God. Rather than being a Jew, in the modern sense, Gabriela seemed to have assimilated the spirit of the Hebrews of biblical times. Mention has been made of her ability to quote whole passages from the Bible and of the parallels critics have found with Job and Jeremiah. But no comment is more apt than that by her friend Díaz Arrieta: "*Hebrea de corazón, tal vez de raza—dejamos el problema a los etnólogos e investigadores—el genio bíblico traza su círculo en torno a Gabriela Mistral y la define.*"[16] Díaz Arrieta drew attention to a passage from the French historian Ernest Renan which defines the Hebrew spirit and illustrates the common, unifying ground between Gabriela and the Hebrews. In effect, the Chilean critic sees in the poet and in the Hebrews an emotional strength capable of crying out against injustices. Both raised a trumpet to God to disabuse man of his unjust ways lest he suffer the consequences of a terrible judgment.

It does not follow, however, that careful study of the Bible led Gabriela to a singular preoccupation with the Jews.[17] Nor is it valid to conclude that the numerous allusions to biblical characters and events in her poetry indicate either a Jewish ancestry or a oneness with contemporary Jewry. Rather, one must consider three different, parallel relationships, too often overlooked, which contribute to a total comprehension of the poet's stand vis-à-vis Judaism.

The first is that study of the Bible led to an affinity with biblical characters, kindled a Hebrew spirit such as that mentioned by Díaz Arrieta, and provided the groundwork for the biblical allusions in the poetry.

The second is that preoccupation with present-day Jewish social problems was part of her encompassing, humanitarian feeling for the persecuted, and not exclusively identification with Judaism. Frequently cited is "Al pueblo hebreo," a poem to elegize the Polish Jews killed in pogroms between 1903 and 1920.[18] By way of homage, this poem shows an empathy that transcends any documentary value it might have: "*Los surcos de tu rostro, que amo tanto, son cual llagas de sierra de profundos*" (p. 8). The identification with persecuted Jews is both particular and universal, personal and general. For Mistral had empathy with all oppressed peoples: undernourished, exploited Indians, Basque children who were victims of the Spanish Civil War (1936-39), underpaid Chilean miners, unprotected mothers, homeless emigrants, and, of course, the hounded Jew, traditional scapegoat of tyrants and religious zealots.

The third point is that Gabriela's personal suffering and her own feeling of persecution, which led her to abandon Chile voluntarily and to become a wanderer and outcast—"*la descastada*," as she sometimes grimly called herself—became associated in her mind with the Jewish people, who wandered as outcasts from tribulations, whether pogroms, persecution, or political grievances. And so in the twilight of her life, musing on her fate, she recalled the suffering Jew, a pariah condemned to wander the earth:

> *Voy mas lejos que el viento oeste*
> *y el petrel de tempestad.*
> *Paro, interrogo, camino*
> *¡y no duermo por caminar!*
> *Me rebanaron la Tierra,*
> *sólo me han dejado el mar.*
> ("Emigrada judía," p. 777)

Gabriela took along a recording of the Kol Nidre on entering the hospital with Doris Dana in Hempstead, New York, where she died on January 10, 1957.[19] This prayer in Aramaic, sung at dusk to begin the Jewish Day of Atonement, asks for release of the individual from personal vows made to God. Gabriela chose to hear this spiritual chant to affirm her independence of institutionalized religion.[20] Furthermore, it is fitting that this last gesture, along with asking that the Psalms be read, should betoken fidelity to the Jewish tradition, because in spirit she had allied herself with the persecuted Jews, including the martyred Jesus, "King of the Jews."[21] Her life cycle closed as it had begun, with the sound of an ancient Hebrew chant, which may have recalled the voice of a wizened grandmother who recited wondrous tales of the Old Testament.

Some critics believe that the Elqui valley in the province of Coquimbo in northern Chile (Gabriela's birthplace and residence until she reached womanhood) is reminiscent of Old Testament descriptions of life and nature. Agricultural in the lowlands and pastoral on the slopes, isolated from centers of learning and provincial in outlook, the Elqui valley could have inspired any idyllic scene in Genesis. Díaz Arrieta calls the region "*paradisíaca*" to emphasize the singular lushness of the vegetation and the pervading sense of solitude.[22] The valley, according to the following description, is a splendrous cornucopia:

> *Todo el valle que fecunda ese río es una esmeralda tendida al sol, fragante a surcos sembrados, ricos en viñedos y olivares. A semejanza de la huerta valenciana, sus pobladores saben de una primavera continua. Los frutos de esa región, regados por acequias sonoras como cuerdas de arpa, son jugosos y lozanos. Tierra pródiga, en las enramadas cuelgan las maduras cargas como un milagro de dulzura, que ponderan propios y extraños.*[23]

Chilean scholar Fernando Alegría claimed that the verdant Elqui valley is the actual model for Gabriela's poems that allude to the Bible:

> The reason might be the Elqui Valley where Gabriela was born; a land that seems to have been lifted from the Bible and set down in Chile for the good of our poetry and the danger of our souls. A valley through whose ample heavens huge clouds race to infinity. [It is] a land of warm and strange scents. Elqui produces the sweetest raisins and the most disturbing mystical individualists. It could be the land of the Song of Songs suffering under a blight of human selfishness and injustice. Gabriela has rejoiced in the eternal spring, but has also grieved among the miseries of mankind. She has been pure Chilean when she has spoken with the voice of the prophets about the inhabitants of the Elqui Valley.[24]

Although intuition underlies Alegria's impression that Gabriela's poetry fused the landscape of her childhood with the world represented in the Bible, his opinion gains credence in the light of similar judgments: "*Gabriela recordó el valle de Elqui en relación con descripciones de la Biblia, en una confusa imagen de luces y palabras.*"[25] Another study, by St. John's University scholar Marie-Lise Gazarian Gautier, avers that the Elqui valley determined the course of Gabriela Mistral's poetry and life:

> *El Valle de Elqui y la totalidad de Chile están a la base del encuentro de Gabriela Mistral con la naturaleza. Es en su país que aprendió a conocer los elementos y a fundirse con ellos para gozar universalmente de la naturaleza. La vida rural representa la infancia feliz, la unión del niño con la tierra, el contacto directo con las materias, la participación con las cosas por medio del tacto, del olor, del sabor, en vez de estudiar la botánica y la zoología en los libros fríos de la escuela.*[26]

Professor Gazarian's main point is that Gabriela learned from these early experiences to be at one with the world of nature[27] and to love flora and fauna because of her belief that everything in nature reflects God's divine will.[28]

Gabriela's "Tierra chilena" lends support to the preceding opinions, that nature in her poetry and in the Bible have much in common. Nevertheless, the poet reserves for that valley a generosity she does not accord the land of Leah and Rachel:

> *Danzamos en tierra chilena,*
> *más bella que Lia y Raquel;*
> *la tierra que amasa a los hombres*
> *de labios y pecho sin hiel ...*
> (p. 220)

Undeniably, the poet's hyperboles are motivated by the sense of absolute freedom and beauty which prevails in this New World Eden. Like Paradise, the Elqui valley, she believes, antedates the Fall of Man because serenity and love govern the communal dance:

> *Mañana abriremos sus rocas,*
> *la haremos viñedo y pomar;*
> *mañana alzaremos sus pueblos*
> *¡hoy sólo queremos danzar!*
> (p. 221)

Unlike the bounties of Paradise — and not for this reason less idyllic — Elqui's do not exist gratuitously. Elqui's inhabitants pay for their earthly facsimile of Paradise with hard work. More realistic than idealistic, "Tierra chilena" does not subordinate the imperatives of duty, sacrifice, and love to an escapist dance. The dance is the necessary prologue to a fraternity that renews faith, energy, and dedication for the empire building that awaits the Chilean people.

The poet understood nature because she had become attuned to its moods at an early ago. She felt, too, that man partakes of his natural surroundings as he works with the inanimate, by caring for crops, planting trees, pressing grapes for wine, and tending sheep. Interdependence between man and nature assures survival of both. Man and nature are God's creatures bound to earth to flourish and die. Thus they continue a cycle over which neither has control. Gabriela ultimately saw that man and nature, in their bleakness and in their plenty, remained weak before the power of God. The Bible also treats nature as a reflection of God's will, and with this fine thread the poet began to interweave her own pastoral world and that of the Bible. Having experienced simultaneously God's voice in the tempest and his sweetness in the honey of the bee, Gabriela united the world of the Elqui valley with that of Job and Ruth, and it became a world in which she was spectator, participant, and, ultimately, creator.[29]

Old Testament Women and Infertility

The Russian-born, Argentinean actress Berta Singerman has compared Gabriela Mistral with the prophetess Deborah, who distinguished herself as a strong-willed woman and as a "mother in Israel" for having delivered the Israelites from the hands of Jabin.[30] Gabriela was not a prophetess. On the other hand her indefatigable willpower cannot be disputed. That Gabriela was a "mother in Israel" has more validity as metaphor than as fact. But her friends inferred elements in her psyche and demeanor that led them to cast her as a Jewish matriarch, eager to cradle the budding writers of South America. At the age of forty, the elements consisted of her serious, austere demeanor, her love for the Old Testament, and also the inclusion of biblical women in her poetry: "*No bien doblara el cabo de la cuarentena, se hizo para siempre la Sara vieja y a todo joven escritor tratábalo como a un adolescente Benjamín.*"[31] More trenchant, though, are comments from the Uruguayan writer Sarah Bollo, who saw Gabriela's biblical heroines as women imbued with strength, sacrifice, and heroism: "*Gabriela ama aquellas recias almas templadas en el sacrificio, deslumbradas por Jehová, aureoladas del fulgor del heroísmo.*"[32] Neither of these commentaries, however, goes to the ontological heart of the matter. The biblical women most akin to Gabriela were those who, like herself, had been denied a child. She saw in their barrenness her own, and this sign of God's disfavor with them suggested her own divine abandonment.

The roots of her childlessness lay, to a degree, in Gabriela's unfeminine personality and appearance which kept most traditional, would-be suitors at bay. Asceticism and a rigid code of ethics precluded romantic closeness to most men who courted her. Marriage was improbable, if not impossible, for this vigorous woman who sought solitude and simplicity; chastity, however, was a matter of speculation. González Vera mentions a mysterious suitor whom Gabriela thought worthy, but upon further reflection she rejected him as short and ugly ("*bajo, casi retaco*").[33] Her fondness for the boy friend Romelio Ureta, discussed earlier, had little chance of leading to marriage, given their divergent interests; and, of course, his engagement to another girl and his suicide ended any possibility. Her father's desertion and her mother's subsequent despair raised grave doubts about the permanence and felicity of marriage. In short, Gabriela possessed the virtues and the faults that could turn young girls into pious spinsters.

It is important to reconcile the devotion to children and the stress on fertility and maternity in her poetry with the insurmountable barrier she set up to frustrate these very goals in her personal life. A plausible response is that, having decided that marriage was improbable or out of the question, she dedicated herself with greater zeal to the children in her schools. But this does not explain the impassioned outcries in her poetry for the dead sweetheart, for the eventual union of the two in immortal love. In her poetry, she did not accept loneliness with calm, but, instead, proceeded to curse fate for her lover's deception. More important still, she cursed him for having doomed her heritage as a woman. But the most curious thing is that the tension that gave rise to the poetry was not induced by a desire to have him truly return, or to join him in suicide, or to condemn him and forget him, or to take another lover. On the contrary, the death underscored her true feelings on life and love. Here was the desired but impossible love that held no threat to her freedom, chastity, or creativity. It was a perfect vehicle for the poetry that it inspired. The "love affair" provided everything and took nothing. With utmost caution, it may be suggested that the lover meant more dead than alive, that the love for him became more genuine in the poetry than it could ever have been in real life, and that the true value in her poetry derives from prolonged lack of fulfillment in life, which she tried to sublimate through her art. The lover and the desired child, transfigured, became creations of the poet. The love objects became the husband and the child of the poetry. A widow without ever having been married, and a mother without — it is has been argued here — ever having conceived, the poet achieved marriage and maternity in the only way possible, through the sincere expression of her feelings in poetry.

As noted above, Gabriela shared a common misfortune with certain biblical women who were infertile. Unlike them, though, because each of them eventually received a child through God's blessing, the poet was limited to poetically-created children, school children, children in humanitarian activities, and the adopted "nephew" Juan Miguel. These limitations apparently did not lead to total self-denigration, to the feeling that God had completely deserted her, to the belief that she, being unfertile, was an outcast.[34] She did not succumb to these feelings, rather she dominated them. Not only did she succeed in fashioning her imaginary child, she became guardian mother, vicariously at any rate, to the destitute children of the world. The converse is also possible: The realization that she, like the biblical women, was truly barren and a pariah in God's eyes stimulated her to deny the fact. If this hypothesis is valid, it tends to confirm the theory that the poet tried desperately to dissociate herself from the stigmatized biblical women, a striving that clearly affirms that, she, too, felt stigmatized and in God's disfavor.

Not all the fifteen Old Testament women in her poetry have a direct bearing on the theme of infertility. Several, however, may be singled out for illustration. Sarah, Rebekah, Rachel, and Hannah suffered because God refused each of them a child. They later conceived, owing either to divine intervention, prayer, repentance of envy, or to the promise to dedicate the offspring to God. Leah, Rachel's sister, and Hagar, Sarah's bondwoman, played analogous roles with regard to Jacob and Abraham. Rachel and Sarah offered them to their respective husbands, by whom they bore children. Ruth the Moabite, a widow, fulfilled her destiny with Boaz.

Gabriela's Ruth, like the poet herself, is on a quest for both spiritual fulfillment and motherhood. In the first phase of her search Ruth discovers God through his bounteous harvests. She bears physical hardships for the glory of God because she believes herself in a divine field ("*predio divino*") ("Ruth," p. 12). The second phase is her encounter with Boaz, who sits confidently as patriarch and undisputed leader. But his existence has no meaning because no children bear his name. Love is instantaneous and irrevocable. The third phase entails the nuptials, unfettered by convention and simple in their beauty, in which Ruth, guided by instinct and will, seeks out the pillow of the expectant Boaz.

The three sonnets on Ruth diverge from the biblical account in important ways. It is true that Ruth, as in the Bible, is the instrument by which Boaz fulfills God's pledge to Abraham's descendants that they will have more children than stars ("*más hijos que estrellas*").[35] Gabriela's Ruth, however, is landless and of humble origin ("*no tiene ni un campo mezquino*"), and has no dynastic preoccupations. She is, instead, concerned about individual plenitude. This poetic interpretation of the Book of Ruth concentrates solely on the instinctive nature of the idyllic love affair and the importance of fertility and propagation. The poet chooses to ignore the biblical fact that Ruth is also fulfilling Naomi's destiny. Nor does the poem allude to the legalistic and tribal dicta that must officially precede love's consummation. Boaz and Ruth are not bound by any of the moral restraints of their biblical counterparts. The stars, as extensions of God's creative power, illumine their paths, dictate their duties and obligations, and unite them in eternal love:

> *Ruth vio en los astros los ojos con llanto*
> *de Booz llamándola, y estremecida,*
> *dejó su lecho, y se fue por el campo ...*
>   *Dormía el justo, hecho paz y belleza.*
> *Ruth, más callada que espiga vencida,*
> *puso en el pecho de Booz su cabeza.*
>   (p. 14)

Gabriela compares her own barrenness to that of Sarah who, at ninety, despaired of bearing a child.[36] In "Agua," the poet rebels against her stay in Spain, preferring the verdant lands of Chile, the Antilles, or Italy:

> *Me han traído a país sin río,*
> *tierras-Agar, tierras sin agua;*
> *Saras blancas y Saras rojas,*

> *donde pecaron otras razas,*
> *de pecado rojo de atridas*
> *que cuentan gredas tajeadas;*
> *que no nacieron como un niño*
> *con unas carnazones grasas,*
> *cuando las oigo, sin un silbo,*
> *cuando las cruzo, sin mirada.*
> (pp. 447–448)

"*Tierras-Agar*" ("Hagar's lands") connote Spain, the barren land. The leap from Spain, to Hagar, to "*Saras blancas*" is swift. "White Sarahs" refer to the sterility of the Spanish race. "*Saras rojas*" connote the "red Sarahs" who killed the children they bore, like the "*atridas*." The title, too, is significant: "*Agua*" symbolizes fertility and underscores the poet's aversion to sterility. She associates fertile lands with children and water: "*Quiero volver a tierras niñas; / llévenme a un blando país de aguas*" (p. 448).

Rebekah and Rachel, sisters in a common sorrow, join hands with the poet in "Sal" ("Salt"): "*Mano a la mano nos tenemos / como Raquel, como Rebeca*" (p. 445). Salt has two main and opposite uses in the Old Testament.[37] As a preservative, it prolongs the edibility of foods. It is also a corrosive element that causes pain and ruins land, as such, signifies grief and barrenness. The latter meaning is valid here and throughout her poetry:

> *Ambas éramos de las olas*
> *y sus espejos de salmuera,*
> *y del mar libre nos trajeron*
> *a una casa profunda y quieta;*
> *y el puñado de Sal y yo,*
> *en beguinas o prisioneras,*
> *las dos llorando, las dos cautivas,*
> *atravesamos por la puerta ...*
> (pp. 445–446)

The poet's body is filled with brine ("*salmuera*"), signifying not only bitter years, but also infertile ground in which no seed can bear fruit:

> *La cojo como a criatura*
> *y mis manos la espolvorean,*
> *y resbalando con el gesto*
> *de lo que cae y se sujeta*
> *halla la blanca y desolada*
> *duna de sal de mi cabeza.*
> (p. 445)

In contrast with Pablo Neruda's visions of the saline sea as the origin of life and the terminus of man, for Gabriela the sea means departure, separation, and distance. Gabriela "molds" her *personae* from fuller's marl and delivers them to the same earth in the fashion of Jehovah.

In the contrasting poems of strong and sterile women (respectively, "La mujer fuerte" and "La mujer estéril"), the life force of the former is juxtaposed to the barrenness of the latter. The "*mujer fuerte*" inspires admiration; her feet, although covered with mud, are worthy of kisses, while the image she casts is revered in song by the poet (p. 15). Anguish and isolation, however, beset "*la mujer estéril*": "*...todo su corazón congoja inmensa baña*" (p. 16). As nature repeats the life processes in the fertile woman, so does it intensify, by contrast, the aridity of the barren one: "*El lirio le recuerda unas sienes de infante; / el Ángelus le pide otra boca con ruego.*" The woman incapable of reproducing is shamed by a pregnant beggar woman ("*...una mendiga grávida, cuyo seno florece / cual la parva de enero*").[38] Women who do not bear fruit nor fulfill their biological destiny commit a crime answerable to God, whose will is stated in Genesis 1:22 of the Spanish Bible: "*Y Dios los bendijo diciendo, Fructificad y multiplicad y henchid las aguas en los mares, y las aves se multipliquen en la tierra.*"

The "*mujer estéril*" dies a double death, which is reflected in the double trembling of the cypress trees: "*Con doble temblor oye el viento en los cipreses.*" The "*doble temblor*" also indicates that the mother has not been transcended by the child, and that the child has been denied the right to live, a right implicit in the mere existence of woman, and vouchsafed by the righteous God to all except sinners.

Whether Mistral was biologically childless herself is — as we saw in Chapter III, the section on Juan Miguel Godoy Mendoza — still debated by those with documents and those without them. However, the poet, by choosing the biblical women who were barren, becomes open to questions that thrive on a one-to-one relationship between poetry and poet. It is obvious that the biblical women represent, psychologically, an unfulfilled aspect of the poet's personal life. Yet it is imperative that criticism also focus upon the larger forces and pressures operating on and within the poet, which drew her attention to these women. In the same measure that the women of the Old Testament lamented their barrenness for personal reasons, they despaired that the race and family they represented would not continue. Gabriela Mistral was also conscious of the decline of the Chilean race, owing to high child mortality rates, to diseases that prevented women from bearing healthy children, and to attrition from lack of care and food. The hope for Chile and South America lies in the quantity and quality of its youth. Neither quality nor quantity is possible if the mothers are starved, diseased, and overworked. The poetry on infertility, therefore, is part of the poet's all-embracing concern for the protection of the underprivileged women and children.

But there is more. Mothers and children occupy a preeminent role in the poetry's hierarchy. A religious, mystical aura surrounds the mother and child. It is explained, in part, by the mystery of birth which the poet sees incarnate in women, and which she tries to express in the "Poemas de las madres." Conception is a miraculous, sacred act that involves the direct intervention of God, with the result that every child is in full measure a gift of God. Mothers, by their nature, intuit the divine essence that forms within them: "*Por el niño dormido que llevo, mi paso se ha vuelto sigiloso. Y es religioso todo mi corazón, desde que lleva el misterio.*"[39] The expectant mother is aware of the inexplicable processes that give shape and substance to innocence: "*Que estoy tejiendo en este silencio, en esta quietud, un cuerpo, un milagroso cuerpo, con venas y rostro, y mirada, y depurado corazón.*" Maternity, then, is a holy state because it makes possible the emergence of innocent, God-like life. And since the mission of the artist is beauty ("*embellecerlo todo*"), art ought to ennoble the holiness of this painful and divine state ("*la santidad de este estado doloroso y divino*"). The trinity of mother, child, and poet is inseparable. Each is touched by innocence and beauty, and each, in turn, shares these virtues with the other.

Old Testament Men

Old Testament men in the poetry are not as readily classifiable by theme as are Old Testament women. (Job, the exception, is discussed separately.) The poet had no single overriding purpose in choosing the men; as a group, they do not answer to any clearly defined personal need. Reference to them is limited to about twenty poems, and their significance as a whole is restricted. Taken individually, however, they enhance an image, provide a comparison, deepen an emotion, and add a biblical flavor. The poet realizes their dramatic possibilities, but does not develop them. Frequently, several men are included in one poem, at times one man appears in several poems, or one man may be limited to a small part of one poem. All in all, no distinct pattern is discernible.

The biblical Abel is linked to St. Francis de Sales in the following stanza. Both share God's favor according to the poet's metaphor, "*con su oreja de Abel.*"

> *Y ni alcanzo al segundo Francisco*
> *con su rostro en el atardecer,*
> *tan sereno de haber escuchado*
> *todo mal con su oreja de Abel,*
> *¡corazón desde aquí columpiado*
> *en los coros de Melquisedec!*[40]
> ("Nocturno de la derrota," p. 387)

Here the poet expresses her inability to match her works against the holy works of St. Francis and other Disciples of Christ because, in truth, she has been shaped by the rigorous tradition of the Old Testament. The following stanza tends to validate this interpretation:

> *Yo nací de una carne tajada*
> *en el seco riñón de Israel,*
> *Macabea que da Macabeos,*
> *miel de avispa que pasa a hidromiel,*
> *y he cantado cosiendo mis cerros*
> *por cogerte en el grito los pies.*
> (p. 387)

By stressing her Hebrew affinities, Gabriela emphasizes her inability to come to terms with herself, with others, and with God. By considering herself the original matriarch of the warrior race of Maccabees, she is stressing the stern qualities that have made her outspoken, proud, and defiant.

Abraham of Ur has been mentioned above in connection with Ruth. The poet continues her conception of Abraham as the benevolent father of his race by comparing a friend, Lola Arriaga, with this providential patriarch of the Jewish people.[41] The legend of Abraham and the memory of the rural teacher ("La maestra rural") fuse in the indirect allusion to an ailing Abraham sowing or planting in Israel (*"el doloroso sembrador de Israel"*) (p. 51). Just as the poet enjoys ennobling teachers for their dedication and self-effacement, so she extols divine qualities in Abraham: *"Su reino no es humano."* The obvious analogy between Abraham and the teacher is that each fosters generations that bear the stamp of wisdom, love, and strength. But the adjective "dolorous" (*"doloroso"*) hardly seems apt in connection with Abraham, who possessed power, enjoyed God's love, and suffered none of the afflictions that beset other prophets. It is true that it was not until late in life that his wife bore a son, and that God also told him to sacrifice Isaac.[42] Yet Abraham remained unswervingly dedicated to God's wishes and did not consider those commands unjust. Nor did they produce excessive grief in Abraham. The poet evidently finds rugged majesty in the patriarch of the Jewish people. He provides a lesson in selfless giving, perseverance, and faith.

The "Nocturno de los tejedores viejos" ("Nocturne of the Old Weavers"), written against the backdrop of the Spanish Civil War (1936–1939), records the impossibility of returning to pleasant, carefree days dancing in front of the sea (*"días divinos / de la danza delante del mar"* [p. 389]). Try as people may to disregard war (*"y vendemos la blanca memoria"*), or the warlike instinct in man (*"Nos callamos las horas y el día / sin querer la faena nombrar"* [p. 390]), so that war will not exist or perhaps even pass away (*"porque el nombre no nutra al Destino, / y sin nombre, se pueda malar"*), war, nevertheless, forces all men to row on its endless sea ("*remos negros quo siempre jadean / y que nunca rematan el mar*" [p. 391]), and thus forces them to think about the conditions of life that have caused it and the end that awaits all men. War had roots in the Bible and, to illustrate this, the poet exhumes the ghost of the militant Assyrian general Shalmaneser (727–722 B.C.): "*Han llegado los días ceñidos / como el puño de Salmanazar*"[43] (p. 389). The terrible lessons of aggression depicted in the Bible have not deterred conflict. On the contrary, man has learned from his Biblical forebears, Joseph and Isaac, to destroy others and himself: "*¡Pobre cuerpo que todo ha aprendido / de sus padres José e Isaac!*" (p. 391). It is clear that man has not learned, either, to utilize his past to settle his present condition. He weaves the fabric of his life, unaware of his impending destruction, unaware, too, of the demiurge he has to placate. Eternity is not a splendid extinction, nor is it a glowing reawakening. It is nameless, faceless, painful, and silent.

Mistral revered the Song of Songs perhaps more than any other part of the Old Testament, because the Canticles spoke to her personally on so many levels. For her, they burst forth spontaneously and plumb the meaning of spiritual and physical love:

> *Raza judía, y aun te resta pecho*
> *y voz de miel, para alabar tus lares,*
> *y decir el "Cantar de los Cantares"*
> *con lengua, y labio, y corazón deshechos.*
> ("Al pueblo hebreo," p. 9)

"Elogio de la canción" ("In Praise of Song" [p. 41]) reveals that the cantor is more poet than those who study verse forms, and he is also a greater seer than those who delve into the physical workings of the universe: "*Amad al que trae / boca de canción: / el cantor es madre / de la Creación.*" The singers reveal the inner harmony of man or his turbulence, the order of the world or its disorder. Song captures all because song makes everything possible. Song is a record of past achievement and the stimulus to further progress; it notes failure yet it builds dreams of new conquests. She believes that song enlivens, makes life, *is* life: "*Y cuando le pones / su canto a escuchar, / tus entrañas se hacen / vivas como el mar.*"[44] David, the master singer, is praised in "Todas íbamos a ser reinas" as the worthy groom of young girls with a dream of being queens (p. 521). And God, "El Tañedor" ("The Musician") has ...

> *...un arpa inmensa, cuyas cuerdas*
> *son las entrañas de los hombres.*
> *No hay un solo momento de silencio*
> *sobre el arpa, ni de paz para*
> *la mano del Tañedor ardiente.*[45]

The implication is that great poets are miniature gods capable of enouncing divine truths. But "El Tañedor" overshadows all by caring for all. The poetic chords (*"cuerdas"*) that lead from God's harp to the inner core of men (*"las entrañas de los hombres"*) pulsate in two directions — with God's will and with man's misfortune. The poet is most certainly aware of this, as well as the mystic, who on hearing this harp tore at his wounds in order to ... sing infinitely in heaven's fields: (*"...el místico lo supo, y de oír esta arpa rasgó sus heridas para dar más, para cantar infinitamente en los campos del cielo."*) The poet would not deny that God is the master musician. Nor would she refute the desire of poets to be like gods.

Nowhere does the poet consider the Song of Solomon an extension of theological musings on Jesus Christ, with Christ as bridegroom and either the Church or the soul as bride. The poet comes closer to accepting the profane love implicit in the Canticles — an idea that prompted the Inquisition to imprison the Spanish priest and mystic poet Fray Luis de León (1528–1591) — than formalized, religious pronouncements by either the Synagogue or the Church. She borrows expressions of love to a mortal being, as in "God Loves You" ("Dios lo quiere"), which appears to be a reworking of the Song of Solomon 2:14:

> *Beso que tu boca entregue*
> *a mis oídos alcanza,*
> *porque las grutas profundas*
> *me devuelven tus palabras.*
> *El polvo de los senderos*
> *guarda el olor de tus plantas*
> *y oteándolas como un ciervo,*
> *te sigo por las montañas ...*
> (p. 69)

The frequent mention of *"gacela"* and *"ciervo"* ("gazelle" and "stag") clearly symbols of Christ, probably has its basis in the Canticles.[46] "Dios lo quiere," with its theme of betrayal, is, of course, antithetical to the pure love of the Song of Songs. Yet the intensity that unites the lovers of the Bible is analogous to the passion the woman in love in the poetry displays in order to show her eternal affection for the betrayer, despite his infidelity. More subtle borrowings are in "El ruego" ("The Plea"), where the poet asks God to be merciful to the suicide in the poem because he was basically good and innocent. Compare the language of "El ruego" with the following lush, intimate language of Canticles 4:10–11, taken from the Bible in Spanish:

> *¡Cuán hermosos son tus amores,*
>   *hermana, esposa mía!*
> *¡Cuánto mejores que el vino tus amores*

> *Y el olor de tus ungüentos que todas*
> *Las especias aromáticas!*
>
> *Como panal de miel destilan tus labios,*
>   *oh esposa;*
> *Miel y leche hay debajo de tu lengua;*
> *Y el olor de tus vestidos como el olor del Líbano,*

The following comparison comes from "El ruego":

> *Vengo ahora a pedirte por uno que era mío,*
> *mi vaso de frescura, el panal de mi boca.*
>   *Cal de mis huesos, dulce razón de la jornada,*
> *gorjeo de mi oído, ceñidor de mi veste.*
>   (p. 99)

The opulence and fragrance inherent in the Song of Songs become a wish for fertility and aroma ("*Va a esparcir en el viento / la palabra el perfume de cien pomos de olores / al vaciarse....*" [p. 101]), which would signal the end of the desert-like existence to which God has condemned the unpardoned for his unforgivable sin. God's forgiveness could placate the beasts of the field:

> *Se mojarán los ojos de las fieras,*
> *y, comprendiendo, el monte que de piedra forjaste llorará*
> *por los párpados blancos de sus neveras:*
> *¡toda la tierra tuya sabrá que perdonaste!*
>   (p.101)

The mountain referred to in this sentimental passage may be merely a conceit or the same Mount Hermon of Song of Songs 4:8, with its snow-covered peaks and lions' dens. In any event, this book of the Old Testament served the poet as a source of inspiration and devotion.

Among all the Old Testament men, Job undeniably casts the deepest shadow on Gabriela Mistral's poetry. Statistically, the evidence for his importance is not overwhelming. Job is mentioned only six times, which is insignificant compared with the ubiquitous presence of Jesus Christ. Yet the lamentations, the anger, the self-righteousness at being wronged by God, the wounded body, the direct confrontation with Yahweh — all these reflect the spirit of Job. No mere poetic adornment, the essence of the Book of Job relates to the essence of the poetry: Both epitomize suffering and bitterness at God's unwarranted attacks on the just, thereby depriving them of friends and contentment. Although the poetry raises the question of a God who inflicts undeserved suffering, the poetic and personal response to God's action with regard to Job's afflictions recognizes that Job gained greater stature because of his rocklike faith in God and his ability to absorb pain. Job remains confident of his innocence and sure that God moves in ways unknown to him:

> *Cuando canta el alma de Caín, se trizan los cielos como un vaso; cuando canta Booz, la dulzura hace recordar las altas parvas; cuando canta Job, se conmueven las estrellas como una carne humana. Y Job escucha arrobado el río de su dolor vuelto hermosura.*[47]

In addition to indicating the poet's literary affinity with Job and Thomas à Kempis, the following passage emphasizes that the story of man is the struggle against ever-renewing pain, and that purity, self-discipline, and humility before God have never guaranteed felicity:

> *Nobles libros antiguos, de hojas amarillentas, sois labios*
> *no rendidos de endulzar a los tristes, sois la vieja*
> *amargura que nuevo manto viste:*
> *¡desde Job hasta Kempis la misma voz doliente!*
> ("Mis libros," p. 35)

Abstention and righteous behavior in accordance with God's will actually stress man's inherent defects and his struggle to minimize or eliminate them. Man is trapped in a vicious circle of awareness that he is impure and a potential sinner, which leads to greater self-mortification. The pain endured in trying to do good would be worthwhile and bearable if man were guaranteed immunity from God's wrath. No such warranty is possible. Thus, whether man aspires to greater purity or whether he is a sinner, he is not impervious to divine wrath. The lesson of the Book of Job is that even the righteous can suffer. In addition, the righteous may suffer more than sinners or sycophantic, trembling, do-gooders, such as Job's three friends. Possibly God is testing the strength of man's faith in him, and only the most faithful can offer the proper resistance to his essays. Sinners, by definition, are condemned. Notwithstanding their purity and righteous actions, sycophants and conformists readily acknowledge their sinful lives whenever disaster strikes. Only those, like Job, who are unswervingly convinced of their integrity in the face of God's seemingly unjust ways, provide God with a fair test of human faith in divine power.[48] Job had the strength to recognize his own innocence and to affirm to God, while maintaining his faith, that he did not deserve punishment. Job was both rebel and conformist.[49] He refuted as false logic the long-held principle that affliction, *ipso facto,* proves prior sin. He did not dispute, however, God's capacity to inflict suffering, with or without design, deservedly or undeservedly.

Although the Bible does not link Hagar and Job, the poet binds them in their common anguish and likens her own pain and abandonment to theirs. Their mutual desperation prompts both a simile and an explicit metaphor:

> *Le he abrazado [al espino] como una hermana,*
> *cual si Agar abrazara a Job,*

> en un nudo que no es ternura,
> porque es más: ¡desesperación!
> ("El espino," p. 128)

The title, "El espino" ("The Thorn") suggests the central dessicated symbol. The "horrible God [the] forger" ("*el horrible Dios forjador*") hammered out a world which the poet laments as the "spirit of the desert, / twisted in anguish and sun" (*el espíritu del yermo, / retorcido de angustia y sol*" [p. 127]). The thorn tree may produce aromatic flowers, but its thorns offer no comfort to "*mi nido turbador*."[50] God's wrath, like thorns, has pierced Job, Hagar, and the poet:

> *Me ha contado que me conoce,*
> *que en una noche de dolor*
> *en su espeso millón de espinas*
> *magullaron mi corazón.*
> (p. 128)

Yet there are redemptive factors. Hagar, although abandoned by Abraham and driven away by Sarah, was visited by the "angel of the Lord" who protected her and her child, Ishmael.[51] Job's worthiness could not dispel his suffering, but his lament endured eternally, even after his body had been healed: "*De las greñas le nacen flores. / (Así el verso le nació a Job.)*" (p. 127). So, too, the poet, afflicted by loneliness and abandonment, takes refuge in her irremediable condition by comparing herself with Hagar, who embraces Job out of desperation and discovers, in that terrible act, the tragic sense of her life. The poet is the condemned sufferer, renewing her song in eternal grief.[52]

The allusion to Job in the poem "Una palabra" imputes to him the same "word" the poet also wants to express, but cannot and does not because of possible dire results: "*Si la soltase, quema el pasto vivo, / sangra al cordero, hace caer al pájaro*" (p. 721). Although not stated directly, the "word" that "my father Job ... said, while burning" ("*mi padre Job ... dijo, ardiendo*") most probably concerns the defense of his just actions in the face of God's harsh treatment and the rebukes of friends. Job concludes his apology by saying:

> *Si mi tierra contra mí,*
> *Y lloran todos los surcos;*
> *Si comí su sustancia sin dinero,*
> *O afligí el alma de sus dueños;*
>
> *En lugar de trigo me nazcan abrojos,*
> *Y espinos en lugar de cebada.*
> *Acábanse las palabras de Job.*[53]

The if-clause construction, the prediction of terrible consequences, the use of nature metaphors, the impassioned tone, are common to both "Una palabra" and the above quotation from Job in the Spanish Bible. Since "Una palabra" appears in the section "Luto" ("Mourning"), dedicated to Gabriela's dead nephew, it would also seem that she is caught in an emotional and religious conflict similar to that of Job. God snatched away, unexpectedly and unjustly, her beloved possession. Belief in God was rewarded only by deception; yet, disbelief is capable of producing greater anguish than belief itself.

The influence of "*Padre Job*" is evident in borrowings and interpolations. The poet's strong language reminds one of Job's curses for having been born, and his self-vituperation stems from his mother's fertility: ("*Perezca el día en que yo nací ...*"; "*¿Y para qué las tetas que mamase?*"[54]). The preceding serve as guides to the poet's impassioned question in the "Poem of the Child" ("Poema del hijo"): "*¿Por qué ha sido fecunda tu carne sollozante / y se henchieron [sic] de néctar los pechos de mi madre?*" (p. 104). Job's lament resounds in "*Madre mía, pero tú sabes: / más me hirieron de lo que herí*" ("A la Virgen de la Colina," p. 27). In "El encuentro" ("The Encounter" [p. 60]), she paints a scene reminiscent of Job's boils, i.e., "my God dressed me in sores" ("*mi Dios me vistió de llagas*").[55] The fate of the wicked is not pleasant, as Job says: "*Olvidaráse de ellos el seno materno; de ellos sentirán los gusanos dulzura; Nunca más habrá de ellos memoria, Y como un árbol serán los impíos quebrantados.*"[56] More trenchant still is the prediction for transgressors in "Gotas de hiel" ("Drops of Bile"), where death neither desensitizes the sinner to the gnawing worms nor releases him from a gnawing conscience:

> *Y no llames la muerte por clemente,*
> *pues en las carnes de blancura inmensa,*
> *un jirón vivo quedará que siente la piedra que te*
> *ahoga y el gusano voraz que te destrenza.*
> (p. 36)

The macabre "*gusano*" ("worm") image crops up again in the autobiographical "Credo," where it is suggested that physical death, represented by the worm, cannot destroy man's moral and spiritual fiber or his capacity for love:

> *Creo en mi corazón en que el gusano*
> *no ha de morder, pues mellará a la muerte;*
> *creo en mi corazón, el reclinado*
> *en el pecho de Dios terrible y fuerte.*
> (p. 32)

This passage from "Credo" seems a restatement of the traditional interpretation of resurrection, which Job expresses in verses that might have inspired "Credo": "*Yo sé que mi Redentor vive, Y al fin se levantará sobre el polvo: Y después de deshecha esta mi piel, aun he de ver en mi carne á Dios.*"[57] The poet ultimately declares her faith in the power of love to resist time and death.

Although love may involve sacrifice and pain, and may seem absent in the face of the harsh justice of *"el Dios terrible y fuerte,"* love is not resurrected because it does not die in the first place.

Chapter 30 of the Book of Job appears to have been the basis for "Tribulación" and the point of departure for other poems. Especially suggestive is the transformation of verse 15, *"Hanse revuelto turbaciones sobre, mí; Combatieron como viento mi alma, Y mi salud pasó como nube,"* into Gabriela's:

> *¡Todo se me ha llenado de sombras el camino*
> *y el grito de pavor! ....*
> *y es invierno, y hay nieve, y la noche se puebla*
> *de muecas de locura*
> (pp. 77, 78)

No less provocative is the restructuring, in the same poem, of the last two verses of chapter 30: *"Mi piel está denegrida sobre mí, Y mis huesos se secaron con ardentía. Y hase tornado mi arpa en luto, Y mi órgano en voz de lamentadores."* Apart from the syntactical similarity of the dative (also present in the preceding examples), by substituting *"boca"* for *"piel"* and *"trova"* for *"arpa,"* the same sense of burning, bitterness, and desolation is apparent: *"Me socarró la boca, me acibaró la trova, / y me aventó los días"* (p. 77). It is clear, then, that Job's voice spoke to the poet on the most intimate levels: birth, life, and death. His sense of frustration and his abandonment by God touched responsive chords in Gabriela Mistral, and this led her to make use of passages, constructions, and vocabulary reminiscent of Job.

Jehovah and Jesus

When asked about his conception of God, a Jew usually talks about one supreme creator, the king of the universe, who is the God of justice, truth, and also vengeance. A Christian, on the other hand, faced with the same question about God, would be more inclined to express awe, perhaps fear, of God the Father's absolute and irrevocable power. The reasons that underlie these differing attitudes are too complex for a full analysis here. One point, however, should be made clear. The modern Jew still shares with the early Hebrews his notion of God. Many modern Christians, by contrast, possibly no longer accept what Jesus tried to instill in his brethren about God, that is, God's abiding love.[58] John and Paul unknowingly prepared the ground for the great debates about Jesus' separation but oneness with the Godhead and the Holy Spirit.[59] Later on, theologians, in despair over solving this enigma, which was as much emotional and political as it was religious and philosophical, attempted to reconcile "their Christian belief in three Gods with their inherited Jewish belief in one God."[60] For all the subtleties of the Church Fathers, Christians still do not associate the Old Testament deity with compassion and mercy in order to ascribe these qualities to Christ, who, as the begotten God, came to redeem, and as man, to atone for humanity.[61]

A study of the poet's life and poetry reveals that Mistral knew the Bible, not only from the viewpoint of a Jew, that is, the Old Testament, but from the vantage point of a Christian, for whom the New Testament is the culmination of the prophecies and the laws set forth in the Old. Thus the poet was able to assimilate and accept the apparently opposing views contained in each covenant and, furthermore, felt at home in the spiritual climate of both. The Chilean novelist, Eduardo Barrios, presents this view of Mistral convincingly:

> ... *su espíritu [es] esencialmente hebraico. Esto no me parece absoluto. Yo diría más bien: Es un alma de Israel convertida al cristianismo. No sería grande la enmienda; pero precisaría el matiz. Porque Gabriela Mistral es David, Job y Salomón, en Mateo, Pablo y Juan. Antes de evocar su "Mujer fuerte" y su "Ruth" la moabita "bajo el sol caldeo," nos dijo en occidente su más genuino ardor, "Al oído de Cristo." Su aliento bíblico nos llega siempre aromado en el aliento del Nazareno. Su corazón está henchido por la sangre piadosa del Hijo.*[62]

Jehovah and Jesus Christ, the God of Wrath and the God of Benevolence, fight their duel in Gabriela Mistral's poetry. One brings anguish and loneliness, the other compassion and redemption. The righteous God's violence and strength filter through the Nazarene, lose their destructive force, and become a fount of love.[63] The heritage of suffering, the open wound, the parched earth — symbols of the reproving and unresponsive God — through Jesus' intercession are tolerable, even sought after. Pain, the inescapable factor of her life, of all life, does not disappear but is now a source of pleasure, now a means of sharing Christ's holy sacrifice. Christ and his teachings lead Gabriela from total despair. And although the influence of the Old Testament is strong, at times dominant, eventually and ultimately Christ's ethic prevails.

The quality that gives meaning to the Old Testament God is his self-derived power to fashion and deal with the world and its creatures for reasons and purposes that are beyond the ken of mortals. When addressing the Old Testament God, Gabriela Mistral's poetry recognizes the nature of his omnipotence and, accordingly, regards it with awe, respect, fear — and dissatisfaction. She expresses his immeasurable strength in hyperboles that are incapable of limiting him. Chief among these are "*inmenso*" and "*tremendo*," which are employed repeatedly to describe, not only the vastness of God, but also the summit of pain, the absoluteness of death, and the infinity of nature. Other adjectives of exaggeration are "*enorme*," "*estupendo*," and "*profundo*." His strength keeps worshipers at a respectful distance, which is evidenced by the distancing demonstrative adjective ("Aquel" / "That" [beyond reach]), contained in "*Aquel tremendo y fuerte / Señor*" ("El Dios triste," p. 37). Faith in God's compassion does not negate possible reprisal: "*...creo en mi corazón, el reclinado / en el pecho de Dios terrible y fuerte*" ("Credo," p. 32).[64]

A plea for justice and mercy may go unanswered:

> *¡Mira! De cuantos ojos veía abiertos sobre*
> *mis sendas tempraneras,*
> *sólo los tuyos quedan. Pero, ¡ay!, se van llenando*
> *de un cuajo de neveras ...*
> ("Tribulación," p. 78)

Turning to "El ruego" once again, the snow on the mountain which does not thaw to become water and then tears represents again God's glacial refusal to pardon suicide and human frailties:

> *Se mojarán los ojos de las fieras,*
> *y, comprendiendo, el monte que de piedra forjaste*
> *llorará por los párpados blancos de sus neveras :*
> *¡toda la tierra tuya sabrá que perdonaste!*
> (p. 101)

It is precisely this combination of power and aloofness which inhibits pleas to Yahweh. And the corollary, which is the real sense of the poetry, may also be stated: His total supremacy and tradition of detachment make possible true justice, however painful, because it is divine and impartial.

The disparateness between God's power to create and the abrupt, random manner in which this same creator claims his creatures sets the stage for a vital drama. In a series of meditations on death, elegies to friends and loved ones, and in her allusions to the death of Christ, we see the irrational nature of God and the equally blind passions that infuse the poetry. The fundamental life-giving and life-taking polarity within Jehovah prompts a simile about God's irreconcilable position between extremes and also points up man's impotence before incalculable power: "*El Trópico es como Dios absoluto / y en esos soles se muere o se salva*" ("Recado para las Antillas," p. 577). Silencing all other laments is the one that derives from an awareness of the discrepancy between the belief that God can create or sustain life and man's hopelessness at God's refusal to do so. The dichotomy and the inconsistency involved chain man to his greatest frustration and disillusionment. At the same time, they provide, by contrast, the supreme test of mortal faith in a relentless and all but implacable God.

In the meditation, "La muerte-niña" ("Death-Child") death represented as an innocent child born in a cave—the likeness to the Child Jesus is more than coincidence, as we shall see—comes into a world that enjoys the luxury and smugness of never having known sorrow or loss:

> *¡Tan entero que estaba el mundo!,*
> *¡tan fuerte que era al mediodía!,*
> *¡tan armado como la piña,*
> *cierto del Dios que sostenía!*
> (p. 425)

This world with its creatures endures the disasters that beset Eden after man's Fall:

> *Se envilecieron las mañanas,*
> *torpe se hizo el mediodía;*
> *cada sol aprendió su ocaso*
> *y cada fuente su sequía.*
>
> *La pradera aprendió el otoño*
> *y la nieve su hipocresía*
> *la bestezuela su cansancio*
> *la carne de hombre su agonía.*
> (p. 426)

Each of the enumerated physical creations of God learns the nature of its frailty. Each becomes conscious of life's deception and death's power when its original substance changes to non-substance, or to an abstraction of pain and disillusion. The same world that boasted of God's aid given impartially before death originated, afterward disregards the learnings of his prophets in the face of disaster:

> *Y dejé de gritar mi grito*
> *cuando vi que se adormecían.*
> *Ya tenían no sé qué dejo*
> *y no sé [qué] melancolía ...*
> (p. 427)

Men continue to feel themselves privileged "*reyes*" ("kings"), although they arc victims of death expressed as the humble "*la sierva*" ("the servant") of God. "Muerte" ("Death"), capitalized now in an orthographic and hierarchical sense, reaches glory and fame at thirty years of age and makes possible the perpetuation of spiritual life in the person of Jesus:

> *La Muerte tenía treinta años,*
> *ya nunca más se moriría,*
> *y la segunda Tierra nuestra*
> *iba abriendo su Epifanía.*
> (p. 427)

"*Treinta años*," emblematic of Christ's mission, "*segunda Tierra*," of the Resurrection, and "*Epifanía*," of either birth, baptism, or the miracle at Cana, symbolize the validity of death under the new Savior. The innocent babe of the cave brought awareness to man of his own potential for destruction and of the meaning of true sacrificial death, in contrast with the emptiness of death under the Old Testament God. When told of the miracle of death, men "*se ríen con insanía*" ("laugh crazily") and ask for an unattainable frolic back in Eden: "'*Yo soy de aquellas que bailaban / cuando la Muerte no nacía*'" (p. 427). To summarize, the poem carries us through four successive stages:

1. The period of preconscious tranquility when man is unaware of death;
2. The period of awakening, dim comprehension, and disgust of physical death;
3. The period of resignation, reason, and smugness;
4. And finally, the period of the glory of death, epitomized by Jesus' acceptance of it, a period in which there is a parallel regression on the part of mankind to a false, artificial paradise.

The preceding analysis contrasts the representation of death in an Old Testament setting with that made possible by the coming of Christ. The interpretation may be compared with the opening sonnet in *Desolación,* in the section "Vida" ("Life") — ironically a meditation on death. Here the poet vivifies the bronze "Rodin's Thinker" ("Pensador de Rodin"), lets him remember that he is "flesh from the tomb / fatal flesh before naked destiny" ("*carne de la huesa, / carne fatal delante del destino desnuda*"), and then turns his "burning spring" ("*primavera ardiente*") into a nightmarish autumn[65]:

> *Y en la angustia, sus músculos se hienden, sufridores.*
> *Los surcos de su carne se llenan de terrores.*
> *Se hiende, como la hoja de otoño, al Señor fuerte*
>
> *que le llama en los bronces ... Y no hay árbol torcido*
> *de sol en la llanura, ni león de flanco herido,*
> *crispados como este hombre que medita en la muerte.*
> (p. 3)

Through inference, "*el Señor fuerte*" ("the mighty Lord") reaches down to affect "*el árbol torcido*" ("the twisted tree") and "*el león de flanco herido*" ("the lion wounded in his side"). The metal world, the sea and snow, the trees and plants, the creatures of air and field, common man and the Son of God — all seek to avoid death and to placate God. From one extreme of the poetic spectrum to the other — personified metal to God-made-man — we can establish the meaning of the threat of extinction. In a stanza of "Muerte del mar" ("Death of the Sea"), water's power and ever presence struggles with God's might:

> *Donde él bramaba, hostigado*
> *del Dios que lo combatía,*
> *y replicaba a su Dios*
> *con saltos de ciervo en ira ...*
> (p. 647)

This appears to be an inversion and repudiation of Psalm 42: 1, taken from the Spanish Bible: "*Como el ciervo brama por las corrientes de las aguas, Así clama por ti, oh Dios, el alma mía.*" The poet dislocates the biblical context of "*ciervo brama*" ("stag roars") in favor of "*[mar] bramaba*" ("[sea] roared") and thereby turns the sea into a figurative "*ciervo en ira*" ("angry stag"), which battles the Creator for its existence. Since "*ciervo*" is also a symbol of Christ, presumably it manifests again the duel between Yahweh and Jesus, a duel that reappears more subtly in "La encina" ("The Oak Tree"). Emblem of the sanctified schoolteacher, the tree is rooted in firm ground while it shelters the innocent in its branches and perseveres in spite of inclement weather. The relationship of tree to cross will be discussed in detail in Chapter XIV, "The Poetry of Sacrifice," here it suffices to mention that the sensorial, affective, and moral qualities of the teacher reflect those of Christ primordially. The envoy, a parting wish for eternal serenity, also expresses the hope that the binary correlatives, "*encina-maestra*" ("oak-teacher"), like the "*cruz–Cristo*" ("cross–Christ"), will not suffer indignities from either man or God:

> ¡Encina, noble encina, yo te digo mi canto!
> Que nunca de tu tronco mane amargor de llanto,
> que delante de ti prosterne el leñador
> de la maldad humana, sus hachas; y que cuando
> el rayo de Dios hiérate, para ti se haga blando
> y ancho como tu seno, el seno del Señor!⁶⁶
> (p. 56)

God's lightning may not be punishment necessarily, but it is his terrible swift way of dealing with trees, including those imdued with virtue and divinity.

The foregoing passage contains a perspective of narration which is radically different from the three examples preceding it. This difference effectively explains other expressions of death. The narrative in "La encina" introduces the poet into the living song and fabric: ("¡ ... *yo te digo mi canto!*"). The poetry is highly personal to begin with, but the poet assumes a still closer kinship with the poetry by prefixing the subject pronoun "*yo*" ("I") to the first person singular of the verb.

It is worthwhile referencing, at this juncture, the perceptive literary critic Wolfgang Kayser. He outlines the triple dilemma for the poet and for further poetic analysis:

> *La lírica se presenta como expresión de un yo.*
> *Por consiguiente, el autor tiene que decidir*
> *si quiere hacer de su discurso lírico la expresión*
> *de su propio yo o de un yo indeterminado, o si*
> *quiere ponerlo en boca de determinado personaje.*⁶⁷

XII. The Hebraic Tradition 141

The distinctive and puzzling quality of three poems, "La muerte-niña" (which, apropos, has an indeterminate "I"), "El Pensador de Rodin," and "Muerte del mar" is the objective way in which the poet can personify and animate both the abstract and the material without personal involvement. Objective personification is evident in "La encina," but in the last stanza the poet bids farewell to an admired and beloved friend. The personal solicitation and her direct confrontation with God, absent before "La encina," are hallmarks in the selections to come.[68]

The poet, in "Plegaria por el nido" ("Prayer for the Nest") — with tender affection and cautious optimism — entreats "*el dulce Señor*" ("the sweet Lord") to protect the helpless bird from the vicissitudes of nature. Although the appeal to the Lord is rather gentle, a contrasting tone of distress and disillusionment underlies the supplication:

> *Tú que me afeas los martirios*
> *dados a tus criaturas finas:*
> *la cabezuela de los lirios*
> *y las pequeñas clavelinas,*
>
> *guarda su forma con cariño*
> *caliéntelo tu pasión.*
> *Tirita al viento como un niño*
> *y se parece al corazón.*
>   (p. 335)

The poet uses diminutives, "*plumilla*," "*almohadita*," and "*Conchita*" ("tiny feather," "small pillow," and "petite Conchita") of the second and fourth stanzas and imagery of tiny delicate flowers and the innocent "*niño*," all of which suggest defenselessness. Yet, God is empowered to send wind, rain, and ice to turn against creatures of his own making. Out of her personal disenchantment ("*me afeas*" / "you make me ugly"), she pleads, on behalf of the bird of "heavenly similitudes" ("¡*Y el canto dicen que es divino / y el ala cosa de los cielos!*" [p. 334]), for a benevolent, positive act on God's part ("*Dulce tu brisa sea al mecerlo ...*"), and for a mitigation of the violent, negative aspects of nature:

> *... desvía el vidrio de la helada*
> *y las guedejas de la lluvia;*
> *desvía el viento de ala brusca*
> *que lo dispersa a su caricia*
> *y la mirada que lo busca,*
> *toda encendida de codicia ...*
>   (p. 335)

The intent is to suggest a fairer way of dealing with the unprotected. The poet displays a generosity reminiscent of St. Francis of Assisi: "¡*Dulce Señor, por un hermano pido / indefenso y hermoso: por el nido!*" (p. 334). To the premise that all creatures are manifestations of God's hand and thus of the divinity of God, the poet adds the hypothesis of the fraternity of all living things, so that it becomes inconceivable to countenance the extinction of any form of life. The ramifications of such a belief are frightening, not because the creatures die (since they have to in any event), but because as each creature passes on so, too, God is in part extinguished. That God is instrumental in death doubles the tragedy and leaves a residue of despair in those who appeal for help.

"Plegaria por el nido" hints at the latent strength that could erupt should the prayer to God prove ineffective. "El ruego" brings to a head the verbal skirmish between the poet and God over the former's appeal for pardon for a suicide. Because the poet's main task is to prove the spiritual worth of one who has defied God's commandment not to kill, and who thus is damned in the very act, the argumentation takes subtle turns. From the outset, the poet seeks to justify the ways of men to God. The first and second stanzas (which form a closed unit) iterate the poet's self-proclaimed right to a fair hearing before God in the defense of loved ones. These stanzas also show the attempt to obtain a preferential decision for the deceased on the basis of the poet's purity and her aid to strangers:

> *Señor, Tú sabes cómo, con encendido brío,*
> *por los seres extraños mi palabra te invoca.*
> *Vengo ahora a pedirte por uno que era mío,*
> *mi vaso de frescura, el panal de mi boca,*
>
> *cal de mis huesos, dulce razón de la jornada,*
> *gorjeo de mi oído, ceñidor de mi veste.*
> *Me cuido hasta de aquellos en que no puse nada;*
> *¡no tengas ojo torvo si te pido por éste!*
> (p. 99)

The deceased's attributes merit emphasis and repeated enumeration, as if the poet cannot restrain the desire to convince:

> *Te digo que era bueno, te digo que tenía*
> *el corazón entero a flor de pecho, que era*
> *suave de índole, franco como la luz del día,*
> *henchido de milagro como la primavera.*
> (p. 99)

Here, in ellipsis, the last three adjectival clauses echo the insistent "*te digo*" ("I say to you"). There is a weak try at objective evaluation, in contrast with the unreasoning and emotional justification in the first two stanzas. Most fascinating of all is the unintentional irony of the last clause, which suggests fertility in the actuality of death, sanctification in the face of anathema. Through the poet's voice, God rebuts the preceding demands and initiates the colloquy:

> *Me replicas, severo, que es de plegaria indigno*
> *el que no untó de preces sus dos labios febriles,*
> *y se fue aquella tarde sin esperar tu signo,*
> *trizándose las sienes como vasos sutiles.*
> (p. 99)

Christ's counterthrusts are not refuted, rather, they are parried with the same double-edged sword he wields so expertly: love and pain. Cruelty, sorrow, even sin, can be tempered and forgiven through infinite love, which is the meaning of the following oxymoron:

> *El hierro que taladra tiene un gusto frío,*
> *cuando abre, cual gavillas, las carnes amorosas.*
> *Y la cruz (Tú te acuerdas, ¡o Rey de los judíos!)*
> *se lleva con blandura, como un gajo de rosas.*
> (p. 100)

The overt alliance with the pain of Jesus indicates forbearance, without loss of faith, toward the God of whom she must constantly beseech mercy and pardon, as Jesus himself on the Cross thought that God had forgotten him: "*Padre Nuestro que estás en los cielos, / ¿por qué te has olvidado de mí?*" ("Nocturno," p. 79).

There is even a tenuous zone between Yahweh's severity and Christ's charity, where the former appears less stern. In fact, the poet ascribes attributes she normally reserves for Jesus Christ to Jehovah. "Interrogaciones" exemplifies the problem. It is a poem of non-sacrificial and unexalted death, where the poet seeks to determine Jehovah's role in comforting the deceased:

> *¿O Tú llegas después que los hombres se han ido,*
> *y les bajas el párpado sobre el ojo cegado,*
> *acomodas las vísceras sin dolor y sin ruido*
> *y entrecruzas las manos sobre el pecho callado?*
> (p. 84)

She hopes for redemption and pardon, not a deaf ear and a closed eye:

> *¿No hay un rayo de sol que los alcance un día?*
> *¿No hay agua que los lave de sus estigmas rojos?*
> *¿Para ellos solamente queda tu entraña fría,*
> *sordo tu oído fino y apretados tus ojos?*
> (p. 85)

Rejecting the "*entraña fría*" ("cold inner being") of the God of Justice, through catachresis she uses the terminology of the Eucharist — "I have tasted you like a wine" — to equate Jehovah with Christ and redemption:

> *Tal el hombre asegura, por error o malicia;*
> *mas yo, que te he gustado, como un vino, Señor,*
> *mientras los otros siguen llamándote Justicia,*
> *¡no te llamaré nunca otra cosa que Amor!*
> (p. 85)

Christian theologians who believe in the deity of Christ and in the Holy Trinity, that is, a pre-existent God the Father, may see no dichotomy. Nevertheless, it is there. The poetry consistently relegates to Christ the role of child, martyr, or the resurrected. In matters of love, consolation, and sacrificial death, Christ remains primal. But when death is unwarranted, pain undeserved or too extreme to imagine, God is the Old Testament deity.

The poet's forbearance amid suffering links her to both the Jewish and Christian traditions. Within her spirit, the Jew and the Christian unite in their mutual suffering. All three, then, continually participate in Jesus Christ's unique sacrifice of pain and abnegation. "Al pueblo hebreo" ("To the Hebrew People") exemplifies the bond between Jew and Christian:

> *En tu mujer camina aún María.*
> *Sobre tu rostro va el perfil de Cristo;*
> *por las laderas de Sión le han visto*
> *llamarte en vano, cuando muere el día ...*
>
> *Que tu dolor en Dimas le miraba*
> *y El dijo a Dimas la palabra inmensa*
> *y para ungir sus pies busca la trenza*
> *de Magdalena ¡y la halla ensangrentada!*
> (p. 9)

Christ's martyrdom called for a like commitment by Demas and Mary Magdalene. Since that time other Jews have endured a similar fate. Jew and Christian, then, share a common heritage. The poet, too, steeped in both currents, participates in that heritage.

In summary, the Old Testament is indelibly stamped on both the poet and her poetry. Gabriela Mistral's acquaintances agree that in dress, bearing, and attitude she came close to being a biblical heroine incarnate. Her speech was marked by quotations and phraseology from the Bible, and the biblical flavor intensified the feeling that she had absorbed and was living the role of a biblical character. Her devotion to justice, simplicity, and duty further solidifies this impression. She often recalled the biblical lessons and tales her father, sister, and paternal grandmother had read to her. The importance of the world of nature, the pain and suffering that could be inflicted by an angry God, had a profound effect upon the sensitive and imaginative Lucila Godoy. It seems clear, also, that she identified with the spirit of the ancient Hebrews, to the extent that she empathized with the harassment and perpetual exile of the so-called chosen people. The quest of the Jews for contentment and stability, their sign that God favors them, has its counterpart in the poet's quest for the blessing of God, when she says, "... *sigo por soledades / de Ismael sin patria...*" ("I go on through solitudes / like Ishmael without a country ...").[69]

As Ishmael typifies the abandoned, estranged son, so Gabriela is the castaway daughter in search of her land and her God.[70] Unfortunately, she was reunited with her promised land in the Edenic Elqui valley only after death. Final union and peace with God, although devoutly desired, like the return to Montegrande, came about with grudging compromise, with vacillation and fear, before her sacrifice to God. Her final poem, "Último árbol" ("Last Tree") symbolizes her intransigent spirit which, like that of Job, hesitatingly recognized its own opaqueness and tried desperately to shed its self-righteousness:

> *...soledades que me di,*
> *soledades que me dieron,*
> *y el diezmo que pagué al rayo*
> *de mi Dios dulce y tremendo...*
> (p.798)

The Hebrew spirit that pervades Mistral's poetry consists precisely of this hubris, this insistence upon equal and fair treatment during a direct confrontation with God. The poet repeatedly carries her lament directly to the altar of God for just decisions with regard to suicide, frustrated motherhood, and unmerited death.[71] Still the tears, the lamentations, the estrangement, and the final reconciliation with God despite blind injustice, stamp Gabriela Mistral's poetry with the attributes of the Hebraic tradition.

CHAPTER XIII

A Quest for Religious Harmony

Catholicism and the Clergy

Doña Petronila Alcayaga Rojas de Godoy baptized her daughter, Lucila María del Perpetuo Socorro Godoy Alcayaga, into the Catholic Church on her date of birth, April 7, 1889. The inner religious name, Mary of Perpetual Succor, slips from the shadows to prefigure Lucila's and Gabriela's sacred lifelong mission to succor the less fortunate through teaching, writing, and humanitarian works. Although Lucila attended Mass in her formative years, neither the religious name nor the ritual of Mass bound her to fidelity to the Church's rituals and dogmas throughout her life. By 1909, she had parted informally from the Church without, however, breaking intellectual, spiritual, and emotional ties with Christianity. During the next twenty years, she explored Theosophy and Buddhism in the hope of assuaging her personal grief, albeit in vain, and finding a pathway to God.[1] After her disenchantment with Eastern religions, sometime between 1924 and 1930 (exact dates cannot be given), she gradually mellowed toward the Church. This section surveys her stormy relationship with Catholicism and the clergy and discusses possible reasons for making peace or at least calling a truce. Her interest in Theosophy and Buddhism intervenes between these two phases and provides a connecting link with her religious principles in later life.

It is difficult to ascertain precisely why Gabriela became disenchanted with Catholicism, although the following incidents, some already discussed at length, contributed to a great degree, perhaps out of proportion to their significance. As noted earlier, in 1904, she was accepted into the Escuela Normal de Preceptoras to prepare for the teaching profession. In addition to the respectability that teaching offered, a position would provide sorely needed money. Her father had abandoned the family in 1892, and although her half sister, Emelina, lent financial support, it was far from sufficient. Hence, Lucila felt obligated to accept a larger share of the financial burden. In anticipation of Lucila's matriculation, her mother sold some valuables to buy clothing and necessary supplies. Hope turned to distress, however, when the director refused to admit her because the local capellán thought that her articles and poetry smacked of pantheism, an idea that might adversely affect the other students and her views as a teacher.[2] The true motives for refusing her admittance were not revealed at the time, but when they became known to her, she turned away from the Church with bitterness. Nor did her resentment abate when she finally won teaching jobs after tutoring under Emelina's guidance.

The early setbacks did not entirely shape Lucila's/Gabriela's disdain for the Church. By nature, she was exceptional in her rebelliousness and intransigency. She also possessed a tendency to nurse grudges, which made reconciliation difficult, not only with the capellán who had wronged her when she attempted to enroll in school, but she conflated that incident into a general reproach. Years later, Gabriela the writer and social arbiter rejected the Church for what she and other writers perceived as its indifference to social welfare and its disregard of the needs of exploited workers and peasants.[3] Gabriela's concepts are reinforced by American historians who view the nineteenth- and early twentieth-century Chilean clergy in Chile as a privileged aristocracy obsessed with pomp and materialism, insensitive to the basics of religion, and intent on bettering its own political and economic situation. Gabriela witnessed the clergy's indifference to the Chilean campesino's plight, with poor pay, unhealthy living conditions, and insufficient food: "Pero nuestro catolicismo no ha hecho nada por el campesino chileno, con salarios inverosímiles, viviendas insalubres (año 1924), alimento insuficiente."[4] Here she was stressing that if the Church could redress social issues, it could regain the goodwill of the fervently religious Chileans who had become disillusioned with the clergy.[5] For her, the Church in the United States, through its charitable acts, should have been a template for the Chilean clergy:

> *En los Estados Unidos la fe trabaja socialmente, y las iglesias, desde las protestantes hasta las católicas, son instrumentos vivos para la elevación de las clases humildes. Sus servicios de beneficencia son de una extensión tal, que no pueden compararse con la migaja de lo que hacemos en América del Sur; su preocupación por la Casa del Obrero y del Empleado llega hasta esto: la Iglesia ha obtenido en Nueva York un empréstito enorme para proveer de habitaciones holgadas a cada uno de sus miembros, sin excepción alguna.*[6]

Although the promotion of social welfare is not the prime function of religion, or the highest goal attainable, it is not to be shunned for these reasons since, as Gabriela added, only a handful of men ascend the religious ladder (*"a las cumbres de una religión no asciende sino un puñado de hombres"*). She believed that religion must have its sights on heaven — the sacred — as well as on material sufficiency for the impoverished — the secular. It would be a perversion of religion for the clergy to be indifferent to suffering simply because the Kingdom of Heaven, with its lure of abatement of pain, offered a ready-made rationale for apathy. Her rebellion against the clergy's excesses of privilege did not include destroying the Church or opposing organized religion, for she recognized the importance of religion as an element of culture. Instead, she urged reforms which included democratization of the Church, increased benevolence on the part of the clergy, participation in charitable works, and a united Christian movement free of internecine warfare.[7]

In an article written in 1924, "Cristianismo con sentido social" ("Christianity with a Social Sense"), Gabriela tried to analyze the growing separation between a Church hierarchy minimally aware of social reforms and the masses that desperately needed such reforms. She underlined the alternative that awaited Catholicism should it not "choose the pathway," should it not awaken to the spirit of charity and justice:

> *A los egoístas más empedernidos será bueno decirles que, con nosotros o sin nosotros, el pueblo hará sus reformas, y que ha de salir, en último caso, lo que estamos viendo: la democracia jacobina, horrible como una Euménide y brutal como una horda tártara. Elijamos camino.*[8]

Mistral's clear references in this article to the Russian Revolution prefigured inevitable strife unless the Church was prepared to assume the lead in civic action. The workers and peasants would eventually take by force the bread and shelter ("*pan y techo para los hijos*"), which, through custom and design, had been denied them. (In the light of future developments in Cuba under Fidel Castro, and in Peru with the Liberation Theology movement, her thoughts were prescient.) Still, there was time, according to Gabriela, but only if the Church was serious about the spirit of self-sacrifice and social service:

> *Todo el bien que hoy día puede hacerse al catolicismo y al cristianismo en general, es un sacrificio de intereses materiales. O se da eso, o se declara lealmente que la doctrina de Cristo la aceptamos sólo como una lectura bella, en el Evangelio, o como una filosofía trascendente que eleva la dignidad humana, pero que no es para nosotros una religión, es decir, una conducta para la vida.*

Mistral goes on with the following screed that condemns the philosphical dilettantes of God's words and works:

> *Si somos dilettanti de la Escritura, recitadores estéticos de una parábola, por su sabor griego de belleza pura, es bueno confesar nuestro epicureísmo; nos quedaremos entre los comentadores literarios o filosóficos de la religión. Si somos lo otro, los cristianos totales del Evangelio total, iremos hacia el pueblo.*

> *Ordenaremos un poco sus confusos anhelos sobre reformas de nuestro sistema económico, y mezclados con ellos, hemos de discutir primero y conceder en seguida.*

The more the Church tried to go toward the people as Christ did, become more democratic, the greater the opportunity for a Church triumphant. On the other hand, a religion nourished only by elites must perish. In this sense, Mistral anticipated the era of Pope John XXIII and his doctrine of *mater et magister*.[9]

Gabriela carried her cathedral within and denied reverence for the external forms of religion, certain that man was meant to talk with God directly and to lead a life of service and simplicity.[10] She admitted being a Christian and a believer, but qualified her statement by affirming her personal, non-dogmatic approach to prayer and to God: "*...tengo una concepción muy personal sobre la religion.... Sólo sé decirle que no soy dogmática y que le rezo a Dios, es decir, le hablo a Dios muy a mi manera.*"[11] Avoiding formal prayer, she preferred to talk with God, not because she thought of God as human, and not out of haughtiness or disrespect, but because she wanted to avoid artificiality, cant, and the sacrosanct traditional channels of communication with God:

> *No puedo hacer traición a mis sentimientos ni a las tendencias de la evolución contemporánea. Es otra la norma que me guía: reconocer las virtudes de Jesús, su nombre y su gloria, sin las exterioridades que rodean su culto. Y esto no es una claudicación: es seguir viviendo en la tierra y contemplando las grandezas de otras regiones.*[12]

For Gabriela human intercessors, the clergy, played a minor role. In the style of Martin Buber, she believed in an "I-and-Thou" relationship, devoid of pomp and ceremony and free from the mumblings and platitudes in the Mass that kill the spirit of prayer: "*¡...yo no voy a misa! ... Pero eso no quiere decir que no vaya usted, y que suponga que yo soy anticatólica. ¡Al contrario! Sólo que mis 'padres de la Orden de San Francisco' aceptan que yo lo sea, sin obligaciones litúrgicas, por mi salud.*"[13] She praised the Order of Saint Francis for accepting her manner of prayer as an anguished outburst, not a duty; it united the poet with Jesus Christ directly and eliminated the need for priestly intercession.[14]

Not all clergy merited scorn. Singled out for the highest praise was Don Crescente Errázuriz Valdivieso, archbishop of Santiago, a model of intelligence, moral discretion, and dedication to religious, social, and political justice.[15] The nun Sor Juana Inés de la Cruz, of the Order of Discalced Carmelites and later of the Paulist Order of St. Jerome (1669) — arguably the major intellect in 17th century Mexico — merited acclaim, not only because she was a most gifted poet, but also because she gave up her advantaged and long-sought material world of books, charts, and intellectual conversations and died tending victims of the plague.[16] Mistral also praised that paragon of sixteenth-century Spanish ecclesiastics, the Dominican Fray Bartolomé de las Casas

(1484–1566), the "Apostle of the Indians." He antagonized Spanish colonists and the Inquisition itself by arguing againt the Just War waged against New World Indians, and instead, pleaded the just cause of the natives convinced that man, regardless of his skin color, was a human being and did not by nature merit servitude and apostasy.[17]

Generally, the clerics Mistral esteemed — including St. Francis of Assisi and Santa Teresa de Jesús — zealously fulfilled the message of Jesus. They committed themselves to positive, disinterested acts of charity and benevolence toward their fellowmen urged on by the parable of the Good Samaritan. Mistral, out of her adoration for St. Francis, joined the Order of Franciscans as a tertiary. She could thus live humbly, not as an excuse for disengaging from society or as a means to personal self-enhancement, but because she wanted to serve the less fortunate. This flowering of love in service is a concept found, to be sure, in all truly Christian thought, but stressed particularly by St. Francis and his followers, for whom the entire social economy proceeded from the ideal of service motivated by Christ's law of love. In the case of Mistral it may even be asserted that the primary appeal of Christianity to her as a faith lies in its social implications.[18] Gabriela stated succinctly the essence of her Franciscan concept of service, i.e., humble and full of energy: "*Hay que ser humilde pero enérgico.*"[19] She stressed a vigorous program of physical and spiritual help for the poor. It was false if it were undertaken by clergymen who practiced self-sacrifice and humility merely to ensure their own individual salvation.

Her half-dozen essays advocating more clerical responsibility and Christian unity failed to capture attention. Nor did the essays serve to make the author a religious reformer or leader. Indeed, what reforms she suggested are confined to paper, and there is little evidence that she engaged actively and continually in political or social reform of the Church or of Christianity. Although she recognized the need for changes, her temperamental makeup kept her from joining movements for bettering the Church.

That makeup consisted of independence of spirit, a need for solitude, aloofness, and even haughtiness. Her inability to compromise without lowering herself, or to join an organization without yielding autonomy, prevented her from being an active reformer and had the effect of diminishing her worthwhile ideas on religious reform. Her biographer, Virgilio Figueroa, underscores her position. Figueroa shows her religiosity to be militantly nonreligious when there was the slightest possibility that she might be accused of allowing adherence to doctrine to filter into her teaching duties:

> *Se le objetó que el magisterio debía ser arreligioso y apolítico. Su réplica fue varonil y arrolladura. Expresó que no aceptaba ningún fanatismo, que su incorporación a un culto, en caso de hacerlo, no significaba su renunciación a*

la libertad y que la obediencia ciega e incondicional no comulgaba con su ser íntimo, consciente, pensante y autónomo.[20]

The irony is that, in her few attempts to make the Church more vigorous and more responsive to human misery, Gabriela was generously prescribing aid for others which she could not accept for herself. Even if the Church had been free of taint, it would still have been inconceivable to see her kneeling before altars or participating in the liturgy.

Considering all the preceding arguments, and taking into account Gabriela Mistral's independent intellectual spirit — which, for all its need for freedom from restraint still sought dependence on God — a further reason may be offered to explain her lack of interest in the Church. It is that the Church did not try to elevate its worshipers but, instead, conceded to ritual, offered sentimentality rather than piety, asked for faith and offered no means by which that faith could be sustained. And Gabriela could never entrust religion to human beings no better or purer than herself. Simple folk find less reason to be dissatisfied than intellectuals, who continue to thirst for causes, knowledge, and understanding, all antagonistic to the Church's teaching.[21] Four years before her death in 1957, Gabriela underlined the basic flaw of the clergy in Chile as being deaf to discussion and change: "*Repito que me parecen peligrosas y dañinas las polémicas sobre religión en países como los nuestros en los cuales la sensibilidad católica es demasiado gruesa y sorda y estropea cualquier discusión.*"[22] The Church's failure to present enlightened theology — an oxymoron, a contradiction in terms — forced her to seek fulfillment elsewhere.[23] Noteworthy in this regard is that Theosophy, which attracted her in 1911, in Antofagasta, called for an open, inquiring mind and stressed the rational nature of religion and the importance of self-purification.[24]

Evidence indicates that eventually Gabriela returned to Catholicism, or at least became more sympathetic to the Church. A tone of personal reconciliation and compromise pervades her previously cited article, "Cristianismo con sentido social": "*Yo, que he anclado en el catolicismo, después de años de duda, me he puesto a hacer este buceo, con un corazón dolorido, por lo que mi fe pierde, pero a la vez con una mente lúcida, deseando, más que condenar, comprender el proceso.*" In her overt realignment with Catholicism, she presupposed that Catholicism was capable of affirming Christ's charity and sacrifice, in spite of the blinding effect that wealth and power had on the Church in South America:

> *El catolicismo tiene que hacer la reconquista de lo que, por desidia o egoísmo, ha enajenado, y esto será posible si los católicos demostramos que, en verdad, somos capaces de renunciación, o sea, capaces de la esencia misma de nuestra doctrina.*[25]

The reforms undertaken in Belgium, Germany, and Argentina to benefit the workers persuaded Mistral that the Church was not totally incapable of social action, and therefore was not entirely to be condemned. The basic question was to foment similar action in South America, where the need was greater but the possibilities for change more difficult of achievement.

Furthermore, José Santos González Vera affirmed in a personal letter to me (July 12, 1962), that Gabriela turned towards Catholicism after her stay in Mexico:

> ... volvió al catolicismo cuando estuvo en México y se perseguía allí a los católicos, que eran llamados entonces cristeros.... Su catolicismo fue especial, quizás siempre mezclado a palabras, ideas o fórmulas de otras religiones. Se hizo católica nuevamente como protesta por la persecución que sufrían en México y seguramente también por meditación de lecturas de escritores neocatólicos.

Mistral's sympathy for the Cristero movement of Mexico (1926–1928) is understandable. She opposed governmental suppression of ecclesiastical freedom as fiercely as she deprecated the autocracy of the Church. The Mexican government brutally crushed the increasing physical and spiritual power of the Church to prevent Catholicism from becoming a state religion and a challenge to the civil government. But the federal soldiers, in upholding the anti-clerical Reform Laws of 1857, further strengthened by the Constitution of 1917, acted as barbarously as the fanatic cristeros, who committed many atrocities in the name of Cristo Rey (Christ the King). Gabriela sided with the underdog clergy and those who defended the right to free worship against the oppressive measures of the central government. It is quite conceivable that she evidenced concern for Catholics and Catholicism, but this is not adequate proof that she accepted Church doctrine. It indicates, perhaps, that she favored the lesser of the two evils, the weaker of the two sides. It might be more precise to say that she became less reproachful of the Church than she had been before, during the Guerra Cristera, when the government proved to be even more fanatic in suppressing religion than the Church in teaching it.

Mistral, in Mexico between 1922 and 1924 at the invitation of Minister of Education José Vasconcelos, observed the events leading up to the Guerra Cristera. In keeping with the prevailing anti-clerical ideology of President Elías Calles, she worked to establish secular rural schools and libraries for illiterate Mexican peasant children. The situation was ironical: the Church wanted desperately to regain control over the religious and academic education of the young, but Article 130 of the Constitution of 1917, an outcome of the Mexican Revolution, prohibited it. The Church, moreover, could provide better instruction than the rural schools, in which the children received a poor education and no religious training. Gabriela weighed both sides when she was in a position to organize rural schools and decided in favor of secular education. A faulty education in a democratic environment outweighed a good one in a repressive atmosphere. From 1922 to 1929, she vacillated between praise for the Mexican government for trying to raise the standards of free public education and scorn for that same government when it imposed tyrannical control on the right of free worship.

Mistral evinced contradictory positions with respect to the role of Church and state in the education of children. She exemplified one attitude with Christ's words to the Pharisees on proper tribute (Matthew 22:21): *"Dad, pues, a César lo que es de César, y a Dios lo que es de Dios."*[26] The parable underlines the separation of the secular from the sacred. Her approval of the concept of giving to Caesar what is Caesar's and to God what is God's led her to conclude that Christ believed in the separation of Church and state in matters of education. The Church was to be occupied with teaching morality, ethics, and the Word of God. Yet she reversed this view by denying the atheistic educational theories of one of her mentors, Jean Jacques Rousseau. Together with Maria Montessori and Rabindranath Tagore, both admirers of Rousseau, she wrote articles, translated to French, opposed to godless education in a secular environment:

> *L'Hindou s'inspirant lui aussi des principes pédagogiques de Rousseau, a fondé dans le voisinage de Calcutta une école qui est défendue contre l'odieux rationalisme du Génevois par un riche et admirable enseignement religieux.*[27]

Christian spiritual values have a rightful and necessary place in the school, according to her comment translated to French:

> *Je m'élève également contre l'accusation d'anticléricalisme portée contre moi. Un des buts que je me proposais en allant à cette société de professeurs ... était justement de défendre l'enseignement religieux à l'école. J'ai exalté cet enseignement en butte à des attaques et à des railleries cruelles, me donnant ainsi la joie profonde de défendre le Christ.*

She was also prepared to condemn theocratic Ecuador under President Gabriel García Moreno, where only one state-sponsored religion flourished, and the atheism of the Soviet Union, which had developed excellent schools but tyrannized religious groups. Her basic stance on education vis-à-vis Church and state was to defend the right of Christianity to enter a school system. This was part of her concept of a Christian, democratic philosophy, again expressed in French: *"...que je sais sur le sol éternel de la démocratie chrétienne; mais d'une démocratie chrétienne courageuse et non tiède, loyale à Dieu et aux hommes et non traîtresse à Dieu et aux hommes."*

Mistral's reconciliation with Catholicism had, presumably, been achieved by January 1957, when she lay dying of cancer in Hempstead Hospital, in New York. One must be wary, nonetheless, of declaring with certainty that

Gabriela accepted the Last Sacraments, not only because of her continued refusal to acknowledge Church doctrine, but also because the following data, garnered from persons who witnessed her last days, harbor inconsistencies and differences of opinion. In the first place, her last-minute concern with the Aramaic prayer, Kol Nidre, and the Old Testament Psalms (see Chapter XII, "The Hebraic Tradition") do not suggest orthodox preoccupation with deliverance through Catholic rites but, rather, opposition to the Church's institutionalized religion and willingness to accept the form of atonement reminiscent of a Jew. But it is not worthwhile to belabor her so-called Jewishness at this juncture, because it is also possible to argue that her insistence on hearing Old Testament scriptures and the chant Kol Nidre stemmed from her need for beauty and sadness.

Conflicting testimony of friends and clergymen makes it difficult to determine whether Gabriela consciously requested and comprehended the last rites of the Church. The Reverend Father Joseph E. Dunn of the Church of Our Lady of Loretto in Hempstead affirmed, in his letter to me (December 8, 1965), that Gabriela was in a semiconscious state on January 2, 1958, when the local chaplain (who preferred anonymity) administered the Last Sacraments.[28] Another source averred that Gabriela received the Last Sacraments with devotion and total mental clarity ("con mucha devoción y con toda lucidez de mente") from an American priest.[29] The conflict between the two statements, "semiconscious state" and "mental clarity" ("*toda lucidez de mente*"), is obvious. With regard to the Papal Blessing for the dying, administered January 8, 1958, the Reverend Father Renato Poblete, S.J., affirmed in a letter (December 22, 1965), that she was conscious and accepted the blessing: "*Cuando yo fui a verla aún tenía a mi juicio conocimiento, y le di la bendición para los que están moribundos, que recibió a mi parecer aceptándolos.*" A day-by-day study of her progressively worsening condition made by Josué Monsalve, who supported the idea that Gabriela, with her last breath converted to Catholicism ("*moría como una conversa en el seno de la religión católica*"), declared, in opposition to the preceding opinions, that she was unconscious from January 4 until her death six days later.[30] These statements should not lead to the conclusion that the correspondents alluded to were being untruthful. There is ample proof that the comments were made in good faith, even though the question of Gabriela's consciousness required subjective evaluation.

The presence of many priests certainly indicated that Doris Dana, Gabriela's loyal companion, was adhering to her last wishes. Doris placed a silver cross in the casket that was carried into St. Patrick's Cathedral, in New York City, for the public service officiated over by Francis Cardinal Spellman. St. Patrick's would not have accepted Gabriela for religious services had she been a renegade or had not received the Last Sacraments. The main thrust of the ambiguities presented here concern narrow details of time and the difficult question of determining voluntary, conscious acceptance of the Church and the liturgy in the face of pain-relieving sedatives and coma. Until these inconsistencies are resolved, a residue of doubt continues to linger about Gabriela Mistral's concept toward Catholicism, the clergy, and the liturgy in her last moments.

Theosophy

When Gabriela Mistral renounced the religion imposed upon her from childhood, she consciously sought personal solace and understanding of the nature of God in other religious systems.[31] In pursuing Theosophy, she freed herself from the strictures of theology and the incantations of the clergy without ever denying the essential aspects of Christianity: the teachings, morality, and sacrifice of Jesus Christ. Theosophy, intertwined with Christian and Buddhist concepts, played a decisive role in her understanding and focus of the sacred and the secular for her life and creativity. She absorbed from Theosophy those elements that best answered her particular needs: the idea of the oneness of all creatures and things; the intellectual, rational inquiry into the workings of religions; the need for meditation and contemplation; the belief that there is a course of action which, when followed, frees man from bodily pain; and the feeling that death, with its divesting of the leaden body, allows the individual to find eternal peace.

Theosophy, a term that originates in Late Greek (*the* [God]+*sophia* [wisdom]) and passes to medieval Latin as *teosophia*, God's wisdom, goes beyond any one religion, including Buddhism and Christianity from which it has borrowed heavily. Theosophists study all religions to understand their arcane wisdom. They believe that the primeval period of a religion, when it has not yet been affected by society, theologians, and evolution, is the stage at which religion is a "gift to humanity."[32] A divine authority, whether a messiah or a "savior-teacher," brings to the world exoteric and esoteric doctrine. Exoteric, or secular, doctrine is clear to the masses and deals with morality, right and wrong, the personal conduct of men on earth. Esoteric, or sacred, doctrine, however, is imparted only to the qualified and disciplined initiates in secret organizations. "This aggregate of precious knowledge, this innermost teaching of the gods to mankind is, needless to say, the Ancient Wisdom — is Theosophy. Theosophy, [essentially], claims [to be] the key to all this body of wisdom, which has always been in the world, but never publicly until now."[33] Theosophical doctrine is found in the sacred books of India, China, Persia,

Babylon, Egypt, and Greece. Theosophy embraces Buddhism and Christianity by focusing attention on their common points: Each has its human savior and a similar ethic; each stresses a need for purification. Notwithstanding these general affinities, close scrutiny reveals many differences of method and purpose. The problems of birth and death, the existence of God, activity or quietude, are reconciled in divergent ways.

Biographers of Gabriela Mistral usually give meager accounts of her attachment to Theosophy. As described in Chapter V, section "A Dispute over Catholicism and Theosophy," she attended, starting 1911, a lodge in Antofagasta, Chile, called Destellos (Beams of Light).[34] Carlos Parrau Escobar, who presided, explained the fundamentals of the movement and offered her *La voz del silencio*, and another book by Theosophy's Russian founder, Mme Héléna Petrovna Blavatsky (1831–1891), a volume of short stories. In that lodge, she also met Don Zacarías Gómez, founder of the Librería Orientalista in Santiago, who would supply her with reading materials in the course of their relationship. (See Appendices A and B.)

Gabriela espoused Theosophical doctrine and tradition by contributing poems to two Theosophical journals published in Santiago: *Nueva Luz*, in whose pages "El himno del árbol" appeared (December 1913), and "La charca" (March 1914).[35] For the *Revista Teosófica Chilena*, she wrote (August 1924), the sentimental, but sincere "El placer de servir." During this period, she also submitted poems of a Theosophical nature to a magazine in Chillán, *Primerose*, and to another in Valparaíso, *Luz y Sombra*.[36]

Theosophy requires physical and moral discipline. In this regard, González Vera discerned an intensification of Gabriela's asceticism, brought on by her oriental studies and by an attempt at purification of the body and the spirit.[37] While attending the Destellos Lodge in Antofagasta, she assuaged her mental anguish and stress by performing Yoga exercises, taking long walks, and sunbathing. She avoided meat, but ate, to imitate the high saints of India, vegetables, honey, sweets, and fruit: "*...se alimenta de vegetales (ya siente el influjo de los santones de la India); paladea la miel, se harta de frutas, pasteles y dulces.*" She dressed severely, held herself erect while walking, and combed her hair straight back: "*Viste con sencillez austera, anda erguida y peina sus cabellos hacia atrás.*" At night, in the solitude of the Andes, she enjoyed meditation:

> *Cuando la rodea el silencio nocturno, su espíritu huelga por el universo, se asoma al plano astral, recréase con el aura de los grandes iniciados y se entrega a la meditación pura. Si la embarga una dulce felicidad, permanece minutos y minutos en el nirvana.*[37]

This self-renunciation formed part of her Yoga exercises.[38] The purpose of Yoga is to "penetrate to a transcendent experience, wherein the spirit tears itself away from its connection with the body so that, having thus become bodiless and free, it attains its own, as well as universal, infinity, rides on the wind and enters into ever higher, into even the highest, realms of Being and Essence, in order finally to achieve universal experience."[39] The Western temperament and culture do not adapt to all Yoga practices, so Gabriela Mistral remained more interested in the contemplative, health, and spiritual aspects of Yoga than in the extreme physical manipulations often associated with Yogin.

Mme Blavatsky recognized that only the most fervent could undergo complete self-renunciation with the purpose of understanding the soul. Still, the "modest benefactors of humanity"[40] could also contribute without undergoing the rigors of all Yoga practices." Spiritual exercises, called "Prácticas," manifest the poet's intense dedication to sounding the nature of the self, the universe, and God. The "Prácticas" exemplify an intellectual self-awareness of the presence of the Universal Spirit within the poet and, at the same time, reveal her desire to share this presence with her audience. Here Gabriela stressed the proper physical and mental attitude so that the search for the universal can begin, appropriately, within the individual:

> *Los que quieran obtener resultados por medio de sus fuerzas mentales deben, antes que nada, abstenerse de las discusiones. Estas producen una divergencia absoluta de vibraciones e impiden las fuerzas cósmicas el manifestarse.*[41]

She repeatedly emphasized the prerequisites for a harmonious rapport with the universe: proper breathing (*"respiración recta"*), relaxation (*"todos los músculos están en perfecto descanso"*), and concentration, made possible by orange-colored lights. But foremost they consisted in getting a perfect mental image of one's actions on the organisms (*"obtener una perfecta imagen mental de su acción sobre los organismos"*). These very same exercises for communing with the Universal Spirit, while beneficial for the practitioner in alleviating physical and mental pain, also contributed greatly for spiritual achievement.

Theosophists who are more attentive to the mysteries of the origin of the universe than to moral and ethical concerns are prone to attribute supernatural powers to Theosophy. Relying too much upon the God-spirit within them and not enough upon the rigorous preparation for godliness that the American Theosophist, Dr. Annie Besant (1847–1933), recommended for initiates, some self-appointed oracles use Theosophy to commune with God, or to contact spirits, or even to predict the future on the basis of a prearranged orderly universe. This aspect of Theosophy has at once been the source of its novelty and the reason for its disrepute.[42] Other Theosophists, realizing the metaphoric implications of the universe which Theosophy purports to describe, do not claim special powers on the basis of such knowledge. Rather, they derive personal and spiritual security from their ability to decipher cosmic laws.

The preceding discussion introduces comments on the occult in Gabriela Mistral's life and poetry. Theosophy condones occult practices by its own Fellows initiated in esoteric doctrine, but condemns occultism as charlatanry in the hands of non–Theosophists.[43] And since Theosophy affords to all its adherents an awareness of the spiritual life within and beyond matter and of the mysterious forces operating in the universe and within man, it is obvious that Theosophists have a feeling for occultism. Some critics considered Gabriela an occultist because of her Theosophical studies. This untenable judgment neglects the fact that occultism requires a total physical and emotional surrender, which, in turn, becomes a way of life. It is clear that Gabriela Mistral did not pretend to be an occultist in the extreme sense.

In fact, in the following passage from her "Prácticas" Gabriela demonstrated an aversion to communication with the dead:

> *Algunas almas en oración, al llegar el silencio, se sienten fluctuar en el plano astral o psíquico y allí a los desencarnados. Estos quieren comunicarse con ellos y ser reconocidos. Es esa una tremenda tentación. La experiencia es fascinante, pero debéis desear subir a plano más alto. Si esa intromisión sobreviene, levantáos y rechazar las visiones astrales.*
>
> *Declarad que no es eso lo que buscáis. O decid expresamente: 'Nadie se puede interponer entre el Cristo, puente de toda vida y yo, su criatura.' O bien decid esta oración: 'Tu voluntad, Señor, se haga ahora en mí. "*[44]

Mistral avoided the spiritist, or spiritualist, trap that would have lent an air of fraudulence to her religious convictions. She rejected all divine presences but one, that of Christ:

> *Cada uno do nosotros tiene acceso directo al Cristo que está en nosotros: el Ser de nuestro ser.*
>
> *Para satisfacer espir[itual] de N[uestro] Ser, sólo nos queda el grito nostálgico del niño hacia su Padre-Madre: ¡Abba!*
>
> **Volvéos niños** *y aprended a permanecer silenciosos escuchando lo que JCNS va a decir, a manar, a poner sobre la parte intuitiva nuestra. Esta no es la consciencia sino el espíritu mismo.*
>
> *Ligáos a ese eje, a esa fuente, en todos los momentos de vuestra vida:—"Ven, y juntos razonaremos" [Isaiah 1:18], dice el Señor.*

In these selections Mistral is quite close to spiritual mysticism. Yet it is difficult to determine who the mystic is. The exhortations do not redound exclusively to the poet's private world; rather they are supplications that others act as well. By exclaiming aloud, albeit rhetorically, the silent voice is shattered; the masses may enter where only initiates dare to penetrate. Mistral believed herself an initiate, and this thought prompted her to extend to others what was already hers. It is impossible to overlook the devotion, the intensity, and the pure spirit that prevail in these intimate glimpses into her religious world. As she reaches for the arcane, the divine presence continues to dwell within.

Manifestations of the occult in her poetry lend further insight into the recondite nature of the world she created. In her themes of love, of communion with the dead, of separation, of eternity and nature, astrology has an important part. For example, contemplation of the stars causes Ruth and Boaz to plot their common destiny, he to fulfill the word of Jehovah, she to attain personal satisfaction:

> *Ruth vio en los astros los ojos con llanto*
> *de Booz llamándola, y estremecida,*
> *dejó su lecho, y se fue por el campo ...*
> ("Ruth," p. 14)

On the other hand, in "Sonetos de la muerte," astrological signs augur doom for a perfidious lover:

> *Se hará luz en la zona de los sinos, oscura;*
> *sabrás que en nuestra alianza signo de astros había*
> *y, roto el pacto enorme, tenías que morir ...*
>
> *Malas manos tomaron tu vida desde el día*
> *en que, a una señal de astros, dejara su plantel*
> *nevado de azucenas. En gozo florecía.*
> *Malas manos entraron trágicamente en él...*[45]
> (p. 82)

The sidereal pact of love seems to have been created by forces beyond the control of man and woman, like that foretold in the Prologue to Shakespeare's Romeo and Juliet: "From forth the fatal loins of these two foes / A pair of star-cross'd lovers take their life." In its inexorability, fate as envisioned here is quite similar to the Hindu and Buddhist karma; no pleas, no pardon, can save the lover because he must pay for his sins personally. The sky that prefigured tragedy announces the arrival of the dead in some heavenly region:

> *Oh, no, !Volverlo a ver, no importa dónde,*
> *en remansos de cielo o en vórtice hervidor,*
> *bajo unas lunas plácidas o en un cárdeno horror!*
> ("Volverlo a ver," p. 95)

The death of the Mexican poet Amado Nervo (1870–1919) opened up the possibility of an astral reunion on the Southern Cross: "*...sobre la Cruz del Sur que ... mira temblando ...*" ("In memoriam," p. 23). The death of Gabriela's mother (1929) elicited intimate revelations of the poet's nocturnal pleadings to the constellations for a chance communication:

> *Estoy sola con la Noche,*
> *la Osa Mayor, la Balanza,*
> *por creer que en esta paz*
> *puede viajar tu palabra*
> *y romperla mi respiro*
> *y mi grito ahuyentarla.*[46]
>
> ("Madre mía," p. 728)

Propitious for the communion of souls, the starry night, in "Balada de la estrella" ("Ballad of the Star," pp. 138–139), also permits the poet to voice her own destiny and sadness:

> *Estrella, estoy triste.*
> *Tú dime si otra*
> *como mi alma viste.*
> *— Hay otra más triste.*

And the distant star responds:

> *— Soy yo la que encanto,*
> *soy yo la que tengo*
> *mi luz hecha llanto.*

To be sure, Gabriela's own destiny is as closely linked to the stars as that of Ruth, Amado Nervo, or her mother. By reflecting through the stars the Moabitess' desire for love and purity, the Mexican's search for a God he could understand, and an insignificant Chilean woman's longing for peace in death, Gabriela Mistral is echoing her own sentiments, which also accord with the Theosophical point of view.

The primal distinction between the savior-teachers, Christ and Buddha, is that Christ's ultimate act illustrated the annihilation of physical life in order to attain spiritual exaltation in the Resurrection, whereas Buddha exemplified the extinction of the pleasures of living in order to unshackle man from the pain to which his desires lead him. Similarities between the mission of Buddha and that of Christ are common knowledge, but it is fruitful to draw a parallel between Buddha and St. Francis of Assisi, who, although not God, best epitomized the godlike spirit of Christ among men. For this reason alone the comparison between St. Francis and Buddha is more apt; Buddha was no god either, in spite of his superior attributes. Undoubtedly St. Francis, for whom Gabriela felt a strong attraction, taught and possessed the very ethic and virtues Buddha extolled in the Noble Eightfold Path.[47] Indeed, because of a similar ethic, the philosophies of both men express humility with images similar enough to make clear identification difficult.

If their ethic is similar, their methods and purposes are different. St. Francis flagellated himself with increasing severity; Buddha, after his initial period of extreme asceticism, renounced self-torture as vanity and wanton destruction incapable of leading to the truth.[48] Where St. Francis' extreme penitence reflected atonement for Christ's sacrifice, Buddha's decision to renounce pleasure was motivated by the attempt to eliminate personal suffering. According to St. Francis, suffering for the purpose of sharing Christ's wounds imparted divinity to the victim; Buddha recognized no God, only godlike perfection that man could achieve through his acts of abstinence and truthfulness. In short, St. Francis endured humility in order to strive to equal Christ's total humility symbolized in death; Buddha humbled himself to avoid the pain of living which emanates from a desire for worldly things. With these distinctions made clear, further contrasts are possible with regard to the manner in which Gabriela Mistral's poetry treats the themes of revilement of the self and purification of the spirit through detachment from material objects.

Humility, from the Latin *humus* (earth), appears in the poet's numerous references to clay and mud. The Lord God formed men of the dust of the ground according to the Bible, which validates the theory of the essential worthlessness of the body. And by extension, Gabriela applies the theory to *"siglo engreído"* ("greedy humanity") admirers of physical objects, which, like the body, are composed of *"barro"* ("mud") and have only a transitory nature (*"soy mortal"*):

> *Y que, por fin, mi siglo engreído*
> *en su grandeza material,*
> *· no me deslumbre hasta el olvido*
> *de que soy barro y soy mortal.*
> ("El himno cotidiano," p. 351)

"Arcilla" ("clay") is the poet's often-used metaphor to designate matter without life, therefore matter void of desire.[49] A man fashioned out of clay would not have the passions that could ultimately consume his life:

> *Yo sueño con un vaso de humilde y simple arcilla,*
> *que guarde tus cenizas cerca de mis miradas;*
> *y la pared del vaso te será mi mejilla,*
> *y quedarán mi alma y tu alma apaciguadas.*
>
> *No quiero espolvorearlas en vaso de oro ardiente,*
> *ni en la ánfora pagana que carnal línea ensaya:*
> *sólo un vaso de arcilla te ciña simplemente,*
> *humildemente, como un pliegue de mi saya.*
> ("El vaso," p. 98)

The poverty of the flesh is heightened by avoiding all adornment and by dressing in the coarsest sackcloth. The *"maestra rural"* wears *"sayas pardas"* ("brown skirts"), or the body itself can be the sackcloth, as in *"carne es su propio sayal"* (respectively, "La maestra rural," p. 51, and "Nocturno de los tejedores viejos,"

p. 300). St. Francis, the model of humility, would "sew rough sack upon his own tunic" to intensify the mortification, and because he felt no need for clothing: "This man, being clothed with virtue from on high, was warmed more within by a divine, than without by a bodily garment."[50] The essence of Christian humility is reached when the body has cast off its last possession, has cut away its ties with any symbols of terrestrial worth: "*Ahora suelto la mártir sandalia / y las trenzas pidiendo dormir*" ("Nocturno," p. 80).[51] Sleep, for the humble penitent, means death in the arms of Christ: "*Por eso es que te pido, / Cristo, ... ¡pára mis pulsos, / y mis párpados baja!*" The last lines of "Éxtasis" (p. 65), take Christian humility to its ultimate conclusion — a total submission to the will of Christ: "*Recíbeme, voy plena, / ¡tan plena voy como tierra inundada!*"

Mme Blavatsky summarizes the *raison d'être* of Theosophy in a key phrase: "[It] is essentially the philosophy of those who suffer, and have lost all hope of being helped out of the mire of life by any other means."[52] Of particular significance is "mire of life," which in this context may connote, besides hopelessness and frustration, the unredeemed sinner, the man devoid of spiritual values, or at most, the man who is slave to a false faith. The very same idea impressed itself on Gabriela's works. Its essence is reiterated in "Primavera," "La charca," and "Limpia tu fuente" (respectively, "Spring," "The Stagnant Pool," and "Clean Your Fountain"), the last two in poetic prose. In their unique way, all three are interconnected parables about the transformation of a pool of dirty water into a pristine current. "Primavera" suggests that the change is possible by reflecting upon purity:

> *¡Y hasta una charca pútrida, copiando en su agujero*
> *la turquesa de arriba, se está transfigurando!*[53]

The common issue in all three works is that evil thoughts and surface ugliness mask the underlying beauty that is waiting to be revealed: "*Cuando los seres te parecen mezquinos y la vida se desfloca, parda, como una cepa muerta, es que te han enturbiado tu linfa; limpia tu fuente.*"[54]

"Himno al aire," a paean to life free of pain, suggests man's threefold dilemma and the single solution:

> *Cree en mí con beato ardor, místicamente,*
> *y déjame insuflarte nueva alma y nueva esencia;*
> *que te cambie el espíritu, y la carne y la mente,*
> *cuya triple fatiga mancilla la existencia.*[55]

To achieve freedom from pain, it is first necessary to eliminate desire, which originates in attachment to nonpermanent matter. As an example, the beautiful lotus flower, its roots anchored in the mud, rises above dank and fetid surroundings to the air and sun:

> *Ábrete entero. Así los lotos de cien hojas.*
> *Y vive en mí como ellos viven sobre las aguas,*
> *y me entre por tus venas, como por brechas rojas,*
> *a encenderte la vida como se encienden fraguas.*[56]

Like the lotus, man can rise above the mud, which binds his lower self, to seek union with the Universal Self.[57] By so doing he discards ever-changing matter for immutable matter, which act, in the final analysis, leads to the annihilation of all desire and, concomitantly, to the elimination of all pain.

It appeared to José Santos González Vera that Gabriela's personal correspondence with Annie Besant, her increasing penetration into the history of Theosophy, and her knowledge and concern for Krishnamurti, had an air of fetishism: "*...nadie iguala su saber acerca del niño Krishnamurti, que será dios no bien alcance la edad adulta.*"[58] González Vera's tone may lead to the belief that Gabriela, along with many others, was gullible, and was, therefore, fooled by Jiddu Krishnamurti (1895–1986), the Indian boy Annie Besant adopted in Adyar, India, and educated to become the anointed Christ.[59] Mistral's faith in the olive-skinned, dark-eyed Krishnamurti was not a weakness, but an affirmation of both Christianity and Theosophy. Krishnamurti, until his personal renunciation of Besant's anointment, attested to the potential Christ in every man. In this sense, no one is entirely a sinner or is completely damned. Annie Besant extolled the "Christ of the human Spirit, the Christ who is in every one of us, [who] is born and lives, is crucified, rises from the dead, and ascends into heaven, in every suffering and triumphant 'Son of Man.'"[60] Each man can thus mirror Christ by living in simplicity and by loving God's creatures. (In Chapter XIV, "The Poetry of Sacrifice," Besant's influence on Mistral's concept of sacrifice will be discussed in detail.)

Krishnamurti, as the Christ incarnate, influenced Gabriela Mistral's religious beliefs in several ways. First of all, his appearance refuted the popular illusion that Christ had blond hair, blue eyes, and fair skin. Gabriela also rejected this unjust image of an Anglo-Saxon God on loan to the underprivileged South American peasants and aborigines:

> *Todos los que están allí, vistos a la luz de las estrellas, son gente morena, como nosotros, y debió serlo hasta el reciénnacido, a pesar de los cromos del cristianismo a la inglesa, y tostado sería después, de vivir al sol de los campos y caminar en pespunteo de aldea en aldea.*[61]

In the same vein, she was proud, also, that the Christ Child was born poor, unknown, and under the Roman yoke. These views were in accord with her attitude of trying to dignify the humble and downtrodden:

> *Allegarnos al Dios-Niño sería buscar los pesebres nuestros de Cordillera y selva adentro, por los caminos rurales y las playas no sospechadas, por todas partes de*

> *donde se escape un llanto chiquito que es el mismo de aquella Medianoche y se oiga además el rezo de la María indígena o mulata. Ella reza ahora mismo una oración heroica a lo divino, que está partida en el gajo de la Aleluya y el gajo de la pesadumbre, en el gozo de su alumbramiento y la humillación del ámbito desnudo. Y el lugar donde ocurre lo que digo no es el arenal asiático ni el africano, sino que es la América nuestra de la abundancia botánica, del bosque maderero, del río amazónico y del sol más creador que conozcan los ojos humanos.*

Christ's divinity and innocence suffuse every child, as the "Romance de Nochebuena" (p. 356) suggests:

> *Vamos a buscar*
> *dónde nació el Niño:*
> *nació en todo el mundo,*
> *ciudades, caminos ...*

Peasant stock burdened by the onus of color, poverty, and prejudice is no less divine because of humble beginnings. On the contrary, the poet believes that the peasant's halo is more glorious because the struggle to attain it is more intense. In a sharp allusion to her own status, she said that poverty and humble birth — that is, low economic and social status — do not necessarily mean an enslaved spirit. Theosophy does not abrogate economic poverty, but neither does it try to inure man to that fate. Theosophy teaches the poor that desire begets anguish, that detachment from material objects is conducive to a spiritual life. Thus the poverty-stricken may undeceive themselves about false illusions of wealth and also about the equally deceptive pleasures of a paradise where angels sing and trumpets blare."[62]

Not only is the dignity of the humbly born at stake. In recognizing that the poor may emulate Buddha or Christ, the poet is also attempting to disabuse the rich, the powerful, and the clergy of their exclusive right to God. No human being is entitled to dispense divinity, nor is godliness the privilege of the few. Rather each individual may strive to develop the God-spirit that dwells within:

> *El Reino de los Cielos no vendrá con señales o demostraciones externas. No dirán.—'Helo aquí,' o 'helo allá.' Porque el Reino de los Cielos está dentro de vosotros.*[63]

To this end, Theosophy's claim to the possibility of the knowledge of God "as the inevitable result of the immanence of God" captured Mistral's imagination.[64]

This doctrine leads to the discovery of the true nature of the individual, and thence to the discovery of the nature of God. By disregarding the paraphernalia of religion and by emphasizing the inner life, man may seek God within himself without recourse to intercessors and dogmatic theology. By probing deep, he may transcend the body, the emotions, the passions, and the intellect, and realize his separability from, yet unity with, these faculties. When he has discovered the pure "I," his own pure being, he may be said to have found the God-spirit that resides within all matter. And since, according to this doctrine, "there is but one life in all forms, all forms must be interrelated."

>   *Árbol que no eres otra cosa*
>   *que dulce entraña de mujer,*
>   *pues cada rama mece airosa*
>   *en cada leve nido un ser:*
>   . . . .
>   *haz que a través de todo estado*
>   *— niñez, vejez, placer, dolor —*
>   *levante mi alma un invariado*
>   *y universal gesto de amor.*
>   ("Himno al árbol," p. 349)

This poem illustrates, in conclusión, that the individual partakes of the qualities of the Universal Spirit, and is thereby united with God. Man is bound to all other creatures that are also emanations from the Universal Self in an amalgam of universal brotherhood.

Mary and the baby Jesus—Jews by culture and history—were intentionally omitted from the preceding chapter, "The Hebraic Tradition." The Marian theme could have been placed in the section on Old Testament women and discussed along with the study of infertility and spiritual anguish. But it would have been incongruous to introduce the Virgin Mary among Biblical women who sought, not only the divine hand of God, but also the physical touch of men. In the first place, Mary never felt the blight of God's rejection, which would tend to contrast her life with the intense drama in the lives of some of the Old Testament heroines. But a more crucial reason separates Mary from the others: "To the Jew, maternity not virginity, was praiseworthy, and to him the thought of Jehovah becoming incarnate would be incredible; in fact, the Virgin-birth, so far from being an invention of Jewish Christians, must have been a severe stumbling-block to them in accepting their new faith."[65] How did this concept take root? In A.D. 431, the Council of Ephesus declared the concept of the virgin birth in order to show Mary free of sin, including intercourse, menstrual flow, and afterbirth.[66]

For these reasons, perhaps, Gabriela Mistral's poetry underplays Mary's importance. She appears in the poetry among barn animals, clumsy and unaccustomed to her task, rather than as the medieval painters conceived of her, adorned with a nimbus and in regal vestments:

> *Y la Virgen, entre cuernos*
> *y resuellos blanquecinos,*
> *trastocada iba y venía*
> *sin poder coger al Niño.*
> *Y José llegaba riendo*
> *a acudir a la sin tino.*
> ("El establo," p. 184)

Gabriela again tries to erase the stereotype of the Nativity scene in "Recado de Navidad," an essay that might have been based on "El establo," by painting a grotesque portrait of the stable. "Dung," "dirty water," and "Joseph's dirty tunic" are backdrops for the Three Kings and their gifts of "frankincense, myrrh, and gold":

> *La escena de la noche 1948-ava, de rara se pasa a grotesca: hay en aquel establo el estiércol desparramado y el agua turbia, por servida, del abrevadero y brillan aquí y allá unas copas llenas de incienso, mirra y oro. La túnica sucia de José se roza con las mangazas de los Reyes y la pelambre de los animales.*[67]

Gabriela does not treat Mary with disrespect, but neither is Mary the creature of a papal enactment or a stylized painting. Mary is unique because she symbolizes the divine essence. No woman, however humble—as Mary is represented here—need feel that a child is the fruit of a fortuitous act or an unresponsive God.

The poet's characterization of the Virgin as a clumsy and inept peasant woman contrasts sharply with Mary's position as a delicate and somewhat embarrassed saint in the ensuing panegyric:

> *¡Virgen de las Vírgenes! Ningún rostro de mujer más confuso que el tuyo en la hora de la Anunciación. Tu sonrojo todavía tiñe nuestro paisaje y la zozobra de tu corazón estremece nuestra agua.*[68]

Gabriela reiterates her constant attitude that fecundity is a sign of divine blessing. Even more praiseworthy is divine motherhood, here accepted humbly and with serenity, because it distinguishes Mary from the virgin saints:

> *Las demás vírgenes, las de todos los tiempos, numerosos como los tallos de cuarenta primaveras fundidas, se ajan de humillación: ellas también entraron íntegras en el aire del cielo; pero su vientre no oyó el propio vagido y tuvieron la castidad de los metales. Por eso ellas ahora te hacen un tapiz extendido debajo de las plantas y tú las huellas, con el peso de tu cuerpo, que soporta al Niño.*

In both instances Mistral's unconcern for Mary's outward physical opulence further enhances the Virgin's spiritual inner richness. Yet this last version does not dwell on malodorous animals and exaggerated poverty, but instead concerns itself with hyperdulia, the veneration of Mary by exalting her above all things, persons, and heavenly hosts:

> *Tú eres la Virgen, intocada como las grutas que no acaban, intocada como el fondo del mar que no conoce la atmósfera. Pero más intocada aún que cuantas cosas puras hace la Tierra; más que el fruto que se seca en la frente del árbol y que recibió la palpitación de la siesta.*

The poet dematerializes and turns into abstractions all physical objects to show Mary's transformation from an ordinary woman into the exalted Virgin-Mother, an example of virtue and beauty to both human beings and the angels.

Esoteric Theosophy holds to the solar theory of the birth of a mythic Christ. The sun had always exercised a hypnotic effect on primitive religions, and the theory prevailed that the sun was in fact an incarnation of the Logos, or that it stood for the Logos.[69] In brief, Theosophy maintains that the immanent God-spirit residing in man emanates from the Universal Self "as a ray is an emanation from the sun."[70] The self-limiting, but supreme, God also circumscribes the universe, but he is still "present in every current and atom."[71] From the Supreme Trinity the First, Second, and Third Logoi unfold; "...the ranks of secondary Logoi rule congeries of solar systems." In the Mysteries, Christ became associated with the Logos in the sun.[72] Christians began to celebrate the Nativity on the same date as the pagans dedicated themselves to the birth of the sun:

> *[The sun-god] is always born at the winter solstice, after the shortest day in the year, at the midnight of the 24th of December, when the sign Virgo is rising above the horizon; born as this sign is rising, he is born always of a virgin, and she remains a virgin after she has given birth to her Sun-Child, as the celestial Virgo remains unchanged and unsullied when the Sun comes forth from her in the heavens.*[73]

Although the Church sought to dissociate itself from astrological and pagan symbolism, it was inevitable that the invincible sun came to stand for the birth, power, and majesty of Christ[74]: "Then the festival of His nativity became the immemorial date when the Sun was born of the Virgin, when the midnight sky was filled with the rejoicing hosts of the celestials, and 'Very early, very early, Christ was born.'"[75]

This mythical version of Christ's birth inspired Mistral to write "Dos canciones del Zodíaco." The first "Canción" opens with a lament for the lost child of Virgo, the archetype for future Madonnas, who "is represented in ancient drawings as a woman suckling a child"[76]:

> *Un niño tuve al pecho*
> *como una codorniz.*
> *Me adormecí una noche;*

> *no supe más de mí.*
> *Resbaló de mi brazo;*
> *rodó, lo perdí.*[77]
>
> ("Canción de Virgo," pp. 174–175)

After the loss, Virgo travels the heavens to save the babe from certain death:

> *Sed y hambres no sabía*
> *su boca de jazmín;*
> *ni sabía su muerte.*
> *¡Ahora sí, ahora sí!*

In the heavens the child enjoys complete protection and infinite life. The child belongs to one mother, derives from one father:

> *Era el niño de Virgo*
> *y del cielo feliz.*
> *Ahora será el hijo de*
> *Luz o Abigail.*
>
> *Tenía siete cielos;*
> *ahora sólo un país.*
> *Servía al Dios eterno,*
> *ahora a un Kadí.*

The child's fall to earth symbolizes the coming of Christ and, at the same time, the sadness of the mother. The traditional emotional context of the birth of Jesus, acceptance by the Virgin and elation on the part of the child, does not appear.

The second half of this two-part song envisions the mythological Bull transporting the fallen child across the heavens. The last two stanzas apparently indicate that the child is returned to his sleep, to his mother, and to his God[78]:

> *Dormido irás creciendo;*
> *creciendo harás la Ley*
> *y escogerás ser Cristo*
> *o escogerás ser Rey.*
> *Hijito de Dios Padre*
> *en brazos de mujer.*
>
> ("Canción de Taurus," p. 177)

The Bull represents the sacrificial act of Easter, the time when Christ gave up his life to return to the "*siete cielos*" ("seven heavens"), his place of origin.

With the majority of the poems in her second book, *Ternura* (*Tenderness*) these two share three basic themes: fertility, sleep, and fantasy. The poet's initial attempt to create an eternal child takes place, however, in her first book, *Desolación*:

> *¡Un hijo, un hijo, un hijo! Yo quise un hijo tuyo*
> *y mío, allá en los días del éxtasis ardiente....*
> . . . .
> *¡Un hijo con los ojos de Cristo engrandecidos,*
> *la frente de estupor y los labios de anhelo!*
> ("Poema del hijo," p. 102)

The sequels, in *Ternura*, become less frantic and less violent, but not less passionate. Christ as the Agnus Dei enters the body of the expectant mother:

> *Corderito mío,*
> *suavidad callada:*
> *mi pecho es tu gruta*
> *de musgo afelpada.*
> ("Corderito," p. 159)

The miracle of birth is not expressed only in mother and child. Nature itself delights in producing fruit, wheat, corn, and trees. Mother Earth and "*Dios Padre*" embrace frequently in Gabriela Mistral's poetry:

> *Cantemos mientras el tallo*
> *toca el seno maternal.*
> *Bautismo de luz da un rayo*
> *y es el aire su pañal.*
> ("Plantando el árbol," p. 332)

As a result, "*trigo*" and "*maíz*" ("wheat" and "corn") reflect the continuing symbology of God and Christ in all living things: "*...Sol que cría y Sol que dora / y a la Tierra hija de Dios*" (p. 333). The poet mediates between heaven and earth with the life-giving forces that pulsate in the cosmos.[79] From Christ's descent and incarnation through astral myths, to his appearance in Chilean bread, which is called "*cara de Dios*" ("God's face"),[80] there is a flow of divine spirit.

Eastern Theosophy derived from Hinduism and employed its vocabulary while modifying its aims. Buddhism also evolved naturally from the same parent religion, but did not respect its principles. Theosophy was, in many ways, a fad of the late nineteenth and early twentieth centuries; Buddhism, however, antedated Christianity by five hundred years and has persisted. There are two points here. Gabriela Mistral could combine Theosophy and Buddhism, given their common heritage to suit herself. She passed from one to the other and back again because of their similarities. The second point is that Theosophy lost prestige ten years after World War I. Its ideas turned into a spectacular circus in the twenties, acquired an aura of lunacy, placed emphasis on materialism, and finally waned after the death of its leader, Annie Besant.[81] Theosophy's descent into the arena of public attention caused Gabriela Mistral to become disenchanted with its leadership and to have misgivings regarding its claims:

> *La abandoné cuando observé que había entre los teósofos algo de muy infantil y además mucho confusionismo. Pero algo quedó en mí de ese período — bastante largo: quedó la idea de la reencarnación, la cual hasta hoy no puedo—o no sé—eliminar. Cada vez que me confieso, Padre, no soy ayudada respecto de este asunto tan hincado en mí.*[82]

Buddhism, too, for reasons discussed in the final section of this chapter, ceased to attract the poet. Although Theosophy was moribund, its principal aims, as well as those of Buddhism, did not die. She never forgot their ethical principles, their emphasis on reincarnation, nor could she cease to believe in the "nucleus of a Universal Brotherhood of Humanity without distinction of race, creed, sex, caste or colour."[83] Quite the contrary. From 1932, until the end of her life, Gabriela continued to practice with vigor what had started as a personal escape from pain.

Tagore and Universal Harmony

The Uruguayan critic and poet Sarah Bollo states without evidence that devotion to the French poet Leconte de Lisle probably inclined Gabriela toward a belief in Buddhism.[84] It seems more likely that two other poets — Rabindranath Tagore, the Nobel laureate from Bengal (1861–1941), and the Mexican, Amado Nervo (1870–1919) — exercised a stronger influence.[85] Although she had read the French poet and was aware of his philosophy of maya and his oriental pessimism, it is difficult to envisage that his unemotional, Parnassian verse could have had a positive ideological influence on her. Gabriela absorbed the message of poets only to the extent that it reflected her own sentiments. Virtually the whole of her poetry possesses a romantic or a personal note: emotionalism, anthropomorphism, the pathetic fallacy, a close tie with contemporary national problems, and a certain bluntness of expression. These elements are surely contrary to the goals of Leconte de Lisle. An ideological influence would have had to have come through his poetry, and this does not seem possible in view of their divergence of theme and sentiment. Tagore, however, according to Gabriela's own confession, helped to shape her teaching, thought, feelings, and poetry.[86]

It is important to state at the outset how Tagore, who was not a Buddhist, but belonged to the "reformist Hindu sect of Brahmos,"[87] united the transcendentalism and universalism of the "Upanishads" with the Buddhist harmony of all living things.[88] Tagore took the song, the myth, and the poetry from the Vaishnava ritual and disregarded the theological demands of formal religion. He was a free spirit, a world-wanderer like Gabriela, able and willing to taste of multiple experiences. And this Hindu mystic poet could recognize the virtues Buddhism professed without feeling disgraced, without betraying his own religion, because he had loose ties with Hinduism.

The following stanza of Tagore's "The Earth" shows him on a quest for spiritual union with other beliefs:

> I wish at heart I could
> Live with different races of mankind
> In different lands, as their kith and kin:
> I wish I were an Arab, desert-bred,
> Fed on the camel's milk, untamed and free!
> That I lived at the foot of Tibet's peaks
> Secluded in some town of stone, and moved
> Freely among Buddhist shrines.[89]

In the quest for the "emancipation of consciousness,"[90] man fuses with the fleeting forms of the world and discovers in that fusion wholeness, completion, and then the meaning of beauty. Man not only discovers, thereby, the truth that binds the universe. He also learns through his emotions and feelings the higher truth of love and world harmony between one man and another. It is thus that the Hindu and the Buddhist come together, and it is precisely this harmony that Gabriela recognized in Tagore's poetry and assimilated into her own.

The harmony in question took many forms. Both poets allied themselves with the youth of their respective countries to found schools, establish libraries, and maintain the freedom of education. With regard to this, Gabriela wrote, in a translation to French:

> *L'éstime où je tiens l'école Tagorienne [Santiniketan] est une attitude logique de mon ésprit, car en elle se fondent mon amour de la nature, de l'Esprit et de l'art, les trois forces que le poète a appelées à collaborer à son oeuvre.*[91]

She complemented her inspired teaching with articles she wrote to better the spiritual climate of education. Years before representing Chile on the Children's Relief Committee of the United Nations Economic and Social Council, she had waged her personal battle against cruelty to children by offering the royalties from sales of *Tala* (Buenos Aires: Editorial Sur, 1938), to orphans of Basque descent who became refugees after German Stuka dive bombers had destroyed unyielding Guernica (1937) with Generalíssimo Francisco Franco's blessing in the Spanish Civil War (1936–1939). As if sacrificing the royalties were insufficient, she also politicked to have the orphaned Basque children transported to Chile. The double action served to emphasize, once again, the role of the secular (money and politics) and the sacred (safeguarding innocence). For in rescuing and saving children Mistral and Tagore found the potential realization of their messianic dreams of universal understanding among men of all nations, of frankness born of innocence, of the unsullied spirit seeking purification through life's experiences, and of a world that begins with animal instinct and gradually molds itself through love to beget love in turn.

The mention of *Tala* in this section on Theosophy leads to a useful digression. The esteemed critic Julio Saavedra Molina defined the title as "*llanura*" ("flat plain"), a term that he claimed derives from the Sanskrit word *tala-ö*, "*lengua madre de la teosofía, ... ya que su Tala tiene de llanura, plano astral, desolación y angustia.*"[92] That novel connotation leads to other possibilities. The *Vox Spanish-English Dictionary* offers two definitions of "*tala*" in English that have closer relevance: (1) "havoc" and (2) "clearing of the forest for new planting." Either one seems more convincing than that offered by Saavedra Molina. The title *Tala*, meaning "havoc," could apply to the consequences of the Civil War that was afflicting Spain and its people. But the second definition appears closer to the text and the beliefs of the poet. *Tala* symbolizes a "new planting," a renewal of faith and confidence, possible by a metaphorical hewing down of the sacrificial Cross without denying her Christian spirit. By 1938, she had cut away major sentimental ties with the past: the Chilean motherland, her mother and sister, and the self-absorbed poetry of her first two books, *Desolación* (1922, 1923), and *Ternura* (1924). Her poetic mission no longer exclusively reflected the Chilean landscape or a personal tormented inscape. Instead, she looked beyond Chile, in this period, to European problems of war and peace, and to the pre–Columbian native cultures, where the past informed the present, so that the race and the individual might find their roots. *Tala,* meaning a "clearing of the forest," could also extend to divestment of the leaden body, "*la cobra*" ("the yoke strap"), as Gabriela called the mass that bound her to earthly matter. *Tala*, its possible etymological ties to Theosophy in Sanskrit notwithstanding, signified, to this reader anyway, the transformation of her poetry in form, sentiment, and substance.

Gabriela's suite of "Rondas" invites children of all lands to dance in rounds, with hands clasped in friendship, as in "Dame la mano" ("Give me Your Hand," p. 217):

> *Dame la mano y danzaremos;*
> *dame la mano y me amarás.*
> *Como una sola flor seremos,*
> *como una flor, y nada más ...*

The "Rondas" express the spirit of oneness between man and man, and between man and nature; unity is achieved by sharing similar aspects of nature.[93] The common, unifying element here is a positive act of love, symbolized by hands joined in friendship. And once the dance is in motion, names and faces blur, blend, and become unimportant:

> *Te llamas Rosa y yo Esperanza;*
> *pero tu nombre olvidarás,*
> *porque seremos una danza*
> *en la colina, y nada más ...*
> (p. 217)

Individuation, the source of selfishness, the obstacle to God, yields to self-effacement and group harmony.[94] Immersed in the rhythm, the dancers have no need to voice their love aloud; sense perception diminishes; all outside feeling is banished in preparation for the divine host, Jesus:

> *Danzando, danzando,*
> *la viviente fronda no lo oyó*
> *venir y entrar en la ronda.*
> *Ha abierto el corro, sin rumor,*
> *y al centro está hecho resplandor.*
> ("Jesús," p. 231)

In that same vein is "El corro luminoso" ("The Luminous Chorus"), where a flower is formed, composed of dancers, which blooms on a desert floor:

> *En la tierra yerma,*
> *sobre aquel desierto mordido de sol,*
> *¡mi corro de niñas como inmensa flor!*
> (p. 241)
>
> . . . .
>
> *En la estepa inmensa,*
> *en la estepa*
> *yerta de desolación,*
> *¡mi corro de niñas*
> *ardiendo de amor!*
> (p. 242)

To the image of whirling children transformed into a living flower, the poet adds, by way of contrast, parched land that is incapable of sustaining life. But love is the life spirit of the unified "children-flower," making it a hardy perennial, self-sustaining and self-creating even on barren land.

In a concluding example, "Todo es ronda" ("Everything is a Round," p. 240), the poet envisions a world order whose unifying force is expressed in the "ronda de niños":

> *Los astros son rondas de niños,*
> *jugando la tierra a espiar ...*

> *Los trigos son talles de niñas*
> *jugando a ondular, a ondular ...*
>
> *Los ríos son rondas de niños*
> *jugando a encontrarse en el mar ...*
> *Las olas son rondas de niñas*
> *jugando la Tierra a abrazar ...*

On a cosmic scale, the great elements pulsate in unison. And by equating the stars, the vegetable world ("*trigo*"), the rivers and waves with the "*rondas,*" the poet minifies nature, making it accessible to man, and, more importantly, she affirms that nature can reflect human harmony. She does this by defining the goals of nature in terms of the verb "*jugar*" (to play), which at once removes the mystery inherent in nature and reduces the unknown to the knowable, the hostile to the friendly, namely, to a children's game pervaded by peace and love.

The three "Comentarios a poemas de Rabindranath Tagore" gloss three prose poems of Gitanjali.[95] In the first gloss, "*Sé que también amaré la muerte*" ("I Know that I Shall Love Death"), Gabriela diverges markedly from Tagore's sentiment and philosophy. Where Tagore is delicate, almost feminine, in his expression, Gabriela is forceful, virile, and prone to overstatement. She describes death as "*...un tremendo ardor que desgaja y desmenuza las carnes, para despeñarnos caudalosamente el alma*" ("...a tremendous burning that breaks and crumbles flesh, in order to fling abundantly before us our soul"). And again death is God's terrible love, which she describes relentlessly, shamelessly, as broken bones, a livid face, and a weary tongue: "*Es tu amor, es tu terrible amor, ¡oh Dios! ¡Así deja rotos y vencidos los huesos, lívida de ansia la cara y desmadejada la lengua!*" Death, for the Bengali poet, in contrast, has no more violence than that evidenced by the child who "cries out when from the right breast the mother takes it away, in the very next moment to find in the left one its consolation."

Tagore says, "And because I love this life, I know I shall love death as well."[96] Gabriela holds no such premise, because her life did not abound with joy, rather, it was a struggle against heavy odds. And so she focuses on the second half of Tagore's line and, in so doing, emphasizes further that death offers the only solution to weariness. Death erases wounds and assures a union with God. She justifies salvation after death by affirming that the existence of the living body, created out of God's infinite care and wisdom, proves his love: "*¿Para qué derramarías la luz cada mañana sobre mis sienes y mi corazón, si no fueras a recogerme como se recoge el racimo negro melificado al sol, cuando ya media el otoño?*" The argument is, of course, circular. It does not follow logically (granted that God exists metaphorically and poetically, and is capable of such feats), that because He gives life, God will save those he has created from total annihilation after the body has crumbled and decayed. But love solves the enigma, because love is the preservative. Death is another form of love, another step in man's existence where, devoid of his body, his soul lives on, protected by God's love. For without the feeling that in death she will succeed in uniting with God (since union is impossible or nonexistent in life), and without the will to believe in the salvation of her soul (since her body is a tortured, useless weight in life and in death subject to destruction), she would see only total pessimism.

Although elements of Buddhism are present, the poet's view of death is, of course, not entirely Buddhist. Buddhism is atheistic. Thus no God exists to save souls. Only man himself can prepare the way for salvation by following the eightfold path prescribed by Buddha. No preparation of this sort is present in Gabriela's "Comentarios." There is an appeal to God through questions, and the questioner's self-righteousness precludes humility. Such an appeal has no place in Buddhism. The desire for the immortality of the soul and Gabriela's negation of the suffering body are, however, reminiscent of Buddhist philosophy.

Tagore's prose poem begins: "I boasted among men that I had known you" (No. CII, p. 37). In it, he affirms that he may create everlasting songs about God but, truly, God is incapable of direct explanation. The result is that men in quest of divine knowledge scorn the poet who, in despair, ironically laments to God, "And you sit there smiling."

Gabriela's version includes these facets. In addition, though, there is a curious statement. She actually imputes to the mass of men the desire to know God, and describes God in poetic imagery, ostensibly for their edification. In reality, she herself aspires to this knowledge. Aware that poetry offers no guarantee for communication with God, she attempts to leap beyond all power of discernment to reproduce the unknowable in terms of human qualities, to ascribe to God manlike characteristics, to listen to her own heartbeat and conjure up wings in flight: "*Pero, tú que comprendes te sonríes con una sonrisa llena de dulzura y de tristeza a la par.*" Here, the poet seeks God actively and openly, albeit futilely. He is a god with manlike attributes, created to replace the God that can never come. This manlike god, more man than god, is born of impatience and feverish human desires: "*Lo sabes bien: la espera enloquece y el silencio crea ruidos en torno de los oídos febriles.*" The poet believes this god's voice emanates from the inner whisper. But here is another fiction, a reflection of self, born of desperate measures to corporealize and animate the nonmaterial. In retrospect, there is a conflict between a god of manlike proportions — as in the veiled reference to the half-smiling, but inscrutable, Buddha, with all the attributes of man but none of his warmth — and the God whose presence can only be felt and whose existence cannot, therefore, be verified.

The last "Comentario" by Gabriela stresses the nature of man's dilemma before God's awesome power (No. VI, p. 4). On the one hand, man is insignificant: "*Verdad es que aún no estoy en sazón, que mis lágrimas no alcanzarían a colmar el cuenco de tus manos.*" Insignificant man is also dispensable, a throwaway: "*Verdad es también que no haré falta para tus harinas celestiales; verdad es que en tu pan no pondré un sabor nuevo.*" The negatives and imploring tone suggest self-ridicule and humility. On the other hand, man seeks God's attention to avoid oblivion: "*Por esto quiero suplir con el canto mi pequeñez, sólo por hacerte volver el rostro si me dejas perdida, ¡oh, mi Segador extasiado!*" Aware of God's invisible hand in the welfare of defenseless creatures, the poet fervently believes herself in God's care after death: "*—Así me recogerá, como a la gotita trémula antes de que me vuelva fango: así como al pájaro se cuidará de la última hora.*" Thus the poet's conception of life and death presented here emphasizes the worthlessness of the individual body during a lifelong adoration of God. In contrast, she has faith that in death she will flower under God's protective hand. Death, then, relieves man of the ignominy of having to live tied to a body, of having to abide materialism: "*No tengo raíces clavadas en esta tierra de los hombres.*"

In conclusion, the three "Comentarios" represent a plea to an all-knowing, all-seeing, but unresponsive, God. In spite of silence and the implication of abandonment, Gabriela remains steadfast in her adoration. To mitigate the pain caused by trying to express the ineffable and to know the unknowable, she endows God with human attributes (anthropopathy) and thus makes him at once more understandable and less remote. She comprehends fully that God stems from man's inner voice, that he is describable only in human terms. She also knows that oneness with God, in which she achieves a modicum of respite from pain, is only temporary. Yet she prefers the existence of God, along with the pain, to the blight of a godless world. Without the illusion that a supreme deity exists, neither life nor death would be bearable. In the final "Comentario," the poet has no doubt that God exists, because she has perceived his mode of existence:

> *Mas, ¡de vivir atenta a tus movimientos sutiles, te conozco tantas ternuras que me hacen confiar! Yo te he visto, yendo de mañana por el campo.... Te he visto asimismo, dejar disimuladas en el enredo de las zarzamoras las hebras para el nido del tordo.*

Tagore also captures beautifully the sentiment of religious simplicity which characterizes Gabriela's poetry: "My song has put off her adornments. She has no pride of dress and decoration. Ornaments would mar our union; they would come between me and thee; their jingling would drown thy whispers" (p. 5). Like Gabriela, in worship he eschews formal practices. God is not in the darkened temple: "He is there where the tiller is tilling the hard ground and where the pathmaker is breaking stones" (p. 6). Elegant words and priests ought not to be an impediment to communication between the poet and God. Tagore's influence on Gabriela was not insignificant. She lived with his message of love and his spirit of peace, finding in this kindred soul an affirmation of her own desire for spiritual love.

Nervo and Bergson: A New Synthesis

Mistral allied herself with the "pained" and "serene" Mexican mystic poet, Amado Nervo, "*el místico dolorido y sereno*," whom she eulogized as "*el Tagore de América*."[97] By comparing Nervo with Tagore, Gabriela clearly underscored her common bonds with both of them. All three fervently renounced dogmatic theology and priests; they believed in a universal spirit of love that encompassed all things and all men; they had an abiding affection for children. What is more, in their deeds and beliefs, Tagore and Nervo veered the Chilean poet to a course of action and a philosophy of religion which led her away from proscriptive religion to a view of God, the universe, life, and death which was consistent with Theosophy and Buddhism.

According to the Uruguyan poet Sarah Bollo, the study of Buddhism caused torment in the poet's soul because it separated her from Christ and purely Christian ideas.[98] On the contrary, Christ was never dismissed from either her life or her poetry during her Buddhist phase, as Mistral herself confessed: "*...yo me interné un tiempo en el budismo, pero viviendo* una *experiencia difícil de contar: la de no haber eliminado nunca los gérmenes cristianos más fundamentales.*"[99] Bollo's criticism errs, on the one hand, by deriding Gabriela's adoption of Buddhism as transitory or inconsequential and, on the other, by disregarding the fact that Gabriela studied Buddhism because Catholicism placed stronger emphasis on the need for suffering. Even when Bollo admits to Gabriela's interest in Buddhism, she plays down its importance, as in this comparison with Amado Nervo who was also a Theosophist and Buddhist: "*...agudo problematismo transcendente mezclado a insinuaciones búdicas, más fuertes en Nervo que en Gabriela.*"[100] It is true that Nervo's Buddhist leanings were more overt, as is evidenced in "Místicas," "Las voces," and *El estanque de los lotos*. Still, Gabriela's interest in it was no mere flirtation. Sarah Bollo's remarks are like many others by Catholics who, upon discovering the presence of Buddhism in Gabriela Mistral's life, have declared it insignificant or a sign of frivolous "*herejías*" ("heresies"). She believed in karma for twenty years; she practiced Yoga. This is evidence enough that it is necessary to take her affinity with Buddhism seriously.

A number of parallels exist between Nervo and Mistral which tend to confirm her closeness to the mystic poet-philosopher. For one thing, she imagined that his emotional sensitivity paralleled her own, and that she could find release from suffering through his poetry.[101] This relationship is nowhere better expressed than in a letter to him: "*Le hallo a usted, Amado Nervo, en cada día y en cada llanto mío. Con sus versos en los labios fui yo hacia el amor, ellos me ayudaron a sollozar 'de modo sosegado y acerbo.'*" Surprised that Nervo was grateful for her favorable comments on his poetry, Gabriela continued feeling, instead, grateful to him:

> *¿Es ironía, Amado Nervo? ¡Usted agradecido de mí! ¡Es un colmo! ¿Qué habría entonces de mí hacia usted, a quien debo el alma posiblemente tanto como a Dios, o más, ya que esta alma mía de hoy es otra cosa que la que traje a la vida y le hallo a usted a cada instante en sus pliegues recónditos?*[102]

To honor Nervo's death, Mistral wrote the poetic elegy, "In memoriam" (pp. 22–23):

> *De donde tú cantabas se me levantó el día.*
> *Cien noches con tu verso yo me he dormido en paz.*
> *Aun era heroica y fuerte, porque aún te tenía;*
> *sobre la confusión tu resplandor caía.*
> *¡Y ahora tú callas, y tienes polvo, y no eres más!*

Although the two poets never met, Mistral proposed, in her poem, a meeting beyond time and space, where two lonely souls might find peace on the astral plane:

> *Aún me quedan jornadas bajo los soles. ¿Cuándo*
> *verte, dónde encontrarte y darte mi aflicción,*
> *sobre la Cruz del Sur que me mira temblando,*
> *o más allá, donde los vientos van callando,*
> *y, por impuro, no alcanzará mi corazón?*

And she urges Nervo to shout to God, in whose shade he will rest, what they both have experienced: orphanhood, solitude, and a death wish: "*...que somos huérfanos, que vamos solos, que tú nos viste, / ¡que toda carne con angustia pide morir!*" While the idea of an astral meeting is reminiscent of Theosophy, terrene anguish suggests, in Buddhistic terms, man's inability to diminish his sense of pain and loneliness by appealing to a god. Because Buddhism is atheistic, man controls the quality of his present and future destiny by proper living. For it is not the life of this world he seeks, but the serenity of the afterlife, presumably guaranteed by his righteous acts and his self-denial. Yet neither Nervo nor Mistral rejected the encounter with Jesus Christ or God the Father. Although both had disavowed the Catholic Church and its dogmas, Nervo for faith in the power of rationalism (which he eventually spurned), and Mistral for rational inquiry into Theosophy, neither completely gave up belief in Jesus Christ as God.[103] They lived in the shadow of his suffering, accepting pain as a necessary concomitant of life and love.[104]

Nervo's walk with Buddha led to a continual ascension along the mystic path: "*...melancolía, despego de lo mundano, anhelo de perfección.*"[105] In the poem, "Las voces,"[106] Nervo professes the Buddhist principles of self-denial and stoicism, the fraternity of all living things, the struggle for the eradication of consciousness when the latter impedes a spiritual alliance with the One and the All by focusing on the materiality of existence. Although *El estanque de los lotos* (*The Lotus Pond*) seems to announce Nervo's complete absorption into Buddhism, two factors must be noted. First, Nervo never ceased to believe in Christ, because he saw in Christ divine perfection. Second, Nervo had more sympathy for Buddhism as a literary theme than as a personal religion.[107]

The preceding paragraph, except for the last sentence, could apply as well to Gabriela Mistral. In contrast with Nervo's poetry, hers has few unmistakable references to Buddhism. In the main, what appears as a phenomenon of Buddhism could also be interpreted as a characteristic of Christianity.[108] In secular practices of meditation, Gabriela believed the purificatory acts of Buddhism to be essential to an abatement of grief and to an understanding of the nature of man:

> ... *en verdad lo que influyó más en mí bajo este budismo nunca absoluto, fue la meditación de tipo oriental, mejor dicho, la escuela que ella me dio para llegar a una verdadera concentración. Nunca le recé a Buda; sólo medité con seriedad las manifestaciones de este mundo, la indecible superficialidad de la vida americana toda y más tarde la de la vida europea.*[109]

If this, written in 1953, is to be taken as the final statement of her relationship with Buddhism, it is clear that she did not consider herself adept in all phases of this philosophy.

Investigation reveals that Gabriela Mistral became less antipathetic to Catholicism and the Church after 1924, and that she sought a purer Christianity, undiluted by Buddhism. An autobiographical note offers a significant clue to a religious crisis after 1929, attendant upon the death of her mother. She subsequently realized that blind hate for Chile and its institutions had motivated her estrangement, from her country and its religion, and had caused sharp personal distress:

> *Ella [Chile] se me volvió una larga y sombría posada; se me hizo un país en que viví cinco o siete años, país amado a causa de la muerta, odioso a causa de la volteadura de mi alma en una larga crisis religiosa. No son ni buenos ni bellos los llamados "frutos del dolor" y a nadie se los deseo.*
>
> *De regreso de esta vida en la más prieta tiniebla, vuelvo a decir, como al final de* **Desolación**, *la alabanza de la alegría. El tremendo viaje acaba en la*

> *esperanza de las "Locas letanías" y cuenta su remate a quienes se cuidan de mí alma y poco saben de mí desde que vivo errante.*[110]

Gabriela severed past ties after 1929 with Buddhism. By so doing she achieved, paradoxically, a catharsis that diminished her disgust for Chile and obviated self-flagellation, which in turn made her less dependent on Buddhism and Yoga for surcease from pain.

In 1935, Gabriela Mistral tersely stated that she admired Buddhism, but no longer followed it: "*Admiro, sin seguirlo, el budismo; por algún tiempo cogió mi espíritu.*"[111] And in the 1940's she made a comment about her twenty-year commitment to Buddhism, karma, and subsequently her evolution away from it: "*Yo fui budista durante más de veinte anos; creía en el karma de los orientales, como otros creen en los Moiras de la Mitología. Fui una buena budista, pero evolucioné, así lo creo.*"[112] Paralleling each of these two negative reactions to Buddhism were positive feelings for Christianity: "*Soy cristiana, de democracia total.*" Matilde Ladrón de Guevara records the following words of Gabriela Mistral:

> *[No] suponga que yo soy anticatólica. ¡ Al contrario ... ! Soy cristiana y creyente, pero tengo una concepción muy personal sobre la religión.... Sólo sé decirle que no soy dogmática y que le rezo a Dios, es decir le hablo a Dios muy a mi manera.*[113]

It will be remembered that González Vera attributed Mistral's evolution from Theosophy and Buddhism to Christianity to a deeper sympathy for the Church after the Guerra Cristera in Mexico. The same critic also referred, in passing, to neo–Catholic authors ("*lecturas de escritores neocatólicos*"), which reshaped her philosophy of religion.[114] In this vein, the Puerto Rican author Margot Arce de Vázquez specified that Henri Bergson's *Les Deux Sources de la morale et de la réligion* had a decisive effect on the poet and her reaffirmation of Jesus Christ ("*...vida futura en la paz de Cristo*").[115] Henri Bergson (1859–1941) published *Les Deux Sources* in 1932. Gabriela must have read it during the period of religious crisis brought on by the death of her mother (1929), and by her own physical and spiritual estrangement from Chile. Bergson's philosophy not only provided sufficient bases for rejecting Buddhism (which Gabriela must have been prepared to do in any event), but, more important, his dynamic Christianity offered a new synthesis between Catholicism and Buddhism. It would enlighten the discussion to examine *Les Deux Sources* for a rationale that could have prompted Gabriela to reject Buddhism and to reaffirm the Christian faith.

As a point of departure, an important aspect of Amado Nervo's religious dilemma illustrates Gabriela Mistral's involvement with Buddhism and with Bergson. Nervo was, for a time, unable to reconcile the contradictions inherent in the "God of Christianity, the World-Soul of Pantheism, and the Absolute of Philosophy.[116] He tried, unsuccessfully, to balance and assimilate Christian ideas, monism, and rationalism. With the discovery of "Bergsonism," because Nervo was more interested in method and technique than in the core of Bergsonian *durée* and *revolution créatrice*, he believed he had found an approach to resolving spirit, mind, and matter. The revelation that he no longer was enslaved to a mechanistic and deterministic philosophy set Nervo free, restored the sky, to follow Esther Wellman's image, to a man who had been born with wings.[117] Nervo discovered that human consciousness need not be limited by the body, the brain, and the environment. When man lives in duration and not in space, when his acts are more than the sum total of the parts, when his personality and ego have transcendence beyond his finite body, then man is no longer a robot or a chemical equation, and certainly not a spiritual derelict. Obeying a pattern that was the reverse of Gabriela's, Nervo went from Bergson to Buddha. Like Gabriela, Nervo never renounced Christ. At the end of his life, while still imitating Bergson's endless gazes into the future, Nervo was composing *El estanque de los lotos* with its emphasis on renunciation and love, also prime tenets of Christianity.[118] Unlike Gabriela, Nervo feared to reject any philosophy, perhaps because of the dread of being in error, or his inability to hate anything or anybody. "His sense of the infinite apparently demanded an emotion which contradicted neither his skepticism nor his mysticism. And not only that — but Nervo sought that common ground which exists in the most highly generalized ethics. It was a realm inclusive enough [to permit] ... all his Buddhism, and his Greek Philosophy, and his Christianity [to] ... exist side by side."[119] It is difficult to speculate as to what Nervo's resolution of the problem would have been had he lived to understand Bergson's final position on Buddhism and Christianity in *Les Deux Sources*.

It is not my purpose to challenge Bergson for disclaiming Buddhism in favor of a mystic Christianity, but rather to discover his reasons for doing so, and in this way to provide analogous reasons for Gabriela Mistral to follow the same path.[120] His first argument arises from the atheistic nature of Buddhism. Buddha rejected on principle the myriad gods of Brahmanism before whom worshipers fawningly dedicated themselves to buy redemption through the priestly caste. Buddhism disavowed these "miraculous" gods, believing they too needed deliverance, in favor of man, who could earn spiritual elevation and physical tranquility through a renunciation of desire and dishonesty. While Buddha's ethic is praiseworthy, Bergson believes that a fundamental of religious belief is the incarnation of the Good in humans who seek to reflect the perfection of a supreme God. By definition, he rejects Buddhistic atheism. In his second argument, Bergson attributes to Buddhism — and to oriental religions in general — a passiveness and a skepticism that vitiate active participation in bettering society through technological means. Because Buddhism exalts individual responsibility and personal salvation, and not collective salvation, and because Buddhism has fostered quietism and resignation, millions are helplessly enslaved in pessimism. Bergson would substitute dynamic Christianity for Buddhist passivity. The economic and political advantages of the West could then accrue to the mass of people still doomed under a system that reconciles the poverty-stricken to irremediable suffering by making them insensitive to the virtues of material success.[121]

In the next chapter, "The Poetry of Sacrifice," Gabriela Mistral's pursuit of her vision of the sacredness of God, Jesus Christ, and Christianity in her attitude and thought will be examined as it manifests itself in the seemingly secular objects in her poetry and prose.

CHAPTER XIV

The Poetry of Sacrifice

The Paradoxical Universality of Christian Sacrifice

Allusions to Jesus Christ's sacrifice and pain characterize Gabriela Mistral's poetry. They appear mainly in *Desolacion,* but also inhabit other volumes. Rather than point to these allusions in individual volumes, I have found it advantageous to group them according to theme, type, or idea. Their poetic intent and their function can thus be discussed within definite categories. This arrangement unifies the works and brings order and sense out of poems written at different times and under varying circumstances. These groupings show that Gabriela's poetry develops also within definable linguistic patterns. The rearrangement demonstrates the nuances of a mode of expression, a metaphor, or an analogy. The reader, thus, can compare juxtapositions and similar elements in the whole corpus. The motive, then, borrowing a key phrase from the New School critic Austin Warren's thoughts on the duty of the critic is a "rage for order, a passionate desire to discover, by analysis and comparison, the systematic vision of the world which is the poet's construction, his equivalent of a philosophical or other conceptual system."[1]

The continual reference to the actions of Jesus Christ to represent sacrifice suggests the poet's assimilation of the philosophical and religious sense of Jesus' act. Neither coincidence nor whim guided her in recreating Jesus' sacrifice. Instead, she was influenced by Annie Besant's Theosophical comments in "The Mystic Christ" and in "The Atonement," which derived from her articles and from her book *Esoteric Christianity.*[2] The poet invested her creations with the theories of this Theosophist. Mistral was attracted to Besant's "Law of Sacrifice" [which] underlies our system and all systems, and on it all universes are builded." Besant goes on to say that "all the great religions of the world have declared that the universe begins by an act of sacrifice, and have incorporated the idea of sacrifice into their most solemn rites" (p. 200). More specifically, only when the deity has limited his presence, circumscribed his power, voluntarily destroyed some part of what he might have had, does he become manifest (p. 201).

Sacrifice is inherent and perpetual in the universe, according to Besant's following concept:

> Mineral is sacrificed to vegetable, vegetable to animal, both to man, men to men, and all the higher forms again break up and reinforce again with their separated constituents the lowest kingdom. It is a continual sequence of sacrifices from the lowest to the highest, and the very mark of progress is that the sacrifice from being involuntary and imposed becomes voluntary and self chosen, and those who are recognized as greatest by man's heart are the supreme sufferers, those heroic souls who wrought, endured, and died that the race might profit by their pain.
>
> If the world be the work of the Logos, and the law of the world's progress in the whole and the parts is sacrifice, then the Law of Sacrifice must point to something in the very nature of the Logos; it must have its root in the Divine Nature itself [p. 202].[3]

Sacrifice, in short, is the divine "outpouring of Life directed by Love, a voluntary and glad pouring forth of Self for the making of other Selves" (p. 208).

Ultimately, sacrifice brings boundless joy; only in its superficial connotation does it bring pain. When man learns to dissociate from material existence, from the "wasting and changing forms" that continually need replenishment, and to identify with the "growing persistent life," as espoused by the great teachers, then sacrifice becomes an act of joy and not of pain. Only with surrender, first, of debasing human desires (lust, envy, and greed) does man become an Initiate, a *Chrêstos,* who has learned the exoteric doctrine. Then he may aspire to anointment and the status of *Christos,* with total self-surrender whereby everything and everyone is forsaken (p. 173). At this point, man must learn to "become the God to whom he cries, and by feeling the last pang of separation he finds the eternal unity ..." (p. 220). In the paradox of sacrifice [Besant is quoting I Timothy 3:16], "...every son of man may become such a manifested Son of God, such a Saviour of the world" (pp. 225–226). The sacrifice of the Logos is thus reflected in all subsequent attempts by human beings to partake of the divine. Each man must prepare the way for himself, not only by his acts of giving, but also by the selfless attitude that must sustain them. Mrs. Besant sums up: "Every man may work in that direction by making every act and power a sacrifice, until the gold is purged from the dross and only the pure ore remains" (p. 229).

The Passion of Christ and the traditional symbols surrounding his sacrifice form the core of this chapter. Although some of Mistral's references are covert, the majority are explicit. Few are merely decorative, that is, without reference to the poet's personal grief and her feeling of abandonment. It is not necessary to burden the following discussion of the poetry with Gabriela's life and times, because biographical and historical evidence have already made clear the reasons for her personal grief and her desire for sacrifice and love. Germane, and hitherto unexplored, however, are the specific allusions to Christ betrayed, the journey with the Cross to Calvary, the Crucifixion, apparent divine abandonment, the symbolic representations of Christ's body, the esoteric meaning of his wounds, and the Resurrection and Ascension. These allusions are primal in Gabriela Mistral's poetic works.

Betrayal

In "Nocturno," the treachery that has befallen a faithful, but naive, maiden is reenacted in terms of the betrayal of Christ: "*Me vendió el que besó mi mejilla; / me negó por la túnica ruin.*"[4] Judas' motives and those of the maiden's deceitful lover are materialistic. Judas wanted silver; the betrayers [*think* Romelio, Manuel, and Jorge] another woman ("túnica ruin"). Compounded into one image are two separate, but related aspects of Christ's betrayal. One is Judas' perfidy for thirty pieces of silver. The other is Christ's scarlet (or purple) tunic, a gift from the mocking Herod, for which the soldiers eagerly diced once he was on the Cross.[5]

Neither human nor divine love exists in the poet's Gethsemane:

> *Yo en mis versos el rostro con sangre,*
> *como Tú sobre el paño, le di,*
> *y en mi noche del Huerto, me han sido*
> *Juan cobarde y el Angel hostil.*
> ("Nocturno," p. 80)

Like the permanent impression of Christ's bloody face on Veronica's handkerchief, the blood of the poet is etched in her poetry. The same metaphor reaffirms the constancy of pain in life and art for those who are willing to tread the path of Christ — that is, for those who look for love, who find it is either unrequited or impossible, and who then martyrize themselves to prove their faith in an ideal, just, and impersonal belief.

> *Los que cual Cristo hicieron la Vía-Dolorosa,*
> *apretaron el verso contra su roja herida,*
> *y es lienzo de Verónica la estrofa dolorida;*
> *¡todo libro es purpúreo como sangrienta rosa!*
> ("Mis libros," p. 35)

As a corollary, the worse the human deception, the greater the possibility becomes of sharing the pain of Christ. And to this end, the pain endured becomes worthwhile. The poetry, too, as a projection of personal grief, becomes an eternal song when its basis is undiminished human suffering and when it seeks to emulate the sacrifice of Jesus Christ.[6]

At the universal or impersonal level, the poet feels that Christ is abandoned and betrayed every time man thinks of his own pleasures and the myriad joys of life, forgetting that these are made possible only through sacrifice. The supreme sacrifice was made by Christ, and so in "Viernes Santo" Gabriela asks *"el labrador"* ("the farmer") to refrain from thinking about his harvest before pondering the anguish of others in his behalf:

> *No remuevas la tierra. Deja, mansa*
> *la mano y el arado; echa las mieses*
> *cuando ya nos devuelvan la esperanza,*
> *que aun Jesús padece.*
> (p. 10)

In the next stanza, Simon Peter, whose rashness in acting and in boasting of fidelity stands in marked contrast to his denial of his Master,[7] appears identical to many who boast of love and loyalty and yet, when put to the test, are too weak to uphold principles.

The poet also rebukes the impassive unbelievers, incapable of love, hate, or compassion. She calls them, pityingly, *"estas pobres gentes del siglo [que] están muertas / de una laxitud, de un miedo, de un frío"* ("Al oído del Cristo," p. 5). The inability to call forth a spontaneous emotional response, for fear that it might be harmful, is compared with Lazarus' fetid body, entombed for four days and presumably decomposed:

> *Porque como Lázaro ya hieden, ya hieden*
> *por no disgregarse, mejor no se mueven.*
> *¡Ni el amor ni el odio les arrancan gritos!*[8]
> (p.5)

Now, as in Christ's time, people are afraid to acknowledge love and faith. For this reason Christ raised his voice to God and proclaimed at the raising of Lazarus:

> Father, I thank thee that thou hast heard me. And I knew that thou hearest me always: but because of the people which stand by I said *it,* that they may believe that thou hast sent me.[9]

The heartless regard Christ's sacrifice as bad taste, because the spilled blood and mutilated flesh make an unpleasant picture. They believe that the Crucifixion is like a bad play that nobody heeds after the first performance. Gabriela's words are damning:

> *Tienen ojo opaco de infecunda yesca,*
> *sin virtud de llanto, que limpia y refresca;*
> *tienen una boca de suelto botón*

> *mojada en lascivia, ni firme ni roja,*
> *¡y como de fines de otoño, así, floja*
> *e impura, la poma de su corazón!*
> (p. 6)

Underlying godlessness are materialism, pride, and vanity. Material objects are regarded as everlasting; even the body is exalted, so that people become blind to the perishability of their own flesh:

> *Y que, por fin, mi siglo engreído*
> *en su grandeza material,*
> *no me deslumbre hasta el olvido*
> *de que soy barro y soy mortal.*
> ("El himno cotidiano," p. 351)

Death becomes something that afflicts others; or it may become an abstraction, so remote and tangential that time is not available to ponder death. For some, the cessation of life means the beginning of repose and the suspension of pain. Because of this, the tearless and the heartless, the vain and the haughty, do not need God. Gabriela has a different idea about the destiny of those who disregard the essential of love, Christ's first commandment:

> *Y no llames la muerte por clemente,*
> *pues en las carnes de blancura inmensa,*
> *un jirón vivo quedará que siente*
> *la piedra que te ahoga*
> *y el gusano voraz que te destrenza.*
> ("Gotas de hiel," p. 36)

Furthermore, to those who deny compassion to children, the Kingdom of Heaven is closed (see "Piececitos" and "Manitas," pp. 317–320). Men who are insensitive to the demands of the weak and helpless are also impervious to the helpless Christ on the Cross.[10] With justification, Gabriela can affirm the ungrateful do not deserve God's blessing: "—*Ingratos son los hombres, Señor; / no merecen tus gracias.*" Men seek beauty, and when they find it in material objects, then that beauty is destroyed. The rose appeals to God the Father for help:

> *Quisimos ser gratas al hombre y para ello*
> *realizábamos prodigios: abríamos la corola*
> *ampliamente, para dar más aroma:*
> *fatigábamos los tallos a fuerza de chuparles*
> *savia para estar fresquísimas.*
> *Nuestra belleza nos fue fatal.*[11]

Man destroyed the rose, the God-given symbol of beauty with ruthlessness: "*De tus manos salimos hace poco tiempo íntegras y bellas; henos ya mutiladas y míseras.*"

In conclusion, Christ's betrayal by Judas, the poet's by lovers, and that of humanity by individual human beings have happened because deceit is inherent in the human condition. In Jesus' question — "What, could ye not watch with me one hour?"[12] — to the faithful, but drowsy Peter just before the arrival of the Roman soldiers, he was including all the well-intentioned people throughout the ages who have found it to their advantage to care less for others. He included, by definition, the brutes that pass for human beings and continue in their animalistic ways to deny the poor and the weak, and to deny also the essence of humanity, which is love. Those who deny the agonizing Christ, whom Gabriela Mistral portrays, and prefer a Christ with a halo, dressed in finery, cleaned and combed, are the same people who turn their backs on the helpless. The appeal in this poetry is that man return to an awareness of his capacity for sensitivity, for compassion, and for love:

> *¡Oh Cristo! El dolor les vuelva a hacer viva*
> *l'alma que les diste y que se ha dormido,*
> *que se la devuelva honda y sensitiva,*
> *casa de amargura, pasión y alarido.*
> ("Al oído del Cristo," p. 6)

Denial of this facet of man's nature signifies the potential destruction of man himself. Gabriela offers this possibility:

> *¡Retóñalos desde las entrañas, Cristo!*
> *Si ya es imposible, si tú bien lo has visto,*
> *si son paja de eras ... ¡desciende a aventar!*
> (p. 7)

The God of Love becomes for the moment the God of Wrath, more reminiscent of Yahweh than of Christ. But Gabriela still prefers the counsel of Christ, i.e., to turn the other cheek rather than to take an eye for an eye.[13]

Christ and Suffering

Gabriela would have been among the faithful few who did not desert Christ on Golgotha. In another life, she might have stood beside the Marys who watched tearfully from a neighboring hill.[14] Or she might have imagined herself as Veronica. For her devotion to Jesus, and her tendency to think of her sacrifices in terms of his, lead to the imaginative conclusion that she is reliving a deeply felt personal drama in her poetry. The vision of Christ on the Cross is firsthand: "*Está sobre el madero todavía / y sed tremenda el labio le estremece*" ("Viernes Santo," p. 11). The verbs indicate an act simultaneous with the moment of utterance, not only to imply direct observation of the

Crucifixion, but also to bring into relief an ever-present Christ. The "Canto del justo" presents a similar scene, with the poet again as detailed observer, depreciating her own suffering in the face of the immensity of his:

> *Pecho, el de mi Cristo,*
> *más que los ocasos,*
> *más, ensangrentado:*
> *¡desde que te he visto*
> *mi sangre he secado!*
>   (p. 18)

And, in parallel fashion, the first line of each succeeding stanza lists parts of the pained body: "*Mano,*" "*Brazos,*" "*Costado,*" "*Mirada,*" "*Cuerpo.*" The possessive adjective "*mi*" in each initial verse has more than normal vigor here; it signifies a strong, personal bond. In the penultimate strophe, as before, the present tense of "*mirar*" vitalizes the image:

> *Cuerpo de mi Cristo,*
> *te miro, pendiente,*
> *aún crucificado.*
> *¡Yo cantaré cuando*
> *te hayan desclavado!*
>   (p. 19)

In addition, the adjective "*pendiente,*" the adverb "*aún,*" and the subjunctive "*hayan*" all contribute to the impression of a directly observed, ever-present Christ with whom the poet is in consonance.

The stress on physical destruction of the body, on blood, sweat, nails, and torn flesh, is overpowering. No detail of the martyred Christ is omitted. A rent Savior with "*carnes en gajos abiertas*" and with "*venas vaciadas en ríos*" chills the reader ("Al oído del Cristo," p. 5). There are verbs and phrases that denote violent assault: "*llagar,*" "*tajear,*" and "*el flanco hendido de Cristo, / el ángulo de su boca.*"[15] Instruments of torture reminiscent of those used on the scourged and crucified Christ are enumerated:

> *¡Garfios, hierros, zarpas, que sus carnes hiendan*
> *tal como se parten frutos y gavillas;*
> *llamas que a su gajo caduco se prendan*
> *llamas como argollas y como cuchillas!*
>   ("Al oído del Cristo," p. 7)

The image of flesh sliced like fruit, or cut into bundles of wine shoots, is reiterated: "*Desde tu vertical cae tu carne / en cáscara de fruta que golpean....*"; "*El hierro que taladra tiene un gusto frío, / cuando abre, cual gavillas, las carnes amorosas.*"[16]

Christ's suffering elicits self-hate in the poet: "*¡Odio mi pan, mi estrofa* *y mi alegría, / porque Jesús padece!*" ("Viernes Santo," p. 11). Tearing at her wounds, she tries to increase her anguish to feel, at least in part, his burden: "*...¡desde que te he visto / rasgué mis heridas!*" ("Canto del justo," p. 19). No human sacrifice can equal that of Christ; all comparisons pale:

> *Mano de mi Cristo,*
> *que como otro párpado*
> *tajeada llora:*
> *¡desde que te he visto*
> *la mía no implora!*
> (p. 18)

Yet Gabriela is certain that if absolute suffering can exist on a human basis, no other can match hers, which rivals only Christ's. The parallels are unmistakable: "*Ame mi gozo y mi agonía: / ¡ame la prueba de mi cruz!*"; "*Los que cual Cristo hicieron la Vía-Dolorosa ...*"; and finally in "La cruz de Bistolfi"[17]:

> *Cruz que ninguno mira y que todos sentimos,*
> *la invisible y la cierta como una ancha montaña:*
> *dormimos sobre ti y sobre ti vivimos;*
> *tus dos brazos nos mecen y tu sombra nos baña.*
> (p. 4)

The images of death carry grim reminders of Christ's death, as the poet stresses grammatical variations of nails: "*clavo,*" "*clavar,*" and "*clavarse*"[18]: "*Ha venido el cansancio infinito / a clavarse en mis ojos, al fin*" ("Nocturno," p. 80). Body wounds recall the one in Christ's side: "*¡Llevo abierto también mi costado...!*" (p. 79). To express grief over the death of her nephew, Juan Miguel, she writes about a rent side: "*Otra vez sobre la Tierra / llevo desnudo el costado ...*" ("El costado desnudo," p. 706). As Thomas doubted Christ's wound until he thrust in his finger,[19] the wound in Gabriela's side is also undeniable:

> *Como a Tomás el Cristo,*
> *me hunde la mano pálida,*
> *porque no olvide, dentro*
> *de su herida mojada.*
> ("La obsesión," p. 89)

There is little novelty in the sentiments, images, and attitudes in the poetry selected for this section. Many devotional manuals encourage the pious to bring forth firsthand visions of Christ on the Cross, so that the nature of his sacrifice may remain ever fresh.[20] In periods of temptation or distress or when faith needs renewal, St. Francis de Sales urges that one should "run in spirit to embrace the Holy Cross, as if you saw Jesus Christ crucified before you."[21] The theory is that to receive the maximum impact, the mind should not intellectualize Calvary, nor should the imagination reconstruct it as a play in a theater. As ideation and as secondhand drama the Passion of Christ is limited to theology and vicarious comprehension. The truly devout will attempt to empathize with the physical pain of Christ and so share that pain. The poet, however, must also integrate feeling and thought, sensuous detail, and theological abstraction.[22]

Fray Luis de Granada (Spain, 1504–1588) suggested a method by which the Passion of Christ may acquire greater immediacy. Not through the intellect, but through the imagination, stated this Dominican scholar in his *Libro de la oración y meditación* (published 1849), ...

> ... *debemos figurar [el juicio final, ó el infierno, ó el paraíso] ... de la manera que ella es, ó de la manera que pasaría, y hacer cuenta que allí en aquel mesmo lugar donde estamos pasa todo aquello en presencia nuestra; para que con esta representación de las cosas sea más viva la consideración y sentimiento dellas.*

This phenomenon is quite evident in the poetic examples given, but Fray Luis makes another, even more telling, suggestion: "*Y algunos hay que dentro de su mesmo corazón imaginan que pasa cualquiera cosa destas que piensan; porque pues en él caben ciudades y reinos, no es mucho que pueda caber también la representación y figura destos misterios.*"[23] The stress in the latter passage is on essential oneness between the poet's sentiment and that of Christ. Fray Luis gives a physical description of Calvary as if it were a place to which one could go, albeit with difficulty, or it is so vividly arrayed in the imagination that one can almost perceive it visually. However, man's most difficult challenge, as the poetry suggests, is to inwardly live the suffering of Christ: "*Ame mi gozo y mi agonía: / ¡ame la prueba de mi cruz!*" ("El himno cotidiano," p. 352).

Fray Luis urges a proper perspective on the meaning of Christ's suffering. For him the exercise of devotion is the means to other ends. Man must figuratively ascend the Cross, ladder-like, to reach a total understanding of Christ's love, atonement, and charity. In turn, each pays the debt for Christ's act with eternal gratitude, reverence, and abstention from sin. These, then, according to Fray Luis, are the goals of meditation about Christ. Too long a gaze upon suffering for its own sake could turn the means into the end. In this context, one must ask whether the poet has not exceeded the bounds of discretion. In *Desolación* alone, expressions for wounds, destruction, breaking and tearing the flesh, occur more than eighty-eight times in sixty-three poems. Mere statistics, however, cannot convey the overpowering impression of violence. To everyone's relief, though, the poetry following *Desolación* displays less gore, but no lack of grief.

The Cross, Trees and Wood

By metaphorically developing the symbiosis of Christ with the Cross, the poet transforms secular objects, such as wood or things made of wood, into sacred objects, having been endowed by personal suffering, humility, and death. The leaves, branches, trunks, and roots of trees, through anthropomorphism, turn into hair, arms, bodies, and feet.[24] The wind blowing through the branches makes a moaning sound, similar to a human moan, and carries "...*la fragancia / de su costado abierto!*" ("Tres árboles," p. 126). The lines, "*Tres árboles caídos / ... apretados de amor, como tres ciegos*," represent Christ and the two thieves, Demas and Gestas.[25] One tree, more twisted than the others, turns and

> ...*tiende*
> *su brazo inmenso y de follaje trémulo*
> *hacia otro, y sus heridas*
> *como dos ojos son, llenos de ruego.*
> (p. 126)

Gabriela links her fate to theirs in a pact of pain and love: "*Estaré con ellos.... / Y mudos y ceñidos, / nos halle el día en un montón de duelo*"[26]

Elsewhere she chants a "Himno al árbol" (pp. 347–349), in terms suggestive of the Crucifixion: The tree is rooted and "*clavado por garfios pardos en el suelo.*" Suggested also are heavenly aspiration ("*una intensa sed de cielo*"), purification ("*hazme piadoso hacia la escoria / de cuyos limos me mantengo*"), and refreshing shade and sanctified halo ("*amplia sombra refrescante / y con el nimbo de tu esencia*"). And finally, worship at the tree leads to the mitigation of sin, followed by universal love and beneficence.

In "La encina" ("The Oak"), because of stoic acceptance of adversity, Brígida Walker, the poet's model of the sacrificing teacher, becomes idealized as splendid and perfumed: "...*encina espléndida de sombra perfumada, / por cuyos brazos rudos trepara un mirto en flor*" (p. 54).[27] The trunk bears a sore ("*llagado*"); it is at once delicate and aromatic, stout and straight: "*Pasta de nardos suaves, pasta de robles fuertes*" (p. 54). Walker's unstinting service to education and her love for students, discussed in Chapter IV when she granted Lucila certification, are translated into "*leño heroico [que] se ha vuelto, encina, santo*" (p. 55). The sanctification continues as the poet hopes that the "*encina*," wounded in the side, feels no pain. All humanity ("*el leñador*" / "the woodman") owes her reverence. And finally, in the parting hour, before God the poet says: "¡...*y que cuando / el rayo de Dios hiérate, para ti se haga blando / y ancho como tu seno, el seno del Señor!*" (p. 56). The dedicated teachers bear a cross of sacrifice, but their own body is also the cross to which they are bound until death. The greater the perseverance in life, the more glorious appears the death.

The cypress traditionally designates mourning, perhaps because it is planted in cemeteries, or perhaps because it is associated with the medieval legend that the transverse beam of the Cross was made of cypress.[28] Whatever the source, Mistral combines both connotations in the ensuing metaphors. With regard to the poet's despair over the death of her mother and/or her estrangement from Chile owing to disillusionment with officialdom, her body is an "*alzadura de lento ciprés*" ("Nocturno de la consumación," p. 382). In addition, she has been forgotten by God as Jesus was also apparently forsaken on the Cross. In "Luto," which mourns the death of her nephew, Juan Miguel, the same metaphor occurs: "*Soy yo misma mi ciprés / mi sombreadura y mi ruedo*" (p. 712). The mortification is clear. More central, however, is the desire to become like the trees in order to escape the pain of life.[29] Again, in "Luto" she says: "*...pero yo que me ahogo me veo / árbol devorado y humoso, / cerrazón de noche, carbón consumado, / enebro denso, ciprés engañoso, / cierto a los ojos, huido en la mano.*"

In "Nocturne of the Consummation"— analyzed in Chapter I in a social context, now from a philosophical perspective — her image of the transitoriness of life is a tree consumed in flames, and she, the tree, flees life leaving no trace of ash, merely a wisp of smoke: "*Dame Tú el acabar de la encina / en fogón que no deje la hez*" (p. 384). There is no disintegration of the body, because she has long forgotten the body. She is an open-eyed tree made up of smoke ("*...árbol de humo y con ojos abiertos,*" p. 712), which has died from within and maintains a marginal, almost nonmaterial, contact with existence:

> *Igual que las humaredas*
> *ya no soy llama ni brasas.*
> *Soy esta espiral y esta liana*
> *y este ruedo de humo denso*
>   (p. 711)

In general, trees are the poet, whether buffeted by storms, blanched by the sun, or blooming for short intervals under a gentle rain that heralds fecundity or signifies tears and disaster.[30] The epilogue to the *Poesías completas* bookends with the fittingly titled "Último árbol" ("Last Tree," pp. 797–799). The poem marks a half century of searching for spiritual tranquility. The allusions to the Crucifixion range from the obvious to the subtle: "*...mi costado de fuego*" ("my fiery side"), "*Isla de mi sangre*" ("Isle of my blood"), "*parvedad de reino*" (i.e., humility), "*tamarindo*" (tamarind-like red color and acid core), "*cedro*" ("cedar," i.e., majesty and glory).[31] Blood congeals to "*frescor*" and "*silencio,*" metaphors that emphasize spiritual repose and serenity in death. The poet wants to leave all matter behind, knowing that death awaits in the form of the nameless tree borne like a sightless child ("*...árbol sin nombre /*

que cargué como a hijo ciego"). The "*árbol*," symbol of the body, will soon be carried by the "*Arcángel verdadero / adelantado en las rutas / con el ramo y el ungüento!*" She will be transported by an Archangel to an ultimate resting place, where pain will cease and her soul will deliver itself to God.[32]

"Manos de obreros" ("Workers' Hands") holds one slim clue to the presence of a medieval legend that "makes the cross on which Christ was crucified of the wood of a tree which sprung *[sic]* from a slip of the Tree of Knowledge, thus connecting the fall and salvation of man, which is the story of Christianity."[33] With an almost surrealistic eye, the poet views men as hands, separated from bodies and minds, continually and obediently performing ordinary tasks. In the pertinent stanza, the hands of the workers shape themselves to the wooden handles and they become wood:

> *Parecidas a sus combos*
> *o a sus picos, nunca a su alma;*
> *a veces en ruedas locas,*
> *como el lagarto rebanadas,*
> *y después, Árbol-Adámico*
> *viudo de sus ramas altas.*
> (pp. 738–739)

The poet labels Adam — "Name-Giver" in Hebrew — as the tree trunk from which primitive humanity sprang forth ("Arbol-Adámico"). Adam antedates man's conscience and awareness of the world. Gabriela tellingly divorces the workers' intellectual faculties ("*viudo de sus ramas altas*") from their capacity for physical labor. Yet, in spite of brutishness and ignorance, of being tools and instruments of society, they have the gleam of humanity and compassion in that they sing, dance, work, and fabricate [*homo faber*]. In this regard, they escape the consequences of the Fall of Man and automatically attain salvation: "¡ *...Jesucristo las toma y retiene / entre las suyas hasta el Alba!*" (p. 740).

Adam's role before the Fall is to tend the Garden of Eden in harmony with God's wish. Adam is dependent on God the Father for integrity, peace, and the few liberties accorded him. After tasting of the Tree of Knowledge, he becomes cognizant of the difference between good and evil, and is condemned to work the cursed and grudging soil.[34] Adam pays for disobedience and inquiry; having chosen freely, Adam must continue to exercise his reason and his will in all of life's awesome choices. The rub is that Adam's burden is also that of man: Adam chose for all mankind and thus condemned humanity to estrangement from God the Father. Through Christ, however, man is freed of Adam's onus and returns, as it were, to the stage of innocence, sinless, industrious, and content. The poet is expressing the redemption of mass man through work and through faith in God the Son.[35]

In theology, the "ship" usually represents the Church of Christ; it bears the sinners and the faithful over perilous waters and protects them from the wickedness of the world.[36] It is difficult to reconcile this orthodox sense with that offered in the triad under the general heading "Canciones en el mar" ("Songs on the Sea"). The Church is not the substitute for Christ, the ship of this allegory: "¡*Ay*!, *barco, no te tiemblen los costados, / que llevas a una herida*" (p. 112). Christ is ship, navigator, and polestar: dependable, skilled, and constant. The poet has entrusted her voyage and salvation to the man on the prow who suffers from the sea's buffetings ("[*el*] *hombre que sufre en la proa, / el viento del mar*," p. 115). The union is as painful as it is susceptible of alleviating pain:

> *En la proa poderosa*
> *mi corazón he clavado.*
> *Mírate barca, que llevas*
> *el vórtice ensangrentado.*
> (p. 113)

The double sacrifice on the prow and mast is cleansed by the rushing sea:

> *Sobre la nave toda puse*
> *mi vida como derramada.*
> *Múdala, mar, en los cien días,*
> *que ella será tu desposada.*[37]
> (pp. 113–114)

The relationship offers a promise of everlasting and unwavering faith in Christ. But the poet eventually abrogates her pledge of total faithfulness.

In the aftermath of Juan Miguel's death, Gabriela's images with regard to the Cross imply an opposition to Jesus Christ. Beset by profound anguish, the poet symbolically bares her side again ("El costado desnudo") in the usual sign of martyrdom. She rejects Christ as her ideal and denies that the cross she bears is his, preferring the loneliness of abandonment and suffering to the disillusionment attendant upon placing complete faith in him. She denies that the Cross offers protection:

> ...*y, si duermo, queda expuesto [el costado]*
> *a las malicias del lazo*
> *sin el aspa de ese pecho*
> *a la torre de ese amparo.*
> (pp. 706–707)

And furthermore, Christ is no longer her infallible guide through adversity!

> *Ya no más su vertical*
> *como un paso adelantado*
> *abriéndome con su mástil*
> *los duros cielos de estaño*

*y conjugando en la marcha
el álamo con el álamo.*
(pp. 707–708)

Gabriela's position, reflected through the poetry of this particular period — discussed in detail earlier — should not be considered irrevocable, but rather a result of severe grief. It is true that Jesus would never again be, as he was previously, the total savior or the omnipresent redeemer. Nor, on the other hand, would he inspire the pain-wracked, tortured poetry that derived from her exaggerated dependence on Christ's suffering as a means of redemption and ultimate love.

In the last analysis, Juan Miguel's death created a personal dialectic. The death (thesis), which resulted in anguish (antithesis), forced a synthesis between total reliance upon Christ or complete estrangement from him. The poet became aware that the solution to man's grief, if one were possible, did not lie outside the individual in the acts of others, was not determined by flagellation or symbolic self-crucifixion, and could not be alleviated by constantly reflecting upon anguish. After a slow and lengthy recovery from the shock of Juan Miguel's passing, and having purged herself of the initial rancor toward Christ, Gabriela embarked upon a new spiritual voyage in which the symbolic upright mast no longer guided her, but she had not yet abandoned the "ship." The result was that grief no longer gave rise to poetry in which a bleeding, sacrificed Christ was present.

Blood and Water

In the Passion of Jesus Christ, the water that fills him upon dying is symbolic of God's acceptance of the Son. It is God's response to Christ's prior declaration, "I thirst."[38] The Roman soldiers accepted the words literally and offered a sponge dipped in vinegar to heighten the derision. The vinegar, furthermore, helped to diminish pain. But Christ refused the anodyne because he sought neither liquid refreshment nor surcease from pain. He thirsted for a sign from God that the sacrifice and atonement were not in vain. The Word came as Longinus' lance pierced his side. In death, blood and water issued forth as a sign of God.

In Gabriela's poems, blood does not lose its original symbolic meaning by being transformed into water. But the primal connotation of water and blood as "sustainers of life" is expanded to include certain attributes unique to blood: sacrifice, martyrdom, atonement, and parental love. Besides a literal, physical similarity to blood, water has qualities not possessed by blood. Because water suggests horizontal extension (sea, river), vertical downpour (rain), and movement by river and rain, water serves to propagate and transmit the acquired symbolic meanings of blood. Water is not only the agent of transmission, but also a transformed symbol, coparticipating in the meanings distinctive to blood.

Christ is the main source of all blood: "*...manos que sangraron con garfios y en ríos*" ("La sombra inquieta," p. 43). Figuratively, blood flows, too, from the poet's side, and either joins the river of blood from Christ or else forms a pool of its own. The following citations illustrate these possibilities. The first, in addition, has a particularizing definite article: "*Cristo, el de las venas vaciadas en ríos*" ("Al oído del Cristo," p. 5). The poet, in quiet desperation, is faced with having to live with her personal tragedies: "*...me han dado esta montaña mágica, / y un río y unas tardes trágicas / como Cristo, con que sangrar*" ("Serenidad," p. 116). And again, the exacerbated grief, relentless in its pursuit, continues: "*Vivo una vida entera en cada hora que pasa; / como el río hacia el mar, van amargas mis venas*" ("Poema del hijo," p. 105). The horizontal current never ceases, even when the blood empties into the sea: "*¡Y no untó mi sangre / la extensión del mar!*" ("Balada," p. 76). The sea is limitless and contains the overflow. The poet seems to have in mind the futility suggested by the line from Ecclesiastes 1:7: "All the rivers run into the sea; yet the sea is not full." Ablutions can in no way erase pain or death: "*¿No hay agua que los lave de sus estigmas rojos?*" ("Interrogaciones," p. 85). The sea cannot dilute the emptying rivers of blood; the sea itself turns red to reflect their dual sacrifice.

Christ's blood descending vertically is likened to a summer shower: "*El cielo es como un inmenso / corazón que se abre, amargo. / No llueve: es un sangrar lento / y largo*" ("La lluvia lenta," p. 140). The image copies Christ, but the bitterness belongs to the poet. The purpose of the descending blood is to redden humanity—"*regando la vida*" ("Canto del justo," p. 19)—and thus to apprise it of the sins for which Christ is still paying because of sins that remain and go unpunished.

In *Tala*, blood no longer corresponds to all the prior physical manifestations of water. A river of blood, ascending vertically now, announces the Resurrection. The poet sanctifies and spiritualizes blood and water by dematerializing both when she speaks of a "Río vertical de gracia" ("Locas letanías," p. 399). Then, to introduce a paradox, Christ's blood no longer flows freely, but is dammed up: "*Mi sangre aún es agua de regato; / la tuya se paró como agua en presa*" ("Nocturno del descendimiento," p. 396). Humility is thus expressed by comparing the insignificant trickle to the potential kinetic force in Christ's confined blood. The poet enlarges upon the image of the dammed-up water ("*agua en presa*") by combining antitheses: "*parado y corriendo vivo, / en su presa y despeñado*" ("Locas letanías," p. 399). The second verse is pleonastic; the explanation of the paradox in the first line suffices for the second also. Dramatic tension arises from the juxtaposition of the physical, literal sense of "*parado*" ("stopped") and the spiritualized meaning of "*corriendo vivo*" ("running alive"). His blood has congealed but the significance of the sacrifice is eternal.

In *Lagar*, "*presa de agua*" ("water dam") is a metaphor for Christ, which at first glance seems to evince possible serenity by its association with "*sosiego*" ("tranquility"). The preceding and present contexts of the phrase, however, belie the explicit meaning. Concomitant with "*mi sosiego la presa de agua*" is the paradoxical irony of the line, "...*y mis gozos la dura mina*" ("Recado para la 'Residencia de Pedralbes,' en Cataluña," p. 586). Blood and water flow less freely. They signal restraint, stoicism, and resignation. The fluids have not disappeared or dried up, which would mark the end of suffering, but have merely been held back. If Gabriela's life could have been summed up at that moment, if she could have transmitted a permanent, last message to the young women who reside in the Residencia de Pedralbes in Catalonia, two phrases from the closing stanzas would have served to illustrate her constant anguish. In the first, she wished to be remembered as the "*cierva herida*" ("wounded hind"), another metaphor for the wounded Christ.[39] In the second, she is the sufferer who is no longer deceived by the facile illusion that the fardel of existence can be wished or prayed away. This burden is hers for life. Neither the cessation of tears nor the dried-up blood — even less, the contrary dual feelings associated with "*agua en presa*"— Christ as the reservoir of hope and Christ's love denied to her — can mitigate the suffering when she herself shouts out, "...¡*y doy la cara a mi agonía!*" ("I face my own agony").

Tears, Salt and Sweat

Mistral paints Calvary as the majestic Christian scene. She describes it as "*el resplandor cárdeno del Calvario eterno*" ("Al oído del Cristo," p. 6). On this site, Christ's redemptive blood immersed man in a valley of tears.[40] She calls Christ's wounded hand as "*otro párpado / [que] tajeada llora*" ("Canto del justo," p. 18). Again, with regard to tears, the poet employs the verb "*cuajar*" [usual meaning, "coagulate"] out of its normal context to emphasize that present-day Pharisees avoid weeping before Christ's bloody form: "...*no cuaja en sus ojos dos lágrimas claras*" ("Al oído del Cristo," p. 6).[41] In "Éxtasis," the poet's emotional response to the lover who committed suicide parallels that shown to Christ. After asking Christ for a cessation of pain through absolute humility — that is, for death — she views the relationship with the deceased as an "*amasijo fatal de sangre y lágrimas*" (p. 64).

Mary Magdalene is the archetype of the tearful penitent, prepared to love all the more passionately for having sinned and repented.⁴² Gabriela's poetry re-creates and re-imagines Scripture. The poet mentions Mary twice, but the first allusion, although more poetically pertinent, deviates from the Bible. Mistral positions Christ to regard Mary from the Cross and to annoint his feet: "*...y para ungir sus pies busca la trenza / de Magdalena ¡y la halla ensangrentada!*" ("Al pueblo hebreo," p. 9). It was another Mary, however, the sister of Martha, who wiped Christ's feet with her hair at Bethany. She borrows a false tradition that links Mary Magdalene to the unnamed sinner who earlier had wiped Christ's feet at Capernaum.⁴³ Though it is true that Mary Magdalene did not wipe Christ's feet, she did weep at his sepulcher. It is improbable that Gabriela was unaware of Mary Magdalene's role as the sorrowful penitent, but it is also possible that she believed in the popular, but false, legend. Again in opposition to the Bible, the poetic image has Christ seeking the hair of Mary; in fact, the women sought fervently to cleanse him. But, for the poet, the Bible is the point of departure, not something to copy. Mary Magdalene, as the eternally sobbing woman, is maintained metaphorically if one assumes that blood, the essence of the Crucifixion, and tears, the specialty of Mary, coalesce in the bloody tress ("*trenza ... ensangrentada*").

The poetry written before 1922 is drenched in tears. In it there are more than fifty direct references to combinations of weeping: *llorar, llanto, lágrima,* and *sollozar*. This count does not include the metaphoric versions of *agua, sal,* and *mares*. Nor does it include tears by implication, from wounds, grief, pain, abandonment, and death. Partly owing to a change in her personal life, and partly owing to her growing maturity as a poet, Gabriela Mistral reduced the tearful poetry subsequent to *Desolación*. That is, while tears, compassion, grief, and death still permeated her works, with increasing poetic skill she imagined and crafted new and more subtle expressions for her pain. Whereas emotion led the intellect in her first two books, *Desolación* and *Ternura,* in the last two, *Tala* and *Lagar,* the intellect channeled emotions. The result was beneficial for poetic expression

As blood gives expression to water, having sacrifice in common with it, so water in its dual role of sea and tears connotes salt, a symbol of acerbated grief and oblation. In Leviticus 2:13, salt is required for use in sacrifices and offerings: "...with all thine offerings thou shalt offer salt." In Mark 9:49, the tradition continues: "For every one shall be salted with fire, and every sacrifice shall be salted with salt." The indispensable accompaniment to man's food also spices "God's food."⁴⁴ A vestige of the Crucifixion marks the following image, which treats of deception by an unfaithful lover: "*...y me clavo como un dejo / de salmuera en tu garganta*" ("Dios lo quiere," p. 70). "*Clavo*" ("nail") symbolizes the punishing instrument; "*salmuera*" ("brine") could be the gall given to Christ along with the vinegar.⁴⁵ In effect, the poet is inflicting the penance of sacrifice for perfidy and sin. But, in reverse irony, she is the martyred one and possesses the wounds of the crucified ("*me clavo*" and "*salmuera*"). It is the poet who, having tasted of pain, has drunk of the brine: "*En tu abierto manto no cabe / la salmuera que yo bebí*" ("A la Virgen de la Colina," p. 27).[46] Sacrifice, in this instance, does not entail voluntary submission to a divine force for the purpose of spiritual renewal at the expense of personal comfort. Nor is sacrifice entirely calm acceptance of the evils that destiny can hurl with impunity.

If life is bitter like drinking from the ocean ("*amarga como un sorbo de mares*") ("Tribulación," p. 77), if salt implies total destruction, then the poet, while recognizing the immensity of the task, is nevertheless struggling against bitterness and destruction. To do this, the opposing senses and uses of salt are put into play. Here, salt not only destroys flesh, impoverishes the soil, and symbolically negates life, but it also helps to preserve and, by so doing, sustains life. The life-taking and life-giving functions of salt are an integral part of Gabriela's poetic spectrum in that they reinforce other symbols of death and destruction, life and fertility. Salt always retains its values of bitterness, disintegration, infertility, and desperation.[47]

It may be argued, however, that the presence of salt in sacrifices and oblations dating from biblical times, the enormous importance of salt in preserving food, and its abundance, may lend to the sacrificial act and to the victim sanctity that no other material is capable of giving. That is, salt corrodes the flesh, but by the same token its presence in the sacrifice sanctifies the offering to God; its abundance may be taken as a sign of permanence and eternal life; it destroys living flesh, but preserves the meat of the victim.[40] The most striking support for this theory is in "Canción de los que buscan olvidar" ("Song of Those Who Seek to Forget"), where the poet hopes that an ocean voyage will erase the bitter memories of martyrdom. Nailed to the cross, seemingly for an eternity, the poet asks for release from sacrifice. She asks that the very salt that caused so much pain wash out her wounds:

> *Lávalo, mar, con sal eterna;*
> *lávalo, mar; lávalo, mar;*
> *que la Tierra es para la lucha*
> *y Tú eres para consolar.*
>
> *Lávalo, mar, con sal tremenda,*
> *lávalo, mar; lávalo, mar.*
> *O me lo rompes en la proa*
> *que no lo quiero más llevar.*
>
> (p. 113)

Salt, employed in this fashion, again points up the poet's desire to escape from pain. At the same time, this use of salt emphasizes that, by making salt the balm, there is merely an intensification of sacrifice and self-flagellation.

One of Gabriela's most startling poems appears in *Lagar*. "Una piadosa" is startling, that is, if the metaphors and images are interpreted in the following way. It appears to be the quest of *"una piadosa"* ("a pious woman") for Jesus, following a long absence from his company. The traditional metaphors indicate Christ: "*[el] hombre del faro*"; "*sólo mira al Este, /— emparedado que está vivo—*"; "*el herido*"; "*el hombre que va a contarme / lo terrestre y lo divino*" (pp. 634–635). What causes concern is the confrontation with an apparently superannuated, ineffective Jesus, depicted in the most frightening terms. He is a "*viejo salobre y salino*" ("brackish and saline old man") engrossed in personal suffering, "*escupido de marea*" ("spit out of the tide") and "*parado en sal y olvido*" ("standing in salt and forgetfulness"). This is no caricature, because the pious woman is searching for an answer. She is carrying a token offering of milk ("*jarro de leche*"), which symbolizes, on the one hand, the compassion of mother for child and, on the other, a renewal of the spirit of the sacrificial wine on the Cross ("*sorbo de vino*"). But it appears that neither purifying milk nor sacrificial wine can restore vitality and dignity, and certainly not divinity, to an ineffective god who seems never to have been born "*...¡y de inmóvil, y mudo y ausente, / ya no parece ni nacido!*" (p. 635). It is not clear what particular circumstances stimulated this point of view; it does not tie in with other poems of this same section. It does, however, complement "Luto" and "El costado desnudo."

Some of the more trenchant images have their origin in Luke 22:44: "*Y estando en agonía, oraba más intensamente: y fue su sudor como grandes gotas de sangre que caían hasta la tierra.*" This particular image has several contexts. In "Al oído del Cristo" and "Viernes Santo," almost identical allusions have the same theme: "*Ya sudó sangre bajo los olivos*" and "*en tu sudar sangre*" (pp. 6, 10). They refer to the betrayal of Christ by his disciples and by men who, while attending to private pleasures, care little for Christ's agony. In a parallel context, "*En su sudor de sangre bebieron nuestras raíces,*"[49] the poet refers to the animated and vivified olive trees that witness Christ's agony and respond with deeper fervor to his grief than do Simon Peter or the other disciples. The response of the olives is ontological, not physiological: They shun water and, instead, nourish on Christ's blood. Completely different from the other contexts is the following line in "Luto": "*Soy yo misma ... mi sudario sin costura*" (p. 712). Apart from the confusion of biblical sources,[50] there is no doubt that the poet, twenty-five years after the sanguinary poetry of *Desolación*, uses a quondam expression to reiterate the ineffable anguish evinced by the death of her nephew, Juan Miguel. The poet's body is the sudarium for her own blood.

Whereas one expects blood to flow from open wounds, blood mixed with sweat oozing from pores represents a vigorous dramatization of the poet's intensity and of the Passion of Christ. The full import of these visual and olfactory images includes all the elements of the fluids, blood and water: red color, movement, salt, bitterness, stench, and anguish, as well as the intimate, carnal relationship of blood to sweat.

Wine

The verdant Elqui valley produces the sweetest wine grapes and raisins in Chile. Lucila took part in the gathering and production and delighted in the community viniculture. The poetry reflects that experience, because wine and the multiple variants associated with wine derive from two sources. The first, secular, evokes vivid memories of childhood. The second is the sacred meanings of wine which derive from the New Testament. In the following discussion of the religious connotations of wine, it is necessary to keep in mind the secular, first source that conditioned awareness of wine as a life-sustaining liquid. For her, wine had ontological importance. Not to be forgotten in this regard, either, are Mistral's concerns for the farm workers and the economic benefit afforded by viniculture. And physical contact with the fluid, pulp, grapes, and winepresses left a memory of odors, tastes, colors, and tactile sensations that sustained and formed the substance of her poetic imagery, captured vividly in *Lagar (Winepress)*. The theme at hand is the poetic and religious sense of the metaphors and images, based upon the poet's firsthand knowledge of the essential life-giving and life-taking aspects of wine learned about as a girl in Montegrande.[51]

Blood and wine have sufficient common ostensive properties to make them metaphorically interchangeable. In the poetry, both can betoken life, death, and the suffering in between. The winepress, or *lagar*, symbolizes death: "*Dicen que la vida ha menguado en mi cuerpo, que mis venas se vertieron como los lagares....*"[52] In "Nocturno," the woman betrayed by her lover asks God the Father to crush her, being half-destroyed already, as he had crushed the raceme: "*¡Y en el ancho lagar de la muerte / aún no quieres mi pecho oprimir!*" (p. 79). In her mind's eye, in "Hospital," the poet envisions those wounded in war as "*carnes estrujadas / de lagares que no conozco*" (p. 681). Death awaits them as it does her. Everyone is lost, alone in spite of companionship, and trapped in a "*laberinto blanco y redondo.*"[53] Death does not come mercifully, at one blow, to end the agony of life. Rather, by slow attrition, people disappear, personal capacities wane, and life ebbs: "*Se va de ti mi cuerpo gota a gota.... // ¡Se te va todo, se nos va todo!*" ("Ausencia," p. 535). If there is something of permanence, a reminder of an eternal verity, it is blood, or its equivalent. It is traced on the lips of the sufferers, those who remain to evanesce ("*como humedad de tu cuerpo evaporo*"), recalling the loved ones who were crushed prematurely, like juice from grapes which was not allowed to mellow: "*Sangre sería y me fuese en las palmas / de tu labor, y en tu boca de mosto*"[54] (p. 536). God shows no discrimination, and even less imagination, when it is a matter of dying. The beautiful and the serene may go too soon and undeservedly, while the ugly and pain-wracked may live on beyond endurance: "*Te acordaste del negro racimo / y lo diste al lagar carmesí....*" "*Te acordaste del fruto en Febrero, / al llagarse su pulpa rabí. / ¡Llevo abierto también mi costado, / y no quieres mirar hacia mí!*" ("Nocturno," p. 79).

On the other hand, God cannot reach and control every human action; man can commit suicide. By so doing he does not nullify God's innate love for him, rather man limits his own capacity to love God. Nor does the poet believe that the God of Justice and Righteousness holds sway over the God of Love, with the former choosing victims for slaughter. As man is always the "hard claw" ("*zarpa dura*"), so God is always sweetness: "*¡...el vaso donde se esponjan de dulzura / los nectarios de todos los huertos de la Tierra!*" ("Interrogaciones," p. 85). This view is also found in the New Testament. It is reminiscent of the language of Jesus, which proclaims the love he brings to those who will follow, in terms of wine that should be drunk to symbolize the union of the Redeemer and the redeemed. In Matthew 26:27–28, Christ says, "Drink ye all of it; for this is my blood of the new testament, which is shed for many for the remission of sins." The poet has tasted of redemptive and loving wine: "*...mas yo, que te he gustado, como un vino, Señor, / mientras los otros siguen llamándote Justicia, / ¡no te llamaré nunca otra cosa que Amor!*" (p. 85).

Wine is not imbibed as transubstantiated blood at the church altar, but rather as blood at the Cross, metaphorically endowed with the attributes of blood and wine.[55] This is to say one thing about the poet's religiosity and another about her poetic technique. In the first instance, she seldom prostrated herself before a priest in church; she asked for release from pain from Christ directly. In the second, wine seldom ceases to be an exact metonym for blood, especially where the latter involves pain and love. The poet, borrowing the following passage from Luke 5:39, turns it to her to advantage and illustrates the issue: "*Y ninguno que bebiere del añejo, quiere luego el nuevo; porque dice: El añejo es mejor.*" Where Scripture records the shortsightedness of the disciples, the poet reverses the parable to affirm her dependence upon the blood-wine from the body of Christ, which offers as much joy as it does pain: "*Palpita aún el corazón que heriste: / vive de ti como de un viejo vino*" ("Canciones de Solveig," p. 147).[56]

Interest in wine never ends as mystic inebriation. The open confession of love for Christ is passionate and sincere, but passion and sincerity do not of themselves lead to rapture or ecstasy. There are no stammerings in her emotions and no stutterings of the *no sé qué* variety. Doubts, yes, and overcharged emotion, but no firm *unio,* no dark night of the soul, no inner voices to indicate the inebriated mystic.[57] The direct references to drunkenness touch lightly on mystic connotations, as in "Ixtlazihuatl," the personified Mexican mountain, which seeks purity and offers repose: "*Está tendida en la ebriedad del cielo*" (p. 145). Personified objects and other people are generally drunk, seldom the poet.[58] Drunkenness is also another way of implying uncoordinated, involuntary movements, especially in relation to the wind that moves the trees. The poet refers to "*junco ebrio*" ("La ansiosa," p. 599), and says, "*Juega como los ebrios / el aire que lo ha herido*" ("Enfermo," p. 540). Intoxication can be used as a metaphor for exaggerated feelings and fantastic hallucinations, as with regard to the Old Testament God who is praised for his "*locura embriagada*" ("El Dios triste," p. 37), and as in "*un cuento de hombre beodo*" ("Hospital," p. 682).

The winy term "*falerno*" enters the lexicon. The connoisseur knows Falernum as an Italian wine from the Latium region imbibed by Roman troops. Gabriela, no expert, enjoys tasting wine. However she learned the term, the poet uncovers an aesthetic context: "*…el falerno del viento bebí*"[59] ("Nocturno," p. 79). Falerno intensifies the role of blood and wine fused and permeating the air she breathes. Gabriela employs and amplifies the terminology of the vintage to sum up her philosophy of the continuity of theme and feelings in poetry:

> *Lleva este libro [Tala] algún pequeño rezago de Desolación. Y el libro que le siga—si alguno sigue—llevará también un rezago de Tala. Así ocurre en mi valle de Elqui con la exprimidura de los racimos. Pulpas y pulpas quedan en las hendijas de los cestos. Las encuentran después los peones de la vendimia. Ya el vino se hizo y aquello se deja para el turno siguiente de los canastos….*[60]

It was to be expected, then, that the religious aspect of the poetry would undergo an evolution with, metaphorically speaking, the new wine receiving the bouquet and mellowness of the old, and itself imparting aroma and strength.

Nature and the Legend of Veronica

The darkness that fell over the land at Jesus' death appears re-created as "*cielo de estaño*" and "*cielo de añil.*"[61] "*Estaño*" and "*añil*" ("tin," "indigo") lend chromatic value to the image. "*Estaño,*" particularly, should be noted because in "El costado desnudo," in contrast with "Nocturno," the poet denies her affinity with "*los duros cielos de estaño*" ("the hard skies of tin"), and, by so doing, affirms that if death comes it will not ravage her body or inspire tortured verse like that found in *Desolación*. At the same time, Christ is no longer bloodstained, instruments of torture have disappeared, and the fusion of the poet with the deceased nephew, Juan Miguel, is devoid of violence: "*Han de ponernos en valle / limpio de celada y garfio, / claros íntegros, fundillos como en la estrella los radios...*" " ("El costado desnudo," p. 709). Nature shimmers with scarlet hues. The sunset owes its color to the poet:

> *¿Seré yo la que baño*
> *la cumbre de escarlata?*
>   *Llevo a mi corazón la mano, y siento*
> *que mi costado mana.*
>   ("Cima," p. 137)

Reciprocally, twilight is a reminder of flesh with sores: "*...y en cualquier país las tardes / con sangre serán mis llagas*" ("Dios lo quiere," p. 70). Rather than repose, the darkening hours recall a time of burial: "*Y en la llanura blanca, de horizonte infinito, / miro morir inmensos ocasos dolorosos*" ("Desolación," p. 123). The hyperbolic "*inmenso*" again appears in close association with a cosmic heart which opens to spew forth blood, not rain.[62] The heart changes into a cosmic cup in "La montaña de noche" (p. 133). The cup, always overflowing, is the poet's symbol for the wounded body. Nature does not remain aloof from the pain of the poet or from the suffering of Christ. Nature participates actively and itself shares the color, odor, wetness, and emotions involved in the Crucifixion:

> *El sol de ocaso pone*
> *su sangre viva en los hendidos leños*
> *¡y se llevan los vientos la fragancia*
> *de su costado abierto!*
>   ("Tres árboles," p. 126)

But neither journeys to other countries, the assumption of new challenges, nor total deliverance to Christ can diminish pain or erase unhappy thoughts. Earth- and time-bound, and subject to myriad vagaries, man cannot hope to escape his human condition, for his chief faculties, language, memory, and symbolic ideation, can induce physical and mental suffering in the absence of direct stimulus. Even the most tranquil and breathtaking scarlet sunsets cannot prod the poet into acknowledging the majesty of nature or into paying homage to the divine hand that arranges such splendrous sights. Rather, they recall — borrowing a "magic mountain" image from Thomas Mann's novel — a time of suffering: "*...me han dado esta montaña mágica, / y un río y unas tardes trágicas / como Cristo, con que sangrar*" ("Serenidad," p. 116).

The legend of Veronica does not appear in the New Testament, but derives from the rich folklore surrounding the Crucifixión.[63] Judging from the singular use of her name, her deed, and the results of that deed in the poetry, the poet showed an ardent interest in Veronica. To characterize ineradicable suffering, Gabriela compares her poetic canvas with Veronica's handkerchief, stamped with the impression Christ left on it as he traveled the Via Dolorosa: "*Yo en mis versos el rostro con sangre, / como Tú sobre el paño, le di.*"[64] The chosen few, through sacrifice, accept unalleviated suffering as the essence of life. Christ's deed inspires some, like Veronica, to unparalleled compassion and others, like St. Francis of Assisi, to rigorous self-flagellation. Still others share in Christ's heroism by empathizing with his drama, by regarding personal suffering as a sacrifice for him, and, finally, by transforming that drama and that sacrifice into poetic inspiration. Veronica becomes a metaphor that manifests sacrifice indelibly etched with pain and blood. And the poet is not content to let her own experience lie dormant. Fortified by God's love, she wants to express the pain of life as she feels and sees it, a red stain on the landscape of existence:

> *Creo en mi corazón,*
> *el que yo exprimo para teñir*
> *el lienzo de la vida*
> *de rojez o palor, y que le ha hecho*
> *veste encendida.*
> ("Credo," p. 32)

Sacrifice fosters sacrifice. Sacrifice breeds a dynamic intercourse between the martyred and the aspirants to martyrdom, and within the martyred it inspires further and greater sacrifices. For these reasons, the poet unabashedly hopes that the young women of the Residencia de Pedralbes in Barcelona will model their thoughts and feelings after her: "*La pasión mía me recuerden, / la espalda mía me la sigan.*" And then, transforming an auditive image into a visual one, the poet wishes the students to recall her face in their prayers: "*...y la oración, que es la Verónica, / tenga mi faz cuando la digan*" ("Recado para la 'Residencia de Pedralbes,' en Cataluña," p. 586).

Christ's face appears also in nature. As an implicit metaphor in "Lecturas espirituales," nature, stamped with Christ's tortured face, is offered as a bandage to ease man's wounds:

> *Toda la belleza de la Tierra puede ser venda para tu herida. Dios la ha extendido delante de ti: así, como un lienzo coloreado te ha extendido sus campos de primavera.*[65]

In contrast, in "La huella," saddened and frightened by World War II because it unleashed immense destruction, Gabriela viewed the Holocaust as the culmination of two thousand years of bloodshed. This started, she believes, with Christ's shedding of blood and continues through the present and beyond. Here man has erased his soul, his capacity for love and affection, and has relied on the empty shell of his body to maintain his dignity and pride. The result is that neither body nor soul has survived. Only a trace of blood in the sand reveals the eternal presence of *"el hombre fugitivo"*: *"...¡y la Tierra— Verónica / que me lo balbucea!"* (p. 683). Man seems to be bent on self-destruction from the time he is born. Environment, parents, acquaintances, and the preexisting conditions of life stamp themselves on his consciousness with his first breath. And herein lies one of the significances of the Veronica image, now a symbol: Man seldom ceases to be what conditions force him to be. He may struggle a lifetime for the meaning of his existence, but all the time the answer lies in what he is. In the poet's own quest for serenity in Mexico, she could not escape the sum total of the anguish she had encountered in Chile. Nor could she admit that the beauty of Ixtlazihuatl reflected her own inner state at the time. Rather, she saw her face reflected in the craggy peaks of the Andes:

> *Mas tú la andina, la de greña oscura,*
> *mi Cordillera, la Judith tremenda,*
> *hiciste mi alma cual la zarpa dura*
> *y la empapaste en tu sangrienta venda.*
> ("El Ixtlazihuatl," p. 146)

The dominant meaning of the Veronica theme (and this is consistent with what is already known about the poetry) is that art becomes eternal when the poet's constant pain pervades its substance. Esther de Cáceres also has concluded that Veronica signifies the sum total of the poet's sorrow. As a result of Gabriela's experiences, the song is enriched and thus endowed with what the Uruguayan poet calls *"el gran don de la poesía ontológica"* ("the great gift of ontological poetry").[66] And essentially the poetry of Gabriela Mistral is nothing less than an ontological quest, the baring of a soul, and the opening and reopening of wounds.

The Language of Sacrifice

The concepts of the preceding sections seem to suggest that the poetry of Gabriela Mistral is concerned chiefly with the destructive, pain-producing aspects of Christ's sacrifice, that the poet never grasped the sublime nature of his sacrifice of love for humanity. The violent realism of many images creates a centripetal effect that, lamentably, traps the reader into concentrating on tortured thoughts, abandonment, suffering, and torn flesh. These elements, however, are merely the essential preparation for the first act of a drama that concludes as a paean for love born of sacrifice. Love itself, because of the manner in which the poet expresses it, and because of the fact that it has arisen from grief, tends to be obscured by trenchant language that seemingly contradicts love. In the following paragraphs the nature of sacrifice turned to love has its place. Pain now brings pleasure. Grief is mollified by devotion. The intent is not to minimize or deprecate the suffering—it is sincere enough—but rather to demonstrate that redemption and salvation can emanate from the most desperate situations, that in spite of sacrifice, or really because of it, the individual can surmount perfidy, the death of loved ones, and the essential estrangement of man from man and of man from God.

A study of the language that expresses sacrifice in Gabriela Mistral's poetry reveals that, for many images of destruction and feelings of anguish, there are antithetical (but not contradictory) images or feelings of relief, pleasure, and delight. Through oxymoron, the traditional literary device by which poets can express profound pain turned to joy, her poetry delves into one of the mysteries of religious sentiment.[67] By uniting oxymoron with paradox, the poet affirms the unknowable element in her poetry; there is a knot no critic can untie in spite of his skill. The mystery can perhaps be understood only by those who have made similar sacrifices. The play of opposites allows pain to elicit pleasure, not necessarily to diminish pain, for the intent is to bear the greatest suffering possible, but rather to invest pain with religious meaning in order to make it worthwhile.

Oxymoron, therefore, is not merely a literary device, for the poet endured the wounds that made life more intense, more pleasurable, and more holy. She concludes "El himno cotidiano," a prayer for the lessening of haughtiness and the continuance of unblemished love, with the following guide to personal conduct:

> *Ame a los seres este día;*
> *a todo trance halle la luz.*
> *Ame mi gozo y mi agonía:*
> *¡ame la prueba de mi cruz!*
>
> (p. 352)

The correlative exemplifies that joy and agony do not exist separately, but are concomitant. Each serves as a function of the other. Furthermore, the thrice-repeated possessive adjective *"mi"* ("my" / joy, agony, and cross) stresses the assumption of a personal burden.

Existence, according to the view just presented, is an unending duel between pain and pleasure. The latter is always the result of pain, never of previous joy, and is certainly never to be tolerated for its own sake. Existence owes its tragic nature more to the debt of personal sacrifice Christ imposed on his followers than to Adam's original sinful choice. The onus of pleasure derived only from pain originates in the supreme sacrifice on the Cross: "¡*Estuvimos prendidos, como el hijo a la madre, / a ti, del primer llanto a la última agonía!*" ("La cruz de Bistolfi," p. 4). While sacrifice is inescapable, it is also true that the Cross beckons with continual love:

> *Cruz que ninguno mira y que todos sentimos,*
> *la invisible y la cierta como una ancha montaña:*
> *dormimos sobre ti y sobre ti vivimos;*
> *tus brazos nos mecen y tu sombra nos baña.*
> (p. 4)

This strophe welds opposites by the paradoxical pairing of negative physical qualities with unswerving positive emotions, so that the absence of an actual cross does not erase the personal, intimate sense of sacrifice inherent in human beings.

But even total pleasure — that is, love — is meaningless if the initial impulse to love does not emanate from the lesson of the supreme pain of Christ: "*El amor nos fingió un lecho, pero era / solamente tu garfio y tu leño desnudo*" (p. 4). Total sacrifice, then, is physical death, after which spiritual rebirth ensues. The New School critic Cleanth Brooks, in "The Language of Paradox," cites a line of John Donne's "Canonization": "Wee can dye by it, if not live by love." Brooks offers this explanation of the wounds that confer life and love: "In the sixteenth and seventeenth centuries to 'die' means to experience the consummation of the act of love."[68] Because holy life and pure love originate from an annihilation of the senses, surrender in sacrifice is the discovery of a more intense life. This is the meaning of the metaphor of death, "*clavo de ensueño*," in conjunction with the figurative "*me muero.*" Together they suggest her total participation in the eternal life of Jesus Christ: "*De toda sangre humana fresca está tu madero, / y sobre ti yo aspiro las llagas de mi padre, / y en el clavo de ensueño que le llagó, me muero*" (p. 4). Brooks continues with an exegesis that is particularly applicable to "La cruz de Bistolfi." He says, paraphrasing Donne: "Our death is really a more intense life.... We can afford to trade life (the world) for death (love), for that death is the consummation of life.... After all, one does not expect to live *by* love, one expects, and wants to die *by* it."

Mistral's famous homage to her sister Emelina and to all rural schoolteachers, herself included, encapsulates the life that willingly bears its wounds in order to love more intensely:

> *La maestra era alegre. ¡Pobre mujer herida!*
> *Su sonrisa fue un modo de llorar con bondad.*
> *Por sobre la sandalia rota y enrojecida,*
> *era ella la insigne flor de su santidad.*
> ("La maestra rural," p. 51)

To partake of the joy contingent upon sacrificial death, the victim must possess charitable love in advance: "*Los hierros que le abrieron el pecho generoso / ¡más anchas le dejaron las cuencas del amor!*" (p. 52). The comparative "*más anchas*" ("wider"), indicates that, no matter how sublime the charity within the teacher as a result of unstinting service, the love that originates in the greater pain from sacrifice is more glorious.[69] Like Christ, called "Rabbi" [teacher] by the disciples,"[70] the rural teacher seems destined for a divine apotheosis: "*...y era su vida humana la dilatada brecha / que suele abrirse el Padre para echar claridad*" (p. 53). Repeatedly, the teacher is raised to divine status for a sacrifice born of love: "*...enseñar y amar intensamente sobre la Tierra es llegar al último día con el lanzazo de Longinos en el costado ardiente de amor.*"[71] The true teacher is concerned with wisdom, not knowledge, universal ethics, not manners, and unrewarded dedication, not success. By shunning the ephemeral things in life, the teacher accepts the burden that eventually leads to a spiritual existence: "*Vestía sayas pardas, no enjoyaba su mano / ¡y era todo su espíritu un inmenso joyel!*" ("La maestra rural," p. 51).

It is worth repeating that Gabriela, a rural schoolteacher for more than fifteen years, includes herself among those select few who lead the ignorant from darkness, protect the innocent from evil, and offer love to the unwanted.

The Life Principle: Water, Blood and Milk

For the poet, water can characterize human activities. Moving and stagnant water can represent the quick and the sluggish, the fleeting and the stable, the living and the dead. As water passes over rocks, a song may come forth. And the liquid can be cold or warm. Even more important, the fact that water is indispensable for sustaining life warrants the judgment that water's essence is life. Blood, too, although lacking the more varied physical attributes of water, participates in the latter's most essential meaning. The ancient Hebrews attributed to blood the property of *nephesh*, the "seat of the soul," the source of life.[72] In Hebrew law, to partake of the blood of an animal is to destroy life and to merit tribal ostracism.[73] The "principle of life" is central to both liquids, and the principle is not subverted if blood is spilled in sacrifice or atonement. Although a life is given up in sacrificial death, the victim attains a higher life by his sacrifice for remission of sin. Jesus Christ's sacrifice was unique in that he did not atone for personal sin, but rather for the sins of others. When his body was pierced, blood and water issued forth to extol the new life that his sacrifice proclaimed. It is in this context that blood and water appear most often in the poetry of Gabriela Mistral, essentially endowed with the religious implications of Christ's act.

Actually, Christ's desire for self-sacrifice was really a death wish in expectation of life after death. His body perished in order that his spirit might live eternally.[74] In Gabriela's poetry, a similar process is apparent. Self-humiliation, abstinence, penance, and even a desire for death ("*Ahora, Cristo, bájame los párpados ...*" ["Éxtasis," p. 64]) lead eventually to a hope for spiritual rebirth in the rejuvenating fluids of blood and water:

> *Creo en mi corazón, que cuando canta*
> *hunde en el Dios profundo el flanco herido,*
> *para subir de la piscina viva*
> *como recién nacido.*
>
> ("Credo," p. 31)

A period of emotional and religious crisis can give way to new feeling and new hope. Renewal is manifest also in the ability of the poet to reshape her poetic expression, and to feel, after many bitter verses, cleansed and freed of the suffering that has dogged her. This is implicit in the preceding selection and explicit in the following: "*En estos cien poemas queda sangrando un pasado doloroso en el cual la canción se ensangrentó para aliviarme.*"[75] The personal catharsis was achieved through the poetic bloodletting. Having been joined through poetry to Christ's sacrifice, in the purification attendant upon creative activity she achieved a modicum of serenity.

In the allegorical poem "El barco misericordioso" ("The Merciful Ship"), the suffering poet is on a "*barco,*" a symbol of Christ. Note the familiar "*costados,*" "*rojos frutos,*" "*jarcias vividas,*" "*tiemblen,*" and "*herida*"—all symbols and expressions common to sacrifice and martyrdom—are replaced by "*esperanza*" ("hope") (p. 112). As she had once looked on Christ's blood as the symbol for sacrifice, she now regards the sea as an "*oleaje vivo*" ("living surge of waves") that will bring "*dulzura de rodillas*" ("sweetness of knees"). Elsewhere, in another context, the same dulcifying effect is achieved from Christ's wounds, which become balm to a feverish soul: "*Toda dulzura de su dorso mana; / el valle en ella tierno se reclina*" ("El Ixtlazihuatl," p. 145). With regard to the compassion and mercy of Christ, a vision of a cosmic cup again appears, "*...donde se esponjan de dulzura / los nectarios de todos los huertos de la Tierra!*"[76] This cup, which is the poet's metaphor for the wounded body that pours out its life fluids, has an almost hypnotic power over the poet's fantasy, when, for example, she imagines the enigmatic situation of a "*corazón siempre vertido, pero nunca vaciado*" ("Credo," p. 32). The optimism that underlies this mystery of a "heart always outpouring but never emptied" still suggests that life is sacrifice. Yet it also suggests that, in spite of the loss of "*resinas*" ("resins," a metaphoric variant of vital fluids), the body is never totally emptied while Christ in turn pours back the spiritual liquid of love.

Blood and milk, also, intermingle to intensify the life-giving properties of both fluids. A holy child originates as an aspiration, a dream, which, for its realization, requires the merger of fluids endowed with life:

> *Musgo de los sueños míos*
> *en que te cuajaste,*
> *duerme así, con tus sabores*
> *de leche y de sangre.*
> ("Canción de la sangre," p. 190)

In the famous "Poema del hijo," "*río de mi vida bajando a él, fecundo*" enlarges the above metaphor and adds movement (p. 102). But it does not change the objective, which is to engender miraculously the ideal child. The poet transposes the images of blood and milk to acts of sacrifice and adoration.

Gabriela importunes Christ to care for her dead mother, who had cherished Christ and had extolled his name and innocence. The plea is to a Christ born of woman, as if she were playing on his sympathy, or appealing to his humble, human origin:

> *Cristo, hijo de mujer,*
> *carne que aquí amamantaron*
> . . . .
> *recibe a la que dio leche*
> *cantándome con tu salmo ...*
> ("Locas letanías," p. 398)

In "Lápida filial," which startles by the bold suggestion that the deceased mother was divine and had nursed "*con una leche más que otra viva,*" the poet begs for her resurrection. If resurrection is not possible, an archangel can fashion "*formas y sangre y leche*" from the body of the daughter, who, as recipient of divine sustenance, can now be redeemer of her mother by self-sacrifice. The mother can thus unite with "*...la vasta y santa sinfonía / de viejas madres: la Macabea, / Ana, Isabel, Lía y Raquel.*" (pp. 380–381).

"Campeón finlandés" eulogizes the heroic, outnumbered Finns who, from 1939 to 1941, resisted the Russian invaders, but ultimately succumbed to them. The poem simultaneously pursues two currents of religious feeling, in a process reminiscent of "Al pueblo hebreo," an elegy to the Jews massacred in the Polish pogroms. The spirit and language of the New and Old Testaments coalesce to praise the martyred Finnish people, who tried to save "*el arco-iris de las Vírgenes de Cristo, / y la bautizada frente de tus niños,*" with a display of courage similar to that of the Maccabees, defenders of the Torah and the Jewish state against the heathens: "*¡Partes el cielo, ríes y lloras / al abrazar a Judas Macabeo!*" (pp. 678, 679). The sacrifice of Christ and the strength of the Jews are referred to again:

> *No lloran ni las madres ni los niños,*
> *ni aun el hielo, en la Finlandia enjuta*
> *como la Macabea, que da sudor de sangre*
> *y da de mamar sangre, pero no llora llanto;*
> *y nosotras tampoco lloramos, atizando*
> *el ruedo y los cogollos de tu hoguera.*
>
> (p. 678)

The epithet, "*la Macabea*," unites the complex, multiple allusion to blood and milk. Heroic suffering, both as a Maccabee and as an adherent of Christ, is subsumed in "*sudor de sangre*" ("blood sweat"). Having consecrated their lifeblood to protect their rights as free individuals, and preferring this course to ignominy at the hands of the Russians, the Finnish people are deemed staunch apostles of truth and innocence, who chose martyrdom rather than surrender religious principles.

It may be only coincidence to finish the discussion of the symbols of Christian sacrifice with several references to the Jews. It will be recalled, in contrast, that the chapter "The Hebraic Tradition" concludes with the presence of Jesus Christ in a poem that praises the Jews. The spirit of sacrifice which guided and continues to guide the Jews through adversities contains the seed of religious plenitude. This seed took root and nourished through the supreme act of Jesus Christ, who commended himself, as have persecuted Jews, into the hands of God. For this reason, the Finns of the preceding poem find courage, although death awaits them, in the inspired acts of Jewish and Christian heroes.

Thus the core of the poetry of sacrifice, whether in relation to a poet, a race, or a person with divine inspiration, lies in subsuming individual, earthly destiny to that greater end, which, entrusted to God, becomes a beginning. In the age of two world wars, when faith in God drew laughter, when technology replaced the simplicity of the rural life, when truth and kindness were traded like commodities, Gabriela Mistral exemplified a singleness of purpose which did not sell out fundamental religious principles for an ephemeral, tinseled life of science, machinery, and economics. Nor did her poetry abandon the paths she had hewn out with her own endeavor: love, dedication to the weak, self-sacrifice, and a continual search for the meaning of God.

Through steadfast adherence to the theme of sacrifice, the poetry itself becomes a sacrifice on the altar of new fashions and new techniques. Poetic renewal, however, is not a necessary function of novel experiences, but, rather a concomitant of imagination and spirit. Experiences are fugitive, sensations volatile, but the spirit molded in sacrifice, one capable of suffering and reverence by focusing on the permanent essence of Jesus Christ, need not gild transitory values with artistic respectability. A spirit so dedicated, an imagination so animated, become transformed by spiritual rebirth. Then life and art strive toward integration, so that each responds to the other. Man recreates himself through art, and remakes himself in God's image. In so doing, man strives to ensure the immortality of his works and the transcendence of his being.

CHAPTER XV

Conclusions on the Sacred and the Secular

Among the poetic themes Gabriela Mistral elaborated consistently — love and anguish, life and death, nature and man — none occupies a more pivotal position than her treatment of the sacred meaning of God. The Old Testament God and Jesus Christ, in their respective sternness and charity, appear to share qualities of omniscience and omnipresence. Yet, for Yahweh the poet reserves characteristics rooted in tradition, Scripture, and the collective unconscious. Yahweh's strength negates all possible appeals for mercy and benevolence. Yahweh has absolute power over the life-taking and life-giving aspects of human existence. If man were condemned to face forever the anger of a post–Edenic deity, compassion and love would matter little. What Yahweh tendered grudgingly, Jesus Christ, offered in abundance. The Sinaitic God, therefore, made man aware of his own anguish and insignificance. Christ's sacrifice imparted to man the unique experience of knowing a divine being who shared human pain. This explains Gabriela's appeals to a tortured Jesus Christ, who knew human suffering and promised redemption. If the end is worthwhile, she felt, then, the means must be justifiable. Still, when she ultimately chose the Christian path, she did not cease to recognize that Christian and Jew had a common heritage of suffering. Nor did she disregard the bond of suffering that linked her to both traditions.

Gabriela was on intimate terms with the Old Testament at an early age. Apart from the tales of biblical heroes and heroines memorized at her grandmother's side, she also learned respect for the stern God who fulfills awesome prophecies. The Bible guided her conduct and salved her conscience. Although far from being a Jew in the strict sense of the word, Gabriela Mistral has been characterized as a biblical heroine incarnate. Her spiritual strength and austere demeanor bore this out. In her psyche, she identified herself with the outcast, persecuted Jews. For example, in the references in her poetry to the biblical women who beseeched God for a child, there is more than a trace of her own infertility. For her, as well as for the biblical matriarchs, personal fecundity was secondary to the role of the mother as progenitress of the race. She remained alert to the needs of underprivileged children and, in this respect, accrued the epithet "virgen-madre." Job's rocklike faith and his defiant spirit in the face of God's unjust attacks suggest a parallel with Gabriela's own intransigence, a trait that defined her personality and marks her poetry with the stamp of the Hebraic tradition.

Deeply committed to a universe in which God is central, it might appear incongruous that Gabriela Mistral could be interested in Buddhism, a philosophy that denies the existence of God and the power of miracles. In the quest to reinforce her belief that the divinity of man is a virtue dependent on man's capacity for good or evil and not a grudging concession from Church and clergy, she broke away from institutionalized religion. In Theosophy, which embraces Christian and Buddhist tenets, and holds truth to be the highest form of religion, she was able to maintain her love for Jesus Christ and her oneness with all creatures. To all intents and purposes, then, the study of Theosophy took her closer to God by taking her closer to the spirit of God that resides in all men. What is more crucial, Theosophy frees the individual from the necessity of blindly accepting the judgments of a priestly caste. Gabriela rejected the condescending and selfish edicts of the Church in Chile, because the Church did not seek to elevate its worshipers and, instead, offered sentimentality rather than piety, asked for faith and offered no means by which the faith could be sustained. Inimical to theology, Theosophy depends upon an open, inquiring mind which affirms the rational nature of religion.

Theosophy's stress on the formation of a universal brotherhood without regard to creed, color, sex, or caste had a profound effect on Gabriela Mistral's religious beliefs, even after she had ceased to join in the meetings and investigations of the Theosophical Society. Theosophy, which allied her to Tagore, had a practical and ethical level in addition to a theoretical and religious one. The influence of its practical, secular aspect is evident in her physical, moral, and financial support for the founding of free schools and libraries and the sheltering of homeless, refugee children. On a theoretical level, the brotherhood of man implies the fusion of man with the fleeting forms of the universe for the purpose of achieving wholeness and harmony. Through this act, man fulfills the messianic dreams of universal love and understanding. The fraternal handclasp and the whirling circle of children of the "Rondas" in *Ternura* exemplify a world that forgets its selfishness in order to participate in an act that permits the individual to become one with the totality. This is precisely the meaning, also, of the "Canciones de cuna": "*Dios padre sus miles de mundos / mece sin ruidos. / Sintiendo su mano en la sombra / mezo a mi niño*"

("Meciendo," p. 153). In the "Cradle Songs," as the mother rocks her child in an act of total selflessness, she believes that the hand of God is tilting the cradle and uniting her creation with the vast creation of God.

Contact with Theosophy heightened the poet's awareness of the mysterious, divine spirit that pervades the universe. In her conception of Christ's birth, mission, and sacrifice she describes a cosmic arc. He originates in astral myths; his face appears, transfigured, in the wheat that becomes Chilean bread; and, symbolized by Krishnamurti, the spirit of Christ is ubiquitous, provided man is prepared to acknowledge Christ's sacrifice. The poet displays an aversion to the traditional Nativity scene, with its doting Mary and stereotyped Christ Child, who is born of haloed, white parents in a comfortable inn. She substitutes parents of dark skin to emphasize that Christ belongs also to the underprivileged South American peasants. She opposes the icons that present Christ washed and combed during his ordeal, and offers a trenchant, firsthand image of Christ atoning for man's sins. In this sense, her poetry tends to demythologize comfortable, facile versions of the life of Christ. Europeans and North Americans have invested these versions with their own naivete because of a natural insistence upon religion that does not upset a feeling of supremacy and does not recall sins and suffering.

In contrast with the tender and sentimental note that dominates the poetry to the Christ Child in *Ternura,* the overriding tone of the poetry to the crucified Christ in *Desolación* is strident and violent. The reasons for the display of bitter language and exacerbated grief in connection with Christ's sacrifice are complex, and have to do with the poet's personal feelings of betrayal and persecution and with her concept of religion. It has been established that Gabriela Mistral suffered insults from acquaintances, critics, politicians, and religious leaders, with the result that she felt herself a victim of perfidy and persecution. It is equally clear that Gabriela believed that sacrifice was the noblest form of religious endeavor, as evidenced by Christ's acceptance of sacrifice and his desire to intensify suffering by refusing an anodyne. The poet herself rejected the balm that would have made life more pleasant but less meaningful, and thus may be likened to the legendary Veronica. Her poetry, too, striving to illuminate the pain of Christ with its insistence on blood and sweat, bears the indelible mark of personal and religious tragedy. The poetry of Gabriela Mistral is scarred with the baring, the closing, and the reopening of wounds.

She did not delight in pain for its own sake; sacrifice was not an end in itself. At an early age, Gabriela Mistral was torn between two conflicting views, the Buddhist and the Christian. The Buddhist position is that pain emanates from desire, and its presence proves the a priori existence of desire. To temper her appetite and to forget carnal temptation, she observed Yoga rites of self-purification and contemplation. That is, she performed acts of charity, disciplined her thoughts, and avoided animal flesh in her diet. The Christian concept is the reverse of Buddhism and holds that pain is worthwhile, even necessary, when it emulates the supreme act of Christ. Therefore, pain is not the result of the presence of desire, but of the aspiration to share in sacrifice. The Christian view goes further, and states that existence itself is a duel between pain and pleasure; the latter is always the result of pain and never the result of previous joy. Since pain is inescapable, the Christian view offers a more noble rationalization than Buddhism for delighting in the sacrifices that make anguish more tolerable and life more holy.

Confronted with a religious crisis after 1924, Gabriela Mistral was forced to reconcile her early aversion to the Church with the possible benefits of the Church to society. She had to reconcile also her conscious choice of Theosophy and Buddhism with the discrepancies she could not help but see in them. Impinging on these issues were the three irreconcilable deities of Judaism, Christianity, and Buddhism, each with its own brand of righteousness, pain, and charity. Apart from offering personal fulfillment in a religious life, religion must also point the way to the betterment of society as a whole. In this latter consideration, Gabriela Mistral found the key to the true religion. Influenced in part by Henri Bergson, in part by the Christian Socialists, she began to believe in a dynamic Christianity that would put service and charity above the personal needs of a priesthood. A mystic Christianity takes into account the race, the collective individual. She saw the betterment of the race to be the supreme task of the Church if it was to practice the sacrifice it demanded of others. In the last thirty years of her life, Gabriela Mistral believed the Church, as represented by the Order of Saint Francis, had the potential to initiate the reforms that would enable it to offer a Christianity that would be charitable, dynamic, and uplifting.

Appendices

A. The Theosophical Society of La Serena

Don Ricardo Michell Abós-Padilla, president of the Sociedad Teosófica de Chile, starting 1955, prepared the following "Notas para un Estudio" (November 1966), which outline for the first time his direct knowledge of Gabriela Mistral's commitment to Theosophy and oriental thought. In 1919, he and Gabriela belonged to the Lodge Despertar in La Serena, founded 1917, by Demetrio Salas Maturana. They joined some other members, including Dr. Ramón Clares Pérez, sisters Rosa and Virginia Jácome, Lucy Hinch, and Zacarías Gómez. Zacarías had already befriended Gabriela in the Theosophical Society of Antofagasta (1911–1912). From La Serena he would travel to Santiago to open the Librería Orientalista. Appendix B, "Mistral and Zacarías Gómez: A Personal and Theosophical Relationship," contains many more details.

The members, following discussions of esoteric philosophy in the home of Salas Maturana, frequently visited the nearby beaches. In the sunshine, as an integral part of their dedication to purification practices—all the while philosophizing—they took walks, exercised, and ate a vegetarian lunch. When Gabriela visited Chile in 1925, she renewed her talks and walks with her friends in the La Serena lodge.

The lodge members had free access to one another's private libraries, which contained many esoteric writings. Michell Abós-Padilla recalled distinctly that Gabriela "*devoraba los libros teosóficos*" borrowed from friends. He recalled her reading the following authors and works in Spanish translation:

Annie Besant: *Cristianismo esotérico, Introducción al Yoga,* and *Hacia el templo.*
Charles Leadbeater: *El hombre visible e invisible* and *Formas de pensamiento.*

Besant and Leadbeater: *El hombre: Cómo y dónde vino y a dónde va.*
Jasper Niemans: *Cartas que me han ayudado.*
Anonymous: *Despertad hijos de la luz* and *El espíritu de los por nacer.*
Ernesto Good: *Concentración, Construcción del carácter* and *Métodos y entrenamiento de los hindúes.*
Romain Rolland: *El evangelio de Rusia* and *Jean-Christophe.*
Maurice Maeterlinck: *Senderos en la montaña, El pájaro azul,* and *El gran misterio.*

"Notas para un Estudio sobre Gabriela Mistral y la Teosofía" by Ricardo Michell Abós-Padilla

Ricardo Michell Abós-Padilla's lengthy report outlines the Theosophical movement in La Serena and records, to the best of his memory, the books Gabriela had access to in the members' private libraries and possibly read during her association with the Despertar Lodge. Where his memory flagged or time did not permit, I added missing or additional information in brackets, realigned works with their probable authors, and relocated text for purposes of clarity and emphasis.

Títulos de obras teosóficas que estuvieron en poder de Gabriela Mistral, en La Serena, colocadas en los anaqueles de su biblioteca, o depositadas desordenadamente sobre una mesa u otro mueble al alcance de la poetisa. Algunas de estas obras eran de su propiedad, y otras, las más, las tuvo temporalmente prestadas de la Logia teosófica de esa ciudad, presidida por don Demetrio Salas Maturana, o de las bibliotecas particulares de don Zacarías Gómez, de las hermanas Rosa y Virginia Jácome, del Doctor Ramón Clares Pérez (Médico Cirujano), o de Ricardo Michell Abós-Padilla (actual Presidente de la Sociedad Teosófica de Chile, desde 1955).

Puede haber omisiones, por olvido. También es posible que haya inclusiones indebidas o equivocadas, por falla de la memoria del informante. Este no podría asegurar que Lucila Godoy leyera todos y enteramente los títulos que siguen. Pero sí puede asegurar que ella exhibió interés patente por numerosos temas y pormenores tratados en los libros consignados en este inventario. Por ejemplo, en las tertulias intelectuales tenidas con sus amigos estudiantes de Teosofía serenenses, ella participó más de una vez activamente en el estudio y debate (principalmente en su casa y ocasionalmente en paseos a la playa de La Serena y en el recorrido de unos dos kilómetros por la Alameda que conduce a la orilla del mar) de tópicos como los referentes a: Dhyana — Samadhi — Dharma — Buddhi — Atma — Brahma — Karma — Prana — Kundalini — Manvántara — Pralaya — Kama — Manas — El Logos de un Universo y las Huestes creadoras -La naturaleza trina del hombre: Nous, Psiquis y Soma = La Trinidad: Voluntad, Amor, Sabiduría, encarnada en el Cuaternario: Mente, Emoción, Pasión y Músculo, etc.

Otro ejemplo de su interés por la literatura teosófica, lo dio cuando se trató el tema de la Yoga. Entonces ella demostró tener conceptos claros y exactos sobre cada uno de los sistemas: Raja Yoga, Jnana Yoga, Bhakti Yoga, Hatha Yoga.

En otras ocasiones demostró a sus contertulios haber asimilado bastante de sus lecturas sobre los Misterios de Osiris, de Orfeo, de Thebas, de Mithra, de Krotona.

El informante no ha podido recordar algunos títulos de [Rudolph] Steiner (uno relativo a la sangre *[The Occult Significance of Blood]*, otro referente a la realidad interior del hombre) y otros de Jinarajadasa (concernientes al Arte y a otros temas), que también vio entre las obras teosóficas existentes en la pieza de trabajo y de reunión de Gabriela Mistral con sus amigos.

Annie Besant: *Doctrina del corazón, Lecturas populares sobre Teosofía, El hombre y sus cuerpos, El sendero del discipulado, Constitución septenaria del hombre, Los ideales de la Teosofía, Un mundo en transición, El poder del pensamiento, La sabiduría antigua, La sabiduría de los Upanishads, Reencarnación, Karma, La genealogía del hombre.*
Charles W. Leadbeater: *Un libro de texto de Teosofía, La vida interna, Protectores invisibles, Más allá de la muerte, Los sueños, Clarividencia, A los que sufren, Nuestra relación con los niños, El sistema (solar) a que pertenecemos, El plano astral y el Devakán.*
[Annie] Besant and [Charles] Leadbeater: *Las 30 últimas vidas de Alcione, La química oculta.*
H[éléna] P[etrovna] Blavatsky: *La clave de la Teosofía, Glosario teosófico, Isis sin velos, La voz del silencio, Por las grutas y selvas del Indostán.*
A[lfred] P[ercy] Sinnett: *El Buddhismo esotérico. El mundo oculto.*
Mario Roso de Luna: *Wagner, mitólogo y ocultista.*
Bhagaván Dasa: *La ciencia de las emociones.*
Edouard Schuré: *Los grandes iniciados.*
[George B. S.] Mead: *¿Vivió Jesús 100 años antes de Cristo?, [Pistis Sophia, a Gnostic miscellany], [Apolonio de Thyana].*
Mabel [Cook] Collins: *Luz en el sendero.*
H[enry] S. Olcott: *Catecismo buddhista.*
E[dwin] Arnold: *La luz del Asia.*
Aimé Blech: *Luz y tinieblas.*
[Edward George] Bulwer-Lytton: *Zanoni.*

Dos Chelas: *El hombre: Fragmentos de una historia olvidada.*
Swami Vivekananda: *La filosofía yoga; [Los aforismos de Patán jali].*
Franz Hartmann: *Ciencia oculta en la medicina, [Magia blanca y magia negra en la medicina].*
Scott Eliot: *La perdida Lemuria, La Atlántida.*
Doctor Pascal [?]: *Ensayo sobre la evolución humana, Las leyes del destino, Bases científicas de la Teosofía.*
Jiddu Krishnamurti (Alcione): *A los pies del maestro; La educación como servicio.*
Ralph Wald[o] Trine: *En armonia con el Infinito.*
Miguel de Molinos: *Guía espiritual.*
[Friedrich] Nietzsche : *Así hablaba Zaratustra.*
Paracelsus: *[Four Treatises].*
Meister Eckhart: *[Treatises and Sermons].*
Ramakrishma: *[Gospels of Ramakrishna].*
Rabindranath Tagore: *[Gitanjali].*
Otros autores: Lao-Tse, Confucio, Jacobo Boehme, Porfirio, Plotino, Orígenes.
Otras obras: *El Bhagavad Gita, El Dhammapada, Vida de Pitágoras, Los versos dorados de Pitágoras, Biblioteca de las Maravillas.*
Revistas: *Le Lotus Bleu, El Loto Blanco, Revista Teosófica Chilena, La Nueva Era.*

Mistral's Philosophy Influences Abós-Padilla

Gabriela's sense of justice, free of sectarianism, had a profound and everlasting effect on Ricardo Michell Abós-Padilla. He cherished and preserved the memory of her *"grandeza, serenidad, y majestad"* by offering her own words, which follow:

> *Ricardo, el mundo necesita ser redimido, no importa quién lo ejecute:*
> *Que lo haga el budismo, el islamismo, que lo haga la masonería, o que lo haga el ateísmo, es algo de valor secundario. Lo importante es que el mundo nazca a un mundo nuevo."*

Ricardo continues with a series of thoughts from Gabriela Mistral:

> *El informante recuerda una exposición de ideas que ella hizo en términos aproximadamente a los siguientes:*
> *Dejad que los niños vengan a mí, pues de ellos es el Reino de los Cielos. No habéis de buscar el Reino de los Cielos aquí ni allá ni acullá, porque el Reino de los Cielos está dentro de vosotros. Es un estado de bienaventuranza de que se goza cuando el 'yo' se desvanece, cuando uno se desentiende y olvida de sí*

mismo. Este es el Reino de los Cielos; lo más próximo a nosotros, pues es la naturaleza intrínseca y la esencia primaria de nuestro ser, consubstanciales e idénticas con la naturaleza y esencia de Dios (nuestro Padre que está en los Cielos). En esto consiste la semejanza del Hombre con Dios; vale decir, la identidad, la unidad, de la criatura con el Creador.

Don Ricardo, on helping me with his "Notas," repaid a debt to Gabriela Mistral and to others who afforded him the insights that guided his life.

B. Zacarías Gómez: A Personal Correspondence

Lucila Godoy, along with her friend Fidelia Valdez Pereira, taught in Antofagasta (1911–1912). (This was discussed in Chapter V, "Antofagasta: Desertic North and Arid Behavior.) While Fidelia preferred the company and chit-chat of the *director* of the Liceo Fiscal de Hombres and his Catholic friends—which befit her status as *directora* of the Liceo de Niñas—Lucila opted for the membership and ideas of the Sociedad Teosófica Destellos, presided over by Carlos Parrau Escobar, where she befriended Zacarías Gómez. They met sporadically over the years, especially at meetings of the Theosophical Societies of La Serena and Santiago. In the thirty-five years she lived abroad (1922–1957), their friendship prevailed and flourished through books he mailed to her, chance meetings, tasks he performed, and correspondence.

Scope of the Gómez Marzheimer Family's Correpondence

Don Guillermo Gómez Marzheimer of Santiago graciously granted me permission to read and publish the correspondence between his late father Don Zacarías Gómez and Gabriela Mistral. Because the heirs of Don Zacarías were unwilling to part with valuable documents long enough for them to be transcribed or photocopied, I had to make hurried notes. Absent the originals, I aligned the notes on the contents of the correspondence thematically, and if possible, chronologically. Some of the letters are incorporated into the text and notes, the rest are discussed here.

The correspondence included a postcard dated 1927, and letters embracing fifteen years (1940–1955). Don Guillermo Gómez assumed, however, that more letters existed, and that what survived was only a part of the total correspondence. Some letters could have been lost; others, meant only for his father's eyes, could have been destroyed.

Don Guillermo believed that their philosophical and personal relationship began at La Serena in 1919, when both belonged to the Theosophical Lodge Destellos. Further information corrects this; they had met for the first ime in Antofagasta, from 1911 to 1912. In 1925, they resumed contact when Gabriela visited Chile, a fact substantiated by Ricardo Michell Abós-Padilla (see Appendix A). With her subsequent departure and exile, they began an epistolary exchange.

La Librería Orientalista and Mistral's Readings

Don Zacarías founded the Librería Orientalista in Santiago, located at the time on Calle Catedral 1145. He passed the ownership to his son, Hernán Gómez. While Zacarías was in charge, he generously furnished Gabriela with information and books she wanted on Theosophy and other literary matters. He considered his shop less a source of economic gain and more an extension of a deep religious conviction, which motivated him to aid unselfishly the friends who joined him in seeking truth and wisdom.

During Mistral's stay in Mexico City at the home of Palma Guillén de Nicolau — presumably 1948; the date is illegible — she asked Don Zacarías for Max Heindel's "*libros orientalistas*" on the Rosicrucians: *Principios ocultos de la salud y de la curación, Cristianismo Rosacruz, Filosofía Rosacruz,* and *Cartas a los estudiantes.* She again showed interest in the Rosicrucians (October 3, 1947): "*Extrañas y agudas me parecen esos libros sobre Raja-Yoga. Me interesa saber si ellos no salieron de cabeza nacista ('Jerarquía' descubre eso). Me parece más sano lo Rosacruz.*" Gabriela reiterated her interest in the Rosicrucians in two letters (October 20, 1951, April 18, 1954). The latter note, especially, contains a cryptic, unexplained phrase referring to the Rosicrucians, because one of the assistants who accompanied her to Chile (1954), probably Doris Dana rather than Gilda Péndola, "was a lover of our ideas": "*La compañera que llevaré es una Rosacruz muy amante de nuestras ideas.*"

In her letter of October 3, 1947, Gabriela thanked Don Zacarías for having sent her the copy of *Revista Teosófica* containing an article by Pearl Buck and Ramón Clares. The death of Dr. Clares and of Dr. Bucheli, both Theosophists, prompted Gabriela to inquire about the course of their lives since she had last seen them in La Serena. (For a mention of Dr. Clares, see Appendix A.) To her query Don Zacarías replied (October 7, 1947) obliquely that the restoration of health and the continuance of a good life depend upon maintaining the harmony that Mother Nature illustrates for her children. On the general question of death itself, and specifically regarding the death of Carlos Errázuriz, Don Zacarías wrote (September 15, 1948):

> La muerte es Luz. Entre el mundo visible y el invisible, bien sabe Ud. que no hay otro puente de comunicación que el del pensamiento. Es con lo que mejor podemos ayudar a los que fueron nuestros buenos amigos en la tierra, a que encuentren a su vez buenos y angelicales amigos en su peregrinación hacia el cielo. En el reino de las almas, un sentido y muy humano pensamiento, también puede ser una ayuda y una luz. ¿No pensaremos más o menos lo mismo? ¡Mejor para nuestro buen amigo! Además, no olvidemos que las almas están siempre en manos de Dios, y Dios es siempre justo.

On a sheet of paper inserted among the letters, the bookseller listed some of the material he sent to Gabriela on March 14, 1950. He forwarded magazines: *Sophia, El servidor, El médico del alma, La sabiduría oculta, Meditaciones religiosas, Las llaves del reino interno, La fuerza de la No-violencia,* and *Selecciones de Vivekananda.* In a short note he asked (October 6, 1951) if she had read *En las horas de meditación,* by F. J. Alexander. Gabriela answered (October 20, 1951) that she was reading *Pláticas,* by Annie Besant and Charles Leadbeater.

The sustained correspondence shows, even after her announced separation from Eastern practices, that Gabriela Mistral had an abiding, continued intellectual interest in literature dealing with Theosophy, the Rosicrucians, meditation, the occult, and healing through concentration, prayer, and proper diet.

Overseer of Finances, Relatives, and Editors

Don Zacarías willingly undertook the management of Gabriela's personal and business matters while she was abroad. The job offered no salary, nor did it mean constant attention to her financial affairs. But whenever Gabriela asked for specific help—distributing money to the poor, or sending a check to Emelina, or finding out why her checks were not forthcoming—she always turned to this trusted friend. The letters do away with another myth. Friends have alleged that Gabriela never handled money and purportedly had little taste for finances. The letters reveal an exaggerated concern for money and finances. She asked about the following:

- devaluation of the Chilean peso and the high cost of living in the United States (May 8, 1946);
- a life insurance policy that had expired (1944);
- 35,970 pesos owed her by Editorial Zig-Zag (June 14, 1946);

- 5,000 pesos she gave to the poor children of Montegrande (June 14, 1946);
- $200,000.00 actually paid to María Luisa Bombal but said to have been paid to Mistral (March 1, 1947);
- the loss of two month's salary as consul for Chile (March 1, 1947); and
- travelers' checks for Emelina, which were always under discussion.

On another personal matter, Gabriela Mistral's secretary, Consuelo Saleva, wrote to Don Zacarías from Petrópolis that Gabriela would be extremely grateful if he would inform Emelina about the condition of Juan Miguel Godoy Mendoza: "*Gabriela está muy preocupada y tristísima con la gravedad de Yin-Yin y me encarga Ud. se lo escriba a la Emelina para que ella rece por él.*" The date on this letter is clearly August 16, 1943, just three days after the boy's death. The letter does not allude to death, but, at worst, to serious illness or accident. If the letter is correctly dated, does it mean that Gabriela wanted to break the news to Emelina gradually? But why, then, did she not allow her trusted friend to handle the situation with his usual tact? In short, why was the truth being withheld from Don Zacarías? If the letter is misdated and precedes the boy's death, does this indicate that Juan Miguel was not in good spirits prior to his death, contrary to what Gabriela steadfastly alleged? This letter compounds the confusion noted in the text concerning the death of Yin-Yin.

Don Zacarías evidenced a personal concern for Emelina's poor health and constant pain, although he himself was remarkably free of illness owing to rigorous exercise and a strict vegetarian diet. In a letter dated December 21, 1944, he commented on the possible basis for Emelina's ill health: "*[Ud.] no debe inquietarse por ser algo habitual en ella que no se puede ver libre de dolencias y sufrimientos, por uno y otro motivo; además, según mi parecer, existe en ella una especie de 'gozo' de sufrir, sin el cual no puede tener sentido su vida.*" Don Zacarías' perceptive description of Emelina as being a woman desperate for attention while expecting death could be applied to Gabriela herself. In the next exchange (January 17, 1945), Gabriela answered for herself and for Emelina: "*No crea que yo vivo en racionalista. Después de mi duelo [death of Yin-Yin], he debido coger los pedazos de mí misma y rehacer mi mente. Creo que nuestra vida espiritual no anda distante. Voy a mandar a Eme[lina] una preciosa 'oración de salud,' por ensayar sacarla de su pesimismo tremendo.*" It was Don Zacarías who telegrammed news of Emelina's death to Gabriela (March 28, 1947). It is clear that this gentle man kept alive the mutual love of the sisters by his inordinate concern for both, and his solicitude, in turn, nourished Gabriela's emotional ties to Chile.

The letters also allude to a series of difficulties with the editors of *El*

Mercurio. On September 15, 1948, Gabriela informed her friend that she refused to submit any more articles to *El Mercurio* because Rafael Maluenda, the editor, had never replied to her queries. Furthermore, she was indignant because the administration of the newspaper had treated Don Zacarías with disdain when he had tried to retrieve her checks. To appease Gabriela, Don Agustín Edwards, the publisher, had already sent her a reply on September 2, 1948, through Don Zacarías, asserting that all the articles and poems she had submitted had been printed. Don Agustín, in addition, enclosed a curt, but polite, statement from Maluenda dated August 27, 1948, which affirmed that the elimination of the literary supplement would not mean the suppression of Gabrielas works. On the contrary, Maluenda invited her contributions whenever she had the time to send them.

Zacarías Defines and Identifies with Mistral's Spirituality

On two occasions, Don Zacarías put aside his role as business consultant, intermediary, and bookseller, and concentrated on trying to define Gabriela Mistral's person, message, and earthly mission from his perspective. On June 26, 1946:

> *Para mí es Ud. una verdadera santa laica, que actúa en la humana vida terrenal, como mensajera de la alta Jerarquía que debe reinar en el Reino Eterno; para mí nunca dejará Ud. de ser un alma grande, de sentimientos unitarios y universales, que trabaja, lucha, se esfuerza y se gasta en llevar luz al pensamiento y amor al corazón de los hombres.*

On the second occasion (January 9, 1952), one day short of five years before she died, he tried to resolve the enigma of two souls who were distant from each other in space and time, but who could yet share a common world of sentiment:

> *Yo no la veo con los ojos que la miran los intelectuales, los literatos, los poetas, los filósofos y grandes artistas o pensadores, sino con los ojos del alma, que los da una fraternidad espiritual que ni la misma muerte podrá romper. Por eso, por la identificación de almas, por la familiaridad de sentimientos y afectos del corazón yo la distingo y la quiero como a una hermana espiritual a quien llamo Gabrielita.*
>
> I do not look at you with the same eyes as intellectuals, ... rather through the soul's eyes, which offer a spiritual fraternity that death cannot dissolve. Therefore — through the identification of souls, through the familiarity of the heart — I distinguish you and love you as a spiritual sister whom I call Gabrielita.

C. The Bible: An Intimate Experience

Chapter XII, "The Hebraic Tradition," analyzed the importance that the Bible played in Mistral's life and work and the pivotal role ascribed to her alleged Jewishness derived from her paternal grandmother. The poet's speech, "Mi experiencia con la Bibla," affirmed her oneness with the tone and substance of the Bible and described how the Holy Book, mainly through her grandmother's insistent reading and quizzings, gave shape to her language, emotions, and the creative process.

The speech is crucial, also, to understand Mistral's position vis-a-vis the role that religious reconciliation between Jews and Christians can play in combating fascism, since it is given when militarized Germany threatened Europe and persecuted Jews. Her oration in Argentina, a country of emigrant Jews and Christian Germans, called for a unifying thread of peace and understanding via the Old and New Testaments.

In September 1967, the director of the Sociedad Hebraica Argentina (S.H.A) permitted me to reproduce the speech in my book, *Sensibilidad religiosa de Gabriela Mistral* (Madrid: Editorial Gredos, 1975), 276–288. The speech (April 18, 1938), was published in *Revista S.H.A.* on the following dates in 1938: May 1, May 15 and June 1. Outside of the Argentine Jewish community few were aware of its relevance. To reach a wider audience, S.H.A., the director honored all persons interested in Gabriela Mistral and Judaism by permitting the reproduction of the articles.

"Mi Experiencia con la Biblia" by Gabriela Mistral

Mi primer contacto con la Biblia tuvo lugar en la Escuela Primaria, la muy particular Escuela Primaria que yo tuve, mi propia casa, pues mi hermana era maestra en la aldea elquina de Montegrande. Y el encuentro fue en el texto curioso de Historia Bíblica que el Estado daba a los niños. Aquella Historia tenía tres cuartos de Antiguo Testamento, no llevaba añadido doctrinal y de este modo, mi libro se resolvió en un ancho desplegamiento [sic, "despliegue"] de estampas, en un chorro de criaturas judías que me inundó la infancia.

Yo era más discípula del texto que de la clase, porque la distracción, aparte de mi lentitud mental, medio vasca, medio india, me hacían y me hacen aún la peor alumna de una enseñanza oral.

Con lo cual, mi holgura, mi festín del Antiguo Testamento tenía lugar, no en el banco escolar sino, a la salida de la clase, en un lugar increíble. Había una fantástica mata de viejo jazmín a la entrada del huerto. Dentro de ella, una gallina hacía su nidada y unos lagartos rojos llamados allá liguanas, procreaban a su antojo; la mata era además escondedero de todos los juegos de albricias de las muchachas; adentro de ella guardaba yo los juguetes sucios que eran de mi gusto: huesos de fruta, piedras de forma para mí sobrenatural, vidrios de colores y pájaros o culebras muertos; aquello vená a ser un revuelto basural y a la vez mi emporio de maravillas. Una vez cerrada la Escuela, cuando la bulla de las niñas todavía llegaba del camino, yo me metía en esa oscuridad de la mata de jazmín, me entraba al enredo de hojarasca seca que nadie podó nunca, y sacaba mi Historia Bíblica con un aire furtivo de salvajita que se escapó de una mesa a leer en un matorral. Con el cuerpo doblado en siete dobleces, con la cara encima del libro; yo leía la Historia Santa en mi escondrijo, de cinco a siete de la tarde, y parece que no leía más que eso, junto con Historia de Chile y Geografía del mundo. Cuentos, no los tuve en libros; esos que daba la boca jugosamente contadora de mi gente elquina.

Jacob, José, David, la Madre de los Macabeos, Nabucodonosor, Salmanazar, Rebeca y Judith, son criaturas que no se confundirán nunca en mí con los bultos literarios que vendrían después, que por ser auténticas personas no me dan en el paladar de la memoria el regusto de un Ulises o del retórico Cid, o de Mahoma, es decir, el sabor de papel impreso entintado. Tampoco se me juntarían mis héroes judíos con las fábulas literarias ni aun con otras leyendas sus hermanas. En mi alma de niñita no contó Hércules como Goliat ni la Bella de Monstruo como Raquel, ni más tarde Lohengrin se me hermanó con Elías. Hubo en mi seso una abeja enviciada en cáliz abierto de rosa de Sarón, es decir, en miel hebrea, y es que el patriarcalismo, siendo un clima humano, ha sido particularmente un clima de Sud América. Nada me costaba nada a mí, en el Valle cordillerano de Elqui, ver sentados o ver caminar, oír comer y hablar a Abraham y a Jacob. Mis patriarcas se acomodaban perfectamente a las fincas del Valle; desde la flora a la luz, lo hebreo se aposentaba fácilmente allí, y se avenía con la índole nuestra, a la vez tierna y violenta, con el vigor de nuestro temperamento rural y por sobre todo, con la humanidad que respira y traspira la gente del viejo Chile.

Pero a mi chilenidad le faltaba una condición soberana del hebreo, la mayor y la mejor: el realismo sobrenaturalista, el Jehová o Dios Padre permeando la vida, desde la mesa hasta la vendimia, entreverándose con nuestros días, mota a mota, y siendo, en fin, el cielo de nuestro amparo. El chileno es racionalmente religioso; en su material de hombre no entra el visionario ni lo turba mesianismo alguno; se nos trenza con el cantar a lo humano, el cantar a lo divino. Y como yo necesité de este alimento, parece que apenas tuve una razón, y con la urgencia de un hambre verídica, de un apetito casi corporal, yo me buscaría esta enjundia en la Biblia y de ella comería toda la vida.

Para comenzar, yo había volteado y cogido, arquetipos judíos en el texto escolar que conté. Pero me los habían dado en una versión harto convencional, y con un sabor desabrido. Y lo bíblico, relato o canto, hay que tocarlo directamente, aunque sea en las traducciones; hasta magullado el espíritu de la lengua hebrea asoma en ellas aquí y allá, como los músculos de un prisionero entre el rollo de las cadenas. Toda traducción es una especie de cuerpo cautivo, es decir, mártir pero es preferiblemente siempre la traducción a un arreglo escolar de los relatos.

Mi contacto con la lírica judía, que había de ser la lírica de mi nutrimiento [sic], lo hizo, cuando yo tenía 10 años, mi abuela, doña Isabel Villanueva.

Yo no sé por qué razón, a la altura de eso años de 1898, una vieja católica, de catolicismo provincial, podía ser una chilena con la Biblia, y no sólo con Biblia leída, sino con texto sacro oral, aprendido de memoria en lonjas larguísimas. Pero a aquella curiosa mujer la llamaban los sacerdotes de la ciudad de La Serena 'la teóloga' y tenía una pasión casi maniática de esa cosa grande que es la Teología, desdeñada hoy por la gente banal de nuestras pobres democracias. La frecuentación de la lectura religiosa, que era en ella cotidianidad, como el comer, había construido a esa vieja de 70 años, a la vez fuerte e inválida, de rostro tosco y delicado a un tiempo chilena en los huesos y medio nórdica en la alta estatura, en color rojo y en ojos claros, la pasión de leer textos bíblicos, había dado a esa abuela profundidad en el vivir y un fervor de zarzas ardiendo en el arenal de un raza nueva.

Mi madre me mandaba a ver a la vieja enferma, y doña Isabel me ponía a sus pies en un banquito o escabel cuyo uso era sólo éste: allí se sentaba la niñita de trenzas a oír los Salmos de David.

La nieta comenzaba a recibir aquel chorro caliente de poesía, de entrañas despeñadas por el dolor de un reyezuelo de Israel, que se ha vuelto el dolor de un Rey del género humano. Yo oía la tirada de Salmos que a unas veces eran de angustia aullada y otras de gran júbilo, en locas aleluyas que no parecían saltar del mismo labio lleno de salmuera.

Mi abuela no tenía nada de escriba sentado ni de diaconisa pegada as u misa. La vieja diligentemente iba y venía de la salita a la cocina, preparando su dieta de enferma. Y cuando volvía a sentarse tampoco se quedaba en 'mujer de manos rotas,' como dice el refrán español. Ella vivía de bordar casullas y ornamentos de la iglesia. Sus manos de gigantona se habían vuelto delicadas en las yemas de los dedos y en ademanes por el trabajo de veinte años, gracias al cual ella comía y con el que pagó la escuela de sus hijos mientras crecían; casi todas las casullas de las catorce iglesias de La Serena salían de la aguja de doña Isabel, que subía y bajaba con el ir y venir del cubo de la noria o de los telares indios, servidumbre eterna, esclavitud sin más alivio que el dominical.

Oyendo los Salmos, no recibía sino un momento su vista sobre mí. Al soltar yo un disparate en la repetición, su mano se paraba de golpe, el bordado caía de la falda y sus ojos de azul fuerte se encontraban con los míos. Corregido el error, ella seguía bordando y yo, entre uno y otro versículo tocaba a hurtadillas la tela, que me gustaba sobar, por el tacto del hilo de oro duro en la seda blanda.

Yo entendía bastante los Salmos bíblicos, en relación con mis diez años, pero no creo que entendiese más de la mitad. Un pedagogo francés, sabia gente que da sus clásicos a los niños desde los siete años, diría que lo de entender a medias no es cosa trágica, que lo importante es coger en la niñez el cabo de la cuerda noble y echarse al umbral de un clásico mientras llega el tiempo de entrar a vivir en su casa hidalga.

Entendía yo, en todo caso, algunas cosas de bulto, por ejemplo, que un hombre maravilloso, mi héroe David, gritaba a todo lo ancho del grito de su amor de Dios, como si estuviese voceando sobre el rostro mismo de lo Divino. Yo entendía que ese hombre le entregaba a Jehová sus empresas de cada día. Pero también sus mínimos cuidados de la hora. Yo sabía que el hombre David tomaba su licencia de Él, lo mismo que yo la de mi abuela, así para pelear como para alegrarse o tocar los instrumentos músicos.

Yo comprendía, con el mismo entender de hoy, que Aquel a Quien se hablaba rindiendo cuentas, a Quien se pedía la fuerza para andar y para resolver, y para capitanear hombres era el tremendo y suave Dios Padre, el Dios de la nube rasgada, por donde Él veía vivir a su Israel. Yo entendía que la alabanza del Dios invisible que siendo 'enorme y delicado,' pesa sin pesar sobre cada cosa, era una obligación de loor ligada al hecho de ser hombre, de decir palabra en vez de dar vagido animal, y que cantarlo eras el oficio de aquel David que se llamaba Músico y que daba al Señor el nombre Mayor.

Muchas cosas más entendía, pero las que cuento eran las mayores, y yo creo que ellas fundaban mi alma, me tejían, me calentaban los miembros primerizos de la víscera sobrenatural.

Después del recitado de mi abuela, bastante lento, derretido de fervor, porque nunca lo dijo mecánicamente, aunque se lo supiese como la tabla de multiplicar, venía la parte menos agradable, para mí, la angostura de su exigencia de abuela pedagoga. Doña Isabel volvía a comenzar la hebra de versículos, que yo debía ahora repetir y echarme a cuestas de la memoria. Mi memoria, siempre fue mala, y sobre todo, incapaz de fidelidad, y yo repetía, soltando a cada trecho palabras propias, de las que mi abuela medio se indignaba, medio se reía. Con su risa blanca en la cara roja, me gritaba de que yo podía trocar cosas en cualquier texto menos en esos, en sus Salmos, en su salterio.

¿Por qué ella, en vez de darme puras oraciones de Manual de Piedad, según la costumbre de las viejas devotas de Coquimbo, le daba a su niñita boba, de aire distraído, lo menos infantil del mundo, según piensan los tontos de la Pedagogía? ¿Por qué le echaba ese pasto tan duro de majar y tan salido de tiempo y lugar, esa cadena de salmos penitenciales y de salmos cantos jubilares? Nunca yo me lo he podido comprender, y me lo dejo en misterio porque me echó al regazo de la infan-

cia el misterio y no lo he tirado como tantos y hasta me he doblado los misterios que recogí entonces, por voluntad de guardar en mí la reverencia, el amor de índole reverencial, la adoración ciega, porque ciega es siempre, de lo Divino.

Mi abuela pasó por mi vida parece que sólo para cumplir este menester de proveerme la Biblia, en país sin Biblia popular, de ponerme esta narigada de sal no marítima, sino de sal gema que fortifica y quema a la vez, a mitad de la lengua. Ella no fue la abuela que viste a la nieta de pequeña, pues no asistió a mi primera infancia. Ella no ayudó a mi madre en ningún cuido material de su carne chiquita: ella no me cuidó el sarampión, ni difteria; ella no me vio ser maestra de escuela ni llegaron nunca mis pobres versos a sus ojos rendidos de aguja y Biblia; ella no conoció mi cara adulta, aunque viviría casi 90 años.

Las únicas estampas que yo le guardo son estas de su cara bajada a mí y mi cuello subido a ella, en su porfía para hacer correr de mi seso a mis tuétanos, los Salmos de su pasión.

Y sin embargo, a pesar de las pocas briznas de tiempo que ella me dio y del mal destino que nos había de separar, ella, mi Isabel Villanueva, vieja santa para quienes la convivieron, ella sería la criatura más penetrante que cruzó por mi vida chilena. Pasó de veras como un dardo de fuego, por la niñez mía, como el pájaro ardiendo del cuento balcánico, extraña e inolvidable, diferente de cuanta mujer yo conocí, criatura vulgar por la modestia y a la vez secreta como son todos los místicos. Su vida interna era oculta y sólo por un momento o, a causa de tal o cual signo que ella no alcazaba a hurtar se sabía de golpe que esa mujer del servir y el sonreír constantes, del coser y el bordar con ojos heridos, tenía mucha ciencia del alma y que la industria inefable que es la de pecho adentro, había conseguido logros de culto en esa alma.

El Dios Padre que ella me enseñó, la tenga en su cielo fuerte que no se ralea de vejez. Él le haya dado la dicha que aquí no probó ni en una dedada de miel cananea.

Tiempo después, entre los 15 y los 20 años, y sobra contarlo, porque es la aventura de cualquier sudamericano, les digo que anduve haciendo sesgueos estúpidos y dándome tumbos vergonzosos con lecturas ínfimas, del cinco al diez, con novelas y verso que eran insensateces de hospicio...

Todo ese vagabundeo entre plebes verbales y escrituras, paupérrimas, toda esa larga distracción, no importaban mucho, nada es muy grave cuando la banalidad manosea sólo en nuestros forros y no llegan a la semilla del ser, a hincarse allí por mondarla y tirarla al basurero. La Biblia había pasado por mí y su gran aliento recorría visible o invisiblemente mis huesos, atajada en el punto tal por la torpeza, estorbada más allá por la falta de medio concordante con ella; pero no se había ido de mí, como sale y se pierde nuestro hálito; precisamente a causa de que su naturaleza es la de no irse, cuando se la absorbió en la infancia y su virtud es la de calar en el hombre y no cubrir sólo de cierto yeso y su periferia.

Entre los 23 y los 35 años, yo me releí la Biblia, muchas veces, pero bastante mediatizada con textos religiosos orientales, opuestos a ella por un espíritu místico que rebana lo terrestre. Devoraba yo el budismo a grandes sorbos; lo aspiraba con la misma avidez que el viento en mi montaña andina de esos años. Eso era para mí el budismo, un aire de filo helado que a la vez me excitaba y me enfriaba la vida interna; pero al regresar, después de semanas de dieta budista a mi vieja Biblia de tapas resobadas, yo tenía que reconocer que en ella estaba, no más que en ella, el suelo seguro de mis pies de mujer.

Ella volvía a cubrir siempre con esa anchura que tiene de tapiz tremendo de voces, los tratos y manejos infieles ensayados con lo Divino, ella, a la larga, ganaba en esa pelea de textos orientales que se disputaban mi alma en una lucha absurda, como el de un petrel del aire con el puma de mi quebrada chilena.

Yo no sabría decir cuánto le debo a ella, a mi Madre verbal, a la enderezadora de mi laciedad criolla y a la fatigadora de mis renuncias budistas.

El trato con ciertos libros, pero sobre todo con la Santa Biblia, es intimidad pura y no se puede escarmentarla sin que ella sufra en esta operación verbal lo que una entraña expuesta se dolería en el aire.

Ahora me queda por decir lo formal, que es a la vez lo esencial del contagio de la Biblia sobre mí: pues en lo hebreo andan juntos y entrabadas como carne y tendón el fondo con la forma.

Los Salmos de mi abuela, y después de ellos mi lectura larga y ancha de la Biblia total, que yo haría a los 20 años, me habituaron a su manera de expresión que se avino conmigo como si fuese un habla familiar que los míos hubiesen perdido y que recuperé con saltos de gozo.

Yo sé muy bien que hay en la Biblia muchas líneas de expresión: hay el orden de la crónica, seco y tónico; hay las islas de lo idílico en la historia de José o en la de Ruth; hay el dramático de Job, tan diferente del patético de David; hay el orden clásico del Eclesiastés y los Proverbios y, para no seguir, hay entre las fragosidades de Ezequiel y Jeremías, las colinas medio doloridas, medio felices de Isaías, puente de cuerda echado ya sobre la orilla cristiana. La riqueza es una de las causas de la fascinación que irradia el Santo Libro y que lleva hacia él a fieles e infieles, a finos y a bastos. La variedad constante evita la fatiga de una Escritura, que pudo tener la pesadez mortal de las otras de su género, de todas las demás; la Biblia llega a parecer una geografía continental, en la cual el caminador, siempre fresco, que la recorre, pasa, en turnos como de la mano paterna a mano materna, de esta montaña a aquellos collados y de esos al otro vallecito de gracia. Siempre se anda por la Biblia cogido por el Israel innumerable que, con modo varonil o femenino a grandes tajos de frenético amor, lucha, cree, duda, protesta, y reprende, pero que no duerme nunca, que parece ser la criatura de una vigilia eterna.

Pero existe, en todo caso, un acento bíblico general; hay unos denominadores comunes que valen para aquella masa de documentos colectivos y piezas individ-

uales: existe realmente un verbo hebreo que en el Santo Libro mantiene una columna vertebral, la unidad, o bien el aire de familia entre las figuras del largo fresco.

Para mí —y yo no vengo a decir sino la Biblia mía, en m— la unanimidad del Santo Libro lo dan estas cosas: el riscoso tono verídico; la expresión directa que el judío prefiere, en vertical de despeñadero andino, por el que la maldición o la bendición caen a nosotros; una trama constante de violencia brutal y de una indecibles dulzuras; el realismo que, como el de los españoles, deja circular un airecillo lírico contante, y sobre todo una intensidad extremada, que no se relaja, no se afloja, no se dobla nunca, verdadero misterio de la expresión esencial dada en un ardor que escuece la boca. El hebreo de la Biblia, tal vez el hebreo de todo tiempo, es un hombre henchido y ceñido a la vez, que carga el verbo de electricidad de acción, es el que menos ha pecado contra el baldiísmo de la palabra, el que no cae en el desabrimiento y la laciedad de la expresión.

A los diez años, yo conocí esta vía de la palabra, desnuda y recta y la adopté en la medida de mis pobres medios, a puro tanteo, silabeando sus versículos recios, tartamudeando su excelencia y arrimándome a ella, a la vez con amor y miedo de amor.

Había encontrado algo así como una paternidad para mi garganta, como una tutoría cuando menos en mi amarga orfandad de una niña de aldea cordillerana, sin maestro, y sin migaja de consejo para los negocios de su alma muy ávida, mucho.

De este lote de virtudes expresionales de la Biblia, parece que las que más me hayan atraído sean la intensidad y cierto despojo que no sólo aparta el adorno, sino que va en desuello puro. Heredera del español de América, es decir, de una lengua adiposa, la Biblia me prestigió su condición de dardo verbal, su urgido canal de vena caliente. Ella me asqueó para toda la vida de la elegancia vana y viciosa en la escritura y me puso de bruces a beber sobre el manadero de la palabra viva, yo diría que me echó sobre un tema a aspirarle pecho a pecho el resuello vivo.

La ciencia de decir de la Biblia, el comportamiento del judío con el verbo, aun considerada aparte del asunto religioso, es una enorme lección de probidad dada por Israel a los demás idiomas y a las otras razas. El acento de veracidad de la Escritura, de que hablan los críticos, es lo que en gran parte, ha hecho de la actualidad permanente de la Biblia, esa especie de marcha interrumpida del Santo Libro a través de los tiempos más espesos de materia y más adversos a su orden sobrenatural.

Había en los antiguos tiempos, en ciertos cruceros geográficos del Viejo Mundo, unos lugares de convocación, sitios cruciales de cita donde se juntaban los diferentes, para hablar de algún negocio eterno o temporal.

Vosotros hebreos, y nosotros cristianos, poseemos queramos o no confesarlo, un lugar de convocación, especie de alta y ancha meseta tibetiana, en la cual encontrarnos, vernos al rostro, ensayar siquiera el cerco de la unidad rota; en el cual podemos, sin desatar entero el nudo de nuestro conflicto, ablandar el filo de la tensión, y este país o este clima moral, es, en la Biblia, vuestro Viejo Testamento que nos es común, común, común.

Ay, gozo fresco para nosotros y, anchura dulce, la de esta abra de reunión donde podemos, con los ojos puestos en los ojos, comer igual bocado de oro en nuestro Job, ciudadano del dolor, en el Jacob, abajador [sic] de la Tierra al cielo y en el David, que tañía. Tañedor mejor que el salterio el corazón del género humano.

Hay una alegría grande entre las mayores que fue pulverizada por el vanidoso Siglo XIX y es la de provocar masa y también multitud. Yo no soy poco tribal, o si queréis, medioeval, en todo caso, amiga de comunidad por serlo de comunión, y siento no sé qué euforia viviendo una hora de lo que llama la Iglesia, 'la comunión de los Santos.' Parece que esta dicha sólo podemos lograrla y disfrutarla si acudimos a esos puntos de convocación de que he dicho, como la Biblia, o las viejas leyendas universales.

Por eso he querido hablarles, como quien dice de la peana de la unidad nuestra, y os he traído esta conferencia vergonzantes, sin sentir el bochorno de mi torpeza con tal de que, a lo largo de esta hora, nuestra sangre estuviese batiendo unánime sobre el mismo asunto inmenso e íntimo, terrenal y divino.

Chapter Notes

Chapter I

1. Contradictions surrounding Mistral extended to her eye color. Were they green or brown? The diplomatic passport of June 19, 1933, says "*verdes*"; that of January 31, 1946, says "*pardos*" ("brown"). "Verdes" in *Revista Patrimonio Cultural*, 46 Año XIII (Verano 2008), 47. "Pardos" in *Proyecto, preservación, y difusion del legado literario de Gabriela Mistral*, eds. Magda Arce and Gastón Von dem Bussche (Santiago: Zig-Zag, 1993), 205.

2. Observers also contradict themselves about the color of her clothes. See Arturo Torres-Rioseco, "Gabriela Mistral, Nobel Prize Winner, at Home," *Hispania* XXIX (1946), 72–73. Cf. also Virgilio Figueroa, *La divina Gabriela* (Santiago, El Esfuerzo, 1933), 160. Mistral never wore black, according to Matilde Ladrón de Guevara's very informative, personal account: *Rebelde magnífica* (Santiago: Imprenta de la Central de Talleres, 1957), 34, 46–47, 125. But Manuel Pedro González, in "Profile of a Great Woman," *Hispania* XLI (1958), 428, cites Mistral's confidant, the Latin Americanist Waldo Frank, who says she always wore black. Contradictions about seemingly obvious characteristics affirm the subjective nature of Gabriela's observers and attest to the legendary personality she helped shape.

3. Austerity in dress and austerity in poetry ran parallel, observed Alberto Gerchunoff, in "Gabriela Mistral," *Repertorio Americano* (6 julio 1925), 265.

4. Sergio Fernández Larraín noted her ugliness, in *Cartas de amor de Gabriela Mistral* (Santiago: Editorial Andrés Bello, 1978), 205, note 40. References to physical beauty and ugliness emerge often in the letters and in the poetry.

5. Note the effort at hagiography in the following three titles: Virgilio Figueroa's *La divina Gabriela*; Benjamín Carrión's "Santa Gabriela Mistral," *Letras del Ecuador* X, 100 (1954), 3, 4, 52. Carrión, at the slightest criticism, reiterated his fervor: "Sí, Santa Gabriela Mistral," *Cuadernos Americanos* XVI, 3 (1957), 238–244. Mistral renounced Carrión's deification: "Cartas de Gabriela Mistral a Benjamín Carrión (1927–1955)," *Letras del Ecuador* XI, 105 (1956), 10–11.

6. The Nobel Committee's certified check (Dec. 11, 1945) from the Göteborgs Bank appears in a photo in *Gabriela Mistral: Álbum Personal* (Santiago: Biblioteca Nacional de Chile, 2008), n.p. In 2011, that amount would translate to about 2,200,000 SEK (Swedish Krona), roughly U.S. $350,000.00. Dr. Karl Grandin, director of the Royal Swedish Academy of Sciences, graciously provided his approximate calculations in an E-mail (April 29, 2011).

7. See Mistral's letter to Isolina Barraza de Estay (February 1947), in Héctor Hernán Herrera Vega, *Gabriela Mistral: Vicuña y su gente (1945–1954)* (La Serena, Chile: Editorial del Norte, 2004), 47–49.

8. Pedro Prado, "Al pueblo de Mexico," prologue to *Desolación*, 2nd ed. (Santiago, 1957), 11–12.

9. Hernán Díaz Arrieta, "Interpretación de Gabriela Mistral," *Anales* CXV, 106 (1957), 16. In another variation, the girl blamed the students for stealing the paper, which led them to retaliate by stoning her. A rectification: Díaz Arrieta placed the school in La Unión; it should be in Vicuña. When she was twelve, another teacher expelled her for inattention, claiming she seemed better suited for "*quehaceres domésticos*." See Ladrón de Guevara, 134. See also José Santos González Vera, "Comienzos de Gabriela Mistral," *Anales* CXV, 106 (1957), 22.

10. Díaz Arrieta, "Interpretación de Gabriela Mistral," 16.

11. Ladrón de Guevara, 100, 118–120, 134. People in Vicuña tried to play down Mistral's negative attitude. Don Pedro Moral and Doña Isolina Barraza de Estay, leading citizens and friends of the poet, worked hard during their life to maintain the modest museum in Vicuña dedicated to her, currently supported by the Chilean government and directed by Rodrigo Iribarren.

12. Ibid., 53, 159. Unfortunately the contents of only some letters are available.

13. The rejection was brief or imagined, according to "Cartas de Gabriela Mistral," *Las Noticias de Última Hora* (25 marzo 1962), 4. Alfonso Escudero reported her continuing series of monthly articles in *El Mercurio*, in "La prosa de Gabriela Mistral: Fichas de contribución a su inventario," *Anales* CXV, 106 (1957), 250–256. In 1948, the year in question, she had five articles published. None, however, is indicated from June through November. Appendix B offers new insights on this complex issue.

14. Raúl Silva Castro, *Estudios sobre Gabriela Mistral* (Santiago: Zig-Zag, 1935) 27. Hernán Díaz Arrieta defended her in *Gabriela Mistral* (Santiago: Nascimento, 1946), 57–66.

Gabriela's harsh impressions re Silva Castro intensified after he published his *Estudios* (1935). Prior to that, both displayed conciliatory tones. In the first of two letters to her (Oct. 24, 1929, to Paris), he opens with "mi apreciada amiga," sweetens it with "mi admirada Gabriela," and then proceeds to ask for forgiveness for his clumsiness in defining her ("… he sido tan torpe para definirla"). Is he apologizing for having misunderstood her poetry? For her part, Mistral offers to trust him with a selection of her works. In his second letter, to Genoa (Jan. 24, 1930), he makes suggestions for publishing a defining novel, *El hermano asno*, by mutual friend Eduardo Barrios, with a quality publisher. See *Cartas salidas del silencio*, eds. Pedro Pablo Zegers B., et al. (Santiago: Ediciones LOM, 2003), 31–32, 33–35.

15. Ladrón de Guevara, 159. The "*fondo de vagabundaje*" ("background of wanderlust") alludes to the poet's errant father.

16. Ibid., 53. At the time, Gabriela preferred Italy to all other countries.

17. Figueroa, 96. Quoted in an interview for *El Diario Ilustrado* (22 junio 1922).

18. Luis Vargas Saavedra views "Nocturno" as a repudiation of her "Christian faith" (E-mail, July 2011). See "Nocturno" in *Poesías completas de Gabriela Mistral*, ed. Margaret Bates, 2nd ed. rev. (Madrid: Aguilar, 1962), 384. References to the poetry utilize the Aguilar text.

19. Ladrón de Guevara, 128. Mistral lacked a salary for six months. She received financial support from Eduardo Santos, owner of *El Tiempo de Bogotá*, and from an Englishwoman, Eloise Lewin, who offered a house in Provence, according to Josué Monsalve, in *Gabriela Mistral: La errante solitaria* (Santiago, 1958), 76–77.

20. Díaz Arrieta, in "Interpretación," 15–18, gives an equitable account of this delicate matter.

21. Captured by Herrera Vega, 47.

22. Doris Dana labored over the *Poema* after the poet's death. She continued researching and editing to publication (Barcelona: Editorial Pomaire, 1967). Fragments appeared in *Poesías completas* as "Trozos del 'Poema de Chile,'" 195–509. Margaret Bates wrote a summary: "Gabriela Mistral's 'Poema de Chile,'" *The Americas*, XVII (1961), 261–276. Ladrón de Guevara mentioned it, *Rebelde*, 52, 53, 128, as did Manuel Pedro González, "Profile," 430. Luis Vargas Saavedra has come out with a final edition.

Mary Louise Pratt underrates the *Poema* as "a travel epic," not as a "nation-building" work comparable with analogous themes by Pablo Neruda and José María Heredia. See "Gender, Race, and Nation in the *Poema de Chile*," in *Women, Culture, and Politics in Latin America* (Berkeley: University of California Press, 1990), 66–71.

Mistral wrote neither a "travelogue" nor an "epic," nor the synergistic result of both terms combined. The "nation-building" aspect consisted of unifying a 3,000 mile-long-nation, horizontally and culturally, through its natural phenomena in a peaceful, spiritual way. Unlike the Chilean Neruda or the Cuban Heredia, she was mostly a poet of intimacies, penetrations, and personal details, not one of epic portrayals of generals leading soldiers over the Andes to the blare of trumpets and drum rolls. Although she had the skills to write a Chilean epic that might have featured liberator and nation-builder General José de San Martín, she shied away in person and in poetry from the exploits of colonels and generals, whether home grown or, as with San Martín, from Argentina.

Chapter II

1. An anonymous revealing letter from a friend of the poet in La Serena forms the basis for many statements here. In Virgilio Figueroa, *La divina Gabriela* (Santiago: El Esfuerzo, 1933), 81 ff.

2. Guillermo Rubilar, *Gabriela, maestra y poetisa rediviva* (Santiago: Ediciones Juan Firula, 1972), 11–14.

3. The newspaper story derives from Mistral's collected writings, in *Recopilación de la obra Mistraliana (1902–1922)*, eds. Pedro Pablo Zegers B. et al. (Santiago: Consejo Nacional del Libro y la Lectura/RIL Editores, 2002), 147–148.

4. From *El libro de los Juegos Florales*, an expanded reproduction of Julio Munizaga Ossandón's original version (1914), organized by the Biblioteca Nacional de Chile, Archivo del Escritor (Santiago: LOM Ediciones, 2000).

5. Magallanes Moure's daughter reveals an intimate, painful story of her father and his persevering wife, Amalia, who faced physical and emotional stress owing to her husband's betrayals with Mistral and the beautiful and seductive Sara Hübner Bezanilla. In Mireya Redondo Magallanes, *De mis días tristes: Manuel Magallanes Moure* (Santiago: DIBAM, 1999), 49, 51, 56, 142.

6. From the first letter among 38 love letters compiled by Sergio Fernández Larraín, *Cartas de amor* (Santiago: Editorial Andrés Bello, 1978), 99.

7. Up to and after the Floral Games of December 1914, in which a future Nobel Prize winner's career was launched, Chilean nitrate found eager foreign buyers who used it as fertilizer on nitrogen-poor lands and as the major component of dynamite (trinitrotoluene), an invention of Alfred Nobel (1833–1896). The mineral constituted the principal component of explosives during World War I (1914–1918), and its force carved out the Panama Canal (1903–1914). Eventually, Chile's heavy reliance on nitrates for foreign currency would lead to its economic undoing. Cheaper synthetic nitrates replaced the natural mineral; and Panama's canal eliminated circumnavigation of Cape Horn and a stop in Punta Arenas, depriving the port of Valparaíso and the country of shipping revenues.

8. Ideas on Chile's social classes are interwoven from Elizabeth Horan's book *Gabriela Mistral: An Artist and Her People* (Washington, DC: Organization of American States, 1994), 18, *et seq.*

9. Julio Saavedra Molina, "Gabriela Mistral: Vida y obra," *Revista Hispánica Moderna* III (1937), 110–135. Saavedra Molina reiterated the same theme: "La patética historia de Lucila Godoy," *Antártica*, nos. 15–16 (nov.-dic. 1945), 106 ff.; "Gabriela Mistral: Vida y obra," *Anales* CIV, 63, 64 (1946), 23–104. The latter is also published as "Gabriela Mistral: Su vida y su obra," in *Poesías completas* (Madrid: Aguilar, 1962), xxxix–lv. The matter of tying poetry to life can be slippery and embarrassing, especially since there is a distinct possibility that the poetry pertains to two different situations.

10. According to critics Rene Wellek and Austin Warren, in "Literatura y biografía," from *Teoría literaria*, trans. José María Gimeno Capella (Madrid, 1953), 128: "...*incluso cuando existe íntima relación entre la obra de arte y la vida del autor, nunca debe interpretarse en el sentido de que la obra de arte sea simple copia de la vida.*"

11. The following theory about the postal card is novel, but unprovable: "*Se habla de una tarjeta postal que se habría encontrado entre los papeles del joven luego de su nefanda decisión; pero en ese tiempo las tarjetas postales eran casi un deporte, y se coleccionaban al igual que el 'hobby' filatélico.*" See Augusto Iglesias, *Gabriela Mistral y el modernismo en Chile: Ensayo de crítica subjetiva* (Santiago: Editorial Universitaria, 1949 [1950]), 231, 193–237 *passim*.

12. Erna Fergusson, *Chile* (New York: Knopf, 1943), 25.

13. Dulce María Loynaz, "Lucila y Gabriela," prologue to *Poesías completas*, cxxv–cxxix, cxxxii. Laura Rodig's comments are similar ("Presencia de Gabriela Mistral," *Anales* CXV, 106 [1957], 284): "*Muere él y renace en ella la fe en su siempre profundo amor y es como un gran viento que le anima: nace Gabriela Mistral.*"

Critics disagree regarding the source of the pseudonym. One group holds that Gabriela combined the given name of Gabriel D'Annunzio with the surname of Frederic Mistral. Some exponents of this theory are Silva Castro, *Estudios*, 17; Rafael Heliodoro Valle, "Gabriela Mistral en mis recuerdos," *Anales* CXV, 106 (1957), 68; Juan de Luigi, "Gabriela Mistral en su primera época," *Anales* CXV, 106 (1957), 43. The latter feels unsettled because the poet, in *El Mercurio* (20 feb. 1946), *had renounced this derivation in favor of a "nombre de arcángel con apellido de viento.*"

But before Gabriela's article appeared others had already noted the fusion within the pseudonym of materialized divine essence with invisible earthly matter: Jorge Mañach, "Gabriela: Alma y tierra," *Revista Hispánica Moderna*, 111 (1937), 108; Figueroa, *La divina Gabriela*, 72; and Norberto Pinilla, "Obra de Gabriela Mistral," *Conferencia* I, 3 (1946), 37. Two other critics believe that Dante Gabriel Rossetti and Frederic Mistral gave rise to the pen name: Gastón Figueira, *De la vida y la obra de Gabriela Mistral* (Montevideo, 1959), 10; and Eugenio Labarca, "Literatura femenina chilena," *Atenea* I, 10

(1924), 358. Note also other pseudonyms or variants: Alguien, Alma, Soledad, X. A mistaken pseudonym, Gabriela Mistraly, is discussed in Chapter V, "Antofagasta: Desertic North and Arid Behavior."

She first signed "Gabriela Mistral" for the poem "Del pasado" in the periodical *El Coquimbo* (23 July 1908), according to the National Library of Chile's overview: *Gabriela Mistral: A cien años de su nacimiento (1889–1989)* (Santiago: DIBAM, Undated), 44.

14. Iglesias, 198, 236. Díaz Arrieta ("Interpretación," 17) is also skeptical about the importance to the poet of Romelio Ureta: "*El sujeto pudo ser e nula importancia. Temperamentos como el suyo crean su propio fantasma y resulta secundario que haya o no existido quien lo provoca. Se afirma incluso que los "Sonetos" nacieron de una historia oída, que constituyen un tema retórico. No importa: el clamor traduce una herida profunda y sus huellas ensangrentaron toda su juventud. Sea cual fuere el origen del sufrimiento, hay una atormentada doliente, una víctima abrazada a la cruz, una mujer para quien La existencia se presenta como puro dolor.*"

15. Iglesias, 193–194. José María Vargas Vila, a contentious, eccentric Colombian poet, had a large following among the young romantics. His exhortations on death and suicide were at variance with his own desire for living life to the fullest. Iglesias (53) cites Vargas Vila's famous aphorism from his novel *Ibis*: "*Cuando la vida es una carga, el suicidio es un derecho; cuando la vida es un escarnio, el suicidio es un deber.*" Fortified with this rationale, Gabriela may have viewed Romelio Ureta's death as his own personal necessity. Lucila, under the pen name Alma, in "A Vargas Vila," extolled the Colombian novelist's uniqueness, his "sublime madness." She said, "*Eres único: como el sol.*" From *Penumbras* (La Serena), Año I, 3 (26 mayo 1907); reproduced in *Recopilación*, 131.

16. Private letters published recently mention Manuel Magallanes Moure, Jorge Hübner, and others as Mistral's suitors in Chile. (This is discussed in Chapter VII, "Sexuality, Humanity, and Existential Choices.") But in the fifties and sixties many critics had already surmised their names, but respected confidentialities. Margot Arce de Vázquez confirmed names to me (October 20, 1961), as first alluded to in her *Gabriela Mistral: Persona y poesía* (San Juan, Puerto Rico, 1958), 43–44: "*otra historia de amor*," purportedly "*la más decisiva.*" Dulce María Loynaz, "Lucila y Gabriela," *Poesías completas*, cxxxvi–cxxxviii, corroborated this story.

The aforementioned two critics and Marie-Lise Gazarian Gautier maintain that the poetry of *Desolación* involved two discrete incidents: *Gabriela Mistral, la maestra de Elqui* (Buenos Aires: Crespillo, 1973), 34.

The possibility of a second or third love motif alters the biography, but does not hamper the criticism of the poetry. This eventuality would neither add to, nor detract from, the intensity the poetry already achieves by being considered the result of other adventures.

17. In *Epistolario entre Lucila Godoy Alcayaga y Manuel Magallanes Moure*, eds. María Ester Martínez Sanz and Luis Vargas Saavedra (Santiago: Ediciones Universidad Católica de Chile, 2007), 125.

18. The details about her publications in Coquimbo province derive from Rolando Marzano's careful article, "Recorrer la vida desde la vereda contraria," *Revista Patrimonio Cultural* 46, año XIII (Verano 2008), 10, 11, 14, 15.

19. On "Alguien" and other pseudonyms, see Pedro Pablo Zegers' important "Introducción" to his *Recopilación*, 19.

20. The first group: Raúl Silva Castro, *Estudios*, 17; Rafael Heliodoro Valle, "Gabriela Mistral en mis recuerdos, *Anales* CXV, 106 (1957), 68; Juan de Luigi, "Gabriela Mistral en su primera época," *Anales* CXV, 106 (1957), 43. The second group: Gastón Figueira, *De la vida y la obra de Gabriela Mistral* (Montevideo, 1959), 10; Eugenio Labarca, "Literatura femenina chilena," *Atenea* I, 10 (1924), 358. The third group: Jorge Mañach, "Gabriela: Alma y tierra," *Revista Hispánica Moderna* III (1937), 108; Virgilio Figueroa, *La divina Gabriela*, 72; Norberto Pinilla, "Obra de Gabriela Mistral," *Conferencia* I, 3 (1946), 37. Lucila clarified the issue only after the publication of three corroborating articles from the third group (*El Mercurio* [20 feb. 1946]).

Chapter III

1. Numerous researchers have outlined the poet's personal and family life in Chile. I have relied on Margarita Paz Paredes and Sergio Fernández Larraín. Paz Paredes, "Gabriela Mistral," *Cultura: Revista del Ministerio de Cultura*, No. 17 (oct.-dic. 1959), 162–168. Fernández Larraín carefully documents his information, in *Cartas de amor de Gabriela Mistral* (Santiago: Editorial Andrés Bello, 1978). The numerous pages and notes that follow point to important topics in the text: 13 n. 38, 14 n. 43, 17, 22–23, 25, 29, 36, 41, 205 n. 31, 205 n. 38, 207 n. 72, 207 n. 84. The sequential pagination avoids constant interruptions to the readers.

2. Germán Arciniegas tells anecdotes about the father in "Gabriela, la fantástica chilena," *Cuadernos Israelíes* No. 4 (1960), 23.

3. González Vera, "Comienzos de Gabriela Mistral," *Anales* CXV, 106 (1957), 22. Contrary to standard biographies, the date given for Godoy Villanueva's death is August 29, 1911 (of pneumonia in Copiapó Hospital), by María Sonia Estay Barraza, in "Vida y obra de Gabriela Mistral," *Clímax* (10 enero 1960), 17.

4. Matilde Ladrón de Guevara, *Rebelde magnífica* (Santiago: Imprenta de la Central de Talleres, 1957), 29, notes again that Gabriela shared her father's wanderlust spirit: "*Así somos los Godoy, vagabundos del alma.*" For general information, see Raúl Silva Castro, *Estudios sobre Gabriela Mistral* (Santiago: Santiago: Zig-Zag, 1935), 3–4; also Augusto Iglesias, *Gabriela Mistral y el modernismo en Chile: Ensayo de crítica subjetiva* (Santiago: Editorial Universitaria, 1949 [1950]), 14–19. Virgilio Figueroa transcribes a cradle song of her father's in *La divina Gabriela* (Santiago: "El Esfuerzo," 1933), 42; and Josué Monsalve, *Gabriela Mistral, la errante solitaria* (Santiago: 1958), 9–14, invents some imaginary dialogue between the parents of Godoy Villanueva, and adds that the father truly loved his daughter. Rolando Manzano located the "Poemas de Jerónimo Godoy Villanueva," which he included in the *Revista Patrimonio Cultural,* 46, Año XIII (Verano 2008), 12.

5. The reference to "*padre*" in "Poema del hijo," 104, may be autobiographical. The heroine of the poem no longer regrets never having borne her lover's child, which they had so ardently desired, because the child would have abandoned her as did her lover, and might have turned on her in wrath (as she affirms having done to her father) for having given him life: "*Y el horror de que [mi hijo] un día con la boca quemante / del rencor, me dijera lo que dije a mi padre: / '¿Por qué ha sido fecunda tu carne sollozante / y se henchieron [sic] de néctar los pechos de mi madre?'*"

6. These thoughts are part of an essay on love, sex, and divorce in Latin America. See Gabriela Mistral, "'Un viejo tema': La poetisa chilena comenta el informe de Kinsey," *Life en Español* (26 oct. 1953), 32.

7. Figueroa, 43.

8. This is a deviation from the traditional interpretation that Gabriela assumed the role of "virgen-madre" as a consequence of a frustrated love affair. The traditional view has partial validity, but the precursors of failure in physical love were already sown in her home life, before she met Romelio Ureta. Their amorous encounter and another alluded to by Margot Arce de Vázquez (see n. 36, below), merely clouded her decision to distrust physical love and to find in children the vicarious pleasure of being a mother.

9. *Desolación,* 2nd ed. (Santiago: Editorial del Pacífico, 1957), 11.

10. Ladrón de Guevara, 159.

11. "Lápida filial," *Poesías completas,* 380–381.

12. "La fuga," *Poesías completas,* 377–379. See also Mistral's poem "Madre mía," and in poetic prose, "Evocación de la Madre"; both exalt her mother and by extension motherhood.

13. Two sources, among several, have compiled their letters. See "Gabriela ante la enfermedad y muerte de Emelina," in Héctor Hernán Vega Herrera, *Gabriela Mistral, Vicuña y su gente (1945–1954)* (La Serena, Chile: Editorial del Norte, 2004), 47–53. See also "Cartas familiares," Part 1, in Magda Arce and Gastón Von dem Bussche, eds., *Proyecto, preservación y difusión del legado literario de Gabriela Mistral* (Santiago: Zig-Zag, 1993).

14. The preceding is based on the description by Herrera Vega, 53.

15. The aforesaid is assembled from Veronica Darer, in "Gabriela Mistral as Teacher" (48), and from Elizabeth Horan, in "Mirror to the Nation," (230), both found in Marjorie Agosín, ed., *Gabriela Mistral: The Audacious Traveler* (Athens: Ohio University Press, 2003).

16. The poem to Graciela, the fourth in an initial series of writings, was published Oct. 25, 1904. She had begun her writing career two months earlier, Aug. 11, 1904, in the newspaper *El Coquimbo,* in La Serena. For a list of the names, dates, and places of publication of her first 84 articles and poems (1904–1911), see Rolando Manzano, "Artículos publicados en la prensa regional de Coquimbo," in *Revista Patrimonio Cultural* 46, Año XIII (Verano 2008), 14.

17. Two Chileans knowledgeable about Gabriela and Juan Miguel provided personal assistance: Doña Isolina Barrza de Estay, from Vicuña and a relative of Emelina's, and Professor Luis Vargas Saavedra. They support each other's findings on the boy's biological father and mother. See Barraza de Estay's validation of Juan Miguel's parenthood via the Brazilian Death Certificate, which lists Carlos Miguel Godoy and Martha Mendonza, in *Gabriela Mistral y su sobrino* (La Serena: Editorial del Norte, 1978), 31.

Vargas Saavedra graciously E-mailed me (June 2011) official documents pertaining to Juan Miguel's birth, paternity, and Gabriela's role. See his detailed "Introducción" to *Prosas religiosas de Gabriela Mistral* (Santiago: Editorial Andrés Bello, 1978), 16–17, n. 14; see also his *El otro suicida de Gabriela Mistral* (Santiago: Ediciones Universidad Católica de Chile, 1985), 23–25. In the latter, he cites the Mexican [Andrés] Iduarte and other sources who, quoting Gabriela, said that Yin-Yin derived from a half-brother whose sick wife gave birth in March or April 1925, but died of TB in a Swiss sanitarium.

18. The two headlines: "'Sobrino' de Gabriela Mistral era en realidad su hijo," and "Polémica genera supuesta maternidad de Mistral," *El Mercurio* (6, 7 nov. 1999). Dana repeats the allegation to Cherie Zalaquett Aquea, "Doris Dana, la albacea de la Mistral, rompe el silencio," *Revista El Sábado, El Mercurio* (22 nov. 2002), at http://www.letras.s5.com/gm171004.htm.

19. See Pizarro's "Gabriela Mistral and Brazil: A Journey of Fortitude," trans. Nancy A. Hall, in *Gabriela Mistral: The Audacious Traveler*, ed. Marjorie Agosin (Athens: Ohio University Press, 2003), 164.

20. María Eugenia Román repudiated her father's biological link to Yin-Yin via Mistral: "¡Son mentiras de los chilenos!" *Buen Domingo* (6 junio 1984), 10–12. Despite the denial, Volodia Teitelboim spread Latcham's conjecture in *Gabriela Mistral: Pública y secreta*. 3rd ed. (Santiago: Sudamericana, 1999), 213. Maximino Fernández Fraile also cites Latcham, in "Residencia en Brasil: De dolor y de Gloria," *Revista Patrimonio Cultural* 46, Año XIII (Verano 2008), 22.

21. Luis Vargas Saavedra, *Castilla tajeada de sed como mi lengua: Gabriela Mistral ante España y España ante Gabriela Mistral (1933 a 1935)* (Santiago: Ediciones Universidad de Chile, 2002), 12. The author (242–244) includes a formal letter from Gabriela to d'Ors that asks for his help in the false persecution of Luis Nicolau d'Olwer regarding financial fraud.

See an autobiographical article by d'Ors, "Dice Eugenio d'Ors," *El Mercurio* de Santiago (15 feb. 1925), 7. Found in Patricia Rubio, *Bibliografía Anotada* (Santiago: DIBAM, 1995), 100, No. 808. Rubio summarizes the Catalan's opinion of Mistral's poetry: "*Destaca el 'laicismo' de su obra, en oposición a su 'modo profético' a que parecen empujar a Gabriela Mistral algunos de sus admiradores.*"

22. For the preceding, see Maximino Fernández Fraile, "Residencia en Brasil: De dolor y de Gloria," *Revista Patrimonio Cultural* 46, año XIII (Verano 2008), 21–22.

23. From Dana's already cited interview with Cherie Zalaquett Aquea, "…la albacea de la Mistral, rompe el silencio," at http://www.letras.s5.com/gm171004.htm.

24. The letters are in Vargas Saavedra's *El otro suicida de Gabriela Mistral* 31–34, 34–36. The typed letters from Palma Guillén to Gabriela and to Juan Miguel are also in *Proyecto, preservación y difusión del legado literario de Gabriela Mistral*, eds. Magda Arce and Gastón Von dem Bussche (Santiago: Zig-Zag, 1993). The titles and dates: from Palma to Gabriela, "Hijita muy querida" (29 abril 1943), 103–104; from Palma to Yin-Yin, "Mi querido Juanito" (11 mayo 1943), 105.

Gabriela discussed the boy's death at length in two letters: The first to Victoria Ocampo (Oct. 16, 1943), and the second to four Chilean friends (17 nov. 1943). To Victoria Ocampo in *This America of Ours, The Letters of Gabriela Mistral and Victoria Ocampo*, eds., Elizabeth Horan and Doris Meyer (Austin, Texas: University of Texas Press, 2003), 142–146. The second, "Carta colectiva enviada por Gabriela a varias amigas en Chile," appears in Isolina Barraza de Estay, *Gabriela Mistral y su sobrino* (La Serena, Chile: Editorial del Norte, 1978), 21–25.

Gabriela reiterates her anguish and love for him. She appeased the youth's desires by bringing a German (or French; see note 33) lady friend to live with them. All the while blaming herself for his estrangement by having pulled the boy out of his familiar European surroundings, she continued to condemn xenophobic Brazilian schoolmates for his death.

25. A viewpoint shared by Arce de Vázquez, *Gabriela Mistral: Persona y poesía*, 118.

26. See Vargas Saavedra, *El otro suicida*, 44. Isolina Barraza de Estay gave permission to transcribe factual data about Juan Miguel from her copy of the death certificate from Petrópolis, Brazil: Certidâo de Óbito, no. 01492, leaf 12, book 5 of the Registro de Óbito 3128. The certificate appears also in her *Gabriela Mistral y su sobrino*, 31.

27. Information gathered from interviews with María Urzúa in Santiago (Oct. 24, 1966), and with the poet Manuel Bandeira in Rio de Janeiro (Dec.1966). Despite Gabriela's claims to the boy's good health, she enumerates Yin-Yin's medical problems in her letter to Esther de Cáceres: wounds, scars, and swelling from clumsy use of forceps at birth; a humped back; abnormal growth patterns; delayed puberty. See *El ojo atravesado …*, eds. Silvia Guerra and Verónica Zondek (Santiago: LOM Ediciones, 2005), 48.

28. See Elizabeth Allday's, *Stefan Zweig: A Critical Biography* (Chicago: J. Philip O'Hare, 1972), 238.

29. For Mistral's reaction, see "La muerte de Stefan Zweig: Última conversación con el escritor," *El Mercurio* (9 marzo 1942). See also a letter about Zweig to the Mexican writer Alfonso Reyes (February 1942), in *Tan de Usted: Epistolario de Gabriela Mistral con Alfonso Reyes*, ed. Luis Vargas Saavedra (Santiago: Ediciones Universidad Católica de Chile/Hachette), 136.

30. The double suicide was a cruel and unforgettable blow: "*El autoatentado del autor de 'Amok' y de su mujer era un golpe rudo y difícil de olvidar*," according to Efraím Szmulewicz, *Gabriela Mistral: Bioqrafía emotiva* (Santiago, 1958), 101. On the same topic, see Magda Arce and Gastón Von dem Bussche, eds., in *Proyecto*, 40. Teitelboim, 213, has a similar quotation.

31. V. M., "Jean Michel Godoy," *Tribuna de Petrópolis* (15 agosto 1943), 2.

32. Víctor Alba, "La Mistral vista por su amiga y secretaria," *Anales* CXV, 106 (1957), 93. Appendix B contains a letter that further clouds the issue.

33. These are Gabriela's comments in an interview with Lenka Franulic, "Recado sobre Gabriela Mistral," *Ercilla* (27 mayo 1952), 18.

34. Gabriela Mistral, "Sobre la xenofobia," *La Nueva Democracia* XXIX, 1 (1949), 22 26. Originally a "Mensaje enviado por Gabriela Mistral desde Fortín, Veracruz, a la Conferencia Pro Paz Organizada por los Amigos en Palmira, Morelos, Diciembre 5 al 12 de 1948."

Letter 40 from Gabriela to the Argentine writer Victoria Ocampo (1891–1980), expands on the personal drama with Yin-Yin at home and in public: She disapproved of the older German woman he liked; the boys berated him with the alienating "Frenchy"; two groups of boys, not one, assailed him. The complete letters, edited and translated by Elizabeth Horan and Doris Meyer, are in *This America of Ours* (Austin: University of Texas Press, 2003), 142–146.

35. From Vargas Saavedra, *Prosa religiosa...*, 179–181.

36. Mariná de Morães Sarmento, of Petrópolis, who, when I visited her Sala de Letras e Artes Gabriela Mistral (Dec. 1966), tried not to offend the viewpoint of the poet. Yet twenty years later, the incident was sensitive. She strongly defended the peaceful reputation of the citizens of Petrópolis, whose newspapers carried no factual data pertaining to the cause of the boy's death. For more opinions, see Jorge Inostroza, "96 horas con Gabriela Mistral," *Vea* (15 sept. 1954), 16.

37. Víctor Alba, "La Mistral vista por su amiga y secretaria," *Anales* CXV, 106 (1957), 93.

38. My translation from the original in Horan and Meyer, *This America of Ours*, 306.

39. Both quotations derive from letters to Zacarías Gómez (see Appendix B), on Dec. 10, 1948, and Nov. 2, 1951, respectively. Gabriela answered her letters in pencil (for which she always apologized) to more readily discern the words and to erase as necessary. After Yin-Yin's death, the poet blamed her diminished eyesight on the barbiturates to calm her nerves that her aide and friend Consuelo Saleva "purposely" gave her in Brazil. The above referenced letters to Esther de Cáceres reveal poor vision and possible paranoia. She feared revealing poor eyesight to her superiors for fear of being fired. Owing to perceived and real illnesses, Gabriela accused Consuelo of "stealing" $15,000.00. Afflicted over the charge, Consuelo departed without ceremony only to reconcile years later in California. The events are in Silvia Guerra and Verónica Zondek, *El ojo atravesado*, 102, 104.

Vargas Saavedra summarized Gabriela's illnesses and forgetfulness and when they occurred, in *Tan de Usted*, 25–26. *In El otro suicida...*, 27, he mentioned arteriosclerosis.

40. For a discussion of the psycho-pathology of illness, see Patricia Rubio, "Constructions of the Self: The Personal Letters of Gabriela Mistral," in *Gabriela Mistral: The Audacious Traveler*, ed. Marjorie Agosín (Athens: Ohio University Press, 2003), 217–218, 220–221.

Chapter IV

1. See John A. Crow, *The Epic of Latin America*, 4th ed (Berkeley and Los Angeles: University of California Press, 1992); Bello, 643–644; Sarmiento, 599–603.

2. Gabriela dedicated a poem that extolled Brígida Walker's virtues, "La encina" ("The Oak"). In the *Revista de Educación Nacional* (abril 1915), reproduced in *Recopilacion de la obra mistraliana 1902–1922*, ed. Pedro Pablo Zegers B. (Santiago: RIL Editores, 2002), 228–229.

3. The same official notice granted Fidelia Valdez Pereira certification as "profesora de historia y geografía." See "Liceo de Niñas: El nuevo profesorado," *Recopilación*, 164–165.

Chapter V

1. Pertinent pages from Mario Bahamonde's descriptions of Lucila, Fidelia, and Antofagasta follow in numerical, not thematic, order. *Gabriela Mistral en Antofagasta: Años de forja y va-*

lentía (Santiago: Editorial Nascimento, 1980), 11, 13, 20, 23, 29, 58, 60. Bahamonde's concepts, dates, names, and spellings are followed, even when they might disagree with other sources. I call attention to areas of disagreement.

2. From "El Liceo de Niñas," *El Mercurio* (4 agosto 1911), reproduced in *Recopilación de la obra mistraliana, 1902–1922*, ed. Pedro Pablo Zegers B. (Santiago: RIL Editores, 2002), 165.

3. See Appendices A and B on Theosophy for an in-depth discussion. Appendix B documents the long-lasting relationship with Don Zacarías via their correspondence. She displays interest in Theosophical and Rosicrucian matters, such as diet, meditation, and physical exercises, and includes references to, among others, Yin-Yin, Emelina, and Doris Dana. Chapter XIII, "A Quest for Religious Harmony," especially the section "Theosophy," offers a more complete and integrated review of the complex issues of Theosophy and Buddhism.

Chapter VI

1. She wrote three commentaries in verse and three in prose, which appeared originally in Raúl Ramírez, *Rabindranath Tagore, poeta y filósofo hindú* (Santiago, Imprenta Universo, 1917). They are reprinted in *Recopilacion de la obra mistraliana, 1902–1922*, Pedro Pablo Zegers B., ed. (Santiago: RIL Editores, 2002), 272–276.

2. Volodia Teitelboim, *Gabriela Mistral: Pública y secreta*. 3rd. ed. (Santiago: Editorial Sudamericana, 1999), 55.

3. "La escuela al aire libre," *Atlántida* (4 mayo 1922); reproduced in *Recopilación,* 645–646.

4. Teitelboim, 54, 56.

5. On this period, I brought together the comments by José Santos González Vera in three publications: *Algunos* (Santiago: Nascimento, 1959), 125–150; "Comienzos de Gabriela Mistral" *Anales* CXV, 106 (1957), 22–25; "Gabriela Mistral" *Babel* (Santiago), IX, 31 (1946), 5–16.

6. "Adiós a Laura," 101–103, and "El pensador de Rodin" 339–340, 430, from Zegers, *Recopilación*. "El pensador de Rodin," dedicated to Laura Rodig, was written in Punta Arenas (1919), and is discussed further in Chapter XII, "The Hebraic Tradition."

7. Among many other writings, see Laura Rodig's comments in "Presencia de Gabriela Mistral," *Anales* CXV, 106 (1957), 282–292. Teitelboim, 57–58, describes Laura Rodig as a confidential, protective, and caring person.

Chapter VII

1. Her 80 letters and one telegram are captured in *Epistolario entre Lucila Godoy Alcayaga y Manuel Magallanes Moure*, eds. María Ester Martínez Sanz and Luis Vargas Saavedra (Santiago: Ediciones de la Universidad Católica de Chile, 2007), 11–12.

2. From *Epistolario*, 15.

3. González Vera's remarks are found in *Epistolario*, 181–182.

4. Santiago Aste, the amorous, persistent Italian greengrocer in Los Andes, wooed Lucila for years in vain. A brief description is in Volodia Teitelboim, *Gabriela Mistral: Pública y secreta*, 3rd ed. (Santiago: Sudamericana, 1999), 57–58.

5. Licia Fiol-Matta, *A Queer Mother for the Nation: The State and Gabriela Mistral* (Minneapolis: University of Minnesota Press, 2002), xiv. She first proposed her thesis in "The 'Schoolteacher of America': Gender, Sexuality and Nation in Gabriela Mistral," *¿Entiendes?: Queer Readings, Hispanic Writings*, eds. Emilie L. Bergmann and Paul Julian Smith (Durham, NC: Duke University Press, 1995), 203–229.

Elizabeth Horan uses the cautious phrase "lesbian sensibility," in "Gabriela Mistral," *Latin American Writers on Gay and Lesbian Themes*, ed. David William Foster (Westport, CT: Greenwood Press, 1994), 232. Chilean Diamela Eltit, admittedly without proof, mentioned the "lesbian probability," in "Los tiempos que marcaron una vida," *Revista Patrimonio Cultural* 46, Año XIII (Verano 2008), 31.

In Chile, a book on Lesbian/Gay/Bisexual/Transsexual affairs entices buyers by listing Mistral and other notables on the cover: *LGBT: Homosexualidad en Chile* (2011). It appears to come in a brown paper bag, since it is found on Amazon.com absent the author and date and place of publication.

6. With regard to Ocampo, see *This America of Ours: The Letters of Gabriela Mistral and Victoria Ocampo*, eds. Elizabeth Horan and Doris Meyer (Austin: University of Texas Press, 2003). Regarding the Uruguayans, see *El ojo atravesado: Correspondencia entre Gabriela Mistral y los escritores uruguayos*, eds. Silvia Guerra and Verónica Zondek (Santiago: Lom Ediciones, 2005).

7. Luis Vargas Saavedra analyzes Lucila's system of code words to disguise her love letters with Magallanes Moure in "Estrategias de ocultamientos," in *Epistolario entre Lucila Godoy Alcayaga y Manuel Magallanes Moure*, 2nd ed. (Santiago: Ediciones Universidad Católica de Chile, 2007), 14.

8. See Sylvia Molloy's "Introduction" to

Women's Writing in Latin America: An Anthology (Boulder, CO: Westview Press, 1991), 116.

9. Read the interview by Cherie Zalaquett Aquea online at http://www.letras.s5.com/gm171004.htm, which derives from "Doris Dana, la albacea de la Mistral, rompe el silencio," *Revista El Sábado, El Mercurio* (22 nov. 2002).

10. See *Gabriela Mistral. Niña errante: Cartas a Doris Dana.* The numbers refer to Doris' 15 letters and telegrams: 1, 3, 4, 6, 8, 9, 31, 32, 55, 95, 96, 139, 203, 223, and 245.

11. Ibid., 455–465. Ms. Atkinson's "Epílogo," recounts the affluent and influential Dana family's tribulations with alcohol, violence, and depression. Aunt Doris Dana, she recalls, was a socially-outgoing conversationalist and imbiber, but one who was very cautious about friendships and trust.

12. Extracted from Elizabeth Horan's intimate review: "Las cartas de Doris Dana y Gabriela Mistral," *Chroma* (Aug. 28, 2009), and at http://www.latercera.com/contenido727_175058_9.shtml. See Jorge Marchant Lezcano's complementary analysis, "Gabriela Mistral a Doris Dana: Love Story," at http://letras.s5com/jml120909.html.

On the Chilean public's perception of Ms. Dana's death, see two reports from *El Mercurio's* online newspaper, *emol.com*. First report: To create headlines, *emol.com* falsely and knowingly places Dana's death one day short of the 50th anniversary of Gabriela's death: http://www.emol.com.noticias/magazine/detalle/detallenoticias.asp?idnoticia=242644.

Second report (28 nov. 2007): Doris did not carry secrets to the tomb: http://www.emol.com.noticias/magazine/detallenoticias.asp?idnoticias=241644.]

13. From "La instrucción de la mujer," in *La tierra tiene la actitud de una mujer*, ed. Pedro Pablo Zegers B., 2nd ed. (Santiago: RIL Editores, 1998), 13. Another, broader collection on the same topic is *Gabriela Mistral, Women*, eds. Marjorie Agosín, and Jacqueline C. Nanfito (Buffalo, NY: White Pine Press, 2000).

14. See Mistral's "Organización de las mujeres," *El Mercurio* (5 julio 1925), in Luis Vargas Saavedra's "Introducción," *Prosa religiosa de Gabriela Mistral* (Santiago: Editorial Andrés Bello, 1978), 22, n. 27. For an extended review of feminism in Chile and Mistral's role, see *En batalla de sencillez: Epistolario de Gabriela Mistral a Pedro Prado*, eds. Luis Vargas Saavedra et al. (Santiago: Ediciones Dolmen, 1992), 80–83. A cursory synopsis of Mistral's involvement with feminists appears in Elizabeth Horan, *Gabriela Mistral: An Artist and Her People* (Washington, D.C.: Organization of American States, 1994), 31–36.

Chapter VIII

1. Volodia Teitelboim, *Gabriela Mistral: Pública y secreta* (Santiago: Sudamericana, 1999), 79.

2. The reference is to Scarpa's two volumes, *La desterrada en su patria* [*The Exiled Woman in her Native Land*], subtitled *Gabriela Mistral en Magallanes: 1918–1920* (Santiago: Editorial Nascimento, 1977). Professor Scarpa, by his dedication and thoroughness, has elevated Mistral scholarship. On meeting years ago, he welcomed me to his Instituto de Literatura Comparada. May this book, which tries to adopt his standards of excellence, merit his approval.

3. Mistral's metaphorical and literal uses of "*destierro*" ("exile," "banishment," "remote place"), applied to Punta Arenas and to other sites and situations are captured in *En batalla de sencillez: Epistolario de Gabrieal Mistral a Pedro Prado*, eds. Luis Vargas Saavedra et al. (Santiago: Ediciones Dolmen, 1992), 68–69.

4. Teitelboim, 79–80.

5. "Balada," in *Gabriela Mistral en verso y prosa: Antología*, ed. Cedomil Goic (Lima, Peru: Real Academia Española, 2010), 45–46).

6. The mere thought of betrayal caused Lucila to cease writing letters to Manuel during this period, according to Sergio Fernández Larraín, in *Cartas de amor de Gabriela Mistral* (Santiago: Editorial Andrés Bello, 1978), 63–65, 67.

7. The two articles, written a year apart, appeared in *El Coquimbo*, in La Serena: "Sobre el centenario: Ideas de una maestra" (12 agosto 1909); "Ventajoso canje" (3 sept. 1910). Both are reproduced in *Recopilacion de la obra mistraliana 1902–1922*, ed. Pedro Pablo Zegers B. (Santiago: RIL Editores, 2002), 76–77, 79.

8. Fernando Ortiz Letelier describes the process and outcome in *El movimiento obrero en Chile (1881–1919)* (Santiago: Ediciones LOM, 2005), 202, 206–208.

9. See Teitelboim, 87–91.

10. See Mariana Aylwin et al., for a review of Chile's conflicts with, and armed repressions of, labor movements: *Chile en el siglo XX*, 11th ed. (Santiago, 2002), 62–76.

11. See Mario Garcés Durán's *Crisis social y motines populares en el 1900* (Santiago: Ediciones Documentas, 1991), 139, 141, 143, 144. Ortiz Letelier, 187–188, 203–208, had noted, as had Mistral with chagrin, that the Catholic Church

allied itself with the Conservative Party in opposing workers' rights.

12. See Licia Fiol-Matta, *A Queer Mother for the Nation* (Minneapolis: University of Minnesota Press, 2002), 6. Teitelboim, 87–91, takes up this socio-political theme in great detail. For a wide-ranging discussion of the socio-economic conditions that influenced Chilean women and the poet, see Elizabeth Horan's *Gabriela Mistral: An Artist and Her People* (Washington, DC: OAS, 1994), 12–17.

The idea of annihilating native ethnic peoples for religious, economic, or racial reasons did not originate with the Chileans; in the Americas, the *conquistadores* promoted it and, lamentably, it has continued over the centuries in many countries.

13. This section interweaves comments from Laura Rodig's "Presencia de Gabriela Mistral," *Anales* CXV, 106 (1957), 182–292.

14. See Roque Esteban Scarpa, *La desterrada...*, 303–304, for a summary of Lucila's stinging criticism of the merchant class in *"Entrevista a La Unión de Punta Arenas."* See also Teitelboim, 112.

15. Teitelboim reports on the schemes, 111–112.

Chapter IX

1. See Volodia Tebitelboim, *Gabriela Mistral: Pública y secreta* (Santiago: Sudamericana, 1999), 113.

2. The "Recados" are in *Prosa religiosa de Gabriela Mistal*, ed. Luis Vargas Saavedra (Santiago: Editorial Andés Bello, 1978).

3. A thorough analysis is in *Cartas salidas del silencio*, eds. Pedro Pablo Zegers B. et al. (Santiago: Ediciones LOM, 2003), 150–151.

4. Marie-Lise Gazarian-Gautier's translation in "The Walking Geography of Gabriela Mistral," in *Gabriela Mistral: The Audacious Traveler*, ed. Marjorie Agosín (Athens: Ohio University Press, 2003), 271. The original is in Neruda's *Confieso que he vivido: Memorias* (Buenos Aires: Losada, 1974), 13. Neruda's misplaced simile of "the pitcher" was not an aspersion.

5. For all further quotes herein from *La Mañana*, see *Recopilación de la obra mistraliana, 1902–1922*, ed. Pedro Pablo Zegers B. (Santiago: RIL Editores, 2002), 460–467.

6. Gabriela, while in Punta Arenas (Oct. 1919), had already written "La oración de la maestra," dedicated to César Duayén. It appears in *Gabriela Mistral: Magisterio y niño*, ed. Roque Esteban Scarpa, 2nd ed. (Santiago: Editorial Andrés Bello, 1995), 33–34.

Chapter X

1. *Recopilación de la obra mistraliana, 1902–1922*, ed. Pedro Pablo Zegers B. (Santiago: RIL Editores, 2002), 478.

2. See the annotated documents on Dey and on other matters in *Magisterio y niño*, ed. Roque Esteban Scarpa, 2nd ed. (Santiago: Editorial Andrés Bello, 1995), 16–18.

3. *Recopilación*, 509–511.

4. See the notice and the commemorative piece: *Recopilación*, 475, 509–511.

5. *Recopilación*, 477–478.

6. The life-long dissension between Gabriela and Amanda appears in *This America of Ours: The Letters of Gabriela Mistral and Victoria Ocampo*, eds. Elizabeth Horan and Doris Meyer (Austin: University of Texas Press, 2003), 78, n. 5. See "Labarca Hubertson," *The Encyclopedia of Latin American History & Culture*, 2nd ed. (New York: Gale Cengage Learning, 2008). With Mistral's departure from Chile (1922), Labarca Hubertson continued to play an important role in the feminist movement and educational system of Chile.

7. Letters from vindictive women are not present in *Recopilación*, but two sarcastic letters from Fernando G. Oldini, a supporter of Labarca Hubertson, appear in *Claridad*, "Carta abierta a Gabriela Mistral (4 junio 1921), and "Marginando" (18 junio 1921). See *Recopilación*, 477–478, 480–481.

8. Between 1919 and 1922, Torres Rioseco wrote seven articles in praise of the poet and the poetry, which are noted in Patricio Rubio, *Gabriela Mistral ante la crítica: Bibliografía anotada* (Santiago: DIBAM, 1995), 163.

9. *Recopilación*, 486–487.

10. Read the correspondence between Mistral and de Onís: Jorge Ignacio Covarrubias, "Tras las huellas de Gabriela Mistral en Nueva York," in *Gabriela Mistral y los Estados Unidos*, Gerardo Piña-Rosales et al., eds. (Nueva York: ANLE, 2011), 186–189. Gabriela showed her appreciation to de Onís by dedicating "La maestra rural" to him.

The relationship, at first cordial, soured when Gabriela, in her courses at Columbia University and at a luncheon, outraged de Onís by criticizing Spain's *conquistadores* and by implication the Just War on the natives. De Onís, staunchly pro-Spain, reacted adversely to their political differences. The question of Spain's treatment of native Indians affected Mistral deeply. She sided with their defender, the Dominican Bartolomé de las Casas, who had argued for their humanity ("*seres humanos*") in a public disputation in Sevilla with Juan Ginés de Sepúlveda (1553).

A mutual distrust flared up again in a private letter of vilification (1935) for an alleged earlier lack of respect: "Yo pasé a ser ante Onís una especie de boba grandota.... Me quitó aprecio y saludo, después de haberme ofrecido editar la totalidad de mis artículos que de repente le apestaron a ... indio."

It turns out that before the Spanish Government could declare Mistral officially *persona non grata* as consul for speaking out against the intellectuals in Madrid who criticized her defense of Indians, the Chilean government transferred her from Madrid to Lisbon for having written — in a confidential letter made public in Chile without authorization — a denunciation of the negativity by the intellectuals towards Latin Americans, labeling them, as she claimed Onís did, "*indios*."

The aforesaid derive from *Proyecto, preservación y difusion del legado literario de Gabriela Mistral*, eds. Magda Arce and Gastón Von dem Bussche (Santiago: Zig-Zag, 1993), 102. Vargas Saavedra offers an objective and complete review, in *Tan de usted, Epistolario de Gabriela Mistral con Alfonso Reyes* (Santiago: Ediciones Universidad Católica de Chile, 1990), 26–28. See *Castilla tajeada de sed como mi lengua*, ed. Luis Vargas Saavedra (Santiago: Ediciones Universidad Católica de Chile, 2002), 101. I am appreciative to Luis Vargas Saavedra for pointing out these perspectives in an E-mail (July 2011). I take up this theme again in Chapter IX on the Araucan Indians in Temuco.

11. A personal comment. It is rare that a major U.S. university can contribute to a Latin American woman winning the Nobel Prize. This unheralded event ought to be better known and valued by a wider contemporary audience.

12. Either in anticipation of a position in Mexico or to call the attention of Mexican intellectuals to her, or both, Gabriela published "La cultura Mexicana." The article highlights major figures who will decide her fate and suitability. They are poet and Ambassador Enrique González Martínez; essayist and Minister José Vasconcelos; and philosopher Antonio Caso. Originally in *El Mercurio* (26 agosto 1921), it is reproduced in *Recopilación*, 484–485.

13. See *Recopilación*, 517–519.

14. Reported in *El Mercurio* (22 junio 1922), and reproduced in *Recopilación*, 521–522.

15. The many published final farewells are in *Recopilación*, 517–529.

16. Pedro Prado, "Al pueblo de México," prologue, *Desolación*, 2nd ed. (Santiago Editorial del Pacífico, 1957), 11–12. Pedro Prado, *Mundo Hispánico* X, 107 (1957), 13.

Chapter XI

1. I[vor] A. Richards, *Practical Criticism: A Study of Literary Judgment* (New York, 1955), 2, 13.

2. *Desolación*, 2nd ed. (Santiago: Editorial del Pacífico, 1957), 288.

3. Louis MacNeice, *The Poetry of W.B. Yeats*. (London, 1941), 17.

4. Raúl Silva Castro, *Estudios sobre Gabriela Mistral* (Santiago, 1935), 127.

5. Stuart Holroyd, *Emergence from Chaos*. (Boston, 1957), 15.

Chapter XII

1. Raúl Silva Castro reproached Gabriela for not having had a formal education. He states, condescendingly, that only the Bible and other books of "modesta importancia" influenced her (*Estudios sobre Gabriela Mistral* [Santiago, 1935], 13). Mistral brilliantly clarified the meaning of her biblical formation in a speech before the Sociedad Hebraica Argentina, in Buenos Aires: "Mi experiencia con la Biblia," *Revista S.H.A.* (1, 15 mayo; 1 junio 1938). I uncovered it first (1975) for a wider public; it again fortifies the text in Appendix C. It was also published in *Noah* 1 (1987), 83–90.

2. José Santos González Vera, "Comienzos de Gabriela Mistral," *Anales* CXV, 106 (1957), 22–23. González Vera describes the grandmother's strong personality: "*La abuela, persona altiva y voluntariosa, recibe los domingos a su nieta y le lee, o la hace leer, el Eclesiastés, el Cantar de los Cantares, las Lamentaciones de Jeremías. Así entona el espíritu de la joven maestra.*"

3. See Matilde Ladrón de Guevara, *Rebelde magnífica* (Santiago, 1957), 29.

4. González Vera, "Comienzos," 22, records: "*Apenas pudo entender, su hermana Emelina empezó a contarle episodios de la sagrada historia. Tanto le gustaron que hubo de repetírselos.*"

5. This text references the Casiodoro de Reina version of the Bible. Enrique Lafourcade, the Chilean novelist, recommended it and commented that Gabriela used the Bible translated from the Hebrew by Casiodoro de Reina (1569), revised and corrected by Cipriano de Valera (1602), i.e., the Protestant Bible in the Spanish

language. This is echoed by Julio Saavedra Molina: "Prologue," *Poesías completas de Gabriela Mistral*, Margaret Bates, ed., 2nd ed. rev. (Madrid, 1962), lxxxix.

6. González Vera, "Comienzos," 23. A relevant new work is Darrell B. Lockhart, "Jewish Issues and Gabriela Mistral," 95–112. In *Gabriela Mistral: The Audacious Traveler*, Marjorie Agosín, ed. (Athens: Ohio University Press, 2003).

7. Gabriela presented this annotated Bible to the Liceo No. 6 de Niñas, in Santiago, which she had directed (1921–1922). It now resides with the Order of Saint Francis in Santiago. The following article by Carlos Zurita copied Mistral's prologue and cited some of the biblical passages underlined and annotated by the poet: "La Biblia fue fuente de sabiduría y permanente inspiración para Gabriela," *La Nación* (13 enero 1957), 16. See also Tomás Lago, "Gabriela y el nardo de Las Parábolas," *Anales* CXV, 106 (1957), 96.

8. González Vera, "Comienzos," 25. Enrique Espinoza discusses the Bible's influence on the poet, in "Gabriela Mistral y el espíritu de la Biblia," *Anales* CXV, 106 (1957), 100.

9. Hernán Díaz Arrieta, *Panorama de la literatura chilena durante el siglo XX* (Santiago, 1931), 69–70.

10. *"Llevaba siempre una Biblia y me dijo a propósito de ello: 'Berta, estoy con el Viejo Testamento. Estoy todo el tiempo leyéndolo y releyéndolo.' Me citó un capítulo de memoria."* See Berta Singerman, "Recuerdos de Gabriela Mistral," *Cuadernos Israelíes*, No. 4 (1960), 6. This oftencited issue of *Cuadernos Israelíes* carries important articles.

11. González Vera, "Gabriela Mistral," *Cuadernos Israelíes*, No. 4 (1960), 41. See also Espinoza, "Gabriela Mistral," 100. Cf., also n. 2, above.

12. See Germán Arciniegas, "Gabriela, la fantástica chilena," *Cuadernos Israelíes*, No. 4 (1960), 23; Carlos D. Hamilton, "Raíces bíblicas de la poesía de Gabriela Mistral," *Cuadernos Americanos* XX, 5 (1961), 201.

13. Singerman, "Recuerdos," 60.

14. Cecilia Meireles, "Um pouco de Gabriela Mistral," *Cuadernos Israelíes*, No. 4 (1960), 20.

15. Gabriela Mistral, "Cartas de Gabriela Mistral a Juan Ramón Jiménez," *La Torre* VIII, 31 (1960), 190. "Materna" should be *"paterna"*; typographical error or fantasy?

16. Hernán Díaz Arrieta, *Gabriela Mistral* (Santiago: Nascimento, 1946), 23–24. Quotation and essay reprinted in *Desolación*, 2nd ed. (Santiago: Editorial del Pacífico, 1957), 17. Cf.,

Gabriela's strong images in "Nocturno de la derrota," 387: *"Yo nací de una carne tajada / en el seco riñón de Israel, / Macabea que da Macabeos..."*

17. Fernando Alegría, "Gabriela Mistral Awarded the 1945 Nobel Prize for Literature," *Bulletin of the Pan American Union* LXXX (1946), 29.

18. According to Saavedra Molina, *Poesías completas* (xxiv), it was first published November 1919, in *Renacimiento*, the *"revista israelita de Santiago."*

19. González Vera, "Comienzos," 25.

20. In Josué Monsalve, *Gabriela Mistral: La errante solitaria* (Santiago: Imprenta Lautaro, 1958), 101–103. Monsalve's detailed, clinical account of Gabriela's last days fails to mention her interest in the Kol Nidre. See Chapter XIII for a discussion of her probable acceptance of the last rites of the Catholic Church.

21. In "El ruego" (100), the poet refers to Jesus as *"...¡oh Rey de los judíos!"*

22. Díaz Arrieta, *Gabriela Mistral*, 47.

23. Augusto Iglesias, *Gabriela Mistral y el modernismo en Chile: Ensayo de crítica subjetiva* (Santiago, 1949 [1950]), 154.

24. Alegría, 29–30. Cf. Virgilio Figueroa, *La divina Gabriela* (Santiago: El Esfurzo, 1933), 71.

25. Lago, "Gabriela," 97.

26. Marie-Lise Gazarían, "La naturaleza en la obra de Gabriela Mistral," unpublished M.A. thesis (New York: Columbia University, 1957), 136.

27. Sarah Bollo, in "La poesía de Gabriela Mistral," *Ínsula* II, 6 (1944), 84, offers this personal comment: *"Me contaba Gabriela que en su valle de Elqui, en sus infancias, amaba tanto las montañas que se refugiaba en el huerto de su casa para modelar en barro figuras y actitudes que ella creía contemplar en las piedras y en las laderas; y así primeramente creyó sentir una vocación artística plástica. Siendo niña como a los diez años y habiendo sido situada en el salón de clase de la escuela al lado de la ventana, se distraía en observar el vuelo de los pájaros, el color de los follajes, y el movimiento de los animales, la solemnidad de la cordillera."*

28. Gazarian (81), writes: *"El equilibrio del mundo depende de la interpretación de los elementos y Gabriela Mistral se unifica con cada uno de ellos para expresar el amor que tiene por todas las creaciones de Dios."* And again (130): *"La naturaleza es personal, Dios vive en ella, y Gabriela se integra a ella con un sentido de fraternidad."*

29. Esther de Cáceres synthesized the problem in "Homenaje a Gabriela Mistral," *Revista Nacional* VIII, 90 (1945), 331: "It was in Elqui,

surrounded by nature in all its bleakness and beauty that Gabriela was able to combine within herself the two possibilities of hermeticism and tenderness."

30. Singerman, 6.
31. Espinoza, 100.
32. Bollo, 84.
33. González Vera, "Comienzos," 23.
34. See "Child, Children," *Dictionary of the Bible,* ed. James Hastings (New York, 1963). In biblical times "children were regarded as Divine gifts (Gen. 4:1, 33:5), pledges of God's favour, the heritage of the Lord (Ps. 127:3). It follows naturally that *barrenness* is looked upon as a reproach, i.e., a punishment inflicted by God, and involving, for the woman, disgrace in the eyes of the world."
35. Cf., Gen. 17:2–5.
36. The contrast is between old age and youth, an unproductive body and one that promises: *"...yo con mi cuerpo de Sara vieja / y él con el suyo de cinco años."* The title, "Pan," 412, suggests the permanent, common objects in life which unite the aged with their past and permit a rejuvenation of the spirit through aroma, heat, and texture.
37. See Chapter XIV "The Poetry of Sacrifice" for the Christian concepts.
38. Hagar despised Sarah and felt superior (Gen. 16:4); Rachel envied Leah and cried, "Give me children or else I die" (Gen. 30:1).
39. *Desolación*, 2nd ed. (Santiago: Editorial del Pacífico, 1957), 201, 203, 207–208.
40. In Gen. 14:17–20, Melchizedek, king of Salem, met Abraham on the latter's return from the slaughter of Cherdoloamer. In Ps. 110:4, he is described as an ideal king.
41. In Gen. 12:2, Abraham received the promise to be the founder of a great nation.
42. Gen. 22:1–10. God later recanted.
43. Shalmaneser laid siege to Samaria while king of Assyria (727–722 B.C.) (See II Kings 17:3; 18:9–18.) Cf. the analysis of "Campeón finlandés," in Chapter XIV, "The Poetry of Sacrifice," section "The Life Principle: Water, Blood, and Milk."
44. Gabriela praises universal song writers: Theocritus, Solomon, Anacreon, Omar Khayyam, Petrarch, Netzahualcóyotl, and Tagore.
45. "El arpa de Dios," *Desolación,* 234.
46. See Chapter XIV, "The Poetry of Sacrifice," for references to the wounded stag (*"ciervo herido"*) and Jesus Christ. Gabriela collected figurines of deer and gazelles in order to contemplate their graceful lines and because they symbolized peace. A note by the poet to "Todas íbamos a ser reinas," 807, explains that she first saw these animals and other exotic fauna and flora that excited her imagination, in the *"parque medio botánico y zoológico"* of Don Alfonso Iribarren, in Montegrande.
47. "Lecturas espirituales," *Desolación,* 234.
48. Job 27:5 says: *"Nunca tal acontezca que yo os justifique: Hasta morir no quitaré de mí mi integridad."*
49. Job 34:37.
50. The Bible mentions many species of the thorn tree.
51. Gen. 21:17.
52. Hans Rheinfelder, "Gabriela Mistral," *Anales* CXV, 106 (1957), 51.
53. Job 31:38–40.
54. Job 3:3, 12.
55. Job 2:7.
56. Job 24:20.
57. Job 19:25–26. The traditional view is refuted in the article, "Resurrection," in *The Interpreter's Dictionary of the Bible* (New York, 1960). Nevertheless, this quotation anticipates the Christian concept of resurrection. This passage in Spanish tones down the impact. In English, the same line reads: "And *though* after my skin *worms* destroy this *body,* yet in my flesh shall I see God."
58. N. G. M. van Doornik et al., *A Handbook of the Catholic Faith: The Triptych of the Kingdom* (Garden City, NJ, 1962), 24–25.
59. John 1:1, 17:3; I Cor. 8:6.
60. For a lucid discussion, see Harry Austryn Wolfson, *The Philosophy of the Church Fathers: Faith, Trinity, Incarnation,* Vol. I (Cambridge, MA: Harvard University Press, 1956), 308.
61. Doornik et al., *A Handbook of the Catholic Faith,* 156.
62. Eduardo Barrios, "El primer libro de Gabriela Mistral," *Anales* CXV, 106 (1957), 27. See also Hamilton, "Raíces bíblicas," 21, for this addition: *"Antiguo Testamento para sus gritos de dolor, y Nuevo Testamento, Evangelios, para sus canciones de ternura; Antiguo Testamento en sus tonos proféticos terribles, y también en trozos de emoción suave como el Libro de Ruth; Evangelios para cantar a los niños, los hijos de su alma, y para acercarse a la paz que le da Cristo."*
63. Díaz Arrieta, in *Gabriela Mistral,* 28, affirms that Gabriela believed in the Old Testament God with the tunic of Jesus: *"Su Dios es el Jehová de la Biblia, pero que pasó por la fronda evangélica."* Díaz Arrieta decries, 30, as futile the transforming of Jehovah (*"el Dios vengador"*) into Jesus. For the most part, Gabriela maintained the separateness of Jehovah and Jesus.
64. In "El encuentro," 60, the image, *"...mi*

Dios me vistió de llagas," recalls Job's affliction. Cf., also, "El poema del hijo," 105: "*Y la tregua de Dios a mi no descendiera.*"

65. "Otoño" also symbolizes death and decay. See also "El Dios triste," 37; "La encina," 55; "La espera inútil," 86; "La muerte-niña," 426.

66. Cf., "Último árbol," 798: "*...el diezmo que pagué al rayo / de mi Dios dulce y tremendo.*"

67. Wolfgang Kayser, *Interpretación y análisis de la obra literaria,* 2nd ed. rev. (Madrid, 1958), 296. Kayser states the problem succinctly, but his solution appears inadequate.

68. I am not addressing, of course, the poetry's chronology by choosing this order and selection. Rather, the focus is on illustrating themes and technique.

69. The reference is to Ishmael's desertion by Abraham and the former's settlement in Paran (Gen. 21:14, 21).

70. Cf., on "solitude," Lope de Vega's "*Romance*": "*A mis soledades voy, / de mis soledades vengo.*"

71. Mistral's trust of Margot Arce de Vázquez led her to attest to God's importance:

"*Después pudimos comprobar que Dios era el pensamiento constante, el cotidiano problema de Gabriela Mistral; Dios, el amor y América.*" See *Gabriela Mistral: Persona y poesía* (San Juan, Puerto Rico, 1957), 13.

Chapter XIII

1. Manuel Pedro González, "Profile of a Great Woman," *Hispania* XLI (1958), 428. See also Matilde Ladrón de Guevara, *Rebelde magnífica* (Santiago: Imprenta Central, 1957), 45.

2. Three critics deal with this educational fiasco in Lucila's life: José Santos González Vera, in "Comienzos de Gabriela Mistral," *Anales* CXV, 106 (1957), 23, says Capellán Don Ignacio Munizaga, "*más soldado que pastor de Cristo,*" considered Gabriela's writings "*algo socialistas y un tanto paganos.*" See Hernán Díaz Arrieta in *Gabriela Mistral* (Santiago, 1946), 107–108, and in "Recuerdos de infancia y juventud de Gabriela Mistral," *Revista Nacional de Cultura* XIX, 121–122 (1957), 80–81. Also, Gastón Figueira, *De la vida y la obra de Gabriela Mistral* (Montevideo, 1959), 9.

3. See John A. Crow's discussion of Chile's religious history in *The Epic of Latin America* (New York, 1952), 215–216, 344, 640; see also 4th ed. (Berkeley: University of California Press, 1995).

4. Mistral's remarks to Margarita Cofre Silva occur in "Gabriela Mistral, pensador americano," *Revista de Educación* VI, 34 (1946), 35.

5. See Gabriela Mistral, *Recados: Contando a Chile* (Santiago, 1957), 163.

6. Cofre Silva, "Gabriela Mistral," 35–36, again quotes Mistral, who had already written "El catolicismo en los Estados Unidos," *El Mercurio* (27 julio 1924), 8.

7. See Gabriela Mistral, "Unidad cristiana," *La Nueva Democracia* XXV, 3 (1944), 8–9.

8. Gabriela Mistral, "Cristianismo con sentido social," *Atenea* II, 9 (1925), 477. See the same article (476–477), for the following long passage in the text. This article initiates a tactful polemic with her friends, Alfredo L. Palacios, Romain Rolland, and José Vasconcelos. Their rebuffs follow Mistral's article (477–485).

9. In contrast with Pope John XXIII, Pope Pius XII was surprised to learn from Mistral that millions of South Americans were living in poverty. "*El sólo había conocido el brillo de Buenos Aires, gigantesco y europeo,*" was the poet's tart comment to Germán Arciniegas about the Pope's ignorance of poverty in South America. Arciniegas, in "Gabriela Mistral y Pío XII," *El Tiempo* (13 oct. 1958), 5.

10. Luis Nieto Caballero, "Gabriela Mistral," *Repertorio Americano* (11 enero 1930), 17.

11. Ladrón de Guevara, 44–45. In 1953, the poet admitted her inability for formal prayer: "*Debo confesarle más; no puedo con el Santo Rosario.*" See Francisco Dussuel, "Carta inédita de Gabriela Mistral," *Mensaje,* No. 86 (enero-feb. 1960), 21.

12. Virgilio Figueroa, *La divina Gabriela* (Santiago: El Esfuerzo, 1933), 161.

13. Ladrón de Guevara, 44.

14. Walter Kaufmann discusses the meaning of personal prayer, in *Critique of Religion and Philosophy* (New York, 1961), 367–368.

15. Gabriela Mistral, *Recados,* 158–164. Pedro Lira Urquieta testifies to Mistral's high regard for Monseñor Carlos Casanueva's ability as a priest and as a human being dedicated to excellence and charity, in "Gabriela Mistral y la Universidad Católica," *Finisterrae,* No. 12 (1956), 60.

16. Gabriela Mistral, "Silueta de Sor Juana Inés," *Ábside* XV (1951), 506.

17. Pedro de Alba, "Hispanismo e indigenismo de Gabriela Mistral," *Anales* CXV, 106 (1957), 79. See also Gabriela Mistral, "Fray Bartolomé," *Repertorio Americano* (14 oct. 1933), 210.

18. Sister John Berchmans, O.P., "Gabriela Mistral and the Franciscan Concept of Life," *Renascence* V (1952), 43–44.

19. In José Santos González Vera's letter (July 12, 1962).

20. Figueroa, 160.

21. See Herbert J. Muller, *The Uses of the Past: Profiles of Former Societies* (New York, 1954), 174–181. In tracing the history of Church doctrine, Muller shows the Church's attempts at logic and self-justification.

22. Dussuel, "Carta inédita …, 21.

23. Walter Kaufmann addresses the general inconsistencies of theology and organized religion. See *The Faith of a Heretic* (New York, 1961), 103–148, 201–289. There may be an analogy between Kaufmann and Mistral. Kaufmann, raised Jewish, shows a disregard for organized Judaism reminiscent of Gabriela's for Catholicism.

24. By this I mean a rational inquiry into religious systems, not an enslavement of the mind to science and rationalism. Indeed, Theosophy upholds the Yoga aphorism that "the Mind is the great slayer of the Real. Let the disciple slay the Slayer."

25. "Cristianismo con sentido social," 474, 476, respectively.

26. Mistral's essay on the Cathedral of St. John the Divine in New York deals with the concepts of bigness, equality, and bureaucracy in North American religious life. See "Cómo edifican," *La Nueva Democracia* XII, 1 (1931), 13.

27. Mistral ripostes in a French journal: "Considérations sur Rousseau et autres réfléxions," *Révue de l'Amérique Latine* XI (avril 1926), 324–326. Mistral answers Andrés Montserrat's attack on her ideas on religion and pedagogy: "Gabriela Mistral sur la pente," *Révue de l'Amérique Latine* X (sept. 1925), 270.

28. Carlos Escudero reported that the priest was the Reverend Father William Scrill. See "Sacerdote chileno impartió Bendición Apostólica a poetisa Gabriela Mistral," *El Mercurio* (9 enero 1957), 1.

29. Margaret T. Rudd gave permission (Dec. 4, 1964) to quote from a letter sent to her by Mercedes García-Huidobro de Dublé. Father Ivan Nikolic, S.J., informed Mercedes (Jan. 10, 1957) that Gabriela was conscious and eager to receive the Sacraments. Obviously, Father Nikolic knew this only as hearsay, because he was not allowed to see Gabriela on January 9, 1957, according to his letter to me eight years later (Dec. 1, 1965), in which he reported: "So I returned home without seeing Miss Mistral. Later on I was sorry for not having forced my way to her room doubting very much of the assurances that she had been seen by a priest already." It is difficult to reconcile Father Nikolic's letter of Jan. 10, 1957, unwavering in its convictions, with that of Dec. 1, 1965, remorseful and doubting.

30. Josué Monsalve, *Gabriela Mistral: La errante solitaria* (Santiago, 1958), 103.

31. Cofre Silva observed that Mistral chose a religious path "rationally." See "Gabriela Mistral, pensador americano," 35: "*En materia de religión Gabriela Mistral ha ido buscando racionalmente su camino.*"

32. Alvin Boyd Kuhn, *Theosophy: A Modern Revival of Ancient Wisdom* (New York, 1930), 4.

33. Ibid., 6.

34. Augusto Iglesias, *Gabriela Mistral y el modernismo en Chile: Ensayo de crítica subjetiva* (Santiago, 1949 [1950]), 209–211. Jal B. Dorab, recording secretary of the Theosophical Society, Adyar, India, confirmed (December 12, 1963), this. Ann Kerr Wylie, national secretary of the Theosophical Society in America, assisted. See Appendices A and B regarding Mistral's background in Theosophy.

35. Monsalve, 41.

36. Julio Saavedra Molina, "Gabriela Mistral: Su vida y su obra," in *Poesías completas de Gabriela Mistral*, ed. Margaret Bates, 2nd ed. rev. (Madrid: Aguilar, 1962), xx, lxxxix–xc. See also Raúl Silva Castro, *Producción de Gabriela Mistral de 1912 a 1918* (Santiago: Universidad de Chile, 1957), 37, 40–42.

37. González Vera, "Comienzos," 24.

38. Víctor Alba affirmed her interest in Christian Science and Yoga: "*.. leyó cosas orientales, se interesó luego por la Christian Science y, a su modo practica la oración yoga, de contemplación y concentración.*" See "La Mistral vista por su amiga y secretaria," *Anales* CXV, 106 (1957), 92.

39. Rudolph Otto, *The Original Gita: The Song of the Supreme Exalted One* (London, 1939), 119.

40. Kuhn, 268. Kuhn credits Mme Blavatsky with the following definition of a Theosophist: "Any person of average intellectual capacities and a leaning towards the metaphysical; of pure unselfish life, who finds more joy in helping his neighbor than in receiving help himself; one who is ever ready to sacrifice his own pleasures for the sake of other people; and who loves Truth, Goodness and Wisdom for their own sake, not for the benefit they may confer — is a Theosophist."

41. The quotations and the ideas in this paragraph derive from Reel F, Notebook 64, 8–15, 20, Manuscript Division, U.S. Library of Congress.

42. See Austin Warren's discussion of W. B. Yeats' practice of Theosophy and the occult in *A Rage for Order: Essays in Criticism* (Ann Arbor, 1948), 71–83.

43. See H[éléna] P[etrovna] Blavatsky, *The Key to Theosophy* (London, 1889), 21, 24, 25.
44. Reel E, Notebook 1, July 31, 1944, is the source also for the immediately following quotation.
45. Iglesias, in *Gabriela Mistral*, 208, comments that these sonnets reflect astrological and occult theory (*"...ciertas creencias ocultistas de Gabriela"*).
46. Cf., "La medianoche," 411: *"Oigo / a mi madre dormida / con dos alientos. / (Duermo yo en ella, / de cinco años.)."*
47. See Gabriela Mistral, "Motivos de San Francisco," *Páginas en prosa*, ed. José Pereira Rodríguez (Buenos Aires, 1962), 25–52. Cf. the same work in an edition that distorts Mistral's punctuation and wording: *Motivos de San Francisco*, ed. César Díaz-Muñoz Cormatches (Santiago, 1965). Cf. also two differing reviews of the latter text by Alfredo Lefebvre, in *La Nación* (1 mayo 1966), 5, and by Luis Vargas Saavedra, *Mapocho* XIII, 1 (1966), 256–260.
48. Christmas Humphreys, *Buddhism* (Baltimore: Penguin, 1958), 32.
49. Multiple, symbolic meanings of earth and clay appear in "Motivos del barro," *Desolación*, 2nd ed. (Santiago, 1957), 214–219.
50. St. Bonaventure, *The Mirror of Perfection* (New York, 1951), 257.
51. Cf. Luke 7:38, Isa. 15:2, and Num. 5:18. In these texts, loosening the hair signifies, variously, humility, grief, and abasement.
52. Blavatsky, *The Key*, 37.
53. Silva Castro, *Producción*, 77, offers this poem, called "Primavera," which does not appear in *Poesías completas*. It was first published in *Primerose*, which seems to be a Theosophical publication.
54. "Limpia tu fuente," cited by Silva Castro, *Producción*, 97. Cf. "La charca," *Desolación*, 258, first published in *Nueva Luz* (Órgano de la Rama Teosófica Arundhali), III, 24 (marzo 1914), 570–571.
55. Silva Castro, *Producción*, 75.
56. Ibid., 74. Cf. "La fuga," *Poesías completas*, 378, for a similar Buddhist image: *"...tú eres un agua de cien ojos, / y eres un paisaje de mil brazos."*
57. Humphreys, 92, clarifies the issue: "'Desire is not evil. It is desire to affirm the lower self, to live in it, to cling to it, to identify oneself with it, instead of with the Universal Self, that is evil.'"
58. "Comienzos," 24. See Gabriela's article, "Una explicación más del caso Krishnamurti," *La Nación* (1 agosto 1930), 5–6.
59. Richard Mathison satirizes Annie Besant's exaggerated claims about the divinity of Krishnamurti, in *Faiths, Cults and Sects of America: From Atheism to Zen* (New York: Bobbs-Merrill, 1960), 157–158.
60. AnnieBesant, *Esoteric Christianity or the Lesser Mysteries* (Adyar & Los Angeles: Theosophical Publishing House, 1913), 183.
61. Gabriela Mistral, "Recado de Navidad," *Ábside* XIII (1949), 9. See also p. 13 for the following textual passage.
62. See "Paraíso," 415, where the absence of sound, movement, and time reflects a paradise characterized by surfeited tranquility and stylized beauty.
63. Reel E, Notebook 1, July 31, 1944.
64. See Annie Besant at "Theosophical Society," *Encyclopedia of Religion and Ethics*, ed. James Hastings (New York, 1935).
65. See "Maternity," *Dictionary of the Bible*.
66. See "Sexual Impurity," *Dictionary of the Bible*. For a study of the problems of theology and myth, see E[dwin] O. James, *The Cult of the Mother-Goddess* (New York: Praeger, 1959), 205–206.
67. "Recado de Navidad," 8.
68. All quotations here are from Gabriela Mistral's "Divulgación religiosa. Sentido de las letanías: Virgen de las Vírgenes," *El Mercurio* (12 abril 1925), 3. Cf. also, for theme and tone, her "Alabanzas a la Virgen," (23 agosto 1925), 3. On the proper adoration to Mary, see Hilda Graeff, *Mary: A History of Doctrine and Devotion*, Vol. I (New York: Sheed & Ward, 1963), 73.
69. Besant, *Esoteric Christianity*, 153.
70. Kuhn, 135.
71. Besant, "Theosophical Society."
72. Besant, *Esoteric Christianity*, 166.
73. Ibid., 157.
74. Jacquetta Hawkes, *Man and the Sun* (New York: Random House, 1962), 201–205.
75. Besant, *Esoteric Christianity*, 166.
76. Ibid., 159.
77. Cf. "Recado de nacimiento para Chile," 570: *"...como el niño Jesús en la noche, / lamida del Géminis, el León y el Cangrejo, / cubierta del Zodíaco de enero."*
78. Cf. "Duerme, duerme, niño cristiano," 246: *"Duermo celado / de los humanos, / y recobrado / de lo arcano."*
79. Margot Arce de Vázquez also remarks on the mythic aspect: *"El poeta parece atribuir sentido maternal al universo entero, no sólo a la tierra." Gabriela Mistral: Persona y poesía* (San Juan, Puerto Rico, 1958), 66.
80. On this phrase, see Juan Terlingen, "Cara de Dios," in *Studia Philológica: Homenaje ofrecido a Dámaso Alonso*, Vol. III (Madrid, 1963), 463–478.

81. See Mathison, 148–159.
82. Dussuel, "Carta inédita," 20.
83. Kuhn, 113.
84. Sarah Bollo, "La poesía de Gabriela Mistral," *Revista Nacional* XI (1948), 79.
85. Enrique Espinoza establishes the triad with Nervo and Tagore: "*Tuvo por último relación epistolar con Amado Nervo y conoció en buenas traducciones españolas a Rabindranath Tagore.*" See "Gabriela Mistral y el espíritu de la Biblia," *Anales* CXV, 106 (1957), 100.
86. Raúl Silva Castro, *Estudios*, 8, cites Gabriela's own comments: "*En el arte de regir la vida Dante, Tagore y la Biblia.*"
87. Abinash Chandra Bose, *Three Mystic Poets: A Study of W. B. Yeats, A. E., and Rabindranath Tagore* (Kolhapur, India, 1945), 114.
88. Ibid., 111–112. Edward Thompson states that Tagore "was anti-theosophy" on the ground that Theosophy derived from neo-Hinduism, which advocated force. In *Rabindranath Tagore: Poet and Dramatist*, 2nd. ed. (London, 1948), 98. Tagore's attitude, however, either was unknown to Gabriela or, if it was known, made little difference. The important thing is that Gabriela regarded Tagore with reverence, and saw in his attempts at solidifying man with nature a parallel to Theosophy.
89. Bose's translation is from the Bengali: *Three Mystic Gods*, 127.
90. Ibid., 110. Bose excerpts from *Thoughts from Rabindranath Tagore*, ed. C. F. Andrews (1929), 5.
91. See Mistral's "Considérations," 325.
92. Saavedra Molina, *Poesías completas*, lxxvii–lxxviii. Arturo Torres Rioseco's theory of desolation and death stems from the leafless Tala tree found in Brazil and the Argentine Pampas: "*Tala es otra voz de desolación y muerte, árbol sin sombra, desnudo de pájaros, acribillado de saetas, en tierra de Goyaz o en la pampa argentina.*" See *Gabriela Mistral* (Valencia, 1962), 28–29.
93. Cf. Bose, 112: "In nature he discovers 'harmony of forms, colours, sounds and movements.'"
94. Cf. Blavatsky, *The Key*, 207: "... all pain and suffering are results of want of *Harmony*, and that the one terrible and only cause of the disturbance of Harmony is selfishness. ..."
95. See *Desolación*, 229–231, for the ensuing discussion. Although three revised "Comentarios" appear, originally six were written (including three poems) as prologue to *Rabindranath Tagore: Poeta y filósofo hindú*, trans. Raúl Ramírez (Santiago, 1917). Incidentally, Silva Castro (*Estudios*, 232), says that "Intima" (*Poesías completas*, 66) is a gloss of "Thy Body." Silva Castro (*Producción*, 149–150) adds that "Desvelada" and "El amor que calla" (*Poesías completas*, 72, 63) are based on Tagore's *The Gardener*.
96. Rabindranath Tagore, *Collected Poems and Plays* (New York: Macmillan, 1951), 35. The next four textual references are to this work.
97. Gabriela Mistral, *Epistolario: Cartas a Eugenio Labarca (1915–1916)*, ed. Raúl Silva Castro (Santiago, 1957), 27.
98. Bollo, "La poesía," *Revista Nacional*, 79.
99. Dussuel, 21.
100. Sara Bollo, "La poesía de Gabriela Mistral," *Ínsula* II, 6 (1944), 86. Cf. a comment by Carlos Hamilton: "*Como Amado Nervo, Gabriela había pasado por una vaga época de Teosofismo, en búsqueda desatentada de espiritualidad de qué asirse en la desesperanza.*" See "Raíces bíblicas de la poesía de Gabriela Mistral," *Cuadernos Americanos* XX, 5 (1961), 208.
101. The differences in age, experiences, and environment make non-sequential and asynchronous comparisons necessary. Nervo (1870–1919) had gone through a series of "isms" in literature (realism, naturalism, symbolism, and modernism), and through several in religion and philosophy (Catholicism, positivism, and Buddhism), before Gabriela began writing in 1904.
102. Mistral, *Epistolario*, 30.
103. Esther Turner Wellman, *Amado Nervo: Mexico's Religious Poet* (New York: Instituto de las Españas, 1936), 76.
104. Ibid., 99.
105. Concha Meléndez, *Amado Nervo* (New York: Instituto de las Españas, 1926), 64.
106. Amado Nervo, *Poesías Completas* (Mexico: Latino Americana, 1957), 183–201.
107. See Meléndez, 68, 71.
108. We are stressing the Christianity of Christ and the Buddhism of Buddha, not the development and/or corruption of them by later generations. Note also that Theosophy looks to the founders of religions, not to the followers for inspiration. For this reason, it can embrace the common aspects of all religions.
109. Dussuel, 21.
110. *Poesías completas*, 803. This quotation, an appendix to "Muerte de mi madre," is from *Tala*. The title has already been interpreted as a clearing of the forest for new planting. The meaning can be applied, then, in two senses: a) the end of the suffering for Christ (and his followers), and b) the beginning of his glory in the Resurrection.
111. Silva Castro, *Estudios*, 9.
112. Ladrón de Guevara, 45.
113. In "Profile," 430, Manuel Pedro González states relevantly that Buddhism "co-

incides very closely with the principles of her own stoic convictions — particularly in regard to suffering and grief— and consequently left a deep impression on her soul." González focuses on the two main points elucidated at greater length in this section: "By the time I met her she had already abandoned Buddhism and become a fervent Christian. But her Christianity was completely devoid of rites and external liturgies."

114. In "Gabriela Mistral," Enrique Espinoza Anales, CXV, 106 (1957), 100, singles out neo-Catholic Jacques Maritain, a friend of Gabriela's, who might have contributed to her reconversion: "Y hasta terminó por hacer confusamente católico su teosofismo inicial para sumarse a los llamados social cristianos en boga después de la conversión de Jacques Maritain y su mujer." Espinoza also affirms that it became increasingly difficult to disentangle the multiple religious influences that were operating on her. Gabriela Mistral's religious eclecticism embraced, at different times and in differing degrees, ideas of Georges Duhamel, Charles Péguy, Romain Rolland, Léon Bloy, Thomas Merton, and Oscar Ladislasz de Lubicz-Milosz.

115. *Gabriela Mistral: Persona y poesía,* 78. She adds: "*El capítulo en que Bergson estudia la mística cristiana conmueve al poeta hondamente y lo encamina hacia el anhelo y la búsqueda de la gracia.*" Cf. "Memoria de la gracia," *Poesías completas,* 757: "*Cincuenta años caminando / detrás de la Gracia / gracia de las dos Marías, / y de las dos Anas.*"

116. Wellman, 90.

117. Ibid., 134.

118. See Nervo: "Un año," 714–715; "Al maya," 723–724.

119. Wellman, 24.

120. For a defense of Buddhism against Bergson's arbitrary remarks, see Hjalmar Sundén, *La Théorie bergsonienne de la religion* (Paris: Presses Universitaires, 1947), 195–218, and esp. 207 218.

121. Henri Bergson, *Les Deux Sources de la morale et de la réligion,* 13th ed. (Paris: Librairie Félix Alcan, 1933), 241–212.

Chapter XIV

1. Austin Warren, *A Rage for Order: Essays in Criticism* (Ann Arbor, 1948), preface.

2. Annie Besant, *Esoteric Christianity or The Lesser Mysteries* (Adyar & Los Angeles, 1913), 169–229. Further page references to this work are indicated in the text. Ricardo Michell Abós-Padilla states that Gabriela read *Cristianismo esotérico*. Supported in Appendix A.

3. Besant is quoting from her article, "The Atonement," *Nineteenth Century* (June 1895).

4. *Poesías completas de Gabriela Mistral,* ed. Margaret Bates, 2nd ed. rev. (Madrid: Aguilar, 1962), 80. See this work for all references in the text to the poetry.

5. Matt. 27:28; Mark 15:17; Luke 23:11; John 19:2. Quotations from the Bible are given in English, unless a stylistic comparison is necessary, then they are given in Spanish from the Cipriano Valera, Casiodoro de Reina edition.

6. Esther de Cáceres also makes this point. See "Homenaje a Gabriela Mistral," *Revista Nacional* VIII, 90 (1945), 333. A fuller discussion ensues below in the section, "Nature and the Legend of Veronica."

7. In John 18:10, "*bajo los olivos,*" Simon Peter smites off Malchus' ear to protect Christ. This contrasts with his threefold denial of Christ in Caiaphas' palace (John 18:15–18, 25–27).

See *Poesías*, "La desasida," 604, for a similar reference to Peter: "*Mi enemigo podía injuriarme / o negarme Pedro, mi amigo...*"

8. See John 11:39–4.

9. John 11:41–42.

10. See Matt. 19:13–15; Mark 10:13–16; Luke 18:15–17.

11. "Por qué las rosas tienen espinas," *Desolación,* 2nd ed. (Santiago: Editorial del Pacífico, 1957), 251.

12. Matt. 26:40.

13. Psalm 10:15 promises Yahweh's punishment: "*Quebranta el brazo del malo: Del maligno buscarás su maldad, hasta que ninguna halles.*" Christ also augured war, not peace, destruction, not amity, for those who refused to recognize love (Matt. 10:34 35). Contrast this with Matt. 5:39.

14. Matt. 27:55, 56.

15. Respectively, "La cruz de Bistolfi," 4; "Canto del justo," 18; "Lámpara de catedral," 749.

16. "Nocturno del descendimiento," 397; "El ruego," 100.

17. "El himno cotidiano," 352; "Mis libros," 35. See "Leonardo Bistolfi" (1859–1933), in the *Enciclopedia Italiana* (Milano, 1930). He was a Torinese sculptor known for his religious interpretations of tombs and death. He did a crucifix at Villabasse (1901).

18. For further examples see "La cruz de Bistolfi," 4; "El suplicio," 20–21; "Éxtasis," 64; "Dios lo quiere, 70; "Canción de los que buscan olvidar," 113.

19. An allusion to John 20:27.

20. See Louis Martz, *The Poetry of Meditation: A Study in English Religious Literature of the Seventeenth Century* (New Haven: Yale University Press, 1954), 73.

21. See St. Francis de Sales, *Introduction to a Devout Life,* trans. John K. Evan (New York, 1950), 188.

22. Martz, 79.

23. Fray Luis de Granada, *Obras,* in *Biblioteca de Autores Españoles,* Vol. II (Madrid, 1848), 13.

24. With no attempt at embellishment, the "tree" is used as a simple metonym for the Cross in Acts 5:30, 10:39, 13:29; I Peter 2:24; Gal. 3:13.

25. See Joseph Gaer, *The Lore of the New Testament* (Boston: Little, Brown, 1952), 69–70, 196, 208, 215–216, 221, 228, and 230. See also Gaer's sources, 340, 342.

26. The possible mystic, Franciscan relationship captured the attention of Ulrich Leo. See "La literatura hispanoamericana y los alemanes," in *Interpretaciones hispanoamericanas: Ensayos de teoría y práctica estilísticas, 1939–1958* (Santiago, Cuba, 1960), 194–197.

"Himno al árbol," 347, begins with a typical Franciscan epithet: "Árbol Hermano..."

27. Mary, Martha's sister, anointed Christ's feet with the fragrant oil of spikenard (Mark 14:3; John 12:3). Amos 2:9 has Moab "strong as the oaks," but no match for God.

28. Gaer, 209–211. See 341 for index to sources.

29. This idea is akin to that expressed by Nicaraguan poet Rubén Darío in "Lo fatal."

30. See "Lluvia lenta" and "Pinares," 140–144.

31. "Cedar," *Dictionary of the Bible,* ed. James Hastings (New York: Scribners, 1963). In medieval tradition, the cedar is the upright of the Cross. See Gaer, *New Testament,* 209–211.

32. Arnold Whittick, *Symbols, Signs and Their Meaning* (Newton, MA: Branford, 1960), 279, mentions the complex relationship between God and soul, and tree or stone and body, as discussed by William Robertson Smith, *Lectures on the Religion of the Semites* (New York, 1907), 84.

33. Whittick, 279. For details of the legend, see Gaer, 208–10, 341. Cf. also, "Tree," in George Ferguson, *Signs & Symbols in Christian Art* (New York: Oxford University Press, 1961), 31.

34. See Gen. 2:15, 19–20; 3:23.

35. Cf. a similar discussion on Milton by Roland Mushat Frye, *God, Man and Satan: Patterns of Christian Thought and Life in "Paradise Lost," "Pilgrim's Progress," and the Great Theologians* (Princeton: Princeton University Press, 1960), 43–44. The Spanish painter Diego de Velázquez (1599–1660) hints at the redemption of man through labor in "Las hilanderas," and also in other paintings.

36. Whittick, 262–263, says: "... in some representations the ship is carried on the back of the fish, indicating that members of the Church are piloted trough the seas of life by Jesus." Cf. Christ's power to control the tempest (Matt. 8:24–27), whereby he gains the confidence of the disciples. Incidentally, the word "fish" in Greek, *icthus,* is an acronym for "Jesus Christ God's Son Saviour," according to Ferguson, 18.

37. Apart from the figurative voyage, Gabriela probably wrote the "Canciones en el mar" while traveling from Valparaíso, Chile, to Veracruz, Mexico (1922). The reasons for leaving have already been discussed in Ch. X, "The Transformation: Chile and Beyond."

38. See John 19:28, 34. For a layman's scientific explanation of blood and water in the dead body of Christ, see James A. Bishop, *The Day Christ Died* (New York: Harper, 1957), 309.

30. The *ciervo* (stag) and its counterparts, *venado, cabritillo,* and *gacela,* often appear associated with death, fear, innocence, peace, and swiftness. In three allusions, the *ciervo* points to Christ: "Nocturno de la derrota," 386, 388; "Locas letanías," 399; "Sol del trópico," 458. For a study of *el ciervo herido* ("the wounded stag") in Spanish literature, see María Rosa Lida, "Transmisión y recreación de temas grecolatinos," *Revista de Filología Hispánica* I (1939), 31–52.

40. Cf., Luke 23:27–28; Heb. 13:12. The redemption is possible only through the acceptance of sacrifice — hence the tears resulting from pain and sin.

41. Cf., John 9:37 ff.

42. Perry J. Powers, "Lope de Vega and *Las lágrimas de la Madalena,*" *Comparative Literature* VIII (1956), 279.

43. John 12:3; Luke 7:38.

44. This is an extended interpretation of Lev. 21:8, 17. See "Salt," *Dictionary of the Bible.*

45. Matt. 27:34.

46. By contrast, in "Gracias en el mar," 556, the phrase "*la sal en la garganta*" proclaims farewell, without bitterness, but with a touch of nostalgia and sadness, to a friend from shipboard.

47. For example, in "A la Virgen de la Colina," 27, Gabriela expresses bitterness over not being able to offer physical love adequately: "*...ver que un vaso de hieles di.*" Disintegration of the flesh appears in "Nocturno de la derrota,"

388, as "*con el liquen quemado en sus sales.*" Sterility is a dominant theme. The best illustration is in "Sal," 445, where the poet joins hands with the biblical Raquel and Rebeca. Again in "Sal," 446, the desperation of undeniable and eternal suffering occurs: "*...y el puñado de Sal y yo / en beguinas o en prisioneras, / las dos llorando, las dos cautivas, / atravesamos por la puerta...*"

48. In a sense this is an application of the "Covenant of salt" to Gabriela's poetry. See *Dictionary of the Bible*, which refers to Numbers 18:19; II Chronicles 13:5.

49. "Motivos de la Pasión," *Desolación*, 236.

50. The image confuses a "coat without seam" (John 19:23) with a "sudarium," or "napkin" (John 11:44, 20:7), really a headpiece. "Sudarium" also applies to Veronica's handkerchief.

51. Gabriela enjoyed sipping wine, but did not condone overindulgence and drunkenness, according to Matilde Ladrón de Guevara, *Rebelde magnífica* (Santiago: Imprenta Central, 1957), 21, 22.

52. "Poemas de las madres," *Desolación*, 206.

53. Rev. 19:15 refers to the winepress as a metaphor of death and destruction: "...and he treadeth the winepress of the fierceness and wrath of Almighty God."

54. *Mosto*, or "must" [Latin *mustum*], is grape juice before and during fermentation.

55. It is odd that I find no reference to water becoming wine.

56. Although this is possibly profane love and not directed toward Christ, the New Testament is still the source, and the analogy could be applied as well.

57. Falerno is an Italian still, sweet wine made near Naples. In antiquity, Roman troops drank it.

58. "Éxtasis," 64–65, illustrates the kind of desperation which prompts a desire for death in the arms of Christ and which also causes confusion and stammering, as evidenced by the difficult phrasing, hyperbaton, and pessimism. But ineffability and the desire for plentitude derive from a desire to escape from pain, not from the preparation for a mystic union. On this problem see Lowry Nelson, Jr., "The Rhetoric of Ineffability: Toward a Definition of Mystical Poetry," *Comparative Literature* VIII (1956), 323–336. Mistral's mysticism was not sustained, but responded to momentary crises, according to the thesis of Sister Rose Aquin Caimano, O.P., *Mysticism in Gabriela Mistral* (New York: Pageant, 1969).

59. "Mis libros," 34, alludes to the poet's rapture for the freshness, the pain, and the love in Frédéric Mistral's poetry, as "*yo te aspiré embriagada.*"

60. *Tala*, 3rd ed. (Buenos Aires: Sur, 1946), 153.

61. Matt. 27:45; Mark 15:33; Luke 23:44. Both "Nocturno," 80, and "El costado desnudo," 708, contain the "*cielo de estaño*"; "*cielo de añil*" is in only the former.

62. See "La lluvia lenta," 140: "*El cielo es como un inmenso / corazón que se abre, amargo. / No llueve: es un sangrar lento / y largo.*" Cf. "Cima," 136: "*Hay algún corazón en donde moja / la tarde aquella cima ensangrentada.*"

63. Gaer, 106–167, 204, and 211; esp. 212, 341.

64. "Nocturno," 80. Cf. "Mis libros," 35: "*Los que cual Cristo hicieron la Vía-Dolorosa, / apretaron el verso contra su roja herida, / y es lienzo de Verónica la estrofa dolorida; / ¡todo libro es purpúreo como sangrienta rosa!*"

65. "Lecturas espirituales," *Desolación*, 232.

66. Cáceres, "Homenaje," 333.

67. Eleanor McCann details the subtle antitheses. See her "Oxymora in Spanish Mystics and English Metaphysical Writers," *Comparative Literature* XIII (1961), 16–25.

68. Cleanth Brooks, *The Well Wrought Urn: Studies in the Structure of Poetry* (New York: Harcourt, Brace, 1947), 11–21; esp. 16. Note the possible application of this statement to the famous strophe of Santa Teresa de Jesús: "*Vivo sin vivir en mí, / y tan alta vida espero, / que muero porque no muero.*"

69. Apropos of "La maestra rural," Gabriela said, "*No quiero en ella el arte sino la idea religiosa.*" See *Epistolario: Cartas a Eugenio Laborea (1915–1916)*, ed. Raúl Silva Castro (Santiago, 1957), 271

70. See Matt. 26:25, 49. Mark 9:5, 11:21, and 14:45. John 1:38, 49; 4:31; 9:2; 11:8.

71. "La oración de la maestra," *Desolación*, 198.

72. S.v. "Blood," *Dictionary of the Bible*.

73. Lev. 17:10–14.

74. Maud Bodkin's brilliant analysis of the rebirth archetype suggested the focus of this section. See her *Archetypal Patterns in Poetry: Psychological Studies of Imagination* (New York: Vintage, 1958), *passim*.

75. "Voto," *Desolación*, 259.

76. "Interrogaciones," 85. Cf. "La maestra rural," 51: "*¡Dulce ser! En su río de mieles, caudaloso, / largamente abrevaba sus tigres el dolor.*"

77. The epithet may also refer to the poet. In "Nocturno de la derrota," 387, the poet emphasizes abandonment and intransigence, thus showing spiritual affinity with the Hebrews:
"*Yo nací de una carne tajada / en el seco riñón de Israel, / Macabea que da Macabeos. ...*"

Bibliography

Place of publication of frequently cited journals and newspapers: *The Americas*, Washington, D.C.; *Anales*, Universidad de Chile, Santiago; *Antártica*, Santiago; *Asomante*, San Juan, Puerto Rico; *Atenea*, Concepción, Chile; *Conferencia*, Santiago; *Cuadernos*, Paris; *Cuadernos Americanos*, Mexico; *Cuadernos del Guayas*, Guayaquil; *Cuadernos Israelíes*, Jerusalem; *Cultura*, San Salvador; *Marcha*, Montevideo; *El Mercurio*, Santiago; *Mundo Hispánico*, Madrid; *La Nación* (B.A.), Buenos Aires; *La Nación* (S), Santiago; *El Nacional* (C), Caracas; *El Nacional* (M), Mexico; *Nosotros*, Buenos Aires; *Novedades*, Mexico; *La Nueva Democracia*, New York; *Política y Espíritu*, Santiago; *Repertorio Americano*, San José, Costa Rica; *Revista de América*, Bogotá; *Revista de Educación*, Santiago; *Revista Hispánica Moderna*, New York; *Revista Iberoamericana*, Mexico; *Revista Nacional*, Montevideo; *Sur*, Buenos Aires; *La Torre*, San Juan, Puerto Rico; *El Universal*, Caracas.

Unpublished Materials

The unpublished materials consisted of microfilms, correspondence, and interviews. The first group of microfilm reels, A to S, of Mistral's unpublished writings reside in the Manuscript Division, U.S. Library of Congress, augmented by recent contributions via the Biblioteca Nacional de Chile from the estate of Doris Dana.

This text also incorporates key correspondence from the heirs of Zacarías Gómez (see Appendix B), and letters directly from the following: Sister Rose Aquin, O.P. (March 31, April 11, 1965); Margot Arce de Vázquez (Oct. 20, 1961); Margaret Bates (Nov. 5, 30, 1964); Jal B. Dorab (Dec.12, 1963); Father Joseph E. Dunn (Dec. 5, 1965); José Santos González Vera (July 12, 1962); Father Ivan Nikolic, S.J. (Dec.1, 1965); Father Renato Poblete, S.J. (Dec. 22, 1965); Margaret T. Rudd (Nov. 13, Dec. 4, 1964); and Luis Vargas Saavedra (Oct. 10, 1965).

Important personal interviews took place. With Brazilians: Manuel Bandeira, Rio de Janeiro (Dec. 1966), and Mariná de Morães Sarmento, Petrópolis (Dec. 1966). With Chileans: Isolina Barraza de Estay (Sept. 1966), Enrique Lafourcade (Aug. 1961), Ricardo Michell Abós-Padilla (Nov. 1966), and Maria Urzúa (Oct. 24, 1966).

Cited Works of Gabriela Mistral

"Alabanzas a la Virgen." *El Mercurio* (23 agosto 1925), 3.

"Balada." In *Gabriela Mistral en verso y prosa*: *Antología*, pp. 45–46. Cedomil Goic et al., eds. Lima, Peru: Real Academia Española/Asociación de Academias de la Lengua Española, 2010.

"Berta Singerman y la lengua criolla." In *Recados para hoy y mañana*, pp. 22–26. Luis Vargas Saavedra, ed. Vol. 2. Santiago: Ediciones Universidad Católica de Chile, 1985.

"Cartas de Gabriela Mistral a Juan Ramón Jiménez," *La Torre* VIII, 31 (1960), 190.

"El catolicismo en los Estados Unidos," *El Mercurio* (27 julio 1924), 8.

"La charca." *Nueva Luz* (Órgano de la Rama Teosófica Arundhali, Santiago) III, 24 (marzo 1914), 570–571.

"Cómo edifican." *La Nueva Democracia* XII, 1 (1931), 12–14.

"Considérations sur Rousseau et autres réflexions." *Révue de l'Amérique Latine* XI (avril 1926), 324–326.

"Cristianismo con sentido social." *Atenea* II, 9 (1925), 472–477.

"La cultura mexicana." *El Mercurio* (26 agosto 1921). In *Recopilación,* 484–485.

Desolación. 2nd ed. Santiago: Editorial del Pacífico, 1957.

"Divulgación religiosa. Sentido de las letanías: Virgen de las Vírgenes." *El Mercurio* (12 abril 1925), 3.

"La encina." *Revista de Educación Nacional* (abril 1915). In *Recopilación,* 228–229.

"La escuela al aire libre." *Atlántida* (4 mayo 1922). In *Recopilación,* 209–210.

"Fray Bartolomé." *Repertorio Americano* (14 oct. 1933).

"El himno al árbol." *Nueva Luz* II, 21 (dic. 1913), 500–502.

"La instrucción de la mujer." In *La tierra tiene la actitud de una mujer.* p. 13. Pedro Pablo Zegers B., ed. 2nd ed. Santiago: RIL Editores, 1998.

Lagar. Santiago: Editorial del Pacífico, 1954.

La lengua de Martí. La Habana: Secretaría de Educación, 1934.

Letter to Victoria Ocampo (Oct. 16, 1943). In *This America of Ours: The Letters of Gabriela Mistral and Victoria Ocampo,* pp. 142–146. Elizabeth Horan and Doris Meyer, eds. Austin: University of Texas Press, 2003.

"El Liceo de Niñas." *El Mercurio* (4 agosto 1911). In *Recopilación,* 165.

"Liceo de Niñas: El nuevo profesorado." In *Recopilación,* 164–165.

"Limpia tu fuente." *Luz y Sombra* (Valparaíso) I, 2 (nov. 1915), n.p.

"Mi experiencia con la Biblia." *Revista S.H.A.* (Sociedad Hebraica Argentina, Buenos Aires) (1 mayo 1938) 3, 4; (15 mayo 1938), 6, 7; (1 junio 1938), 6.

"Mi experiencia con la Biblia." *Noah* 1 (1987), 83–90.

"El 'Moisés' de Miguel Ángel." *Revista Católica* (Santiago) (4 oct. 1924), 541–543.

"La muerte de Stefan Zweig: Última conversación con el escritor." *El Mercurio* (9 marzo 1942).

"Organización de las mujeres," *El Mercurio* (5 julio 1925). In "Introducción." *Prosa religiosa de Gabriela Mistral,* p. 22, n. 27. Luis Vargas Saavedra, ed. Santiago: Editorial Andrés Bello, 1978.

"El pensador de Rodin." In *Recopilación,* 339–340, 430.

"El placer de servir." *Revista Teosófica Chilena* V, 6 (agosto 1924), 130.

Poema de Chile. Doris Dana, ed. Barcelona: Editorial Pomaire, 1967.

Poesías completas de Gabriela Mistral. Margaret Bates, ed. 2nd ed. rev. Madrid: Aguilar, 1962. 3rd ed. rev., 1966.

"Prólogo." In *José Martí: Versos sencillos.* La Habana: Secretaría de Educación, 1939.

"Prólogo." In *Rabindranath Tagore: Poeta y filósofo hindú.* Raúl Ramírez, trans. Santiago: Minerva, 1917.

"Recado de Navidad." *Ábside* XIII (1949), 7–13.

Recados: Contando a Chile, ed. Alfonso Escudero. Santiago: Editorial del Pacífico, 1957.

"Siena." *El Mercurio* (7 dic. 1924), 9.

"Silueta de Sor Juana Inés de la Cruz." *Ábside* XV (1951), 501–506.

"Sobre la xenofobia." *La Nueva Democracia* XXIX, 1 (1949), 22–26.

Tala. 3rd ed. Buenos Aires: Losada, 1946.

"Teresa Prats de Sarratea." *El Mercurio* (15 mayo 1922). In *Recopilación,* 475, 509–511.

Ternura. 3rd ed. Buenos Aires: Austral, 1946.

"Tres comentarios a Rabindranath Tagore." In *Recopilación,* 164–165.

"Una explicación más del caso Krishnamurti." *La Nación* (B. A.) (1 agosto 1930), 5–6.

"Unidad cristiana." *La Nueva Democracia* XXV, 3 (1944), 8–9.

"'Un viejo tema': La poetisa chilena comenta el informe de Kinsey." *Life en Español* (26 oct. 1953), 30, 32.

"Yo conozco a Cristo." *La Nueva Democracia* XXIX, 4 (1949), 25.

Collections, Anthologies, and Translations

Agosín, Marjorie, ed. *A Gabriela Mistral Reader.* Fredonia, NY: White Pine Press, 1993.

_____, ed., and Jacqueline C. Nanfito, trans. *Women*, pp. 3–21. Buffalo, NY: White Pine Press, 2000.

Aller, Rosalía, ed. *Gabriela Mistral: Antología poética*. Buenos Aires: Editorial EDAF, 1999.

Arce, Magda, ed. *Gabriela Mistral y Joaquín García Monge: Una correspondencia inédita, 1921–1954*. Santiago: Editorial Andrés Bello: 1989.

_____, and Gastón Von dem Bussche, eds. *Proyecto, preservación y difusión del legado literario de Gabriela Mistral*. Santiago: Zig-Zag, 1993.

Bates, Margaret, ed. *Selected Poems of Gabriela Mistral: A Bilingual Edition*. Baltimore: Johns Hopkins Press, 1962, 1971.

Brown, Monica, trans. *My Name is Gabriela/Me llamo Gabriela: The Life of Gabriela Mistral/La vida de Gabriela Mistral*. A Bilingual Edition. Lanham, MD: Rising Moon Books, 2005.

Couch, Randall, trans. *Madwomen: The "Locas mujeres" Poems of Gabriela Mistral*. A Bilingual Edition. Chicago: University of Chicago Press, 2008.

Dana, Doris, trans. *Selected Poems of Gabriela Mistral: A Bilingual Edition*. Baltimore: Johns Hopkins Press, 1971.

Díaz-Muñoz Cormatches, César, ed. *Motivos de San Francisco*. Santiago: Editorial del Pacífico, 1965.

Falabella, Soledad, ed. *¿Qué será de Chile en el cielo? "Poema de Chile" de Gabriela Mistral*. Santiago: Universidad Alberto Hurtado, 2003.

Fernández Larraín, Sergio, ed. *Cartas de amor de Gabriela Mistral*. Santiago: Editorial Andrés Bello, 1978.

Goic, Cedomil, et al., eds. *Gabriela Mistral en verso y prosa: Antología*. Lima, Peru: Real Academia Española/Asociación de Academias, 2010.

Guerra, Silvia, and Verónica Zondek, eds. *El ojo atravesado: Correspondencia entre Gabriela Mistral y los escritores uruguayos*. Santiago: LOM Ediciones, 2005.

Horan, Elizabeth, and Doris Meyer, eds. *This America of Ours: The Letters of Gabriela Mistral and Victoria Ocampo*. Austin: University of Texas Press, 2003.

Le Guin, Ursula K., trans. *Selected Poems of Gabriela Mistral*. Albuquerque: University of New Mexico Press, 2003.

Martínez Sanz, María Ester, and Luis Vargas Saavedra, eds. *Epistolario entre Lucila Godoy Alcayaga y Manuel Magallanes Moure*. 2nd ed. Santiago: Ediciones Universidad Católica de Chile, 2007.

Pereira Rodríguez, José, ed. *Páginas en prosa*. Buenos Aires: Kapelusz, 1962.

Quezada, Jaime, ed. *Poesías completas*. Santiago: Editorial Andrés Bello, 2001.

Scarpa, Roque Esteban, ed. *La desterrada en su patria: Gabriela Mistral en Magallanes: 1918–1920*. 2 vols. Santiago: Editorial Nascimento, 1977.

_____, ed. *Gabriela anda por el mundo*. Santiago: Editorial Andrés Bello, 1978.

_____, ed. *Gabriela piensa en ...* Santiago: Editorial Andrés Bello, 1989.

_____, ed. *Magisterio y niño*. 2nd ed. Santiago: Editorial Andrés Bello, 1995.

_____, ed. *Prosa escogida*. 2 vols. Santiago: Editorial Andrés Bello, 1979.

Silva Castro, Raúl, ed. *Epistolario: Cartas a Eugenio Labarca (1915–1916)*. Santiago: Universidad de Chile, 1957.

Tapscott, Stephen, ed., trans. *Selected Prose and Prose Poems of Gabriela Mistral*. Austin: University of Texas Press, 2004.

Vargas Saavedra, Luis, ed. *Castilla tajeada de sed como mi lengua: Gabriela Mistral ante España y España ante Gabriela Mistral (1933 a 1935)*. Santiago: Ediciones Universidad de Chile, 2002.

_____, et al., eds. *En batalla de sencillez: Epistolario de Gabriela Mistral a Pedro Prado*. Santiago: Ediciones Dolmen, 1992.

_____, ed. *Prosa religiosa de Gabriela Mistral*. Santiago: Editorial Andrés Bello, 1978.

_____, ed. *Recados para hoy y mañana*. 2 vols. Santiago: Editorial Sudamericana, 1999.

_____, ed. *Tan de Usted: Epistolario de Gabriela Mistral con Alfonso Reyes*. Santiago: Ediciones Universidad Católica de Chile, 1991.

_____, ed. *Vuestra Gabriela: Cartas inéditas de Gabriela Mistral a los Errázuriz Echeñique y Tomás Errázuriz*. Santiago: Zig-Zag, 1995.

Von dem Bussche, Gastón, ed. *Reino: Gabriela Mistral, Poesía dispersa e inédita, en verso y prosa*. Valparaíso: EUV/UCV, 1983.

Zegers B., Pedro Pablo, ed. *Cartas salidas del silencio*. Santiago: DIBAM/Ediciones LOM, 2003.

_____, ed. *Gabriela Mistral: Álbum personal*. Santiago: Biblioteca Nacional de Chile/Pehuén, 2008.

_____, ed. *Gabriela Mistral. Niña errante: Cartas a Doris Dana*. Barcelona: Lumen, 2010.

_____, ed. *Recopilación de la obra mistraliana 1902-1922*. Santiago: RIL Editores, 2001.

_____, ed. *La tierra tiene la actitud de una mujer*. Santiago: RIL Editores, 1998, 1999.

Bibliographical Sources

Albanell, Norah, and Nancy Mango. "Los escritos de Gabriela Mistral y estudios sobre su obra." In *Gabriela Mistral*, pp. 49-90. Washington: Pan American Union, 1958.

Escudero, Alfonso M., O.S.A. *La prosa de Gabriela Mistral: Fichas de contribución a su inventario*. Santiago: Universidad Católica de Chile, 1950.

_____. "La prosa de Gabriela Mistral: Fichas de contribución a su inventario." *Anales* CXV, 106 (1957), 250-265.

Piña-Rosales, Gerardo. "La recepción de la obra Mistraliana en los EE.UU.: Bibliografía selecta." In *Gabriela Mistral y los Estados Unidos*, pp. 309-325. Gerardo Piña-Rosales et al., eds. Nueva York: ANLE, 2011.

Pinilla, Norberto. *Bibliografía crítica sobre Gabriela Mistral*. Santiago: Universidad de Chile, 1940.

Rosenbaum, Sidonia C. "Gabriela Mistral." In *Modern Women Poets of Spanish America*, pp. 262-264. New York: Hispanic, Institute, 1945.

_____. "Gabriela Mistral: Bibliografía." *Revista Hispánica Moderna* III (1937), 135-140.

Rubio, Patricia. *Gabriela Mistral ante la crítica: Bibliografía anotada*. Santiago: DIBAM, 1995.

Critical Studies on Gabriela Mistral

Academia Literaria "Teresa de Jesús." *La nostalgia de vida, de hogar, en la obra literaria de Gabriela Mistral*. Concurso. Panamá: Colegio de las R. R. Esclavas del Sagrado Corazón de Jesús, 1960.

Acereda, Alberto. "Apostillas a una polémica editorial en torno a Gabriela Mistral." In *Gabriela Mistral en los Estados Unidos*, pp. 49-64. Gerardo Piña-Rosales et al., eds. Nueva York: ANLE, 2011.

Adams, Mildred. "Speaking of Books." *New York Times* (Jan. 27, 1957), sec. 7, 2.

Agosín, Marjorie, ed. *Gabriela Mistral: The Audacious Traveler*. Athens: Ohio University Press, 2003.

Aguilera, Honorio. "El alma cristiana de Gabriela Mistral." *La Revista Católica de Santiago* LXVII (1959), 2481-2484.

Alba, Pedro de. "Dádivas espirituales de Gabriela Mistral." *La Nueva Democracia* XXVII, 3 (1947), 52-55.

_____. "Elogio de la Peregrina Iluminada." *La Nueva Democracia* XXV, 9 (1944), 16-18.

_____. "Hispanismo e indigenismo de Gabriela Mistral." *Anales* CXV, 106 (1957), 79-80.

_____. "Mistral por los caminos de América." *Boletín de la Unión Panamericana* LXXX (1946), 123-131.

_____. "Oración por Gabriela Mistral." *Filosofía y Letras* XXXI (1957), 237-244.

Alba, Víctor [pseud. Pere Pagés]. "Gabriela Mistral; la gran poetisa chilena, que conquistó el Premio Nobel, vista por Palma Guillén de Nicolau, que la acompañó en su estancia en nuestro país." *Hoy* (México) (30 agosto 1952), 36-37.

_____. "La Mistral vista por su amiga y secretaria." *Anales* CXV, 106 (1957), 91-94.

Albareda, Ginés de. "Figuras literarias del mundo hispánico." *Revista Javeriana* (Bogotá), XXXII, 158 (1949), 149-152.

Alegría, Ciro. *Gabriela Mistral, íntima*. Bogotá: Editorial Vieja Negra, 1980.

_____. "Visita a Gabriela Mistral." *Norte* (New York), VIII, 8 (1948), 27, 50-51.

Alegría, Fernando. "Gabriela Mistral Awarded the 1945 Nobel Prize for Literature." *Bulletin of the Pan American Union* LXXX (1946), 29-33.

_____. *Genio y figura de Gabriela Mistral*. Buenos Aires: Eudeba, 1966.

_____. "Hacia una definición de la poesía chilena." *Atenea* XXXIV, 378 (1957), 170-185.

_____. "La poesía chilena: Una conferencia de Eduardo Anguita." *Cultura*, No. 5 (1955), 119-122.

_____. "La prosa de Gabriela Mistral." *Boletín de la Academia Norteamericana de la Lengua Española* 8 (1992), 81–93.

Alonso, Carmen. "Hacia Gabriela." *El Nacional* (M) (3 feb. 1957), Suplemento Semanario, 6.

Ambroggio, Luis Alberto. "Gabriela Mistral: El sentido de extranjería." In *Gabriela Mistral y los Estados Unidos*, pp. 97–112. Gerardo Piña-Rosales et al., eds. Nueva York: ANLE, 2011.

Anastasía Sosa, Luis V. "El sentido de la vida en algunas imágenes de Gabriela Mistral." *Revista Iberoamericana de Literatura* (Montevideo), II, III (1960–1961), 5–78.

Anhalt, Diana. "The Inconvenient Heroine." In *Gabriela Mistral: The Audacious Traveler*, pp. 146–159. Marjorie Agosín, ed. Athens: Ohio University Press, 2003.

Anonymous. "Falleció Doris Dana, albacea de Gabriela Mistral." *El Mercurio* (09 enero 2007), http://www.emol.com.noticias/magazine/detalle/detallenoticias.asp?id noticia=242644.

_____. "Gabriela Mistral en Norteamérica." *La Nueva Democracia* V, 7 (1924), 20–31.

_____. "Gabriela Mistral y los principales acontecimientos en su vida." *Antártica*, Nos. 15–16 (nov.-dic. 1945), 113.

_____. "Gabriela Mistral y 'Selva Lírica.'" *Antártica*, Nos. 15–16 (nov.-dic. 1945), 112.

_____. *El Mercurio* (28 nov. 2007), http://www.emol.com.noticias/magazine/detal lenoticias.asp?idnoticias=241644.

_____. "Polémica genera supuesta maternidad de Mistral." *El Mercurio* (7 nov. 1999).

_____. "Puntos de vista." *Atenea* XXXIV, 374 (1957), 2–7.

_____. "'Sobrino' de Gabriela Mistral era en realidad su hijo." *El Mercurio* (6 nov. 1999).

Arancibia Laso, María de. "Homenaje a Gabriela Mistral." Speech. Palacio de Bellas Artes, México City (December 18, 1945).

Arango, Rubén. "Vida, pasión y poesía de Gabriela Mistral." *Revista de las Indias* (Bogotá), no. 101 (enero-feb. 1948), 293–305.

Araquistain, Luis. "Magisterio y poesía." *Repertorio Americano* (23 marzo 1925), 52–53.

Arce, Magda. "Presencia de Gabriela Mistral." *Anales* CXV, 106 (1957), 31–38.

_____. "Presencia de Gabriela Mistral." *Educación* (Caracas), VI, 43 (1946), 3–34.

Arce de Vázquez, Margot. *Gabriela Mistral: Persona y poesía*. San Juan, Puerto Rico: Asomante, 1958.

_____. *Gabriela Mistral: The Poet and Her Work*. Helene Masslo Anderson, trans. New York: New York University Press, 1964.

_____. "Vida y poesía de Gabriela Mistral." *Asomante* II, 2 (1946), 5–13.

Arciniegas, Germán. "Gabriela, la fantástica chilena." *Cuadernos Israelíes*, No. 4 (1960), 22–26.

_____. "Gabriela Mistral y Pío XII." *El Tiempo* (Bogotá) (13 oct. 1958), 5.

_____. "El poema inédito de Gabriela." *Cuadernos*, No. 23 (marzo-abril 1957), 17–19.

_____. "Recado sobre Gabriela Mistral." *Novedades* (3 marzo 1957), "México en la Cultura," 3.

Arias, Augusto. "Vida de Gabriela Mistral." *Cuadernos Israelíes*, No. 4 (1960), 43–44.

_____. "Zweig y Gabriela Mistral." *Letras del Ecuador* XII, 107 (1957), 1, 8, 23.

Arias, Irene de. "Ada Negri y Gabriela Mistral." *Criterio* (Buenos Aires) (12 dic. 1946), 560–564.

"Arribo a Chile de Gabriela Mistral." *Atenea* XXXI, 349–350 (1954), 173.

Arrigoitía, Luis de. "Gabriela Mistral: Ideas pedagógicas en su periodismo americano." *Pedagogía* (Univ. de Puerto Rico), XII, 1 (1964), 85–97.

Asturias, Miguel Angel. "Gabriela Mistral." *Ficción* (Buenos Aires), No. 8 (1957), 49–50.

_____. "Gabriela Mistral." *El Nacional* (C) (1 agosto 1957), sec. lit., 3.

Bahamonde, Mario. *Gabriela Mistral en Antofagasta: Años de forja y valentía*. Santiago: Editorial Nascimento, 1980.

Balensi, Jean. "Gabriela Mistral ha vuelto a encontrar en Francia su patria de elección." *Revista de la Universidad del Cauca* (Popayán, Colombia), No. 9 (junio 1946), 33–37.

Baquerizo Moreno, Alfredo. *Ensayos, apuntes y discursos*. Guayaquil, Ecuador: Biblioteca Guayaquil, 1940.

Baquero, Gastón. "Gabriela Mistral en la Selva de Nieve." *Diario de Centro-América*, sec. inf. (29 enero 1946), 3; (30 enero 1946), 3; (31 enero 1946), 3.

Barraza de Estay, Isolina. *Gabriela Mistral y su sobrino.* La Serena: Editorial del Norte, 1978.

Barrios, Eduardo. "El primer libro de Gabriela Mistral." *Anales* CXV, 106 (1957), 26-30.

Bates, Margaret. "A propos an article on Gabriela Mistral." *The Americas* XIV (1957), 145-151.

———. "Gabriela Mistral." *The Americas* III (1946), 168-189.

———. "Gabriela Mistral's 'Poema de Chile.'" *The Americas* XVII (1961), 261-276.

Becerra y Córdoba, Esaú. "Gabriela Mistral, producto indoamericano." *Universidad de Antioquia* (Medellín), Nos. 75-76 (enero-feb. 1946), 483-485.

Bello, Christian. "Francia y Gabriela Mistral." *Antártica,* Nos. 15-16 (nov.-dic. 1945), 103-105.

Berchmans, Sister John, O.P. "Gabriela Mistral and the Franciscan Concept of Life." *Renascence* V (1952). 40-46, 95.

Bergés, Consuelo. "Cuando sus labios ya no cantan." *Ínsula* (Madrid) (15 feb. 1957), 1, 4.

Bergmann, Emilie, and Paul Julian Smith, eds. *¿Entiendes? Queer Readings, Hispanic Writings.* Durham, NC: Duke University Press, 1995.

Bermejo, Vladimiro. "Itinerario de Gabriela Mistral." *Revista Excelsior* (Lima) (3 enero 1935), 27.

Bianchi, Soledad. "Descubriendo la prosa de Gabriela Mistral." *Araucaria de Chile* 6 (1979), 9-19.

Biblioteca Nacional de Chile. Archivo del Escritor. Colección Legado Gabriela Mistral.

———. *Chile, o una voluntad de ser: Legado de Gabriela Mistral.* Santiago: DIBAM, 2008.

———. *Gabriela Mistral: A cien años de su nacimiento (1889-1989).* Santiago: DIBAM, 1989.

———. *El libro de los Juegos Florales (1914).* Copy of Julio Munizaga Ossandón's original version. Santiago: LOM Ediciones, 2000.

———. *Revista Patrimonio Cultural,* 46, Año XIII (Verano 2008), 47.

Bietti, Oscar. "Evolución de la poesía de Gabriela Mistral." *Nosotros,* 2a época, VI, 68 (1941), 187-193.

Binvignat, Fernando. "Gabriela." *Atenea* XV, 158 (1938), 245-250.

Blanco Segura, Ricardo. "Gabriela Mistral." *Cuadernos Israelíes,* No. 4 (1960), 30-38.

Bohemia Poblana. "Homenaje a Gabriela Mistral." No. 160 (1957), 1, 13, 21, 23.

Bollo, Sarah. "Gabriela Mistral: Una voz lírica continental." *Revista Nacional* VIII, 90 (1945), 324-328.

———. "La poesía de Gabriela Mistral." *Ínsula* (B.A.), II, 6 (1944), 83-92.

———. "La poesía de Gabriela Mistral." *Revista Nacional* XI (1948), 79.

Bonilla, Marcelina. "Mujeres de América." *Pan-América* (Tegucigalpa) X, 120 (1954), 11.

Brenes Mesén. Roberto. "Gabriela Mistral." *Nosotros* XXIII, 245 (1929), 5-22.

Bueno, Salvador. "Aproximaciones a Gabriela Mistral." *Anales* CXV, 106 (1957), 58-67.

Bufill, Elio Alba. "Gabriela Mistral como crítica literaria a la luz de los estudios de Onilda Jiménez." In *Gabriela Mistral en los Estados Unidos,* pp. 149-165. Gerardo Piña Rosales et al., eds. Nueva York: ANLE, 2011.

Bulnes, Alfonso. "Notas acerca de Gabriela Mistral." *Andean Quarterly* (Santiago) (Fall 1946), 5-8.

Bunster, Enrique. "Triunfo póstumo de los 'Recados de Gabriela Mistral.'" *La Prensa* (B.A.), (20 abril 1958), 2a sec., 5.

Bussche, Gastón Von dem. "Análisis estilístico del poema 'La copa' de Gabriela Mistral." *Anales* CXIV, 101 (Primer trimestre 1956), 159-163.

———. "Gabriela Mistral: Chilena universal." *Quaderni Ibero-Americani* III, 23 (1959), 503-506.

———. "Visión de una poesía." *Anales,* CXV, 106 (1957), 176-194.

Cáceres, Esther de. "Alma y poesía de Gabriela Mistral." In *Poesías completas de Gabriela Mistral,* pp. xv-xci. 3d ed. rev. Madrid: Aguilar, 1966.

———. "Homenaje a Gabriela Mistral." *Revista Nacional* VIII, 90 (1945), 328-336.

———. "La poesía de *Lagar,* último libro de Gabriela Mistral." *El País* (Montevideo) (13 enero 1957), 3.

Caimano, Sister Rose Aquin, O.P. *Mysticism in Gabriela Mistral.* New York: Pageant, 1969.

Campoamor, Fernando G. "Recado a la maestra insepulta." *Cuadernos Israelíes,* No. 4 (1960), 39-40.

Capdevila, Arturo. "¡Paz, Gabriela Mistral!" *Cuadernos Israelíes,* No. 4 (1960), 2–4.
Cardona Peña, Alfredo. "Murió sin juntarse con el sol, su marido." *Novedades* (3 marzo 1957), "México en la Cultura," 3.
Caronno, Atilio E. "A propósito de un artículo de Gabriela Mistral." *Nosotros* XX, 208 (1926), 142–143.
Carranza, Eduardo. "Gabriela Mistral." *Cuadernos Israelíes,* No. 4 (1960), 27–29.
———. "Gabriela Mistral, madre cantando." *Voces de América* (Cartagena, Colombia), III, 17 (1946), 195–196.
Carrera, Julieta. "Gabriela Mistral." *Pensamiento Peruano* (Lima) (nov.-dic. 1945), 47–53.
———. *La mujer en América escribe: Semblanzas.* México: Ediciones Alonso, 1956.
Carrera Andrade, Jorge. "Muerte y gloria de Gabriela Mistral." *Cuadernos,* No. 23 (marzo-abril 1957), 26–28.
———. "Muerte y gloria de Gabriela Mistral." *El Nacional* (C) (25 abril 1957), sec. lit., 8.
———. "La quinta de Gabriela Mistral." *Revista de América* VIII, 23 (1946), 153–160.
Carrillo, Morita. "Letanías otoñales a Gabriela." *El Universal* (22 enero 1957), ind. lit., 4.
Carrión, Benjamín. "Cartas de Gabriela Mistral a Benjamín Carrión (1927–1955)." *Letras del Ecuador* XI, 105 (1956), 10–11.
———. "Meditación sobre Gabriela Mistral." *Anales* CXV, 106 (1957), 70–78.
———. "La palabra maldita." *Cuadernos Americanos* XIV, 3 (1955), 7–14.
———. "Santa Gabriela Mistral." *Letras del Ecuador* X, 100 (1954), 3, 4, 52.
———. *Santa Gabriela Mistral (Ensayos).* Quito: Casa de la Cultura Ecuatoriana, 1956.
———. "Sí, Santa Gabriela Mistral." *Cuadernos Americanos* XVI, 3 (1957), 238–244.
Carrión, Fanny Natalia. "Tu corazón de flor." *Filosofía, Letras y Educación* (Quito), XI, 26 (1958), 199–200.
Casa de la Cultura Ecuatoriana. "Homenaje a Gabriela Mistral." *Revista del Núcleo del Azuay* (Cuenca, Ecuador), VIII, 12 (1957), 119–181.
Castellanos, Enrique. "Gabriela Mistral." *El Universal* (29 enero 1957), ind. lit., 3.
Castellanos Taquechel, Enrique. *Tres Recados de Gabriela Mistral.* Santiago: Publicaciones del Instituto de Segunda Enseñanza, 1957.

Castro-Klarén, Sara, et al., eds. "Introduction." In *Women's Writing in Latin America: An Anthology,* pp. 6–11. Boulder, CO: Westview Press, 1991.
Céspedes, Mario. "Prologue." *Gabriela Mistral en el Repertorio Americano.* San José, Costa Rica: Editorial Universitaria de Costa Rica, 1978.
Chacón y Calvo, José María. "Gabriela Mistral en una asamblea franciscana." *Boletín de la Academia Cubana de la Lengua* VI, 14 (1957), 111–118.
Chávez-Silverman, Susana, and Librada Hernández, eds. *Writing the Ambiente: Queer Sexualities in Latino, Latin American, and Spanish Culture.* Madison: University Wisconsin Press, 2000.
Chile. Ministerio de Educación. "Gabriela Mistral." *Revista de Educación,* Nos. 69, 70, 71 (marzo-dic. 1957).
———. Ministerio de Instrucción Pública. *Gabriela Mistral: Homenaje de la educación primaria y normal.* Santiago: Escuela Nacional de Artes Gráficas, 1954.
Clavería, Carlos. "El americanismo de Gabriela Mistral." *Bulletin of Spanish Studies* XXIII (1946), 116–127.
Cofre Silva, Margarita. "Gabriela Mistral, pensador americano." *Revista de Educación* VI, 34 (1946), 32–38, 42.
Cohen, Jonathan. "Toward a Common Destiny on the American Continent: The Pan-Americanism of Gabriela Mistral." In *Gabriela Mistral: The Audacious Traveler,* pp. 1–18. Marjorie Agosín, ed. Athens: Ohio University Press, 2003.
Colín, Eduardo. "Gabriela Mistral." *Nosotros* XIX, 195 (1925), 481–484.
Collantes de Terán, Juan. "Gabriela Mistral." *Estudios Americanos* (Sevilla), XIII, 69–70 (1957), 367–370.
Colombia. *"Homenaje de Colombia a Gabriela Mistral."* Bogotá: Empresa Nacional de Publicaciones, 1957.
Concha, Jaime. *Gabriela Mistral.* Madrid: Ediciones Júcar, 1987.
Concha Arenas, Rubén Enrique. "Escenario de Gabriela Mistral." *Cuadernos del Guayas* IV, 7 (1953), 3, 9,12.
Conde, Carmen. "De mi recuerdo de Gabriela Mistral en España." *El Universal* (12 marzo 1957), ind. lit., 2.
Contreras, Pedro, and Albertina Contreras. "Estudio sobre la obra poética de Gabriela

Mistral." *Revista de Educación* VI, 36 (1946), 161–168.

Cord, William O. "Major Themes in the Poetry of Gabriela Mistral." Unpublished M.A. thesis. St. Louis, MO: Washington University, 1948.

Cordoba, Diego. "Gabriela Mistral, poeta evangelista." *El Universal* (12 feb. 1957), ind. lit., 2.

Correa, Carlos René. *Poetas chilenos.* Santiago: La Salle, 1944.

———. *Quince poetas de Chile.* Santiago: "Orbe," 1941.

Couch, Randall. "Translating the the Hidden Machine in Gabriela Mistral in English." In *Gabriela Mistral: The Audacious Traveler*, pp. 179–202. Marjorie Agosín, ed. Athens: Ohio University Press, 2003.

Covarrubias, Jorge I. "Tras las huellas de Gabriela Mistral en Nueva York." In *Gabriela Mistral en los Estados Unidos*, pp. 183–223. Gerardo Piña-Rosales et al., eds. Nueva York: ANLE, 2011.

Croes, Guillermo. "Gabriela Mistral." *El Universal* (29 enero 1957), ind. lit., 4.

Cruchaga Santa María, Ángel. "Resplandor de Gabriela Mistral." *Antártica*, Nos. 15–16 (nov.-dic. 1945), 96–99.

———. "Un sencillo recuerdo de Gabriela Mistral." *Antártica*, No. 14 (oct. 1945), 1.

Cruz, Pedro Nolasco. *Estudios de la literatura chilena.* Vol. III. Santiago: Nascimento, 1940.

Cuadra, Pedro Antonio. "Gabriela Mistral." *Cuadernos Israelíes*, No. 4 (1960), 55–57.

Cuadernos Israelíes. "En homenaje a Gabriela Mistral." No. 4 (1960).

Cuneo, Ana María. "El discurso religioso en Mistral, Uribe, y Quezada." *Revista Chilena de Literatura*, 45 (1994), 19–38.

Darer, Veronica. "Gabriela Mistral as Teacher." In *Gabriela Mistral: The Audacious Traveler*, pp. 47–63. Marjorie Agosín, ed. Athens: Ohio University Press, 2003.

Daydí-Tolson, Santiago. "Walking South: Gabriela Mistral's Chilean Journey ["Poema de Chile]." In *Gabriela Mistral: The Audacious Traveler*, pp. 132–145. Marjorie Agosín, ed. Athens: Ohio University Press, 2003

De los Ríos de Lampérez, Blanca. "Gabriela Mistral entre nosotros." *Raza Española* VI (nov.-dic. 1924), 47–55.

Díaz Arrieta, Hernán [pseud. Alone]. *Las cien mejores poesías chilenas.* Santiago: Zig-Zag, 1949.

———. *Los cuatro grandes de la literatura chilena durante el siglo XX.* Santiago: Zig-Zag, 1963.

———. *Gabriela Mistral.* Santiago: Nascimento, 1946.

———. "Interpretación de Gabriela Mistral." *Anales* CXV, 106 (1957), 15–18.

———. *Panorama de la literatura chilena durante el siglo XX.* Santiago: Nascimento, 1931.

———. "Recuerdos de infancia y juventud de Gabriela Mistral." *Revista Nacional de Cultura* (Caracas), XIX, 121–122 (1957), 78–84.

———. "Los últimos libros de Gabriela Mistral y Pablo Neruda." *Revista Nacional de Cultura* XVII, 110 (1955), 102–109.

Diego, Gerardo. "La nueva poesía de Gabriela Mistral, Premio Nobel de Literatura 1945." *Revista de Indias* (Madrid), VI (1945), 811–820.

Dinamarca, Salvador. "Gabriela Mistral y su obra poética." *Hispania* XLI (1958), 48–50.

Domínguez, Ramiro. "Gabriela Mistral como ausencia." *Cuadernos Israelíes*, No. 4 (1960), 63–66.

Dominican Republic. *Homenaje a Gabriela Mistral.* Ciudad Trujillo: Secretaría de Educación y Bellas Artes, 1946.

Donoso, Armando. *La otra América.* Madrid: Calpe, [1925].

Donoso, Francisco G. *Al margen de la poesía.* Paris: Agencia Mundial de Librería, 1927.

Donoso Torres, Vicente. "El alma de Gabriela Mistral a través de sus poemas." *Cuadernos Israelíes*, No. 4 (1960), 11–18.

Dorn, Georgette. "Gabriela Mistral y la Biblioteca del Congreso." In *Gabriela Mistral en los Estados Unidos*, pp. 235–240. Gerardo Piña-Rosales et al., eds. Nueva York: ANLE, 2011.

D'Ors, Eugenio. "Dice Eugenio d'Ors." *El Mercurio* (15 febrero 1925), 7. In *Gabriela Mistral ante la crica: Bibliografía Anotada*, p. 100. No. 808. Patricia Rubio, ed. Santiago: DIBAM, 1995.

Doyle, Henry Grattan. "Gabriela Mistral: Nobel Prize Winner." *Hispania* XXIX (1946), 69.

Dussuel, Francisco. "Carta inédita de Gabriela Mistral." *Mensaje* (Santiago), No. 86 (enero-feb. 1960), 19–21.

———. "El Cristo de Gabriela Mistral." *Mensaje*, no. 11 (agosto 1952), 382–392.
———. "El panteísmo de Gabriela Mistral." *El Diario Ilustrado* (Santiago) (2 mayo 1954), 3.
"Edición en homenaje a Gabriela Mistral, Premio Nobel de la Literatura." *Pro Arte* (Santiago) (31 agosto 1951), 1–5.
Elliott, Jorge. *Antologia crítica de la nueva poesía chilena*. Santiago: Nascimento, 1957.
Eltit, Diamela. "Los tiempos que marcaron una vida." *RevistaPatrimonio Cultural*, 46, Año XIII (Verano 2008), 30–31.
Entwistle, William J. "A Visit to Gabriela Mistral." *Latin American World* (London), XXVI, 1 (1945), 28–29.
Escudero, Carlos. "Sacerdote, chileno impartió Bendición Apostólica a poetisa Gabriela Mistral." *El Mercurio* (9 enero 1957), 1, 16.
Espinosa, Aurelio Macedonio. "Gabriela Mistral." *The Americas* VII (1951), 3–40.
Espinoza, Enrique. "Gabriela Mistral y el espíritu de la Biblia." *Anales* CXV, 106 (1957), 99–101.
Estay Barraza, María Sonia. "Vida y obra de Gabriela Mistral." *Clímax* (La Serena) (10 enero 1960), 17–24.
Fergusson, Erna. *Chile*. New York: Knopf, 1943.
———. "Gabriela Mistral: Impression of a Noted Chilean Poet, Consul in Brazil, by a United States Authoress." *Inter-American Monthly* (Washington), I, 4 (1942), 26–27.
Fernández-Cuervo, Luis. "Gabriela Mistral en la tierra de su infancia." *Mundo Hispánico* XIII, 150 (1960), 13–15.
Fernández Fraile, Maximino. "Residencia en Brasil: De dolor y de Gloria." *Revista Patrimonio Cultural*, 46, Año XIII (Verano 2008), 20–23.
Fernández Larraín, Sergio. "Prologue." *Cartas de amor de Gabriela Mistral*. Santiago: Editorial Andrés Bello, 1978.
Ferrer Canales, José. "Gabriela Mistral." *Humanismo* (México), No. 42 (1957), 77–80.
Figueira, Gastón. *De la vida y la obra de Gabriela Mistral*. Montevideo: Talleres Gráficos, 1959.
———. "La depuración estilística en Gabriela Mistral." *Cuadernos Israelíes*, No. 4 (1960), 69–79.
———. "Evocación de Gabriela Mistral." *La Nueva Democracia* XXXVII, 3 (1957), 16–24.
———. "Gabriela Mistral." *Revista Iberoamericana* XVI (1951), 233–244.
———. "Recordemos a Gabriela Mistral." *Cuadernos del Guayas* VIII, 15 (1957), 1, 3,19.
Figueroa, Virgilio. *La divina Gabriela*. Santiago: "El Esfuerzo." 1933.
Fihman, Pablo Rubén. "Lo Bíblico en Gabriela Mistral." *Davar*, No. 72 (sept.-oct. 1957), 13–35.
Finlayson, Clarence. "Amor y paisaje en Gabriela Mistral." *Revista Universitaria* (Univ. Católica de Chile, Santiago), XXIII, 3 (1938), 65–71.
———. "Panorama al vuelo: Algunos poetas chilenos." *Revista Universitaria*, Número especial (1938), 166–189.
———. "Spanish American Poet: The Life and Ideas of Gabriela Mistral." *Commonweal* (Dec. 5, 1941), 160–163.
Fiol-Matta, Licia. *A Queer Mother for the Nation: The State and Gabriela Mistral*. Minneapolis: University of Minnesota Press, 2002.
———. "The 'Schoolteacher of America': Gender, Sexuality, and Nation in Gabriela Mistral." In ¿*Entiendes? Queer Readings, Hispanic Writings*, pp. 201–229. Emilie Bergmann and Paul Julian Smith, eds. Durham, NC: Duke University Press, 1995.
Flasche, Hans. "Gabriela Mistral und ihre Sprachkunst (Der Hymnus 'Sol del Trópico')." In *Studia románica: Gedenkschrift für Eugen Lerch*, pp. 187–219. Charles Bruneau and Peter M. Schon, eds. Stuttgart: Port Verlag, 1955.
Florit, Eugenio. "Paisaje y poesía en Gabriela Mistral." *Miscelánea de Estudos a Joaquim de Carvalho* (Figueira da Foz, Portugal), No. 7 (1961), 712–718.
Franco, Jean. "'Loca y no loca': La cultura popular en la obra de Gabriela Mistral." In *Re-leer hoy a Gabriela Mistral: Mujer, historia, y sociedad*, pp. 27–42. Gastón Lillo and Guillermo Renart, eds. Santiago: Editorial Universitaria, 1997.
Frank, Waldo. "Gabriela Mistral." *Cuadernos Israelíes*, No. 4 (1960), 47–48.
———. "Gabriela Mistral." *Nation* (Jan. 26, 1957), 84.
———. "La poesía de las madres, de los niños." *Novedades* (3 marzo 1957), "México en la Cultura." 3.

Franulic, Lenka. *Cien autores contemporáneos.* 3rd ed. Vol. II. Santiago: Empresa Ercilla, 1952.

———. "Recado sobre Gabriela Mistral." *Ercilla* (27 mayo 1952), 16-18.

Fraser, Howard M. "Gabriela Mistral's Sonnets to Ruth." *Studies in Twentieth-Century Literature,* 3 (1978), 5-21.

Fuentes, Víctor. "Gabriela Mistral en California." In *Gabriela Mistral en los Estados Unidos,* pp. 31-47. Gerardo Piña-Rosales et al., eds. Nueva York: ANLE, 2011.

Fuenzalida, Héctor. "Gabriela Mistral en la última vuelta." *Anales* CXV, 106 (1957), 84-90.

Furness, Edna Lue. "The Divine Gabriela." *Western Humanities Review* X (1955-56), 75-77.

Gallegos, Rómulo. "Ejemplo de dignidad espiritual." *Cuadernos,* No. 23 (marzo-abril 1957), 24-25.

García Huidobro McAuliffe, Cecilia. "Preguntas terrenales: Tras la búsqueda de la mujer cotidiana." *Revista Patrimonio Cultural,* No. 46, Año XIII (Verano 2008), 35.

———. "Tareas pendientes." *Revista Patrimonio Cultural,* No. 46, Año XIII (Verano 2008), 25.

Garrido Palacios, Manuel. "Leyendo a Gabriela Mistral en Nueva York." In *Gabriela Mistral en los Estados Unidos,* pp. 137-140. Gerardo Piña-Rosales et al., eds. Nueva York: ANLE, 2011.

Gazarian, Marie-Lise [Gautier]. "El anhelo de eternidad: El mundo personal de Miguel de Unamuno y de Gabriela Mistral." *American Hispanist* (1976), 129-145.

———. *Gabriela Mistral, la maestra de Elqui.* Buenos Aires: Crespillo, 1973.

———. *Gabriela Mistral: The Teacher from the Valley of Elqui.* Chicago: Franciscan Herald Press, 1975.

———. "La naturaleza en la obra de Gabriela Mistral." Unpublished M.A. thesis. New York: Columbia University, 1957.

———. "La prosa de Gabriela Mistral, o una verdadera joya desconocida." *Revista Chilena de Literatura,* 36 (1990), 17-27.

———. "Recordando a Gabriela Mistral." In *Gabriela Mistral en los Estados Unidos,* pp. 141-147. Gerardo Piña-Rosales et al., eds. Nueva York: ANLE, 2011.

———. "The Walking Geography of Gabriela Mistral." In *Gabriela Mistral: The Audacious Traveler,* pp. 270-286. Marjorie Agosín, ed. Athens: Ohio University Press, 2003.

Gerchunoff, Alberto. "Gabriela Mistral." *Repertorio Americano* (6 julio 1925), 265-267.

Goic, Cedomil. "Cadenillas en la poesía de Gabriela Mistral." *Atenea* XXXIV, 374 (1957), 44-50.

Gómez Hoyos, Rafael. "Gabriela Mistral, poetisa cristiana." *Boletín de la Academia Colombiana,* 168 (abril-junio 1990), 34-35.

González, Manuel Pedro. "Conocimiento de Gabriela Mistral." *El Nacional* (C) (14 feb. 1957), sec. lit., 8.

———. "'La huella': Poesía inédita [y comento] por Gabriela Mistral." *Modern Language Forum* XXXII, 3-4 (1947), 49-58.

———. "Profile of a Great Woman." *Hispania* XLI (1958), 427-430.

González, María Rosa. "Recado de Gabriela Mistral a la América Hispana." *La Nación* (B.A.) (7 abril 1957), 2a sec., 2.

González Lanuza, Eduardo. "Detrás de Gabriela." *El Hogar* (B. A.) (18 enero 1957), 52.

González Montes, Yara. "Gabriela Mistral: Lírica trashumante." In *Gabriela Mistral en los Estados Unidos,* pp. 113-128. Gerardo Piña-Rosales et al., eds. Nueva York: ANLE, 2011.

González Vera, José Santos. *Algunos.* Santiago: Nascimento, 1959.

———. "Comienzos de Gabriela Mistral." *Anales* CXV, 106 (1957), 22-25.

———. "Gabriela Mistral." *Babel* (Santiago), IX, 31 (1946), 5-16.

———. "Gabriela Mistral." *Cuadernos Israelíes,* No. 4 (1960), 41-42.

Goyeneche, Ilona, and Sebastián Cerda. "Falleció Doris Dana, albacea de Gabriela Mistral." *El Mercurio* [Emol.com], (9 enero 2007).

Grandin, Karl. "Gabriela Mistral's Nobel Prize Award." Stockholm, Royal Swedish Academy of Sciences, E-mail, April 29, 2011.

Guillén, Palma. Letter to Gabriela Mistral: "Hijita muy querida" (29 abril 1943). In *Proyecto, preservación y difusión del legado literario de Gabriela Mistral,* pp. 103-104. Magda Arce and Gastón Von dem Bussche, eds. Santiago: Zig-Zag, 1993

_____. Letter to Juan Miguel Godoy Mendoza: "Mi querido Juanito" (11 mayo 1943). In *Proyecto, preservación y difusión del legado literario de Gabriela Mistral*, p. 105. Magda Arce and Gastón Von dem Bussche, eds. Santiago: Zig-Zag, 1993.

Gullón, Ricardo. "Sobre Margot Arce de Vázquez y *Gabriela Mistral: Persona y poesía*." *La Torre* VIII, 25 (1959), 230–234.

Gumucio, Alejandro. *Gabriela Mistral y el Premio Nobel*. Santiago: Nascimento, 1946.

Hamilton, Carlos D. "Gabriela de Hispanoamérica." *Revista Iberoamericana* XXIII (1958), 83–92.

_____. "Raíces bíblicas de la poesía de Gabriela Mistral." *Cuadernos Americanos* XX, 5 (1961), 201–210.

Havana City. Departamento de Cultura. *Homenaje de la ciudad a Gabriela Mistral*. La Habana: Molina y Cía., 1938.

Heliodoro Valle, Rafael. "Alabanza de Gabriela Mistral." In *Gabriela Mistral*, pp. 31–41. Washington: Pan American Union, 1958.

_____. "Gabriela Mistral en mis recuerdos." *Anales* CXV, 106 (1957), 68–69.

Henríquez Ureña, Max. "Vida y angustia de Gabriela Mistral." *Revista Cubana* XXXI, 2 (1957), 47–69.

Hernández de Trelles, Carmen D. "Del mito al misticismo: El símbolo religioso judeocristiano en la poesía de Gabriela Mistral." *La torre* V, 18 (1991), 157–169.

Herrera Vega, Héctor Hernán. *Gabriela Mistral: Vicuña y su gente (1945–1954)*. La Serena, Chile: Editorial del Norte, 2004.

"Homenaje a Gabriela Mistral." *Atenea* XXVIII, 312 (1951), 521–585.

Homsy, Gwendolene. "The Poems of Gabriela Mistral." Uupublished M.A. thesis, Los Angeles, CA: University of Southern California, 1953.

Horan, Elizabeth. "Alternative identities of Gabriel(a) Mistral, 1906–1920)." In *Writing the Ambiente: Queer Sexualities in Latino, Latin American, and Spanish Culture*, pp. 147–177. Susan Chávez-Silverman and Librada Hernández, eds. Madison: University of Wisconsin Press, 2000.

_____. "Las cartas de Doris Dana y Gabriela Mistral." *Chroma* (August 28, 2009), at http://www.latercera.com/contenido727_175058_9.shtml.

_____. "Gabriela Mistral." In *Latin-American Writers on Gay and Lesbian Themes*, pp. 221–235. David William Foster, ed. Westport, CT: Greenwood Press, 1994.

_____. *Gabriela Mistral: An Artist and Her People*. Washington, DC: Organization of American States, 1994.

_____. "Gabriela Mistral: 'Language is the Only Homeland.'" In *A Dream of Light and Shadow: Portraits of Latin American Women Writers*. Marjorie Agosín, ed. Albuquerque: University of New Mexico Press, 1995.

_____. "Mirror to the Nation." In *Gabriela Mistral: The Audacious Traveler*, pp. 224–249. Marjorie Agosín, ed. Athens: Ohio University Press, 2003.

_____. "Sor Juana and Gabriela Mistral: Locations and Locutions of the Saintly Woman." *CHASQUI: Revista de literatura latinoamericana* 25, No. 2 (Nov. 1996), 89–103.

Hübner, Manuel Eduardo. "En torno a la prosa de Gabriela Mistral." *La Nación* (S) (9 nov. 1957), 4.

_____. "México, Gabriela y los escritores mexicanos." *La Nación* (S) (15 nov. 1957), 4.

_____. "El secreto de Gabriela." *La Nación* (S) (18 enero 1957), 4.

Ibáñez, Sara de. "A Gabriela Mistral." *Revista Nacional* VIII, 90 (1945), 337–338.

Iduarte, Andrés. "En torno a Gabriela Mistral." *Cuadernos Americanos* V, 2 (1946), 240–256.

_____. *Pláticas hispanoamericanas*. México: Tezontle, 1951.

Iglesias, Augusto. *Gabriela Mistral y el modernismo en Chile: Ensayo de crítica subjetiva*. Santiago: Editorial Universitaria, 1949 [1950].

Illanes Adaro, Graciela. "Elqui en la obra de Gabriela Mistral." *Atenea* XXIII, 248 (1946), 171–180.

Inostroza, Jorge. "96 horas con Gabriela Mistral." *Vea* (Santiago) (15 sept. 1951), 16–17.

Insúa, Alberto. "Gabriela Mistral, una imitadora de Cristo." *Repertorio Americano* (2 feb. 1925), 328–334.

Iribarren Avilés, Rodrigo, and Fernando Graña Pezoa. "Relación de la poeta y Vicuña: Un ejemplo inspirador." *Revista Patrimonio Cultural*, 46, Año XIII (Verano 2008), 18–19.

Izquierdo Ríos, Francisco. "Gabriela Mistral

ha muerto." *Cultura Peruana* (Lima), XVII, 103 (1957).
Jan, Eduard von. "Die Selbstdarstellung im Werke Mistrals." In *Form, in ehr Selbstdarstellung: Festgabe für Fritz Neubert*, pp. 175–186. Günter Reichenkron, ed. Berlin: Duncker & Humboldt, 1956.
Jaramillo Valderrama, Armando. "Letter." *Zig-Zag*, No. 850 (4 junio 1921). In *Recopilación de la obra mistraliana 1902–1922*, p. 478. Pedro Pablo Zegers B., ed. Santiago: RIL Editores, 2001.
Jehenson, Myriam Ivonne. "Four Women in Search of Freedom." *Revista Iberoamericana*, 12 (1982), 87–99.
Joffre, Manuel Alcides. "Indeterminación de los roles maternos y recepción crítica de la obra de Gabriela Mistral." *Literatura y lingüística*, 3 (1992), 15–33.
Jonckheere, Karel. "Gabriela Mistral." *Niew Vlaams tijdschrift* (Antwerpen) (April 1946), 109–112.
Kiew, Dimas. "Gabriela Mistral." *El Universal* (22 enero 1957), ind. lit., 4.
Labarca, Eugenio. "Literatura femenina chilena." *Atenea* I, 10 (1924), 357–361.
Labarthe, Pedro Juan. "Gabriela como te recuerdo." *Repertorio Americano* (20 enero 1957), 185–187.
_____. *Gabriela Mistral: Cómo la conocí yo, y cinco poemas*. San Juan, Puerto Rico: Campos. 1963.
Ladrón de Guevara, Matilde. *Rebelde magnífica*. Santiago: Imprenta de la Central de Talleres, 1957.
Lago, Tomás. "Gabriela y el nardo de Las Parábolas." *Anales* CXV, 106 (1957), 95–98.
Lagos Carmona, Guillermo. *Gabriela Mistral en México: Biografía y antología*. Biblioteca Enciclopédica Popular, No. 87. México: Secretaría de Educación Pública, 1945.
Lamothe, Luis. "Gabriela Mistral en la poesía hispanoamericana." *El Nacional* (M) (2 junio 1957), Suplemento Semanario, 2.
Landínez, Vicente. *Almas de dos mundos*. Tunja, Colombia: Imprenta Departmental, 1958.
Lastra, Pedro. "Para una poética de Gabriela Mistral." *Revista Patrimonio Cultural* 46, Año XIII (Verano 2008), 41.
Latcham, Ricardo A. "El sentimiento americano de Gabriela Mistral." *El Nacional* (C) 31 enero 1957), sec. lit., 1.

Latorre, Mariano. *La literatura de Chile*. Buenos Aires: Facultad de Filosofía y Letras de la Universidad de Buenos Aires, 1941.
Lefebvre, Alfredo. "Nuevo libro de Gabriela Mistral: *Motivos de San Francisco*." *La Nación* (S) (1 mayo 1966), 5.
_____. *Poesía española y chilena: Análisis e interpretación de textos*. Santiago: Editorial del Pacífico, 1958.
Leguizamón, María Luisa C. "América y Gabriela Mistral." *Revista de Humanidades* (Córdoba, Argentina), II (1959), 129–139.
Leo, Ulrich. "La literatura hispanoamericana y los alemanes." In *Interpretaciones hispanoamericanas: Ensayos de teoría y práctica estilísticas, 1939–1958*, pp. 189–207. Santiago, Cuba: Universidad de Oriente, 1960.
Letona, René. "La prosa de Gabriela Mistral." *Cuadernos Hispanamericanos*, 472 (1989), 85–92.
Lida, Raimundo. "Palabras de Gabriela." *Cuadernos Americanos* XVI, 3 (1957), 234–237.
Lihn, Enrique. "Elegía a Gabriela Mistral: Fragmento." *Revista Patrimonio Cultural* 46, Año XIII (Verano 2008), 30.
Lillo, Gastón, and Guillermo Renart, eds. *Releer hoy a Gabriela Mistral: Mujer, historia y sociedad*. Santiago: Editorial Universitaria, 1997.
Lindo, Hugo. *Cuatro grandes poetas de América*. Buenos Aires: Librería Perlado, 1959.
Lira Urquieta, Pedro. "Gabriela Mistral y la Universidad Católica." *Finisterrae*, No. 12 (1956), 60–61.
Livacic Cazzano, E., and A. Roa. *Literatura chilena; manual y antología*. Santiago: Editorial Salesiana de Textos Escolares, 1955.
Llach, Leonor. "Gabriela Mistral." *Tribuna Israelita* (México), XII, 147 (1957), 16–17.
Lobo, Fernando. "Tribute to the Memory of Gabriela Mistral." *Annals of the Organization of American States* (Washington), IX (1957), 106–109.
Lockhart, Darrell, B. "Jewish Issues and Gabriela Mistral." In *Gabriela Mistral: The Audacious Traveler*, pp. 95–112. Marjorie Agosín, ed. Athens: Ohio University Press, 2003.
Loynaz, Dulce María. "Gabriela y Lucila." *Poesías completas de Gabriela Mistral*, pp. cxv–cxxxix. 2nd ed. rev. Madrid: Aguilar, 1962.

Luby, Barry Jay. "La naturaleza en la poesía de Gabriela Mistral." Unpublished M.A. thesis. New York: New York University, 1961.

Luigi, Juan de. "Gabriela Mistral en su primera época." *Anales* CXV, 106 (1957), 39–43.

Machado de Arnao, Luz. "Yo conocí a Gabriela Mistral." *Anales* CXV, 106 (abril-junio 1957) 81–83.

Madariaga, Salvador de. *Homenaje a Gabriela Mistral.* London: Hispanic and Luso-Brazilian Councils, 1958.

Maiz, Magdalena, and Luis H. Peña, eds. *Modalidades de representación del sujeto auto/bio/gráfico femenino.* San Nicolás de los Garza, México: Facultad de Filosofia y Letras, Universidad Autónoma de Nuevo León, 1997.

Mañach, Jorge. "Gabriela: Alma y tierra," *Revista Hispánica Moderna* III (1937), 106–110.

———. "Gabriela y Juan Ramón: La poesía 'nobelable.'" *Cuadernos,* No. 40 (enero-feb. 1960), 57–61.

Mancilla, Óscar. "Siguiendo la huella de Gabriela Mistral." *Revista Patrimonio Cultural* 6, Año XIII (Verano 2008), 16–17.

Mandlove, Nancy. "Gabriela Mistral: The Narrative Sonnet." *Revista/Review Interamericana,* 12 (1982), 110–114.

Marchant Lezcano, Jorge, "Gabriela Mistral a Doris Dana: Love Story." *La Nación* (6 sept. 2007), and at http://letras.s5com/jml120909.html.

Marín, Juan. "Recuerdos de Gabriela Mistral." In *Gabriela Mistral,* pp. 7–13. Washington: Pan American Union, 1958.

Marzano, Rolando. "Recorrer la vida desde la vereda contraria." *Revista Patrimonio Cultural* 46, Año XIII (Verano 2008), 10, 11, 14, 15.

Mauro, Walter. "Ricordi di Gabriela Mistral." *Fiera Letteraria* (26 aprile 1959), 5.

Mayo, Margarita de. "Gabriela Mistral, maestra." *Cuadernos Hispanoamericanos* (Madrid), XCIX (marzo 1958), 360–366.

McInnis, Judy B. "Gabriela Mistral: La Judith chilena." In *Modalidades de representación del sujeto auto/bio/gráfico femenino,* pp. 157–169. Magdalena Maiz and Luis H. Peña, eds. San Nicolás de los Garza, México: Facultad de Filosofía y Letras, Universidad Autónoma de Nuevo León, 1997.

Mediano Flores, Eugenio. "Ha venido el cansancio infinito." *Mundo Hispánico* X, 107 (1957), 17.

Medina, José Ramón. "La humana figura de Gabriela Mistral." *El Universal* (19 feb. 1957), ind. lit., 1.

Meirelles, Cecilia. "Um pouco de Gabriela Mistral." *Cuadernos Israelíes,* No. 4 (1960), 19–21.

Mengod, Vicente. "Gabriela Mistral en mi recuerdo." *Atenea* XXXI, 351–352 (1954), 57–60.

———. "Matices en la obra de Gabriela Mistral." *Atenea* XXXIV, 374 (1957), 13–21.

Miller, Beth. "Gabriela Mistral's Ideology." In *Women in Hispanic Literature: Icons and Fallen Idols.* Berkeley: University of California Press, 1985.

Molina Müller, Julio. "Naturaleza americana y estilo en Gabriela Mistral." *Anales* CXV, 106 (1957), 109–124.

Molloy, Sylvia. "Female Textual Identities: The Strategies of Self-Figuration." In *Women's Writing in Latin America: An Anthology,* pp. 107–124. Sara Castro-Klarén et al., eds. Boulder, CO: Westview Press, 1991.

Moncada, Julio. "Un testimonio sobre Gabriela Mistral." *Marcha* (22 feb. 1957), 21.

Monsalve, Josué. *Gabriela Mistral: La errante solitaria.* Santiago: Imprenta Lautaro, 1958.

Montenegro, Pedro Paulo. "Gabriela Mistral: Vida e obra." *Clã* (Fortaleza, Brazil), VIII, 17 (1958), 110–118.

Monterde, Francisco. "Gabriela Mistral (1889–1957)." *Revista Iberoamericana* XXII (1957), 333–337.

Montes, Hugo. *Poesía actual de Chile y España: Presencia de Gabriela Mistral, Pablo Neruda, y Vicente Huidobro en la poesía española de hoy.* Barcelona: Sayma, 1963.

Montes I. Bradley, R.-E. "En torno del epistolario de Gabriela Mistral." *El Nacional* (M) (10 marzo 1957), Suplemento Semanario, 10.

Montserrat, Andrés. "Gabriela Mistral sur la pente." *Révue de la Amérique Latine* X (sept. 1925), 270.

Mora, Gabriela. "La prosa política de Gabriela Mistral." *Escritura: Revista de Teoría y Crítica Literarias,* 16, 31–32 (1991), 192–103.

Mora, José A. "Las ideas americanistas de

Gabriela Mistral." In *Gabriela Mistral*, pp. 43–48. Washington: Pan American Union, 1958.

Moreno Mora, Vicente. "Tres poetas chilenos." *El Tres de Noviembre* (Cuenca, Ecuador), Nos. 80–81 (agosto-sept. 1942), 349–305.

Moreno Villa, José. "Con Gabriela Mistral y Germán Arciniegas." *Repertorio Americano* (1 enero 1951), 24.

Mota del Campillo, María R. *La poesía humana de Gabriela Mistral*. Buenos Aires: Asociación Cultural "Clorinda Matto de Turner," 1948.

Mujica, Eduardo. "Gabriela Mistral, Premio Nobel de la Literatura." *Revista de Educación* VI, 34 (1946), 28–31, 42.

Mujica, Juan. "Aventura y gloria de Gabriela Mistra." *Mundo Hispánico* X, 107 (1957), 13–17.

Müller, Heinz. "Gabriela Mistral." *Ruperto-Carola Mitterlungen der Vereinigung der Freunde der Studentenschaft der Universität Heidelberg* IX (1957), xxi, 21–25.

Mulnich, Susan. "El sentimiento de abandono en los textos de Violeta Parra y Gabriela Mistral." *Atenea*, 475 (1997), 123–136.

Muñoz, Eugenia. "The Death of the Beloved in the Poetry of Gabriela Mistral." In *Gabriela Mistral: The Audacious Traveler*, pp. 77–94. Marjorie Agosín, ed. Athens: Ohio University Press, 2003.

Nieto Caballero, Luis. "Gabriela Mistral." *Repertorio Americano* (11 enero 1930), 17.

Ocampo, Victoria. "El credo de Gabriela." *Ibérica* (15 abril 1957), 7–8.

——. "Gabriela Mistral y el Premio Nobel." *Sur* XIV, 134 (1945), 7–15.

——. "Y Lucila que hablaba a río. Gabriela Mistral. 1889–1957." *La Nación* (B.A.) (3 marzo 1957), 2a sec, 1.

Onís, Federico de. *España en América*. Madrid: Ediciones de la Universidad de Puerto Rico, 1955.

——. "Gabriela Mistral." *Anales* CXV, 106 (1957), 19–20.

Orellana, María Isabel. "Protectora de su intimidad: Una militante del silencio." *Revista Patrimonio Cultural* 46, Año XIII (Verano 2008), 26–27.

Oroz, Rodolfo. "Nota al poema 'Ceras eternas' de Gabriela Mistral." *Romanistisches Jahrbuch* (Hamburg), V (1952), 289–292.

Ortiz Vargas, A. "Gabriela Mistral." *Hispanic-American Historical Review* XI, 1 (1931), 99–102.

——. "Gabriela Mistral, Chile's Teacher-Poet." *Poet Lore* XLVI (1940), 339–352.

Osses, Mario. "Casticismo de Gabriela Mistral." *Atenea* XXVI, 286 (1949), 121–156.

——. "Gabriela Mistral: Poetisa de la pasión." *Conferencia* II, 6–9 (1947), 24–41.

——. "La poesía." *Antártica*, Nos. 15–16 (nov.-dic. 1945), 111.

Oyarzún, Luis. "Gabriela Mistral." *Atenea* XXXIV, 374 (1957), 34–39.

——. "Gabriela Mistral en su poesía." *Anales* CXV, 106 (1957), 11–14.

——. "El mundo poético de Gabriela Mistral." *Histonium* (B. A.), XI, 124 (1949), 53–54.

——. "El sentimiento americano en Gabriela Mistral." *Antártica*, Nos. 15–16 (nov.-dic. 1945), 100–102.

Oyarzún, Mila. "Gabriela Mistral." *Atenea* XX, 218 (1943), 173–183.

Paz Paredes, Margarita. "Gabriela Mistral." *Cultura*, No. 17 (oct.-dic. 1959), 162–168.

Peers, E. Allison. "Gabriela Mistral: A Tentative Evaluation." *Bulletin of Spanish Studies* XXI (1946), 101–116.

Peña, Concha. "Recordando a la Inmortal Cantora de América, Gabriela Mistral." *Cuadernos Israelíes*, No. 4 (1960), 58–62.

Peralta Peralta, Jaime. "El paisaje original de Gabriela Mistral." In *Los ángeles burladores: Cuentos y ensayos*, pp. 61–78. Madrid, 1961.

Pérez, Galo René. "La poesía de Gabriela Mistral." *Anales* (Univ. Central del Ecuador, Quito), XC, 345 (1961), 241–265.

Pérez Botero, Luis. "Gabriela Mistral y Odón Betanzos Palacios ('Sonetos de la muerte')." In *Gabriela Mistral y los Estados Unidos*, pp. 83–96. Gerardo Piña-Rosales et al., eds. Nueva York: ANLE, 2011.

Peri, Hiram. "Gabriela Mistral." *Cuadernos Israelíes*, No. 4 (1960), 1.

Petit, Magdalena. *Biografía de Gabriela Mistral*. Santiago: Editorial La Salle, 1946.

Picón Salas, Mariano. "En homenaje a Gabriela Mistral." *Asomante* II, 2 (1946), 14–16.

——. "Gabriela Mistral." *Atenea* XXXIV, 374 (1957), 40–43.

——. "Homenaje a Gabriela Mistral." *El Nacional* (C) (17 enero 1957), sec. lit., 8.

Pillement, Georges. "In memoriam." *Larousse Mensuel Illustré* (Paris), XIV, 511 (1957), 234.

Piña-Rosales, Gerardo et al., eds. *Gabriela Mistral y los Estados Unidos*. Nueva York: ANLE, 2011.

Pincheira, Dolores. *Gabriela Mistral, guardiana de la vida*. Santiago: Editorial Andrés Bello, 1989.

Pinilla, Norberto. *Biografía de Gabriela Mistral*. Santiago: Tegualda, 1946.

———. "Boceto crítico sobre Gabriela Mistral." *Revista Iberoamericana* XI, (1946), 55–62.

———. "Obra de Gabriela Mistral." *Conferencia* I, 1 (1946), 28–39.

———. "Perfil de Gabriela Mistral." *Antártica*, No. 14 (oct. 1945), 3–7.

Piontek, Heinz. "Gabriela Mistral." *Welt und Wort* XIV (1959), 104–105.

Pizarro, Ana. "Con identidad transgresora: Referente simbólico de la nación." *Revista Patrimonio Cultural*, 46, Año XIII (Verano 2008), 24.

———. "Gabriela Mistral and Brazil: A Journey of Fortitude." Nancy A. Hall, trans. In *Gabriela Mistral: The Audacious Traveler*, pp. 160–178. Marjorie Agosín, ed. Athens: Ohio University Press, 2003.

———. "Mistral, ¿qué modernidad?" In *Releer hoy a Gabriela Mistral: Mujer, historia y sociedad*, pp. 13–26. Gastón Lillo and Guillermo Renart, eds. Santiago: Editorial Universitaria, 1997.

Plá y Beltrán, Pascual. "Gabriela Mistral: Humanidad y poesía." *Cultura Universitaria* (Caracas), No. 59 (1957), 27–37.

Porter, Katherine Anne. "Latin America's Mystic Poet." *Literary Digest International Book Review* IV, 5 (1926), 307–308.

Portes, Grace Marie. "Gabriela Mistral: A Study of Motherhood in Her Prose and Poetry." Unpublished M.A. thesis. New York: Columbia University, 1947.

Posada, Germán. "Recuerdo a Gabriela Mistral." *Cuadernos Americanos* XXXI, 88 (1957), 102–104.

Prado, Pedro. "Al pueblo de México: Prologue." *Desolación*, pp. 11–24. 2nd ed. Santiago: Editorial del Pacífico, 1957.

———. "El Premio Nobel de la Literatura se adjudica a Gabriela Mistral." *Revista Nacional* VIII, 89 (1946), 306–307.

Pratt, Mary Louise. "Gender, Race, and Nation in the *Poema de Chile*." In *Women, Culture, and Politics in Latin America*, pp. 66–71. Berkeley: University of California Press, 1990.

Preston, Sister Mary Charles Ann, S.S.N.D. *A Study of Variants in the Poetry of Gabriela Mistral*. Studies in Romance Languages and Literatures. Vol. LXX. Washington, DC: Catholic University of America Press, 1964.

P. V. F. "Gabriela Mistral." *El Universal* (15 enero 1957), ind. lit., 4.

Rabanales, Ambrosio. "Tendencias métricas en los sonetos de Gabriela Mistral." In *Studia Philológica: Homenaje ofrecido a Dámaso Alonso*, pp. 13–51. Vol. III. Madrid: Gredos, 1963.

Ramírez Márquez, Alister. "Gabriela Mistral en la Estatua de la Libertad (1930): Reflexiones sobre la prosa mistraliana." In *Gabriela Mistral en los Estados Unidos*, pp. 129–135. Gerardo Piña-Rosales et al., eds. Nueva York: ANLE, 2011.

Ramírez Rausseo, J. A. "Gabriela Mistral." *El Universal* (14 mayo 1957), ind. lit., 3.

Redondo Magallanes, Mireya. *De mis días tristes: Manuel Magallanes Moure*. Santiago: DIBAM, 1999.

Retamales, Jaime. "Una creadora que no nos pertenece." *Revista Patrimonio Cultural* 46, Año XIII (Verano 2008), 39–41.

Reyes, Alfonso. "Himno a Gabriela." *Anales* CXV, 106 (1957), 19.

———. "El Premio a Gabriela." *Tiras de Colores* (México), II (dic. 1945-enero 1946), 1–2.

———. "Sobre Gabriela Mistral." *Cuadernos Israelíes*, No. 4 (1960), 52–54.

Rheinfelder, Hans. "Gabriela Mistral." *Anales* CXV, 106 (1957), 44–57.

———. *Gabriela Mistral: Motive ihrer Lyrik*. München: Verlag der Bayerischen Akademie der Wissenschaften, 1955.

Riestra, Gloria. "La influencia de Tagore en Gabriela Mistral." *Sembradores de Amistad* (Monterrey, Mexico) (mayo 1965), 5–9.

Rincón, César David. "Gabriela Mistral, mística del futuro." *Ciencia y Cultura* (Maracaibo), II, 7 (1957), 135–148.

Ríos Espejo, Rebeca. "La sintaxis en la expresión poética de Gabriela Mistral." *Boletín de Filología* (Santiago), IX (1956–57), 121–176.

Rodig, Laura. "Presencia de Gabriela Mistral." *Anales* CXV, 106 (1957), 282–292.

Rodríguez Luis, Julio. "Relaciones entre

Gabriela Mistral y Juan Ramón Jiménez." *La Torre* VIII, 32 (1960), 93–95.

Rodríguez Monegal, Emir. "La gruta de aire acondicionado." *Marcha* (Montevideo) (22 feb. 1957), 21.

———. "Valor poético y valor humano en Gabriela Mistral." *Marcha* (Montevideo) (18 enero 1957), 21–22.

Rodríguez Sardiñas [Rossardi], Orlando. "Los rostros de Gabriela." In *Gabriela Mistral en los Estados Unidos*, pp. 17–30. Gerardo Piña-Rosales et al., eds. Nueva York: ANLEs, 2011.

Rojas, Nelson. "Eje temporal y estrategia discursiva en 'Los Sonetos de la Muerte.'" *Revista Chilena de Literatura*, 49 (1996), 27–46.

Rojas Molina, Armando. *Semblanza de Gabriela Mistral*. Iquique: Imprenta El Porvenir, 1959.

Román, María Eugenia. "¡Son mentiras de los chilenos!." *Buen Domingo* (6 junio 1984), 10–12.

Romero, Elvio. "Sobre Gabriela Mistral." *Alcor* (Asunción), II, 107 (1957), 13.

Rosenbaum, Sidonia Carmen. "Criollismo y casticismo en Gabriela Mistral." *Cuadernos Americanos* XII, 1 (1953), 296–300.

———. *Modern Women Poets of Spanish America*. New York: Hispanic Institute, 1945.

Rouillon, Guillermo. "La voz universal de Gabriela Mistral." *Cuadernos Israelíes*, No. 4 (1960), 67–68.

Rubilar, Guillermo. *Gabriela, maestra y poetisa rediviva*. Santiago: Ediciones Juan Firula, 1972.

Rubio, Christian. "Los artículos de Gabriela Mistral en *La Nueva Democracia* de Nueva York." In *Gabriela Mistral en los Estados Unidos*, pp. 65–81. Gerardo Piña-Rosales et al., eds. Nueva York: ANLE, 2011.

Rubio, Patricia. "Constructions of the Self: The Personal Letters of Gabriela Mistral." In *Gabriela Mistral: The Audacious Traveler*, pp. 203–223. Marjorie Agosín, ed. Athens: Ohio University Press, 2003.

———. "Sobre el indigenismo y el mestizaje en la prosa de Gabriela Mistral." *Taller de Letras* (Chile), Número especial (1996), 25–40.

Ryan-Kobler, Maryalice. "Beyond the Mother Icon: Rereading the Poetry of Gabriela Mistral." *Revista Hispánica Moderna*, 2 (1997), 327–334.

Saavedra Molina, Julio. "Gabriela Mistral: Su vida y su obra." In *Poesías completas de Gabriela Mistral*, pp. xv–cxi. Margaret Bates, ed. 2nd ed. rev. Madrid: Aguilar, 1962.

———. "Gabriela Mistral: Vida y obra." *Anales* CIV, 63, 64 (1946), 23–104.

———. "Gabriela Mistral: Vida y obra." *Revista Hispánica Moderna*, III (1937), 110–135.

———. "La patética historia de Lucila Godoy." *Antártica*, Nos. 15–16 (nov.-dic. 1945), 106–110.

Sabat Ercasty, Carlos. "La Gabriela que yo vi." *Cuadernos Israelíes*, No. 4 (1960), 80–87.

———. "Homenaje de la Universidad de Montevideo a Gabriela Mistral." *RepertorioAmericano*, 14 (abril-mayo 1957), 209–213.

Sabella, Andrés. "Curso y discurso de una vida." *Atenea* XXXIV, 374 (1957), 22–33.

———. "El hijo desconocido de Gabriela Mistral." *Atenea* XXII, 246 (1945), 228–236.

Salinas, Pedro. "Vindicación de la distraída (Gabriela Mistral)." *Revista de América* VII, 19 (1946), 65–70.

Samatán, Marta Elena. *Los días y los años de Gabriela Mistral*. México: Editorial José M. Cajica, Jr., 1973

Sánchez, Luis Alberto. "Ahora los 'recados' de Gabriela." *El Nacional* (C) (5 junio 1958), sec. lit., 6.

———. "Gabriela Mistral." *Asomante* XII, 2 (1956), 39–47.

———. "Un ser y una voz inconfundibles." *Cuadernos*, No. 23 (marzo-abril 1957), 20–24.

Sánchez, Luis Amador. "El existencialismo cristiano de Gabriela." *La Nueva Democracia* XXXVII, 3 (1957), 42–49.

Sánchez-Grey Alba, Esther. "Un análisis de la prosa mistraliana desde la perspectiva crítica de Eugenio Florit." In *Gabriela Mistral en los Estados Unidos*, pp. 167–181. Gerardo Piña-Rosales et al., eds. Nueva York: ANLE, 2011.

Santandreu, Cora. *Aspectos del estilo en la poesía de Gabriela Mistral*. Serie Roja, No. 15. Santiago: Universidad de Chile, 1958.

Savoia, Alicia Raquel. "El mundo infantil de Gabriela Mistral." *Universidad* (Santa Fe, Argentina), No. 46 (oct.-dic. 1960), 215–240.

Schultz de Mantovani, Fryda. "Imagen de Gabriela Mistral." *Revista de la Universidad de Buenos Aires* II, 1 (1957), 26–40.

Schiefelbein, Ernesto. "Gabriela Mistral: Visionaria reformadora de la formación docente." *Revista Patrimonio Cultural*, 46, Año XIII (Verano 2008), 28–29.

Sedgwick, Ruth. "Gabriela Mistral's Elqui Valley." *Hispania* XXXV (1952), 310–314.

Sepúlveda, Emma. "Gabriela Mistral's Political Commentaries." Trans. Darrell B. Lockhart. In *Gabriela Mistral: The Audacious Traveler*, pp. 250–259. Marjorie Agosín, ed. Athens: Ohio University Press, 2003.

Silva Castro, Raúl. "Algunos aspectos de la poesía de Gabriela Mistral." *La Nueva Democracia* V, 9 (1923), 8–9, 30.

____. *Estudios sobre Gabriela Mistral*. Santiago: Zig-Zag, 1935.

____. *Producción de Gabriela Mistral de 1912 a 1918*. Serie Roja, no. 11. Santiago: Universidad de Chile, 1957.

____. *Retratos literarios.*, pp. 151–162. Santiago: Ercilla, 1932.

Silva Castro, Raúl, ed. *Epistolario: Cartas a Eugenio Labarca (1915–16)*. Serie Roja, no. 13. Santiago: Universidad de Chile, 1957.

Singerman, Berta. "Recuerdos de Gabriela Mistral." *Cuadernos Israelíes*, No. 4 (1960), 5–7.

Slaughter, Joseph R. "'A Wor[l]d Full of X's and K's'. Parables of Human Rights in the Prose of Gabriela Mistral." In *Gabriela Mistral: The Audacious Traveler*, pp. 19–46. Marjorie Agosín, ed. Athens: Ohio University Press, 2003.

Sobrino Pôrto, Leónidas. *Dios en la poesia de Gabriela Mistral*. Río de Janeiro: Escola Tipográfica Pío X, 1957.

Suárez de Artieda, Matilde. *Gabriela Mistral: Ensayo*. Quito: Surcos, 1957.

Subercaseaux, Bernardo. "Gabriela Mistral: Espiritualismo y canciones de cuna." *Cuadernos Americanos*, 205 (1976), 208–225.

Szmulewicz, Efraím. *Gabriela Mistral: Biografía emotiva*. Santiago: Atacama, 1958.

Taracena, Alfonso. "Epistolario de Gabriela Mistral." *Vida Universitaria* (Mexico) (3 enero 1957), 5.

Taylor, Martin C. "Darío y Mistral." In *Gabriela Mistral*. Centro de Investigaciones Lingüístico-Literarias. Veracruz, México: Cuadernos de Texto Crítico, 1980.

____. "Darío y Mistral." Speech, Symposium on Gabriela Mistral. New York: Barnard College, 1978.

____. "Gabriela Mistral y sus escritos tempranos." Speech, Second Conference on Latin-American Women Writers. San José, CA: San José State University, 1978.

____. *Gabriela Mistral's Religious Sensibility*. Vol. 87, Series in Modern Philology. Berkeley: University of California Press, 1968.

____. "Parálisis y progreso en la crítica mistraliana." In *El ensayo y la crítica literaria en Iberoamérica*, pp. 185–190. Toronto: University of Toronto Press, 1970.

____. "Parálisis y progreso en la crítica mistraliana." Speech, XIV Instituto Internacional de Literatura Iberoamericana. Toronto: University of Toronto, 1970.

____. Prologue, "La metáfora de Dios y el Tiempo: Las dos Lucilas [Lucila Velásquez/Lucila Godoy Alcayaga]." In Lucila Velásquez, *El tiempo irreversible*, pp. 2–10. Caracas: Editorial Pomaire, 1995.

____. *Sensibilidad religiosa de Gabriela Mistral*, Pilar García Noreña, trans. Rev. ed. Madrid: Gredos, 1975.

____. "La trayectoria espiritual de Gabriela Mistral a la luz de 60 escritores." *Revista Patrimonio Cultural*, 46, Año XIII (Verano 2008), 36–38.

____. "Women Intellectuals of Chile." In *Studies on Latin-American Women Writers*. Pittsburgh: Carnegie-Mellon University Press, 1978.

____. "Women Intellectuals of Chile." Speech, First Conference on Latin-American Women Writers. Pittsburgh: Carnegie-Mellon University, 1975.

____, and Saúl Sibirsky. *Language into Language: Cultural, Legal and Linguistic Issues for Interpreters and Translators*. Jefferson, NC: McFarland, 2010.

Teitelboim, Volodia. *Gabriela Mistral: Pública y secreta*. 3rd. ed. Santiago: Editorial Sudamericana, 1999.

Tellería Solari, María. "Postrera visita de Gabriela Mistral a Lima." *Mercurio Peruano* XXXVIII, 358 (1957), 111–114.

Tilliette, X. "Deuil de Gabriela Mistral." *Études* (Paris), XC, 5 (1957), 242–253.

Tomic, Radomiro. "Homenaje a Gabriela Mistral." *Política y Espíritu* XIII, 173 (1957), 10–11.

Torre, Guillermo de. "Aproximaciones de 'Tala,'" *Sur* VIII, 45 (1938), 70–75.

———. "Benjamín Carrión: San Miguel de Unamuno y Santa Gabriela Mistral." *Cuadernos,* No. 27 (nov.-dic. 1957), 99–100.

———. "Evocación de Gabriela Mistral." *El Nacional* (C) (7 feb. 1957), sec. lit., 4.

Torres Bodet, Jaime. "Homenaje a Gabriela Mistral." *Cuadernos,* No. 23 (marzo-abril 1957), 16.

Torres-Rioseco, Arturo. "Gabriela Mistral." *Anales* CXX, 125 (1962), 65–73.

———. *Gabriela Mistral.* Valencia: Editorial Castalia, 1962.

———. "Gabriela Mistral, Nobel Prize Winner at Home." *Hispania* XXIX (1946), 72–73.

Trigueros de León, Ricardo. "Recuerdo de Gabriela Mistral." *Cuadernos Israelíes,* No. 4 (1960), 45–46.

Triviño, Consuelo. "Con tu verso me he dormido en paz: Gabriela Mistral." *Quimera,* 123 (1994), 1–2.

Uribe Echeverría, Juan. "Gabriela Mistral: Aspectos de su vida y su obra." In *Gabriela Mistral.* Washington: Pan American Union, 1958.

Uruguay. Asamblea General. Cámara de Representantes. *"Homenaje a Gabriela Mistral."* Sesión extraordinaria (15 enero 1957). Montevideo, 1957.

Urzúa, María. *Gabriela Mistral: Genio y figura.* Santiago: Editorial del Pacífico, 1981.

Vailakis, Ivonne Gordon. "A Hungry Wolf: The Mask and the Spectacle in Gabriela Mistral." In *Gabriela Mistral: The Audacious Traveler,* pp. 113–131. Marjorie Agosín, ed. Athens: Ohio University Press, 2003.

Valenzuela-Fuenzalida, Álvaro. *La vocación vertical: El pensamiento de Gabriela Mistral sobre su oficio pedagógico.* Valparaíso: Ediciones Universitarias de Valparaíso, 1992.

Valerín A., Celina. "Homenaje a Chile en Gabriela Mistral." *Repertorio Americano* (feb.-marzo 1957), 207–208.

Valéry, Paul. "Gabriela Mistral." *Atenea* XXIV, 269–270 (1947), 313–322.

Valle, Carmen. "Gabriela y su palabra del dolor." *Política y Espíritu* XIII, 173 (1957), 12–13.

Vandercammen, Edmond. "Pasión y espiritualidad de Gabriela Mistral." *Les Langues Néolatines* LIII (1959), 1–8.

Varas, Parttricia. "Gabriela Mistral: Meritorious Member of the Sandinista Army." In *Gabriela Mistral: The Audacious Traveler,* pp. 64–76. Marjorie Agosín, ed. Athens: Ohio University Press, 2003.

Vargas Saavedra, Luis. "Gabriela Mistral and the United States of America." In *Gabriela Mistral: The Audacious Traveler,* pp. 260–269. Marjorie Agosín, ed. Athens: Ohio University Press, 2003.

———. "Motivos de San Francisco." *Mapocho* (Santiago), XIII, 1 (1966), 256–260.

———. "Obra inédita de Gabriela Mistral: 'Lagar' II." Unpublished Ph.D. dissertation. Madrid: University of Madrid, 1966.

———, ed. *El otro suicida de Gabriela Mistral.* Santiago: Ediciones Universidad Católica de Chile, 1985.

Vázquez, Pura. "En la muerte de Gabriela Mistral." *El Universal* (15 enero 1957), ind. lit., 4.

Velázquez, Alberto. "Salutación a Gabriela Mistral bajo el cielo de Cuba." *Cuadernos Israelíes,* No. 4 (1960), 49–51.

Veloso, Agostinho. "Da poesia de hoje, à poesia de sempre." *Brotéria* (Lisbon), LXIV, 6 (1957), 626–642.

Vitier, Cintio. *La voz de Gabriela Mistral.* Santa Clara, Cuba: Universidad Central de las Villas, 1957.

V. M. "Jean Michel Godoy." *Tribuna de Petrópolis,* (15 agosto 1943), 2.

Wais, Kurt Karl Theodor. *Zwei Dichter Südamerikas: Gabriela Mistral, Rómulo Gallegos.* Berlin: H. Luchterhand, 1955.

Welden, Alicia G. "Gabriela Mistral: The Christian Matriarch of Latin America." In *Náhuatl to Rayuela,* pp. 23–33. Dave Oliphant, ed. Austin: Harry Ransom Humanities Research Center, University of Texas Press, 1992.

Yankas, Lautaro. "Responso a Gabriela Mistral: Pedagogía y diplomacia." *Atenea* XXXIV, 374 (1957), 51–59.

Yépez, Luis. "Gabriela Mistral." *El Universal* (22 enero 1957), ind. lit., 4.

———. "El hombre y la piedra." *El Universal* (15 enero 1957), ind. lit., 4.

Zalaquett Aquea, Cherie. "Doris Dana, la albacea de la Mistral, rompe el silencio." *Revista El Sábado. El Mercurio* (22 nov. 2002). At http://www.letras.s5.com/gm/171004.htm.

Zamborain, Lila. "Modalidades de representación del sujeto lírico en la poesía de Gabriela Mistral." Unpublished Ph. D. dissertation. New York: New York University, 1997.

Zamorano Baier, Antonio. "Gabriela Mistral y la crítica." *Atenea* XXIII, 248 (1946), 183–199.

Zardoya, Concha. "Desde 'Desolación' a 'Lagar,'" *Revista Hispánica Moderna* XXII (1956), 137–138.

_____. "La poesía de Gabriela Mistral." *Índice de Artes y Letras* (Madrid), No. 113 (junio 1958), 9–11.

Zegers B., Pedro Pablo. "Mistral y Estados Unidos: Un vínculo intenso y ambiguo." In *Gabriela Mistral y los Estados Unidos*, pp. 241–252. Gerardo Piña-Rosales et al., eds. Nueva York: ANLES, 2011.

_____. "Revisión en Washington: Un sueño cumplido," *Revista Patrimonio Cultural*, 46, Año XIII (Verano 2008), 5.

Zum Felde, Alberto. "Gabriela Mistral, Premio Nobel." *Revista Nacional* VIII, 90 (1945), 338–343.

Zurita, Carlos. "La Biblia de Gabriela Mistral." *La Nueva Democracia* XXXVII, 2 (1957), 23–25.

_____. "La Biblia fue fuente de sabiduría y permanente inspiración para Gabriela." *La Nación* (S) (13 enero 1957), 16.

Studies on Religion, Poetry, Literary Criticism and Social Issues

Agosín, Marjorie, ed. *A Dream of Light and Shadow: Portraits of Latin American Women Writers*. Albuquerque: University New Mexico Press, 1995.

Allday, Elizabeth. *Stefan Zweig: A Critical Biography*. Chicago: J. Philip O'Hare, 1972.

Alonso. Amado. *Materia y forma en poesía*. Madrid: Gredos, 1955.

Alonso, Dámaso. *La poesía de San Juan de la Cruz (Desde esta ladera)*. Madrid: Aguilar, 1946.

_____. *Poesía española: Ensayo de métodos y límites estilísticos*. 3rd ed. Madrid: Gredos, 1957.

Aylwin, Mariana, et al. *Chile en el siglo XX*. 11th ed. Santiago: Editorial Planeta, 2002.

Battenhouse, Henry M. *Poets of Christian Thought: Evaluations from Dante to T.S. Eliot*. New York: Ronald Press, 1947.

Bergson, Henri. *Les Deux Sources de la morale et de la religion*. 13th ed. Paris: Librairie Félix Alcan, 1933.

Besant, Annie. *Esoteric Christianity or The Lesser Mysteries*. Adyar & Los Angeles: Theosophical Publishing House, 1913.

_____. "Theosophical Society." *Encyclopedia of Religion and Ethics*. James Hastings, ed. New York: T.&T. Clark, Scribner's, 1935.

Bishop, James A. *The Day Christ Died*. New York: Harper, 1957.

Blavatsky, Helena P. *The Key to Theosophy*. London: Theosophical Publishing Society, 1889. 3rd rev., 1893.

_____, trans. *The Voice of the Silence*. New York: Elliott Page, 1899.

Bodkin, Maud. *Archetypal Patterns in Poetry: Psychological Studies of Imagination*. New York: Vintage Books, 1958.

Bonaventure, St. *The Little Flowers of St. Francis. The Mirror of Perfection. The Life of St. Francis*. New York: E. P. Dutton, 1951.

Bose, Abinash Chandra. *Three Mystic Poets: A Study of W. B. Yeats, A. E., and Rabindranath Tagore*. Kolhapur: School and College Bookstall, 1945.

Brooks, Cleanth. *The Well Wrought Urn: Studies in the Structure of Poetry*. New York: Harcourt, Brace, 1947.

Carpenter, William B. *The Religious Spirit in the Poets*. London: Isbister, 1900.

Chase, Mary Ellen. *Life and Language in the Old Testament*. London: Collins, 1950.

Crow, John A. *The Epic of Latin America*. New York: Doubleday, 1952. 4th ed. Berkeley: University of California Press, 1992.

Doornik, N. G. M. van, et al. *A Handbook of the Catholic Faith: The Triptych of the Kingdom*. Garden City: Image Books, 1962.

Doty, Alexander. *Making Things Perfectly Queer: Interpreting Mass Culture*. Minneapolis: University of Minnesota Press, 1993.

Drew, Elizabeth. *Poetry: A Modern Guide to Its Understanding and Enjoyment*. New York: Dell, 1959.

Enciclopedia Italiana di Scienze, Lettere ed

Arti. Milano: Instituto Giovanni Treccani, 1930. 36 vols.

Encyclopedia of Latin-American History & Culture. 2nd ed. New York: Gale Cengage Learning, 2008.

Ferguson, George. *Signs & Symbols in Christian Art.* New York: Oxford University Press, 1961.

Fowlie, Wallace. *A Guide to Contemporary French Literature : From Valéry to Sartre.* New York: Meridian Books, 1957.

Francesco de Assisi, St. *The Writings of Saint Francis of Assisi.* Philadelphia: Dolphin Press, 1906.

Francis de Sales, St. *Introduction to a Devout Life.* Trans. John K. Evan. New York: Harper, 1950.

Frye, Roland Mushat. *God, Man and Satan: Patterns of Christian Thought and Life in "Paradise Lost," "Pilgrim's Progress," and the Great Theologians.* Princeton: Princeton University Press, 1960.

Gaer, Joseph. *The Lore of the New Testament.* Boston: Little, Brown, 1952.

Garcés Durán, Mario. *Crisis social y motines populares en el 1900.* Santiago: Ediciones Documentas, 1991.

Graeff, Hilda. *Mary: A History of Doctrine and Devotion.* Vol. 1. New York: Sheed and Ward, 1963.

Granada, Fray Luis de. *Obras.* In *Biblioteca de Autores Españoles.* Vol. II. Madrid, 1848.

Halverson, Marvin, ed. *A Handbook of Christian Theology.* New York: Meridian Books, 1958.

Hamilton, Edith. *Mythology.* New York: New American Library, 1956.

Hastings, James, ed. *Dictionary of the Bible.* Rev. ed. New York: Scribner's, 1963.

———. *The Interpreter's Dictionary of the Bible,* 4 vols. New York: Abingdon Press, 1962

Hatzfeld, Helmut. *Trends and Styles in Twentieth Century French Literature.* Washington: Catholic University of America Press, 1957.

Hawkes, Jacquetta. *Man and the Sun.* New York: Random House, 1962.

Holroyd, Stuart. *Emergence from Chaos.* Boston: Houghton Mifflin, 1957.

Hopper, Stanley Romaine, ed. *Spiritual Problems in Contemporary Literature.* New York: Harper, 1957.

Humphreys, Christmas. *Buddhism.* Baltimore: Penguin, 1958.

James, E[dwin] O. *The Cult of the Mother-Goddess: An Archaeological and Documentary Study.* New York: Praeger, 1959.

Kaufmann, Walter. *Critique of Religion and Philosophy.* New York: Doubleday, 1961.

———. *The Faith of a Heretic.* New York: Doubleday, 1961.

Kayser, Wolfgang. *Interpretacion y análisis de la obra literaria.* 2nd ed. rev. Madrid: Gredos, 1958.

Kepler, Thomas S. *A Journey with the Saints.* Cleveland and New York: World Publishing Company, 1951.

Kuhn, Alvin Boyd. *Theosophy: A Modern Revival of Ancient Wisdom.* New York: Henry Holt, 1930.

Lewis, C. Day. *The Poetic Image.* London: Jonathan Cape, 1958.

Lida, María Rosa [de Malkiel]. "Transmisión y recreación de temas grecolatinos." *Revista de Filología Hispánica,* 1 (1939), 20–63

MacNeice, Louis. *The Poetry of W. B. Yeats.* London: Oxford University Press, 1941.

Maritain, Jacques. *Creative Intuition in Art and Poetry.* New York: Meridian Books, 1955.

Martz, Louis. *The Poetry of Meditation: A Study in English Religious Literature of the Seventeenth Century.* New Haven: Yale University Press, 1954.

Mathison, Richard. *Faiths, Cults and Sects of America: From Atheism to Zen.* New York: Bobbs-Merrill, 1960.

McCann, Eleanor. "Oxymora in Spanish Mystics and English Metaphysical Writers." *Comparative Literature* XIII (1961), 16–25.

Meléndez, Concha. *Amado Nervo.* New York: Instituto de las Españas en los Estados Unidos, 1926.

Meyer, Sister Mary Edgar, O.S.F. *The Sources of Hojeda's La Cristiada.* Ann Arbor: University of Michigan Press, 1953.

Montero, Lázaro, ed. *Poesía religiosa española.* Madrid: Ebro, 1950.

Montes, Hugo, and J. Orlandi. *Historia de la literatura chilena.* Santiago: Editorial del Pacífico, 1955.

Muller, Herbert J. *The Uses of the Past: Profiles of Former Societies.* New York: New American Library, 1954.

Nelson, Lowry, Jr. "The Rhetoric of Ineffability: Toward a Definition of Mystical Poetry." *Comparative Literature* VIII (1956), 323–336.

Nervo, Amado. *Poesías completas*. México: Latino Americana, 1957.

Nisis de Rezepke, Sima, comp. *Chile escribe a Israel*. Santiago: Editorial Andrés Bello, 1982.

Ortiz Letelier, Fernando. *El movimiento obrero en Chile (1891–1919)*. Santiago: Ediciones LOM, 2005.

Otto, Rudolph. *The Original Gita: The Song of the Supreme Exalted One*. London: G. Allen and Unwin, 1939.

Parkes, James. *Judaism and Christianity*. Chicago: University of Chicago Press, 1948.

Powers, Perry J. "Lope de Vega and *Las lágrimas de la Madalena*." *Comparative Literature* VIII (1956), 273–290.

Ramírez, Raúl. *Rabindranath Tagore, poeta y filósofo hindú*. Santiago, Imprenta Universo, 1917.

Richards, I[vor] A. *Practical Criticism: A Study of Literary Judgment*. New York: Harcourt, Brace, 1955.

Rideau, Emile. *Le Dieu de Bergson: Essai de critique réligieuse*. Paris: Librairie Félix Alcan, 1932.

Rukeyser, Muriel. *The Life of Poetry*. New York: A. A. Winn, 1949.

Sáinz Rodríguez, Pedro. *Espiritualidad española*. Madrid: Ediciones Rialp, 1961.

Sinnett, Alfred Percy. *Esoteric Buddhism*. Boston: Houghton Mifflin, 1895.

Sommer, Doris. "Jorge Isaacs." In *Jewish Writers of Latin America*, pp. 268–274. Darrell B. Lockhart, ed. New York: Garland, 1997.

Stace, Walter T. *The Teachings of the Mystics*. New York: New American Library, 1960.

Stallman, Robert Wooster, ed. *Critiques and Essays in Criticism, 1920–1918*. New York: Ronald Press, 1949.

Sundén, Hjalmar. *La Théorie bergsonienne de la religion*. Paris: Presses Universitaires de France, 1947.

Tagore, Rabindranath. *Collected Poems and Plays*. New York: Macmillan, 1951.

Tate, Allen, ed. *The Language of Poetry*. Princeton: Princeton University Press, 1942.

Terlingen, Juan. "Cara de Dios." *Studia Philológica: Homenaje ofrecido a Dámaso Alonso*, pp. 463–478. Vol. III. Madrid: Gredos, 1963.

Thompson, Edward. *Rabindranath Tagore: Poet and Dramatist*. 2nd ed. London: Oxford University Press, 1948.

Warren, Austin. *A Rage for Order: Essays in Criticism*. Ann Arbor: University of Michigan Press, 1948.

———. *Richard Crashaw: A Study in Baroque Sensibility*. Ann Arbor: University of Michigan Press, 1957.

Wellek, René, and Austin Warren. *Teoría literaria*. Trans. José Maria Gimeno Capella. Madrid: Gredos, 1953.

Wellman, Esther Turner. *Amado Nervo: Mexico's Religious Poet*. New York: Instituto de las Españas en los Estados Unidos, 1936.

Whittick, Arnold. *Symbols, Signs and Their Meaning*. Newton, MA: Branford, 1960.

Wolfson, Harry Austryn. *The Philosophy of the Church Fathers: Faith, Trinity, Incarnation*. Vol. I. Cambridge: Harvard University Press, 1956.

Index to Mistral's Works

"A la Virgen de la Colina" 134, 199, 254*n*47
"A Vargas Vila" 239*n*15
"Adiós a Laura" 68–69, 243*n*6
"Agua" 124–125
"Al oído del Cristo" 186–187, 188–189, 197, 198, 201
"Al pueblo hebreo" 119, 129, 144, 145, 199, 212
"Alabanzas a la Virgen" 251*n*68
"El amor que calla" 252*n*95
"La ansiosa" 204
"El arpa de Dios" 248*n*45
"Ausencia" 202

"Balada" 83–84, 197, 244*n*5
"Balada de la estrella" 160
"El barco misericordioso" 211; *see also* "Canciones en el mar"

"Campeón finlandés" 113, 248*n*43
"Canción de la sangre" 212
"Canción de los que buscan olvidar" 200, 253*n*18; *see also* "Canciones en el mar"
"Canción de Taurus" 168
"Canción de Virgo" 167–168
"Canción del hombre de proa" *see* "Canciones en el mar"
"Canciones de cuna" (section) 215
"Canciones de Solveig" 203
"Canciones en el mar" 195, 254*n*37
"Canto del justo" 197, 198, 253*n*15, 254*n*37
"Carta a Emelina" 32
"Carta a José Santos González Vera" 150*n*19
"Carta a Mercedes Dublé-Urrutia" 107
"Carta inédita de Gabriela Mistral" 149*n*11, 151*n*22, 170*n*82, 179*n*109, 249*n*11, 250*n*22, 252*n*82
"Cartas a Doris Dana" 77
"Cartas a Pedro Prado" 65*n*3, 83
"Cartas a Zacarías Gómez" 43

"Cartas de amor a Manuel Magallanes Moure" 21, 23, 72, 238*n*6, 239*n*16
Cartas de amor de Gabriela Mistral 239*n*1
"Cartas de Gabriela Mistral" 237*n*13
"Cartas de Gabriela Mistral a Juan Ramón Jiménez" 118*n*15, 247*n*15
"El catolicismo en los Estados Unidos" 147*n*6, 249*n*6
"La charca" 156, 162, 251*n*54
"Cima" 205, 255*n*62
"Comentario sobre el feminismo" 80
"Comentario sobre la muerte de Yin-Yin" 41*n*33
"Comentario sobre la mujer y la civilización" 79*n*13
"Comentario sobre mi cristianismo" 180*n*113
"Comentarios a poemas de Rabindranath Tagore" 174–177, 243*n*1, 253*n*95
"Cómo edifican" 250*n*26
"Considérations sur Rousseau et autres réflexions" 153*n*27, 171*n*91, 250*n*27, 252*n*91
"Coplas" 29
"Corderito" 169
"El corro luminoso" 173
"El costado desnudo" 190, 195–196, 201, 204, 205, 255*n*61
"Credo" 44–45, 134–135, 137, 206, 211
"Cristianismo con sentido social" 148–149, 151–152, 249*n*8, 250*n*23
"La Cruz de Bistolfi" 69, 209, 253*nn*15 and 18
"La cultura mexicana" 246*n*12

"Dame la mano" 72
"La desasida" 253*n*7
Desolación (book) viii, 12, 22, 23, 91, 102, 108, 109, 139, 172, 191, 199, 201, 205, 248, 239*n*16, 240*n*9, 246 Ch. XI*n*2, 247*n*16, 248*nn*39 and 47, 251*nn* 49 and 54, 252*n*95, 255*nn*49, 52, 71, and 75
"Desolación" (poem) 113, 205

"La desvelada" 252n95
"Dios lo quiere" 130, 199, 205, 253n18
"El Dios triste" 137, 204, 249n65
"Divulgación religiosa. Sentido de las letanías: Virgen de las Vírgenes" 166–167n68
"Dolor (section) 22
"Dos canciones del Zodíaco" 167–168
"Duerme, duerme, niño cristiano" 251n78

"Elogio de la canción" 129–130
"Emigrada judía" 119
"En la siesta de Graciela" 33, 240n16
"La encina" 140, 192, 242n2, 249n65
"El encuentro" 134, 248n64
"Enfermo" 204
"Entrevista a La Unión de Punta Arenas" 245nn16 and 44
Epistolario: Cartas a Eugenio Labarca (1915–1916) 177n97, 178n102, 252n102, 255n69
"Epistolario entre Lucila Godoy Alcayaga y Manuel Magallanes Moure" 243 *ch*VIn1
"La escuela al aire libre" 243n3
"La espera inútil" 249n65
"El espino" 132–133
"El establo" 166
"Evocación de la madre" 240n12
"Éxtasis" 162, 198, 211, 253n18, 255n58

"Fray Bartolomé" 149–150, 249n17
"La fuga" 240n12, 251n56

Gabriela Mistral: Álbum personal viii, 236n6
"Gabriela Mistral sur la pente" 250n27
"Gotas de hiel" 134, 187
"Gracias en el mar" 254n46

"Himno al aire" 162–163
"Himno al árbol" 156, 165, 192, 254n26
"El himno cotidiano" 101, 161, 187, 208, 253n17
"El himno del árbol" 156
"Hospital" 202, 204
"La huella" 206

"In memoriam" 159, 178
"La instrucción de la mujer" 244n13
"Interrogaciones" 143–144, 197, 203, 205n76
"Íntima" 252n95
"El Ixtlazihuatl" 204, 206, 211

"Jesús" 173

Lagar viii, 12, 42, 198, 199, 201, 202
"Lampara de catedral" 253n15
"Lápida filial" 212, 240n11
"Lecturas espirituales" 132n47, 206, 248n47, 255n65

"El Liceo de Niñas" 243 Ch. Vn2
"Limpia tu fuente" 162, 251n54
"La lluvia lenta" 197, 254n30, 255n62
"Locas letanías" 197, 212, 254n39
"Luto" (poem) 42, 193, 201
"Luto" (section) 134

"Madre mía" 160, 240n12
"La maestra rural" 33, 128, 161–162, 209–210, 255nn69 and 76
"Manitas" 187
"Manos de obreros" 194
"Meciendo" 216–217
"La medianoche" 251n46
"Memoria de la gracia" 253n115
"Mensaje enviado por Gabriela Mistral ..." 242n34
"Mi experiencia con la Biblia" 228–235, 246 Ch. XIIn1
"Mis libros" 117, 132, 185, 253n17, 253n49, 255nn59 and 64
"La montaña de noche" 255n49
"Motivos de la Pasión" 158n49, 255n49
Motivos de San Francisco 251n47
"Motivos del barro" 251n49
"Muerte de mi madre" 31, 179–180, 252n110
"La muerte de Stefan Zweig" 242n29
"Muerte del mar" 139–140
"La muerte-niña" 137–138, 249n65
"La mujer estéril" 126
"La mujer fuerte" 126, 136

"Navegando" 58
"Nocturno" 143, 162, 185, 190, 202, 203, 204–205, 206n64, 237n18, 255nn61 and 64
"Nocturno de la consumación" 13, 193
"Nocturno de la derrota" 127, 247n16, 254nn39 and 47, 255n77
"Nocturno de los tejedores viejos" 128, 161–162
"Nocturno del descendimiento" 197, 253n16
Notebooks 164, 250n41, 251nn44 and 63; *see also* "Prácticas"

"La obsesión" 190
"La oración de la maestra" 99, 104, 245n6, 255n71
"Organización de las mujeres" 244n14
"Otoño" 249n65
"La otra" 84

"Pan" 248n36
"Paraíso" 251n62
"El Pensador de Rodin" 69, 139, 141, 243n6
"El perdón de una víctima" 24
"Piececitos" 187
"Pinares" 254n30
"El placer de servir" 156

"Plantando el árbol" 169
"Plegaria por el nido" 141–142
Poema de Chile viii, 12, 17, 42, 237*n*22
"Poema del hijo" 134, 169, 197, 212, 237*n*22, 240*n*5, 244*n*23, 249*n*64
"Poemas de las madres" 127, 255*n*52
Poesías completas de Gabriela Mistral 193, 237*nn*18 and 22, 238*nn*9 and 12, 240*n*12, 247*nn*5 and 18, 250*n*36, 251*nn*43 and 56, 252*nn*92, 95 and 110, 253*nn*4 and 7
"Por qué las rosas tienen espinas" 187*n*11, 253*n*11
"Prácticas" 157–159, 250*n*41, 251*nn*44 and 63; see also unpublished materials
"Primavera" 163, 251*n*53
"'Prólogo' a la Biblia" 115–116*n*7
"'Prólogo' a *La Desterrada en su patria*" 88
La prosa de Gabriela Mistral 237*n*13
Prosa religiosa de Gabriela Mistral 241*n*17, 245*n*2

"Recado de nacimiento para Chile" 251*n*77
"Recado de Navidad" 163–164, 166, 251*nn*61 and 67
"Recado para la 'Residencia de Pedralbes,' en Cataluña" 198, 206
"Recado para las Antillas" 137
"Recado sobre los Tlalocs" 95
"Recado sobre música araucana" 95
"Recado sobre Quetzalcoatl" 95
Recados: Contando a Chile 145*n*5, 149*n*14, 249*nn*5 and 15
Recopilación de la obra mistraliana viii, 238*n*3, 242*n*3, 243*nn*1 and 2, 245*ch*X*n*1
"Romance de Nochebuena" 164
"Rondas" (section) 172–173, 216
"El ruego" 130–131, 137, 142–143, 247*n*21, 253*n*16
"Ruth" 124, 136, 159

"Sal" 125–126, 254*n*47

"Señor Nuestro" 42
"Serenidad" 197, 205
"Silueta de Sor Juana Inés" 149*n*16, 249*n*16
"Sobre el centenario: Ideas de una maestra" 244*n*7
"Sobre la muerte de Yin-Yin" 42
"Sobre la xenofobia" 242*n*34
"Sol del trópico" 254*n*39
"La sombra inquieta" 197
"Sonetos de la muerte" 18, 20–21, 22, 23, 239*n*14
"El suplicio" 253*n*18

Tala viii, 12, 31, 56–57, 104, 130, 171, 172, 197, 199, 252*nn*92 and 110, 255*n*60
"Teresa Prats de Sarratea" 104–105
Ternura viii, 12, 101, 115, 116, 129–130, 168, 172, 199
"Tierra chilena" 121
"Todas íbamos a ser reinas" 130, 248*n*46
"Todo es ronda" 173–174
"Tres árboles" 192, 205
"Tribulación" 135, 137, 200

"Último árbol 143, 193–194, 249*n*66
"Una explicación más del caso Krishnamurti" 251*n*58
"Una palabra" 133–134
"Una piadosa" 201
"Unidad cristiana" 249*n*71
unpublished materials 163; see also "Prácticas"

"Ventajoso canje" 244*n*7
"Vida" (section) 139
"'Un viejo tema': La poetisa chilena comenta el informe de Kinsey" 28–29, 240*n*6
"Viernes Santo" 186, 188–190, 201
"Volverlo a ver" 159
"Voto" 255*n*75

Index to Names and Places

Numbers in ***bold italics*** indicate pages with photographs.

Abel 127
Abós-Padilla, Ricardo Michell 219–223
Abraham 12, 128, 133, 248nn40 and 41, 249n69
Acts of the Apostles 254n24
Adam 194, 209
Agosín, Marjorie 240n15, 244n13
Agüero Wood, Óscar/Panchi 62
Aguirre Cerda, Pedro 14, 66, 82, 86, 88, 90, 91–95, 102, 109–110
Alba, Pedro de 249n17
Alba, Víctor 242nn32 and 37, 250n38
Alcaluf Indians 84, 87, 89, 95
Alcayaga Rojas de Godoy, vda. de Molina, Petronila (Lucila's mother) 27, ***30***–31, 33, 56, 68, 146, 159, 180
Alegría, Fernando 120, 241n17
Alessandri Arturo 105–107, 109
Amos, Book of 254n27
Angels/Archangel 25, 194
Antofagasta 56, 57–61, 63, 67, 83, 88, 101, 115, 151, 156, 242n1
Aquinas, Thomas 114
Araucan Indians 95, 246n10
Arce, Magda 236n1, 240n13, 241n24, 242n30
Arce de Vázquez, Margot 4, 5, 71, 180, 239n16, 240n8, 241n25, 249n71, 251n79
Arciniegas, Germán 117, 247n12
Arriaga, Lola 128
Aste, Santiago 73–74, 243n4
Astrology 16, 159–160, 167–168, 251nn45 and 77; *see also* Occultism
Atkinson, Doris 4, 76, 78, 244n11
Aubert, Jean 54
Aylwin, Mariana 244n10

Bahamonde, Manuel 57–59, 61, 242n1
Bandeira, Manuel, 39, 241n27
Barraza de Estay, Isolina 34, 35, 38, 236n7, 237n11, 240n17, 241nn24 and 26
Barrios, Carlos Omar 19
Barrios, Eduardo 74, 136, 91, 237n14, 248n62
Barros Luco, Ramón 19
Basque 117, 119, 171
Bates, Margaret 237nn18 and 22
Bécquer, Gustavo Adolfo 47
Bello, Andrés 51–53
Benjamín 122
Berchmans, John 249n18
Bergmann, Emilie L. 243n5
Bergson, Henri 180, 182, 218, 253n115, 253nn120–122
Besant, Annie 60, 63, 157, 163, 169, 183–184, 251n59, 60, 64, 69, 71–73, 75, and 76, 219–221, 253nn1 and 2
Bible (Biblia) 116, 118, 121 *passim*, 126, 129, 130, 132, 134, 140, 161, 215, 228–235, 246chXIIn5, 247nn7, 8, 10, and 12, 248nn62 and 63, 252n86; *see also* New Testament; Old Testament
Bistolfi, Leonardo 69, 253n17
Blavatsky, Héléna Petrovna 6, 63, 156, 157, 162, 250n40, 251nn43 and 52, 252n94
Boaz (Booz) 124, 159
Bodkin, Maud 255n74
Bolívar, Simón 51
Bollo, Sarah 122, 177, 247n27, 252nn84 and 98
Bombal, María Luisa 226
Bose, Abinash Chandra 252nn87–90, and 93
Brahmanism 181
Brazil 13, 15, 34, 38, 39, 44, 241nn19 and 22

280

Index to Names and Places

Brooks, Cleanth 209, 255n68
Buber, Martin 149
Buddha, Gautama 160–161, 164
Buddhism 146, 155, 159, 169–171, 177–182, 216–218, 243chVn3, 251n56, 252–253n113

Cáceres, Esther de 39, 74, 207, 241n27, 242n39, 247n29, 253n6, 255n56
Caimano, Rose Aquin 255n58
Caín 132
California 9, 15, 16, 32, 44, 76
Calles, Plutarco Elías 152
Calvary (Calvario) 191, 198
Canticles *see* Song of Songs
Capellán *see* Munizaga, Capellán Miguel Ignacio
Carrión, Benjamín 37, 236n5
Casa del Pueblo de Magallanes 98
Casanueva, Carlos 249n15
Castro Ruz, Fidel 148
Cathedral of St. John the Divine 250n26
Catholic Church 41, 49, 60, 88, 146–155, 178, 179, 195, 216–218, 244n11, 247n20, 250n21
Catholicism 146, 147, 151–155, 155, 178, 179, 249n6, 250n23
Chileanization 82, 86, 87–89, 95, 102
Christian Science 250n38
Christianity 99, 155nn108, 113, 180, 181, 182, 215, 216, and 217–218, 249nn7 and 8, 250n25
Chronicles, Second Book of 255n48
Church Fathers 136
Clares Pérez, Ramón 219, 220
Cofre Silva, Margarita 249nn4 and 6, 250n31
Congreso de Escritores Martianos 44
Coquimbo 1, 16, 20, 24, 31, 49, 70, 106, 119, 239n18, 240n16
Corinthians, First Epistle to 248n59
Cossío de Villegas, Ema 36, 38
Council of Ephesus 165
Covarrubias, Jorge Ignacio 245chXn10
Covenant of Salt 125, 198–202, 254–255nn44, 46, 47, and 48
Cristero uprising 152
Cross of Jesus Christ *see* Crucifixion
Crucifixion 185, 186, 189, 192–194, 199, 205, 206
Cruchaga Santa María, Ángel 71

Dana, Doris 4, 5, 17, 36, 37, 74, **75**–76, 77–**78**, 119, 154, 237n22, 241nn18 and 23
D'Annunzio, Gabriel 23, 25, 238n13
Darer, Veronica 240n15
Darío, Rubén 47–48, 95, 254n29
David 115, 129, 136
Deborah 16, 122
De la Cruz, Juana Inés 149

De la Cruz Barraza, José 33
Demas (Dimas) 144, 192
Destellos *see* Theosophical Lodges
Dey de Castillo, Josefina 103, 105, 245chXn2
Díaz Arrieta, Hernán, (pseud., Alone) 71, 72, 74, 116, 118, 120, 236nn9 and 10, 237nn14 and 20, 239n14, 247nn9, 16, and 22
Domingo Silva, Víctor 9, 10, 17, 20, 55, 61, 63, 74
Donne, John 209
Donoso, Armando 95
Dorab, Jal B. 250n34
D'Ors, Eugenio 3, 36–37, 71, 73, 74, 242nn20 and 21, 241nn20 and 21
Dostoevsky, Feodor 65
Duayén, César 245chIXn6
Duhamel, Georges 155n114
Dunlop, Grace 5
Dunn, Joseph E. 154
Dussuel, Francisco 249n11, 250n23, 252 nn82 and 109

Eça de Queiroz, José María 65
Ecclesiastes (Eclesiastés) 246n2
Eden 120–121, 138, 139, 194, 215
Edwards, Agustín 237
Elqui valley 11, 16, 31, 46, 49, 83, 119–121, 145, 201, 247nn27 and 29
Eltit, Diamela 243n5
Epiphany (Epifanía) 138–139
Ercilla, Alonso de 47, 95
Errázuriz, Carlos 126
Errázuriz Valdivieso, Crescente 149
Escudero, Alfonso M. 4, 237n13
Escuela-Hogar "Gabriela Mistral" 110
Escuela Normal de Preceptoras 49, 146
Espinoza, Enrique 247n8, 252n85, 253n114
Eucharist 143
Evangelio 148

Fajardo, Adelina 65
Fall of Man 121, 138, 194
Ferguson, George 254n33
Fergusson, Erna 238n12
Fernández Fraile, Maximino 36, 37, 241nn20 and 23
Fernández Larraín, Sergio 236n4, 238n6, 239n1, 244n6
Figueira, Gastón 238n13, 239n20
Figueroa, Virgilio 150, 236nn2 and 5, 237nn17 andchIIn1, 238n13, 239n20, 240nn4 and 7
Finnish people 212–213
Fiol-Matta, Licia 3, 74, 79, 243chVIIn51, 244n1
Floral Games (Juegos Florales) 19–22, 23, 24, 48, 67, 68, 70, 71, 238nn4 and 7

France 16
Franco, Francisco 171
Frank, Waldo 236*n*2
Freud, Sigmund 39

Gaer, Joseph 254*nn*25, 28, 31, and 33, 255*n*63
Galatians, Epistle to 254*n*24
Gallo, Domingo 47
Garcés Durán, Mario 244*n*11
García Moreno, Gabriel 153
Gazarian Gautier, Marie-Lise 121, 239*n*16, 245*ch*IX*n*4, 247*nn*26 and 28
Genesis, Book of 126, 248*nn*34, 35, 38, 40-42 and 51, 249*n*69, 254*n*34
Gestas 192
Gide, André 114
Gitanjali see Tagore, Rabindranath
God the Father (Dios Padre) 114, 116, 121, 123, 127, 128, 131-135, 140-145, 146, 153, 155, 157, 166, 180, 181, 184, 186-188, 192, 193, 196, 202-205, 213-214, 215-218, 247*n*28, 248*n*42, 249*n*71, 254*nn*27, 32, and 36, 255*n*53
Godoy Alcayaga, Lucila 144, 146, 190, 193, 195, 196, 202, 205; pseudonyms of, 24-25, 58, 238-239*nn*13, 15, 19, and 20; *see also* Mistral, Gabriela
Godoy Mendo[n/ç]za, Juan Miguel (Yin-Yin, Lucila's nephew) 3, 15, 17, 26, 28, **34**-37, **38**, 42, 71, 123, 126, 190, 193, 195, 196, 200, 205, 240*n*17, 241*nn*17, 18, 20, 24, 26, and 27, 242*nn*31 and 34, 243*n*1
Godoy Villanueva, Juan Jerónimo (Lucila's father) 8-9, 12, 26, **27**-30, 115, 122, 123, 146, 240*nn*3-5, 241*n*24
Godoy Villegas, Carlos Miguel (Lucila's half brother) 3, 35, 36, 37, 240*n*16
Goic, Cedomil 244*n*5
Golgotha 188
Gómez, Zacarías 9, 60, 66, 74, 156, 219, 223-227, 242*n*39, 243*n*3
Gómez Marzheimer, Guillermo 223-224
González, Manuel Pedro 249*n*1, 252-253*n*113
González Martínez, Enrique 47, 246*n*12
González Vera, José Santos 67, 71, 72, 74, 96, 116, 122, 152, 156, 165, 236*n*9, 240*n*3, 243*ch*VI*n*5, 243*ch*VII*n*3, 246*ch*XII*nn*2 and 4, 247*nn*6, 11, and 19, 249*n*19, 250*n*37
González Videla, Gabriel 11-12
Good, Ernesto 220
Gorky, Maxim 65
Graeff, Hilda 251*n*68
Granada, Luis de 191, 254*n*23
Grandin, Karl 236*n*6
Guerra, Silvia 241*n*27, 242*n*39, 243*n*6
Guerra Junqueiro, Abílio Manuel 66-67

Guillén de Nicolau, Palma 13, 36-39, 44, 74, 125, 241*n*24

Hagar (Agar) 124-126, 132-133, 248*n*38
Hamilton, Carlos 117, 247*n*12, 252*n*100
Hastings, James 254*n*31
Hawkes, Jacquetta 251*n*74
Hebrew people 118, 144, 145, 210, 213, 215, 216
Hebrews, Book of 254*n*40
Heliodoro Valle, Rafael 238*n*13, 239*n*20
Hempstead Hospital 153
Heredia, José María 237*n*22
Herod 185
Herrera Vega, Héctor Hernán 16, 236*nn*7 and 21, 240*n*14
Hinduism 168-171
Holroyd, Stuart 114, 246*ch*XI*n*5
Horan, Elizabeth 238*n*8, 240*n*15, 241*n*24, 242*nn*34 and 38, 243*n*5, 244*nn*12 and 14, 245*n*12
Hübner Bezanilla, Jorge 3, 67, 70, 71-73, 79, 239*n*16
Hübner Bezanilla, Sara 70, 71, 73, 238*n*5
Hugo, Victor 47
Huidobro, Vicente 101
Humphreys, Christmas 251*nn*48 and 57, 253*n*122

Ibáñez del Campo, Carlos 6-7, 13-14, 144*n*16
Iglesias, Augusto 23, 71, 238*n*11, 239*nn*14 and 15, 240*n*4, 247*n*23, 250*n*34, 251*n*45
Inostroza, Jorge 242*n*36
Institute of International Cooperation 14, 36
Institute of International Sciences of París 30, 111
Iribarren, Alfonso 248*n*46
Isaac 115, 128, 129
Isaiah, Book of 115, 251*n*51
Ishmael (Ismael) 145, 150, 249*n*69
Israel 122, 128, 136
Italy 10, 15, 16, 44, 78, 124

Jabin 122
Jacob 115, 124
Jácome, Rosa/Virginia 220
James, Edwin O. 251*n*66
Jaramillo Valderrama, Armando 102, 103, 106, 109
Jasso, Eloísa 44
Jehovah 116, 122, 135, 136, 137, 143, 144, 159, 165, 204, 215, 248*n*63; *see also* God the Father; Yahweh
Jeremiah (Jeremías) 116, 118, 246*ch*XII*n*2
Jesus Christ (Jesucristo) 8, 41-42, 130, 136, 140, 144, 149-151, 155, 158, 162-164, 167-169, 177, 185-188, 192-216

Index to Names and Places 283

Jiménez, Juan Ramón 247n15
Job 115, 116, 118, 121, 127, 131–135, 136, 145, 215, 248nn48–57
Job, Book of 131, 132, 135
John, Gospel of 149n59, 156nn5, 7, 8, 9, and 19, 157nn27, 38, 41, and 43, 158n50, 159n70, 253nn7, 8, 9, and 19, 254nn27, 38, 41, and 43, 255nn50 and 70
John XXIII, Pope 149, 150, 249n9
Jonah 115
Joseph (son of Jacob) 115, 129
Joshua (Josué) 116
Judas Iscariot 185, 188
Judith 207
Juegos Florales *see* Floral Games

Kaufmann, Walter 249n14, 250n23
Kayser, Wolfgang 140, 249n67
Kings, Second Book of, 248n3
Kol Nidre 119, 154, 247n20
Krishnamurti, Jiddu 163, 217, 251nn58 and 59
Krusche, Anna 50, 53–54
Kuhn, Alvin Boyd 250nn32 and 40, 251n70, 252n83

Labarca, Eugenio 74, 238n13, 239n20
Labarca Hubertson, Amanda 11, 80, 103, 105–109, 245chXnn6 and 7, 255n69
Labarca Hubertson, Guillermo 105, 106, 109
Ladrón de Guevara, Matilde 180, 236nn2 and 9, 237nn11, 15, 19, and 22, 240nn4 and 10, 246chXIIn3, 249nn11 and 13, 252n112
Lafourcade, Enrique 147, 246chXIIn5
Lagos, Ricardo 4
Las Casas, Bartolomé de 149–150, 246n10, 249n17
Latcham, Ricardo 36, 241n20
Lazarus (Lázaro) 186
Leadbeater, Charles 219, 221
League of Nations 14, 36
Leah (Lía) 121, 124, 212, 248n38
Leconte de Lisle, Charles Marie René 47, 170
Leo, Ulrich 130
León, Luis de 130
lesbianism 74, 243chVIIn5
Letelier del Campo, María 20
Leviticus, Book of 199, 254n44, 255n73
Lewin, Eloise 237n19
Liberation Theology 148
Liceo Número 6 de Niñas 100–102, 104–105, 110–111, 247n7
Lida, María Rosa 254n39
Lira Urquieta, Pedro 249n15
Locke, John 52
Lockhart, Darrell B. 247n6
Logos 167, 184
Longinus 99, 196, 209, 210

Los Andes (town) 62–69, 70, 82
Loynaz, Dulce María 22–23, 238n13, 239n16
Lubicz-Milosz, Oscar Vladislas de 253n114
Luigi, Juan de 238n13, 239n20
Luke, Gospel of 201, 203, 253nn5 and 10, 254nn40 and 43, 255n61

Maccabees (Macabea, Macabeos) 128, 212–213, 255n77
MacNeice, Louis 113, 246chXIn3
Madonna 167
Maeterlinck, Maurice 220
Magallanes Moure, Manuel 3, 7, 19–21, 23, 29, 37, 47, 48, 67, 70–71, 72–74, 79, 239n16, 243n7
Maluenda, Rafael 5, 11, 12, 128, 227
Mañach, Jorge 238n13, 239n20
Mann, Horace/Mary 52
Mann, Thomas, 96, 205
Marchant Lezcano, Jorge 244n12
Maritain, Jacques 253n14
Mark, Gospel of 199, 253nn5 and 10, 254n27, 255nn61 and 70
Martí, José 44, 47, 101
Martínez Sanz, María Ester 239n17, 243chVIIn1
Martz, Louis 254nn20 and 22
Mary (María, Martha's sister) 199, 254n27
Mary (María, mother of Jesus) 30, 165–67, 217
Mary Magdalene 144, 198–199
Marzano, Rolando 239 n18, 240nn4 and 16
Mathison, Richard 251n59
Matte, Jorge 30
Matthew, Gospel of 136, 153, 203, 253nn5, 10, 12, and 14, 254nn36 and 45, 255nn61 and 70
Meirelles, Cecília 117–118, 247n14
Melchizedek (Melquisedec) 248n40
Mendonç[z]a, Marta 34, 35, 41, 240n16
Merton, Thomas 253n114
Mexico 1, 12, 14, 15, 24, 44, 68, 71, 76, 79, 83–84, 88, 104, 107, 111, 152–153, 204, 254n37
Mistral (wind) 25
Mistral, Frédéric 25, 47, 48, 238n13, 255n59
Mistral, Gabriela: on abortion 37; awards 1, 5, 10, 14–16, 24, 44, 254n27; basis for creativity of 184–185; Biblical studies of 26–27, 115–116; on compulsory education 86–90; dealings with Catholicism 146–149, 151, 153–154, 216, 249nn6–7, 250nn23, 25, and 26; death of 14, 20, 46, 54–55, 153–157; on death and suicide 23, 40–41, 123, 137–145, 239n15, 241n24, 242nn29 and 30, 249nn65 and 66; in defense of aborigines 84–89, 95, 243n12, 245n10, 246n10; as director of schools 82–83, 94–95, 100–102, 110; educa-

tion of 46–50; Elqui valley's influence on 21–22, 101, 119–121, 202, 204–205, 247nn26–28; exile of 1, 6, 7, 79, 31, 83–84, 111–112, 237n14, 240n4, 244n3; family of 3, 8–9, 10, 11–14, *15, 16*–19 passim, 26, 47, 60, *64, 110*, 126, 127, 129–137, 146–147; female companions of 4, 38–39, 44, 62, 67, 68–69, 74–78, 90–94; on feminism 79–80, 244n14; on God's centrality 41–42, 114, 136, 151, 175–177, 181, 196–198, 215, 249n71; health of 14–15, 42–47, 57, 242nn39–40; hostility of 4–7, 128, 179, 143n10, 144n16; hostility to 8–13, 103–104, 105–107, 108–109, 236n9, 245nn6–7, 246n1; as humanitarian 2; internationalism of 5, 15; Jewishness of 18–20, 29, 45–46, 116–119, 136, 144–145, 215–216, 247n20; on marriage 23–24, 122–123; on mystic Christianity 150, 158, 159, 180–182, 183, 217–218, 251n79; outcast 13, 119, 77, 145; physical appearance of 3, 122, 143nn1 and 2; *Poema de Chile* 17; poverty and finances of 8–9, 29, 32, 164, 225–226, 236n6, 237n19; on prayer 149, 249n11; protector of children and women 2, 30, 119, 126, 171–173, 216, 240n28; public exaltation of 4–5, 16, 67, 93, 98, 236n8, 237n11, 246n16; self-declared ugliness of 8, 21; self-renunciation 7, 21, 156–157, 236nn1–4; on sexuality 2, 3, 8, 29, 68, 74, 77, 79, 81, 122, 240n6, 243nn5–8, 243chVIIn73; social/class inferiority of 21, 105–109; suffering of 3, 7, 8, 12–13, 26, 37, 42, 77, 95, 111, 114, 116, 162, 184, 188–190, 248–249n64; suitors of 2–3, 23, 37, 70–71, 73–74, 122, 239n14, 239n16; on teaching 24, 46, 48–50, 62, 64–65, 94, 99; and theosophy and Buddhism 155–170, 177–180, 216–217; uprootedness 12, 77; wanderlust of 59; willfulness and perseverance of 9, 45, 59, 122, 128, 145; on workers' rights 2, 88–89, 119, 147–149, 164, 244nn8–11; Yoga practices of 155–157

Moab 254n27
Molina de Barraza, Emelina (Lucila's half sister) 19, 24, *31*–33, 46, 51, 54, 56, 63, 115, 147, 209, 226
Molina de Barraza, Graciela Amalia (Emelina's daughter) 33, 63, 68, 240n15
Molina de Barraza, Marta Amelia (Emelina's daughter) 33
Molina Rojas, Rosendo 32
Molloy, Sylvia 74, 243–244n8
Mondaca, Carlos 74
Monsalve, Josué 155, 237n19, 240n4, 247n 20, 250nn30 and 35
Montegrande 11, 16, 17, 19, 26, 32, 33, 41, 248n46

Montessori, Maria 153
Montserrat, Andrés 250n27
Montt, Manuel 51–52
Morães Sarmento, Mariná de *see* Sala de Letras e Artes Gabriela Mistral
Moral, Pedro 237n11
Moses (Moisés) 116, 118
Mount Hermon 131
Muller, Herbert J. 250n21
Munizaga, Capellán Miguel Ignacio 49, 54, 147, 249n2
Munizaga Ossandón, Julio 20, 238n4
Murillo Le Fort, Fernando 58
Mussolini, Benito 15

Naomi 25
National Prize for Literature (Premio Nacional de Literatura) 5, 10, 15, 44
Nazarene 136
Nelson, Lowry, Jr. 255n58
Neruda, Pablo 95–96, 97, 125, 237n22, 245chIXn4
Nervo, Amado 159, 160, 170, 177–181, 252nn85, 100, 101, and 103–107
New School of Criticism 113, 183, 209
New Testament 136, 199, 202, 203, 255n56
New York 15, 16, 76
Nikolic, Iván 250n29
Nobel, Alfred 238n71
Nobel Prize 1, 8, 10, 11, 14, 25, 36, 39, 42, 46, 47, 48, 64, 76, 238n7, 246n11
Numbers (Números), Book of 251n51, 255n48

Ocampo, Victoria 42, 74, 241n24, 242n34, 243n6
Occultism 158–161, 250n42, 251nn45 and 46; *see also* Astrology
Old Testament (Antiguo Testamento) 2, 26, 116, 118, 119, 122, 125, 128, 129, 131, 136, 139, 144, 204, 212, 215; men of 127–135; women of 122–127, 132
Oldini, Fernando G. 105, 245chXn7
Olegario Sánchez, Pedro 60
Olivares, Adelaida 10, 33
Onís, Federico de 9, 107–108, 245–246chXn10
Order of Saint Francis 4, 11, 150, 218, 247n7, 249n18
Ortiz Letelier, Fernando 244nn8 and 9
Ossandón, Bernardo 48, 49
Otto, Rudolph 250n39

Palacios, Alfredo L. 249n8
Panama 86, 108, 238n7
Paradise *see* Eden
Parrau Escobar, Carlos 60, 156
Passion of Christ 184, 190, 191, 196, 202
Péguy, Charles 253n114

Index to Names and Places

Pérez Galdós, Benito 47
Peter, First Epistle of 253n7, 254n24
Piña-Rosales, Gerardo 245chXn10
Pinilla, Norberto 238n13, 239n20
Pinochet, Augusto 4
Pius XII, Pope 249n9
Pizarro, Ana 36, 241n19
Poblete, Renato 154
Portales, Diego 51
Portugal 15
Powers, Perry J. 254n42
Prado, Pedro 9, 30, 37, 74, 91, 111–112, 246n16
Prats de Sarratea, Teresa 54, 104–105
Pratt, Mary Louise 237n22
Premio Nacional de Literatura *see* National Prize for Literature
Psalms (Salmos), Book of 119, 140, 154, 248nn34 and 40, 253n13
Punta Arenas 14, 17, 66, 68, 82–92, 101, 243n6, 244n3, 245chIXn6

Quezada, Jaime 4

Rachel (Raquel) 121, 123–125, 212, 255n47
Rebekah (Rebeca) 123, 25–126, 255n47
Redondo Magallanes, Mireya 20
Reina, Casiodoro de 246n5, 253n5
Renan, Ernest 118
Resurrection 134–135, 160, 248 n57, 252n110
Revelation, Book of 255n53
Reyes, Alfonso 36, 242n29
Reyes, Neftalí Ricardo *see* Neruda, Pablo
Richards, Ivor A. 113, 246chXIn1
Rimbaud, Arthur 47
Rocuant, Miguel Luis 20, 47, 48
Rodig, Laura 36, 44, 67, 68–69, 90–94, 102, 238n13, 243nn6 and 7, 245n13
Rodin, Auguste 69, 139, 141
Rodó, José Enrique 65
Rojas, Fernando de 118
Rolland, Romain 220, 249n8, 253n111
Román, María Eugenia 36
Rosicrucians 125, 126, 243chVn8
Rossetti, Dante Gabriel 25, 238n13
Rousseau, Jean-Jacques 52, 153
Rozas, Juan Manuel de 52
Rubilar, Guillermo 238n2
Rubio, Patricia 4, 43, 241n21, 242n40, 245n8
Rudd, Margaret T. 250n29
Ruiz, Amantina 44
Russian Revolution 88
Ruta Patrimonial Camino de Gabriela Mistral 49
Ruth, Book of 115, 116, 121, 124, 159, 160

Saavedra Molina, Julio 22, 172, 238n9, 247n18, 250n36, 252n92

Saint Francis of Assisi 141, 149, 150, 160–162, 206, 251n47, 254n26
Saint Francis of Sales 127–128, 190, 254n21
Saint John (Juan) 135, 136
Saint Patrick's Cathedral 154
Saint Paul (Pablo) 135, 136
Saint Thomas 190
Sala de Letras e Artes Gabriela Mistral 242n36
Salas Maturana, Demetrio 220
Saleva, Consuelo 38, 39, 74, 76, 242n39
Sanfuentes, Luis 82, 86, 95
San Martín, José de 237n22
Santa Teresa de Jesús, 150, 255n68
Santelices, Isauro 22, 74
Santiago, Chile 14, 61, 68, 101–112
Santos, Eduardo 237n19
Sarah (Sara) 122, 124–125, 138
Sarmiento, Domingo Faustino 51–53, 66, 89
Sartre, Jean-Paul 81
Scarpa, Roque Esteban 83, 88, 244n2, 245n14, 245chIXn6, 245chXn2
Schiavetti Gallo, Ofelia 72
Scrill, William 250n28
La Serena 16, 32, 48, 49, 59, 240n16, 244n7
sexuality 3, 70–81
Shakespeare, William 159
Shalmaneser (Salmanazar) 129
Silva, José Asunción 47
Silva Castro, Raúl 12, 58, 114, 237n14, 238n13, 239n20, 240n4, 246chXIIn4, 251nn53, 55, and 56, 252nn86, 95, 97, and 111, 255n69
Simon Peter 186, 188, 201, 156n7, 253n7
Singerman, Berta 116, 117, 122, 247n10
Social Christians 253n14
Sociedad de Instrucción Popular de Magallanes 85
Sociedad Hebraica Argentina 228, 246n1
Sociedad Teosófica de Chile 6, 22, 156, 215, 216, 219, 251n54
Solomon (Salomón) 136; *see also* Song of Songs
Son of God *see* Jesus Christ
Song of Songs (Cantar de los Cantares) 117, 129, 130, 131, 246n2
Soviet Union 153
Spain 12, 15, 35, 36, 47, 51, 95, 124, 125, 245chXn10
Spanish Civil War 119, 128–129, 171, 172
Spellman, Francis Cardenal 154
Szmulewicz, Efraín 242n30

Tagore, Rabindranath 63, 65, 153 170–171, 174–177, 216, 243chVIn1, 252nn85–90, 93, 95, and 96
Teitelboim, Volodia 36, 241n20, 242n30,

243nn2, 3, and 7, 243chVIIn4, 244chVII-1nn1 and 9, 245nn12 and 15, 245chIXn1
Temuco 14, 66, 68, 93–99, 101
Terlingen, Juan 251n80
Theosophical Lodges: Destellos 56, 60; Despertar 121, 125
Theosophical Society of Adyar, India 250n34, 251n60
Theosophical Society of the United States 250n34, 251nn64 and 71
theosophy 47, 66, 146, 151, 155–170, 177, 178, 180, 216–217, 218, 243n3, 246n10, 250n24, 251nn53 and 54, 252nn100 and 108
Thomas à Kempis 132
Timothy, First Epistle to 184
Tolstoy, Leo 65
Torres Rioseco, Arturo 107, 108, 236n2, 245chXn8, 252n92

Unamuno, Miguel de 47, 95
United Nations 80, 171
Universal/God Spirit 156, 157, 163, 165, 216
Universal Self 163, 166, 167, 251n57
Ureta Carvajal, Romelio, 2, *18*–19, 23, 28, 72, 122, 238nn14 and 15, 240n8
Urzúa, María 36, 37, 39, 241n27

Valdez Pereira, Fidelia 50, 54, **55**, 57, 58, 59, 62, 84, 223, 242n1
Valera, Cipriano de 235n5
Vargas, Getúlio 39
Vargas Saavedra, Luis 4, 5, 35, 36, 38, 71, 72, 80, 237nn18 and 22, 239n17, 240n17, 241nn21, 24, and 26, 242nn29, 35, and 39, 243n7, 244n14, 245chIXn2, 246n10
Vargas Vila, José María 23, 47, 239n15
Vasconcelos, José 14, 44, 47, 66, **109**, 110, 246n12

Verlaine, Paul 47, 65
Veronica, Legend of 185, 188, 204–207, 253n6, 255nn50 and 64
Vicuña 11, 16, 33, 79, 236n9, 237n11, 240n13
Videla Pineda, Alfredo 3, 73
Villanueva de Godoy, Isabel (Lucila's paternal grandmother) 26, **27**, 115, 117, 118, 119, 228, 230–235, 246chXIIn2, Jewishness of 18–19, 228
Virgo 167–168
Von dem Bussche, Gastón 4, 236n1, 240n13, 241n24, 242n30

Walker, Brígida 50, 54, 56, 63, 192, 242n2
Warren, Austin 183, 238n10, 240n42, 253n1
Wellek, René 238n10
Wellman, Esther, 181, 252n103
Whitman, Walt 66
Whittick, Arnold 254nn32, 33, and 36
Wilde, Oscar 66
wine 202–204, 255nn51, 53, 54, 55, and 59
Wylie, Ann Kerr 250n34

Yahweh 131, 137, 140, 188, 215, 253n13
Yin-Yin *see* Godoy Mendo[n]za, Juan Miguel
Yoga 60, 63, 156–157, 177, 180, 217–218, 116–117

Zalaquett Aquea, Cherie 75, 77, 241n18, 244n9
Zegers B., Pedro Pablo viii, x, 237n14, 238n3, 239n19, 243nn1 and 6, 244n13, 245n3, 245chIXn5
Zweig, Stefan/Charlotte 39–40, 241n28, 242nn29 and 30

www.ingramcontent.com/pod-product-compliance
Lightning Source LLC
Chambersburg PA
CBHW051211300426
44116CB00006B/519